CULTURE AND ECONOMY IN THE AGE OF SOCIAL MEDIA

Understanding social media requires us to engage with the individual and collective meanings that diverse stakeholders and participants give to platforms. It also requires us to analyse how social media companies try to make profits, how and which labour creates this profit, who creates social media ideologies, and the conditions under which such ideologies emerge. In short, understanding social media means coming to grips with the relationship between culture and the economy. In this thorough study, Christian Fuchs, one of the leading analysts of the Internet and social media, delves deeply into the subject by applying the approach of cultural materialism to social media, offering readers theoretical concepts, contemporary examples, and proposed opportunities for political intervention.

Culture and Economy in the Age of Social Media is the ultimate resource for anyone who wants to understand culture and the economy in an era populated by social media platforms such as Twitter, Facebook, and Google in the West and Weibo, Renren, and Baidu in the East. Updating the analysis of thinkers such as Raymond Williams, Karl Marx, Ferruccio Rossi-Landi, Jürgen Habermas, and Dallas W. Smythe for the twenty-first century, Fuchs presents a version of Marxist cultural theory and cultural materialism that allows us to critically understand social media's influence on culture and the economy.

Christian Fuchs is Professor of Social Media at the University of Westminster. He is author of *Social Media: A Critical Introduction* (Sage, 2014), *Digital Labour and Karl Marx* (Routledge, 2014), *OccupyMedia!* (Zero Books, 2014), *Foundations of Critical Media and Information Studies* (Routledge, 2011), and *Internet and Society* (Routledge, 2008).

CULTURE AND ECONOMY IN THE AGE OF SOCIAL MEDIA

Christian Fuchs

NEW YORK AND LONDON

First published 2015
by Routledge
711 Third Avenue, New York, NY 10017

and by Routledge
2 Park Square, Milton Park, Abingdon, Oxon OX14 4RN

Routledge is an imprint of the Taylor & Francis Group, an informa business

© 2015 Taylor & Francis

Library of Congress Cataloging-in-Publication Data
Fuchs, Christian.
Culture and economy in the age of social media/Christian Fuchs.
pages cm
Includes bibliographical references and index.
1. Social media—Economic aspects. 2. Online social networks. I. Title.
HM742.F83 2015
302.30285—dc23
2014029193

ISBN: 978-1-138-83929-8 (hbk)
ISBN: 978-1-138-83931-1 (pbk)
ISBN: 978-1-315-73351-7 (ebk)

Typeset in Bembo
by Swales & Willis Ltd, Exeter, Devon, UK

Printed and bound in the United States of America by Publishers Graphics,
LLC on sustainably sourced paper.

DEDICATION

This book is dedicated to the memory of the life and work of Raymond Williams and Dallas W. Smythe.

May Critical Political Economy of the Media/Communication and Critical Cultural Studies forever unite under the banner of Marxist Media, Communication, and Cultural Studies!

CONTENTS

FIGURES

TABLES

1

INTRODUCTION

Social media has become a common term for signifying the usage of social networking sites, microblogs, blogs, (user-generated) content sharing sites, or wikis. The question of which media are social and which are not is often asked when people discuss social media. And how to answer it depends on how one defines what it means to be social—engaging with thoughts of others, communicating, engaging in communities, co-operative work, etc. (Fuchs 2014b, chapter 2). Facebook, Twitter, YouTube, Baidu, Renren, Weibo, WeChat, or WhatsApp are some of the most well-known social media. Large, transnational corporations operate them: Facebook Inc. (Facebook, WhatsApp), Twitter Inc., Google Inc. (YouTube), Sina Corp (Weibo), Tencent (WeChat), Baidu Inc. (Baidu), and Renren Inc (Renren). Targeted advertising finances many of these online platforms. The companies that run them are the largest advertising agencies in the world that have access to millions or billions of users' personal data.

Understanding social media requires us to engage with the individual and collective meanings that users, platform owners/CEOs/shareholders, companies, advertisers, politicians, and other observers give to these platforms. It also requires us to analyse how the companies operating social media try to make profits; how and which labour creates this profit; the development, contradictions, and crisis tendencies of the social media market; who creates social media ideologies; the conditions under which such ideologies emerge, etc. Understanding social media means coming to grips with the relationship of culture and the economy.

This book takes a fresh look at how we can best think about the connection of culture and the economy. It provides theoretical concepts, application examples, and political interventions for understanding culture and the economy in times of social media.

When observers such as consultants, managers, journalists, analysts, scholars, and intellectuals talk about "the economy", they often focus on discussing the growth/stagnation/shrinkage of the gross domestic product, market developments, innovations, international competition, profits, revenues, prices, etc. and tend to care less about working conditions. This is partly because they assume that people are doing well if the economy is doing well. This can, however, not be taken for granted. The approach taken in this book and by critical political economists is different because they assume that all the just-mentioned phenomena are created by labour and that it therefore matters a lot to look at how people work and the conditions under which they do so. This book therefore has a special focus on the relationship of labour and culture. But talking about labour means in contemporary society that one also has to talk about non-labour—capital—and the relationship between the two—class. So we have to focus on culture and capitalism for understanding contemporary social media.

Part I focuses on theoretical foundations. Part II is about specific questions that concern social media's temporalities. It focuses on social media's cultural political economy of time. Part III takes a global view on the world of social and digital media. Its focus is on social media's cultural political economy of global space. Part IV talks about alternatives to social media controlled by private companies and state institutions.

Each part consists of two chapters that each discuss a specific question:

Part I: Theoretical Foundations
Chapter 2: How are culture and labour connected?
Chapter 3: How are ideology and labour connected?

Part II: Social Media's Cultural Political Economy of Time
Chapter 4: What is the role of labour time in the value creation on social media?
Chapter 5: How is value created on social media?

Part III: Social Media's Cultural Political Economy of Global Space
Chapter 6: Which forms of digital labour are there and how are they connected on a global level?
Chapter 7: What does the political economy of social media platforms (e.g. Baidu, Weibo, Renren) look like in China?

Part IV: Alternatives
Chapter 8: What are alternatives to the existing problems of social media and can the notion of the public sphere help us to better understand social media alternatives and their requirements?
Chapter 9: What conclusions can we draw from the presented chapters for understanding social media's culture and economy?

In his book *Culture & Society: 1780–1950*, Raymond Williams studies British literature in the context of the rise of capitalism, which is framed by the fact that "the concept of culture, in its modern senses, came through at the time of the Industrial Revolution" (Williams 1958, ix). Whereas Williams focused on an analysis of the works of authors such as George Eliot, George Bernard Shaw, T.S. Eliot, D.H. Lawrence, or George Orwell, this book is about contemporary social media such as Google, Baidu, Twitter, Weibo, Facebook, and Renren. Literature is as alive today as it was in the nineteenth century and written expression has taken on additional forms such as the blog. What has not changed, however, is that just like in the late eighteenth and the nineteenth and twentieth centuries that Williams studied, in the twenty-first century, which is the temporal context of this book, we still live in a capitalist society. Capitalism is the major context for twenty-first-century social media just like it was for eighteenth-, nineteenth- and twentieth-century British literature and communication that Raymond Williams studied. We therefore require a critical political economy of media and culture for understanding historical and contemporary modes of communicative expression.

PART I
Theoretical Foundations

2

CULTURE AND WORK

Christian Fuchs and Marisol Sandoval

2.1. Introduction

This chapter discusses the relationship between culture and work. It applies a materialist perspective that is especially inspired by Raymond Williams's works that he characterized as cultural materialism. Williams has been described by observers as "the greatest cultural theorist of modern Britain" (McGuigan 2014, xv) and "the first to see the essential interconnectedness of economic, political, social and cultural developments" (Scannell 2007, 111). "Williams's importance lies precisely in his at times highly critical but nonetheless lifelong allegiance to socialism as a political movement and to historical materialism as an intellectual project" (Garnham 1988, 130).

Section 2.2. introduces a cultural-materialist perspective on theorising culture. Section 2.3. discusses a materialist concept of cultural work based on this approach. Section 2.4. draws a distinction between cultural work and cultural labour. Section 2.5. introduces a typology of the dimensions of working conditions. Section 2.6 discusses the anti-work philosophy and argues against it to revive William Morris and Herbert Marcuse's understandings of work. We draw some conclusions in section 2.7.

There is a latent debate between Vincent Mosco and David Hesmondhalgh about how to define cultural and communication work and where to draw the boundaries. According to Hesmondhalgh cultural industries "deal primarily with the industrial production and circulation of texts" (Hesmondhalgh 2013, 16). Thus cultural industries include for him broadcasting, film, music, print and electronic publishing, video and computer games, advertising, marketing and public relations, web design. Cultural labour is therefore according to this understanding all labour conducted in these industries. Cultural labour deals "primarily with the industrial production and circulation of texts" (Hesmondhalgh 2013, 17).

Following this definition Hesmondhalgh describes cultural work as "the work of symbol creators" (Hesmondhalgh 2013, 20).

Vincent Mosco and Catherine McKercher argue for a much broader definition of communication work, including "anyone in the chain of producing and distributing knowledge products" (Mosco and McKercher 2009, 25). In the case of the book industry, this definition includes not only writers but equally librarians and also printers.

Hesmondhalgh's definition of cultural industries and cultural work focuses on content production. Such a definition tends to exclude digital media, information and communications technology hardware, software, and Internet phenomena such as social media and search engines. It thereby makes the judgment that content industries are more important than digital media industries. It is idealistic in that it focuses on the production of ideas and excludes the fact that these ideas can only be communicated based on the use of physical devices, computers, software, and the Internet. For Hesmondhalgh (2013, 19) software engineers for example are not cultural workers because he considers their work activity as "functional" and its outcomes not as text with social meaning. Software engineering is highly creative: it is not just about creating a piece of code that serves specific purposes, but also about writing the code by devising algorithms, which poses logical challenges for the engineers. Robert L. Glass (2006) argues that software engineering is a complex form of problem solving that requires a high level of creativity that he terms "software creativity". Software is semantic in multiple ways: (a) when its code is executed, each line of the code is interpreted by the computer which results in specific operations; (b) when using a software application online or offline our brains constantly interpret the presented information; (c) software supports not only cognition but also communication and collaboration and therefore helps humans create and reproduce social meaning. Software engineers are not just digital workers. They are also cultural workers. Considering software engineers as functional dupes, as Hesmondhalgh does, is a form of Arnoldian elitism that separates the realm of digital work from the activities performed by the creators of popular culture who are considered as higher beings performing higher forms of work.

Hesmondhalgh opposes Mosco's and McKercher's broad definition of cultural work because "such a broad conception risks eliminating the specific importance of *culture*, of *mediated communication*, and of the *content* of communication products" (Hesmondhalgh and Baker 2011, 60). Our view is that there are many advantages of a broad definition as

- It avoids "cultural idealism" (Williams 1977, 19) that ignores the materiality of culture;
- It can take into account the connectedness of technology and content; and
- It recognizes the importance of the global division of labour, the exploitation of labour in developing countries, slavery, and other blood and sweat inducing forms of labour.

Probably most importantly, a broad conception of cultural work can inform political solidarity:

> A more heterogeneous vision of the knowledge-work category points to another type of politics, one predicated on questions about whether knowledge workers can unite across occupational or national boundaries, whether they can maintain their new-found solidarity, and what they should do with it.
>
> *Mosco and McKercher 2009, 26*

The creation of many cultural and digital goods and services depends on a global division of labour. If there is a strike in one place, then transnational corporations may move one production step to another place. If workers in all or several places involved in the division of labour of a specific commodity protest or go on strike, then they can seriously challenge and put transnational corporations under pressure. A broad concept of cultural work foregrounds the need for transnational struggles in order to challenge global capitalist rule.

Also Eli Noam opposes the separation of hardware and content producers and argues for a broad definition of the information industry: "Are the physical components of media part of the information sector? Yes. Without transmitters and receivers a radio station is an abstraction. Without PCs, routers, and servers there is no Internet" (Noam 2009, 46). Noam argues for a materialist unity of content and hardware producers in the category of the information industry.

While some definitions of creative work and creative industries are input- and occupation-focused (Caves 2000; Cunningham 2005; Hartley 2005), the broad notion of cultural work we are proposing focuses on industry and output. Input- and output-oriented definitions of cultural work/industries reflect a distinction that already Fritz Machlup (1962) and Daniel Bell (1974) used in their classical studies of the information economy: the one between occupational and industry definitions of knowledge work. Our approach differs both from input-oriented definitions and narrow output-oriented definitions.

We argue that cultural workers should be seen as what Marx termed *Gesamtarbeiter*. Marx describes this figure of the collective worker (*Gesamtarbeiter*) in the *Grundrisse* where he discusses labour as communal or combined labour (Marx 1857/58, 470). This idea was also taken up in *Capital, Volume 1*, where he defines the collective worker as "a collective labourer, i.e. a combination of workers" (Marx 1867, 644), and argues that labour is productive if it is part of the combined labour force:

> In order to work productively, it is no longer necessary for the individual himself to put his hand to the object; it is sufficient for him to be an organ of the collective labourer, and to perform any one of its subordinate functions.
>
> *Marx 1867, 644*

The collective worker is an "aggregate worker" whose "combined activity results materially in an aggregate product" (Marx 1867, 1040). The "activity of this aggregate labour-power" is "the immediate production of surplus-value, the immediate conversion of this latter into capital" (Marx 1867, 1040).

The question of how to define cultural labour has to do with the more general question of how to understand culture. It therefore makes sense to pay some attention to the works of one of the most profound cultural theorists: Raymond Williams.

2.2. Cultural Materialism

Raymond Williams was a genuine Marxist theorist with a profound knowledge of Marx's works. Jim McGuigan and Marie Moran (2014) argue that his influence in sociology has been marginalised after his death in 1988 because of the decline of Marxism's influence and the rise of neoliberalism. In 1958, he argued in his early work *Culture and Society* that his approach is grounded in Marxist theory: "We are interested in Marxist theory because socialism and communism are now important" (Williams 1958, 284). Seventeen years later, Williams confirmed his deep commitment to Marxist thought: he argued that he has "no real hesitation" to define himself as a historical materialist, if this position means demanding "the destruction of capitalist society", "the need to supersede" capitalist society and "to go beyond" it "so that a socialist society" is established (Williams 1975, 72). He wrote that Marxism that extends its scope to the totality of culture is "a movement to which I find myself belonging and to which I am glad to belong" (Williams 1975, 76).

Williams (1983) points out that culture comes from the Latin word *colere* that means to inhabit, cultivate, protect, and honour with worship. The association of culture with cultivation and being cultivated, culture as civilisation and process of human development, became especially important with the Enlightenment and the bourgeois revolution. Williams argues that there are three modern meanings of the term *culture*:

1   the "general process of intellectual, spiritual and aesthetic development, from C18",
2   "a particular way of life, whether of a people, a period, a group, or humanity in general",
3   "the works and practices of intellectual and especially artistic activity. This seems often now the most widespread use: culture is music, literature, painting and sculpture, theatre and film" (Williams 1983, 90).

Meanings (1) and (3) have been closely related. Williams (1961, 61) described these three ways of defining culture also as (1) the ideal definition, (2) the social definition, and (3) the documentary definition.

He has especially stressed the second type of definition in his works. In *Culture and Society, 1780–1950*, Williams (1958, xviii) defined culture as "a whole way of life", "a mode of interpreting all our common experience, and, in this new interpretation, changing it." A "culture is not only a body of intellectual and imaginative work; it is also and essentially a whole way of life" (Williams 1958, 325). In *The Long Revolution*, Williams repeated this definition: Culture "is a description of a particular way of life, which expresses certain meanings and values not only in art and learning but also in institutions and ordinary behaviour" (Williams 1961, 61). Understood this way, elements of culture would be e.g. meanings, values, intellectual and imaginative works, traditions, the organisation of production, family structures, institutional structures, or forms of communication, experiences, structures of feeling, the popular (Williams 1961, 62, 69, 78). Terry Eagleton stresses that Williams's reason for foregrounding this definition of culture is that restricting "culture to the arts and intellectual life is to risk excluding the working class from the category" (Eagleton 2000, 35).

In his early works, Raymond Williams was trying to understand working-class culture in contrast to bourgeois culture, which illustrates his genuinely socialist position and interest in culture. But although Williams stresses the focus on totality, i.e. culture as "the way of life as a whole" (Williams 1958, 281) and "a general social process" (Williams 1958, 282), he in his early works tended to categorically separate culture and the economy: "even if the economic element is determining, it determines a whole way of life" (Williams 1958, 281). This notion of determination implies that the two realms of the economy and culture are connected, but that in the first instance they are also separate.

In 1973, Williams discussed the question of the relationship of base and superstructure in his article *Base and Superstructure in Marxist Cultural Theory*. He argues in this essay that the base is a process that is "setting [. . .] limits" and exerts "pressure" on the superstructure (Williams 1973, 34). He understands the base as "the specific activities of men in real social and economic relationship", the "productive forces", and the superstructure as the "range of cultural practices" (Williams 1973, 34). Williams argues that the superstructure is "from the beginning, basic" because productive forces mean the "material production and reproduction of real life" (Williams 1973, 35). Williams here argues on the one hand that the separation of culture from production is artificial and ideological, but on the other hand asserts this separation by providing definitions of the base as production and the superstructure as cultural practices. But if the superstructure is part of the base, then the two categories do not make sense in the first place, so there is no need for defining them in the way that Williams does.

Whereas in *Culture and Society* (Williams 1958) and the *Long Revolution* (Williams 1961) the question of cultural work was not crucial for Williams, he more and more approached it in his later works, which becomes apparent in his 1973 essay, although in a still ambivalent way. Raymond Williams's engagement with Marxist theory for understanding culture probably was most thorough in his 1977 book *Marxism and Literature*. He in this book formulated a genuinely cultural materialist position and a specific form of cultural Marxism.

Later, in his "major theoretical work" (McGuigan and Moran 2014, 172) *Marxism and Literature*, Raymond Williams questioned Marxism's historical tendency to see culture as "dependent, secondary, 'superstructural': a realm of 'mere' ideas, beliefs, arts, customs, determined by the basic material history" (Williams 1977, 19). Cultural materialism is for Williams an approach that avoids "both economic reductionism and [. . .] idealist cultural reductionism" (McGuigan and Moran 2014, 173). "Williams [. . .] developed a notion of culture that pays heed to Marx's materialist supplication that we must analyse ideas, values and cultural forms in the social conditions of their production and circulation" (McGuigan and Moran 2014, 175). Williams discusses various notions that Marxist theories have used for conceptualising the relationship of the economy and culture: determination, reflection, reproduction, mediation, homology. He argues that these concepts all assume a relationship between the economy and culture that to a varying degree is shaped by causal determination or mutual causality. But all of them would share the assumption of "the separation of 'culture' from material social life" (Williams 1977, 19) that Williams (1977, 59) considers to be "idealist". In Williams's view the problem with these approaches is not that they are too economistic and materialist, but on the contrary that they are not "materialist enough" (Williams 1977, 92). For Williams, culture is not a superstructure independent from an economic base, but rather culture understood as "language, ideas, values, beliefs, stories, discourses and so on" is for him "itself material" (McGuigan and Moran 2014, 176).

Williams (1977, 78) argues that Marx opposed the "*separation* of 'areas' of thought and activity". Production would be distinct from "consumption, distribution, and exchange" as well as from social relations (Williams 1977, 91). Productive forces would be "all and any of the means of the production and reproduction of real life", including the production of social knowledge and co-operation (Williams 1977, 91). Politics and culture would be realms of material production: ruling classes would produce castles, palaces, churches, prisons, workhouses, schools, weapons, a controlled press, etc. (Williams 1977, 93). Therefore Williams highlights the "material character of the production of a social and political order" and describes the concept of the superstructure as an evasion (Williams 1977, 93). Here, Williams reflects Gramsci's insight that "popular beliefs" and "similar ideas are themselves material forces" (Gramsci 1988, 215).

Ngai-Ling Sum and Bob Jessop (2013, 117) argue that Williams "placed culture 'inside' the economic base and, indeed, whether Williams recognized it or not, marked a return to the Marx and Engels of *The German Ideology*." One gets the impression that Sum and Jessop assume that Williams has an interesting approach, but did not engage enough with Marx's works. Such an assumption is, however, based on a reading of Williams that is not thorough enough. Works such as *Marxism and Literature* (Williams 1977) and *Marx on Culture* (Williams 1989, 195–225) are among the most thorough discussions of Marx's ideas on culture, including the *German Ideology*. These works show that Williams was not only a thorough reader of Marx, but that he really engaged with the meanings of Marx's works by discussing which specific meanings of terms such as *ideology* and *culture* specific sentences written by Marx convey. Sum and Jessop (2013, 120: table 3.1) also overlook that Williams not just used Gramsci for introducing the notion of the structures of feeling, but that he also used Gramsci's concept of hegemony for conceptualising culture's role in society (Williams 1977, 108–114: chapter 6).

Raymond Williams (1977, 111) formulates as an important postulate of cultural materialism that "[c]ultural work and activity are not [. . .] a superstructure" because people would use physical resources for leisure, entertainment and art. Combining Williams's assumptions that cultural work is material and economic and that the physical and ideational activities underlying the existence of culture are interconnected means that culture is a totality that connects all physical and ideational production processes that are connected and required for the existence of culture. Put in simpler terms this means that for Williams the piano maker, the composer, and the piano player all are cultural workers.

Williams (1977, 139) concludes that cultural materialism sees "the complex unity of the elements" required for the existence of culture: ideas, institutions, formations, distribution, technology, audiences, forms of communication and interpretation, worldviews (138–139). A sign system would involve the social relations that produce it, the institutions in which it is formed, and its role as a cultural technology (Williams 1977, 140). In order to avoid the "real danger of separating human thought, imagination and concepts from 'men's material life-process'" (Williams 1989, 203), one needs to focus on the "totality of human activity" (Williams 1989, 203) when discussing culture: We "have to emphasise cultural practice as from the beginning social and material" (Williams 1989, 206). The "productive forces of 'mental labour' have, in themselves, an inescapable material and thus social history" (Williams 1989, 211). Marx expressed the basic assumption of cultural materialism well by stressing that the "production of ideas, of conceptions, of consciousness, is at first directly interwoven with the material activity and the material intercourse of men" (Marx and Engels 1845/46, 42). The production of ideas is therefore the "language of real life" (Marx and Engels 1845/46, 42). "Men are the producers of their conceptions, ideas, etc., that is, real, active men, as they are conditioned by a definite development of their productive forces and of the intercourse corresponding to these, up to its furthest forms" (Marx and Engels 1845/46, 42). "Consciousness can never be anything else than conscious being, and the being of men is their actual life process" (Marx and Engels 1845/46, 42). Consciousness, thought, information, and communication are for Marx part of the actual social and material production process that enables human life. Thinking and communicating for Marx are processes of production that are embedded into humans' everyday life and work. Human beings produce their own capacities and realities of thinking and communication in work and social relations.

In his later works, Williams stressed that it is particularly the emergence of an information economy in which information, communication, and audiences are sold as commodities that requires rethinking the separation of the economy and culture and to see culture as material. "[I]nformation processes [. . .] have become a qualitative part of economic organization" (Williams 1981, 231). "Thus a major part of the whole modern labour process must be defined in terms which are not easily theoretically separable from the traditional 'cultural' activities. [. . .] so many more workers are involved in the direct operations and activations of these systems that there are quite new social and social-class complexities" (Williams 1981, 232).

As information is an important aspect of economic production in information societies, the culture concept cannot be confined to popular culture, entertainment, works of art, and the production of meaning through the consumption of goods, but needs to be extended to the realm of economic production and value creation. Cultural labour is a crucial concept in this context.

In contemporary capitalism, pianos, compositions (via intellectual property rights), and music are all three commodities. So what unites the cultural work of the piano maker, the composer, and the musician is that the commodity form mediates their works. Raymond Williams argues that this circumstance requires us to think of culture as material and economic. But he adds that in the first instance all of these practices are material because they produce use-values of different kinds.

Terry Eagleton (2000, 1) stresses that the word *culture* has its origins in husbandry, agriculture, and therefore the realm of nature. The phrase "cultural materialism" therefore for Eagleton "is something of a tautology". The problem is, however, that the materiality of culture is today too often forgotten and dualist thought tends to separate the concept of culture from the economy, matter, nature, technology, and labour. The notion of cultural materialism reminds us of the inherent materiality of all culture and is therefore not a tautology, but a critique of dualist worldviews. Why does cultural materialism matter today? We can find a new separatism in the study of the information economy that tends to separate technology/content, non-creative (functional)/creative, production/circulation, productive/unproductive, labour/ideology, work/communication when analysing culture and information.

2.3. A Materialist Notion of Cultural Work

Williams (1981, 207) suggests that culture is "a realized signifying system" that is distinct from the economy and politics, but that all social systems have their own signifying systems, which makes culture part of any system. But any social system also has ownership structures and decision-making structures, which shows that the economic, the political, and the cultural are three crucial dimensions of the social. A "signifying system is intrinsic to any economic system, any political system, any generational system and, most generally, to any social system" (Williams 1981, 208). Culture would nonetheless be a "system in itself", in which humans produce language, thoughts, consciousness, works of art, and ideologies (Williams 1981, 208). Culture would be "the signifying system through which necessarily (though among other means) a social order is communicated, reproduced, experienced and explored" (Williams 1981, 13). Signification appears as "language, [. . .] as a system of thought or of consciousness, or, to use that difficult alternative term, an ideology; and again as a body of specifically signifying works of art and thought" (Williams 1981, 208). Culture involves "signifying institutions, practices and works" (Williams 1981, 208). "All social systems, then, involve signification, but not all of them are signifying or 'cultural' systems" (Eagleton 2000, 34).

What can we make of Williams's work? On the one hand he refuses the separation of culture and the economy as well as base and superstructure. On the other hand he maintains that culture as a signifying system is a distinct system of society. How can we make sense of these claims that at a first sight seem to be mutually exclusive?

Inspired by Raymond Williams's cultural materialism, it is feasible to argue for a broad understanding of cultural labour that transcends the cultural idealism of the early digital labour debate and some positions within the cultural industries school. If one thinks dialectically, then a concept of culture as material and necessarily economic and at the same time distinct from the economy is feasible: culture and politics are dialectical sublations (*Aufhebung*) of the economy. In Hegelian philosophy sublation means that a system or phenomenon is preserved, eliminated, and lifted up. Culture is not the same as the economy: it is more than the sum of various acts of work, it has emergent qualities—it communicates meanings in society—that cannot be found in the economy alone. But at the same time, the economy is preserved in culture: culture is not independent from work, production, and physicality, but requires and incorporates all of them.

On the level of specific qualities of the subsystems of society, we can distinguish between the economy, the political system and culture. There are three interconnected systems of society (Fuchs 2008):

- The economy: the system of the production of use-values that satisfy human needs; labour produces use-value within specific social relations of production.
- The political system: the system of the production of collective decisions that regulate society.
- Culture: the system of human reproduction and the production of meanings and moral judgements that define what is assessed as good and bad. Culture is the system that organises the re-creation of the human—its body and as part of the body also the human mind. "Culture means the domain of social subjectivity" (Eagleton 2000, 39). Culture is therefore about medicine and

psychology, cycling and chess, food/restaurants and cooking, painting and visiting galleries, practicing sports and watching sports, the architecture of churches and the practice of praying in them, schools as institutions and learning as the practice of acquiring skills, the family and friendships as social systems, love as feeling and practice, etc. Culture is not just mind, thought, and ideas. It is at the same time body and matter. The mind is part of the body and thought is an organisational form of matter.

All three systems are material because they are systems of production. Matter is the process-substance of the world (Fuchs 2003c): systems are constituted by permanent reproduction and the creation of novelty that emerges out of existing structures. Production guarantees human existence and reproduction. The world is material because it has the capacity to produce itself and new forms of organisation. Society is material because in it humans produce structures, their own sociality, and ever-newer human practices so that society can reproduce itself and exist over time. This reproduction includes the production of use-values, decisions, and definitional and judgemental meanings.

The Austrian philosopher of information Wolfgang Hofkirchner has introduced stage models as a way for philosophically conceptualising the logic connections between different levels of organisation. In a stage model, "one step taken by a system in question—that produces a layer—depends on the stage taken prior to that but cannot be reversed! [. . .] layers—that are produced by steps—build upon layers below them but cannot be reduced to them!" (Hofkirchner 2013, 123–124). Emergence is the foundational principle of a stage model (Hofkirchner 2013, 115): a specific level of organisation of matter has emergent qualities so that the systems organised on this level are more than the sum of their parts, to which they cannot be reduced. An organisation level has new qualities that are grounded in the underlying systems and levels that are preserved on the upper level. These elements/systems produce through synergies new qualities of the upper level. In the language of dialectical philosophy this means that the emergent quality of an organisation level is a sublation (*Aufhebung*) of the underlying level.

Using a stage model allows us to identify and relate different levels of cultural and digital work (see Figure 2.1). *Cultural work* is a term that encompasses organisational levels of work that are at the same time distinct and dialectically connected: cultural work has an emergent quality, namely, information work that creates content, that is based on and grounded in physical cultural work, which creates information technologies through agricultural and industrial work processes. Physical work takes place inside and outside of culture: it creates information technologies and its components (cultural physical work) as well as other products (non-cultural physical work) that do not primarily have symbolic functions in society (such as cars, tooth brushes, or cups). Cars, tooth brushes, or cups do not primarily have the role of informing others or communicating with others, but rather help humans achieve the tasks

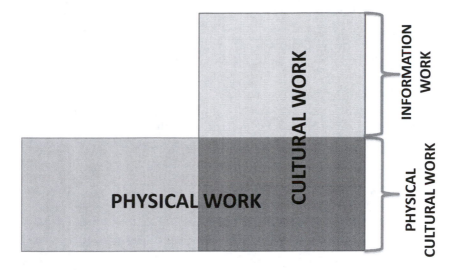

FIGURE 2.1   A stage model of cultural work

of transport, cleanliness, and nutrition. Culture and as part of it information work, however, feed back on these products and create symbolic meanings used by companies for marketing them. Cultural work is a unity of physical cultural work and information work that interact with each other, are connected and at the same time distinct.

All culture involves cultural work and effects of cultural products in society (meaning-making). The production of meaning, social norms, morals, and the communication of meanings, norms, and morals are work processes: they create cultural use-values. Culture requires on the one hand human creativity for creating cultural content and on the other hand specific forms and media for storage and communication. Work that creates information and communication through language is specific for work conducted in the cultural system: information and communication work. For having social effects in society, information and communication are organized (stored, processed, transported, analysed, transformed, created) with the help of information and communication technologies, such as computers, TV, radio, newspapers, books, recorded films, recorded music, language, etc. These technologies are produced by physical cultural work. Culture encompasses (a) physical and information work that create cultural technologies (information and communication technologies) and (b) information work that creates information and communication.

Williams questioned the separation of realms of society and therefore also of culture and economy (McGuigan and Moran 2014). On the one hand the relationship between societal realms changes historically (McGuigan and Moran 2014). On the other hand, given that humans interact in various social roles and through their everyday social practices connect various social roles and realms, social realms are never separated from each other, but dialectically mediated and overgrasping into each other. Culture is at the same time part and no-part of the economy: it requires cultural work that produces cultural structures, i.e. social meanings that help organising communication everywhere in society.

These two types of work act together in order to produce and reproduce culture. Meanings and judgements are emergent qualities of culture that are created by information work; they take on relative autonomy that has effects inside but also outside the economic system. This means that specific forms of work create culture, but culture cannot be reduced to the economy—it has emergent qualities.

Following Williams, communication is the "passing of ideas, information, and attitudes from person to person", whereas communications means the "institutions and forms in which ideas, information, and attitudes are transmitted and received" (Williams 1962, 9). Information and communication are meaning-making activities created by information work. Physical cultural work creates communications as institutions and forms that organise the creation and passing on of information in social processes.

Marx identified two forms of information work: the first results in cultural goods that "exist separately from the producer, i.e. they can circulate in the interval between production and consumption as commodities, e.g. books, paintings and all products of art as distinct from the artistic achievement of the practising artist". In the second, "the product is not separable from the act of producing" (Marx 1867, 1047–1048). The first requires a form, institution, or technology that stores and transports information, as in the case of computer-mediated communication; the second uses language as main medium (e.g. theatre). The first requires physical cultural work for organising storage, organisation, and transport of information; the second is possible based only on information work.

Cultural goods are not just information that expresses and communicates meanings. These meanings also express moral norms, values, judgements. Culture is therefore inherently political. In class societies, culture tends to be antagonistic, an arena of intellectual and symbolic struggle, in which class distinctions are made by and through symbols that communicate differences and hierarchies and contestation of these differences. Class culture is on the one hand shaped by struggles and on the other hand by ideologies: dominant groups express their values in practices that can result in crystallised cultural forms. They try to convince others that society works the way the dominant class imagines. Such a dominant culture can be said to be ideological if claims are made that do not correspond to reality in order to justify or reproduce dominative social relations. The culture of subordinated classes has its own specificities that range on a continuum that runs from reproducing dominative values to challenging them. There can also be mixed cultural forms that mix elements of dominative and oppositional culture. Edward P. Thompson stresses that culture in class societies is often contested and shaped by cultural struggles: "culture is also a pool of diverse resources, in which traffic passes between the literate and the oral, the superordinate and the subordinate, the village and the metropolis; it is an arena of conflictual elements" (Thompson 1991, 6).

Nicholas Garnham (1990, 25) argues that Raymond Williams's approach "suffers from a misleading reductionism by failing to distinguish between the material and the economic." For Garnham, cultural labour are activities that "produce and disseminate symbols in the form of cultural goods and services, generally, although not exclusively, as commodities" (Garnham 1990, 156). Garnham distinguishes between a social and a cultural form. The social form would be "a series of social relations", the cultural form would not itself be material, but have "material support" (Garnham 1990, 26). "Cultural forms become effective only when they are translated into social forms which do have material effectivity" (Garnham 1990, 26). Garnham separates culture and matter by saying that culture is immaterial and that "cultural production directly services the wider system of material production" (Garnham 1990, 13).

Garnham, however, does not consistently use the notion of culture as immaterial and contradicts himself in the very same book. He says in the same book that culture is "the production and circulation of symbolic meaning", "a material process of production and exchange, part of, and in significant ways determined by, the wider economic processes of society with which it shares many common features" (Garnham 1990, 155). Williams does not clarify the difference between the economy and culture, but in Garnham's work it is not clear what it means that something is material.

Terry Eagleton was a student and faculty colleague of Raymond Williams at the University of Cambridge. He commemorated Williams as having "transformed cultural studies from the relative crudity in which he found them to a marvellously rich, resourceful body of work" so that "he altered irreversibly the intellectual and political map of Britain, and put hundreds of thousands of students and colleagues and readers enduringly in his debt" (Eagleton 1989a, 9). Eagleton is Williams's comrade in arms in the struggle against capitalism, but is also critical of the cultural materialist perspective that the author of *Marxism and Literature* advanced.

Eagleton describes himself as "a defender of the classical doctrine" (Eagleton 1989b, 166) and states that "some activities are more fundamentally determining than others" (Eagleton 1989b, 169). He is therefore sceptical of Williams's out-Marxising of the Marxists that is "pressing the Marxist logic to an extreme" and thereby undoes "the 'base'/'superstructure' distinction" (Eagleton 1989a, 6). Williams would collapse all reality into matter:

> If *everything* is 'material', can the term logically retain any force? From what does it differentiate itself? From an actual realm of phenomena which could properly be said to be non-material, or from an ideological misperception of properly material objects as ideal ones?
>
> *Eagleton 1989b, 169*

Eagleton overlooks that a logic that assumes that there is matter and non-matter in the world violates the philosophical law of ground that says that every phenomenon must have a ground. The philosophical law of ground is,

> "Everything has a sufficient ground or reason."—In general, this means nothing but this: Anything which *is*, is to be considered *to exist* not as an immediate, but as a posited; there is no stopping at immediate existence but a return must rather be made from it back into its ground, and in this reflection it is a sublated being and is in and for itself.
>
> *Hegel 1812, 11.294*

If outside of matter there is always non-matter, as assumed by Eagleton, then the world cannot in the first and last instance have a sufficient ground. One ends up with having to assume the fundamental existence of two substances: matter and spirit. The question that can then, however, not be answered is what the ground of matter and spirit is in the first and last instance. The question remains either unanswered or one must assume that God created the world out of nothing. This argument can then take on two forms: (a) That God is the endless expression of spirit in the first and last instance and that God created matter, or (b) That God is something endless that created both spirit and matter. In any case there is no proof for the existence of God. A materialist position that assumes that the entire world is material and that matter is the process-substance of the world (see Fuchs 2003c) does not face this problem: matter is a causa sui, a cause of itself. It is its own ground, which means that matter and therefore the universe are self-organising and capable of producing new levels of the organisation of matter through which the existence of matter reproduces itself (see Fuchs 2003c). That matter is its own ground is a sufficient explanation for the existence of the world that does not have to revert to religious or esoteric explanations. It furthermore has atheistic implications. It is a better elucidation because it has fewer assumptions, which makes it according to the principle of Occam's razor the superior explanation of the world. Raymond Williams has a monist conception of the world, whereas Eagleton holds on to a dualist version that thought to the end is a form of idealism.

Eagleton (1989b, 170) argues that Williams sets up the concept of the "immaterial superstructure" as straw-target in order "to replace 'ideology' with 'hegemony'". Williams does not however, construct a straw-target, but rather criticises Marxists who use concepts such as determination, reflection, reproduction, mediation, and homology as being dualists. They cannot explain society's common ground. Williams in contrast argues that matter is the common ground of society, the world, and the universe. But he does not dissolve the concept of ideology, but rather understands it as "class outlook" (Williams 1977, 109) that, as Eagleton remarks himself, is for Williams part of the more general concept of hegemony.

It is in no way an "idealist reading of superstructures" (Eagleton 1989b, 171) to assume that hegemony involves ideology and other forms of domination (such as direct and structural violence).

Eagleton misses one crucial argument that Williams stressed again and again since the late 1970s: that an important reason why we need cultural materialism is the fact that the superstructure has been industrialised, commodified, and capitalised in the twentieth century by the emergence of the culture industry and the rising importance of information work. We have argued in this chapter that information work is an economic process that produces culture that has effects inside and outside of the economy. So culture necessarily takes place inside and outside of the economy. What economy and non-economy share is that they are both material systems: they are grounded in human transformative action that changes and reproduces structures that enable the continuity of social actions that bring about further changes and reproductions of structures in space-time (Fuchs 2003a, 2003b, 2008). Cultural work is economic in that it creates informational use-values that have emergent qualities that at a sublated level outside of the economy impact the whole of society. Matter is the process-substance of the world and therefore also of society. Society is a specific human organisational form of matter that has emerged in the history of the self-organisation of the universe. All society and human beings are material. Therefore also all of capitalist societies are material. All dimensions of capitalism are material. And this includes both physical and informational domains that are interconnected. Raymond Williams reminds us that culture is part of the material universe of the world and society and must therefore be produced and reproduced by humans in work processes, and at the same time develops dialectically in such a way that it sublates—i.e. preserves, eliminates, and uplifts—its own economicity and takes on emergent qualities in the whole of society.

Eagleton (1989b, 173) justifies the base/superstructure separation by saying that exploitation is primary and that superstructures support, "regulate and ratify" exploitation. He overlooks that both politics and culture do not simply exist, but need to be created and re-created in actual work and labour processes and have therefore their own economies. Eagleton concedes that culture has both an infrastructure and a superstructure, but says that "reading a literary text"—or we could more generally say using any form of medium—means that we are "treating it 'superstructurally'" (Eagleton 1989b, 174). Eagleton disregards that reading, watching, listening, and using are not pure free time and pure consumption activities, but also take place as part of labour activities and have increasingly due to the rise and extension of the culture industry and advertising culture become productive labour—watching, reading, and listening as working, play labour, and prosumption. These developments make Williams's cultural materialism an approach that is compelling and much needed today. His perspective allows us to better understand the interlocking and tendency of the liquefaction of boundaries between culture/economy, private/public, leisure/labour, spare time/labour time, labour/play, production/consumption, home/factory and office, fixed and stationary/mobile, information content/information technology, etc.

Eagleton remains trapped in the orthodoxy that eating is primary and more important than communicating. A baby that is not fed will die. A baby that is socially isolated and to whom nobody talks will, however, also die. What food and language have in common is that they are both material phenomena, because they emanate from nature and the human brain that both have in common that they are material systems.

Given the notion of cultural work and a cultural-materialist framework inspired by Raymond Williams, we can next ask the question what is specific about the digital mode of cultural labour.

2.4. Cultural Work and Cultural Labour in Modern Society

If culture were merely symbolic—mind, spirit, "immaterial", superstructural, informational, a world of ideas—then cultural labour as expression of culture clearly would exclude the concrete works of mining and hardware assemblage that are required for producing media technologies. Williams's cultural materialism, contrary to the position of cultural idealism, makes it possible to argue that cultural labour includes both the creation of physical products and information that are required for the production and usage of digital technologies. Some digital workers create hardware, others hardware components, minerals, software, or content that are all objectified in or the outcome of the application of digital technologies. Some workers, e.g. miners, contribute not just to the emergence of digital media, but to different products. If one knows the mines' sales and financial figures, then it is possible to determine to what extent the performed labour is digital or other labour.

In order to illustrate this point that culture is material, we now return in greater detail to a passage where Marx reflects about the work of making and playing the piano. He wrote:

> Productive labour is only that which produces capital. Is it not crazy, asks
> e.g. (or at least something similar) Mr Senior, that the piano maker is a
> productive worker, but not the piano player, although obviously the piano
> would be absurd without the piano player? But this is exactly the case. The
> piano maker reproduces capital; the pianist only exchanges his labour for
> revenue. But doesn't the pianist produce music and satisfy our musical ear,
> does he not even to a certain extent produce the latter? He does indeed:
> his labour produces something; but that does not make it productive labour
> in the economic sense; no more than the labour of the madman who pro-
> duces delusions is productive. Labour becomes productive only by produc-
> ing its own opposite.

Marx 1857/58, 305

Williams remarks that today, other than in Marx's time, "the production of music (and not just its instruments) is an important branch of capitalist production" (Williams 1977, 93).

If the economy and culture are two separate realms, then building the piano is work and part of the economy and playing it is not work, but culture. Marx leaves no doubt, however, that playing the piano produces a use-value that satisfies human ears and is therefore a form of work. As a consequence, the production of music must, just like the production of the piano, be an economic activity. Williams (1977, 94) stresses that cultural materialism means to see the material character of art, ideas, aesthetics, and ideology and that when considering piano making and piano playing it is important to discover and describe "relations between all these practices" and to not assume "that only some of them are material."

Apart from the piano maker and the piano player there is also the composer of music. All three forms of work are needed and necessarily related in order to guarantee the existence of piano music. Fixing one of these three productive activities categorically as culture and excluding the others from it limits the concept of culture and does not see that one cannot exist without the other. Along with this separation come political assessments of the separated entities. A frequent procedure is to include the work of the composer and player and to exclude the work of the piano maker. Cultural elitists then argue that only the composer and player are truly creative, whereas vulgar materialists hold that only the piano maker can be a productive worker because he works with his hands and produces an artefact. Both judgments are isolationist and politically problematic.

There is a difference if piano makers, players, and music composers conduct these activities, just as a hobby or for creating commodities that are sold on the market. This distinction can be explored based on Marx's distinction between work (*Werktätigkeit*) and labour (*Arbeit*): Brigitte Weingart (1997) describes the origins of the terms *work* in English and *Arbeit* and *Werk* in German. In German, the word *Arbeit* comes from the Germanic term *arba*, which meant slave. The English term work comes from the Middle English term *weorc*. It was a fusion of the Old English terms *wyrcan* (creating) and *wircan* (to affect something). So to work means to create something that brings about some changes in society. *Weorc* is related to the German terms *Werk* and *werken*. Both *work* in English and *Werk* in German were derived from the Indo-European term *uerg* (doing, acting). *Werken* in German is a term still used today for creating something. Its origins are quite opposed to the origins of the term *Arbeit*. The result of the process of *werken* is called *Werk*. Both *werken* and *Werk* have the connotative meaning of being creative. Both terms have an inherent connotation of artistic creation. Arendt (1958, 80–81) confirms the etymological distinction between *ergazesthai* (Greek)/ *facere, fabricari* (Latin)/*work* (English)/*werken* (German)/*ouvrer* (French) and *ponein* (Greek)/*laborare* (Latin)/*labour* (English)/*arbeiten* (German)/*travailler* (French).

Raymond Williams (1983, 176–179) argues that the word "labour" comes from the French word *labor* and the Latin term *laborem* and appeared in the English language first around 1300. It was associated with hard work, pain, and trouble. In the eighteenth century, it would have attained the meaning of work under capitalist conditions that stands in a class relationship with capital. The term "work" comes from the Old English word *weorc* and is the "most general word for doing something" (Williams 1983, 334). In capitalism the term on the one hand has, according to Williams (1983, 334–337), acquired the same meaning as labour—a paid job—but would have in contrast also kept its original broader meaning. In order to be able to differentiate the dual historical and essential character of work, it is feasible to make a semantic differentiation between labour and work.

The meaning and usage of words develops historically and may reflect the structures and changes of society, culture, and the economy. Given that we find an etymological distinction between the general aspects of productive human activities and the specific characteristics that reflect the realities of class societies, it makes sense to categorically distinguish between the anthropological dimension of human creative and productive activities that result in use-values that satisfy human needs and the historical dimension that describes how these activities are embedded into class relations (Fuchs 2014a). A model of the general work process is visualized in Figure 2.3.

Human subjects have labour power. Their labour in the work process interacts with the means of production (object). The means of production consist

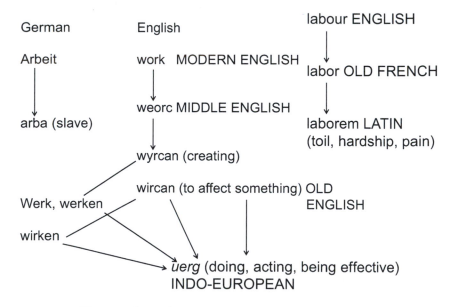

FIGURE 2.2 The etymology of the terms "work", "labour", and *Arbeit*

Marx's dialectic of subject and object in the economy

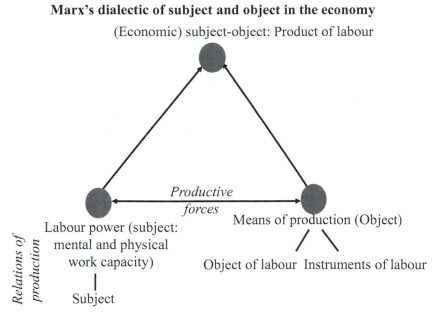

FIGURE 2.3   The general work process

of the object of labour (resources, raw materials) and the instruments of labour (technology). In the work process, humans transform an object (nature, culture) by making use of their labour power with the help of instruments of labour. The result is a product that unites the objectified labour of the subject with the objective materials s/he works on. Work becomes objectified in a product and the object is as a result transformed into a use value that serves human needs. The productive forces are a system, in which subjective productive forces (human labour power) make use of technical productive forces (part of the objective productive forces) in order to transform parts of the nature or culture so that a product emerges.

The general work process is an anthropological model of work under all histori-cal conditions. The connection of the human subject to other subjects in Figure 2.3 indicates that work is normally not conducted individually, but in relation with others. A society could hardly exist based on isolated people trying to sustain them-selves independently. It requires economic relations in the form of co-operation and a social organisation of production, distribution, and consumption. This means that work takes place under specific historical social relations of production. There are different possibilities for the organisation of the relations of production. In gen-eral the term *labour* points towards the organisation of labour under class relations, i.e. power relationships that determine that any or some of the elements in the work process are not controlled by the workers themselves, but by a group of economic controllers. *Labour* designates specific organisational forms of work, in which the human subject does not control his/her labour power (s/he is compelled to work for others) and/or there is a lack of control of the objects of labour and/or the instruments of labour and/or the products of labour.

Karl Marx pinpoints this lack of control by the term *alienation* and understands the unity of these forms of alienation as exploitation of labour:

> The material on which it [labour] works is alien material; the instrument is likewise an alien instrument; its labour appears as a mere accessory to their substance and hence objectifies itself in things not belonging to it. Indeed, living labour itself appears as alien vis-à-vis living labour capacity, whose labour it is, whose own life's expression it is, for it has been surrendered to capital in exchange for objectified labour, for the product of labour itself. [. . .] labour capacity's own labour is as alien to it—and it really is, as regards its direction etc.—as are material and instrument. Which is why the product then appears to it as a combination of alien material, alien instrument and alien labour—as alien property.
>
> *Marx 1857/58, 462*

Figure 2.4 visualizes potential dimensions of the labour process as alienated work process.

Gramsci's (1971, 1988) concept of hegemony makes clear that a ruling class not only rules economically but also has to ensure political and moral leadership in society, which it achieves through the state and ideology. A "hegemonic apparatus" aims at creating "a new ideological terrain" and "introducing

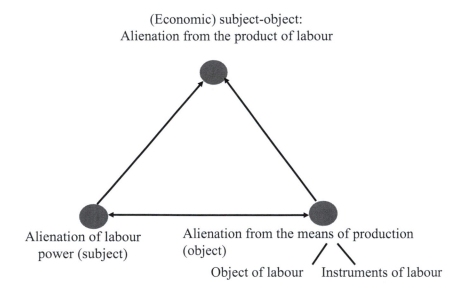

FIGURE 2.4   Labour as alienated work process

a new morality in conformity with a new conception of the world" (Gramsci 1988, 192).

The state has an "educative and formative role" (Gramsci 1971, 242). "Its aim is always that of creating new and higher types of civilisation; of adapting the 'civilisation' and the morality of the broadest popular masses to the necessities of the continuous development of the economic apparatus of production" (Gramsci 1971, 242). The state is "the entire complex of practical and theoretical activities with which the ruling class not only justifies and maintains its dominance, but manages to win the active consent of those over whom it rules" (Gramsci 1971, 244). Hegemony means "an active and voluntary (free) consent" (Gramsci 1971, 271). The law, military, police system, secret services, and prison system are the repressive elements of the state system that aim at guaranteeing internal and external defence of the system. The state school system is for Gramsci (1971, 258) the most important element of state hegemony that aims at creating active consent. Both "force and consent" (Gramsci 1971, 271) are exercised for constituting, maintaining, and reproducing the state system. But there are also elements of "cultural hegemony" (Gramsci 1971, 258) outside direct state control, such as religions/churches, associations, newspapers, theatre, films, radio, other media, public meetings, language and dialects, folklore and traditions, conversations, and morals (Gramsci 1988, especially 356).

The question that arises is if civil society and culture stand outside the state or are part of it. Gramsci says that "civil society and the state are one and the same" (Gramsci 1988, 210), so for him the "State = political society + civil society" (Gramsci 1971, 263) and he speaks of "hegemony protected by the armour of coercion" (Gramsci 1971, 263). A concept of the state that conceives it as the unity of coercive and ideological state apparatuses (Althusser 1970) inflates the state concept to a maximum and does not leave any conceptual space for conceiving parts of culture as neither controlled by the state nor capitalism, but as the people's common culture.

Hegel, who is considered as one of the most influential writers on civil society (Anheier et al. 2010, 338), described civil society as political and as a sphere that is separate from the state and from the private life of the family (Hegel 1821, §§157, 261). Jürgen Habermas's (1989a) seminal work *The Structural Transformation of the Public Sphere* describes that eighteenth-century France and Germany were characterised by a separation of spheres. Civil society was the private "realm of commodity exchange and social labor" (Habermas 1989a, 30) that was distinct from the public sphere and the sphere of public authority. This understanding was reflected in liberal market-driven civil society conceptions of thinkers like Locke and Smith that positioned economic man at the heart of civil society (Ehrenberg 1999). The structural transformation of the public sphere has in the nineteenth and twentieth century according to Habermas resulted in an increasing collapse of boundaries between spheres so that "private economic units" attained "quasi-political character" and from "the midst of the publicly relevant sphere of civil society was formed a repoliticized social sphere" that formed a "functional complex that could no longer be differentiated according to criteria of public and private" (Habermas 1989a, 148). One can say that the structural transformation Habermas describes meant the emergence of the modern economy as a separate powerful sphere of modern society and the separation of the economy from civil society. This notion of civil society could be found in the works of Montesquieu, Rousseau, and Tocqueville and has today become the common understanding of this notion (Ehrenberg 1999). In later works, Habermas (1987, 320) as a result describes contemporary modern society as consisting of systems (economic system, administrative system) and the lifeworld (private sphere, public sphere). Civil society as part of the lifeworld now exists in his theory of "associational networks" that "articulate political interests and confront the state with demands arising from the life worlds of various groups" (Habermas 2006, 417). Civil society's "voluntary associations, interest groups, and social movements always strive to maintain a measure of autonomy from the public affairs of politics and the private concerns of economics" (Ehrenberg 1999, 235). Habermas (2006) mentions as examples for civil society actors: social movements, general interest groups, advocates for certain interests, experts, and intellectuals. Qualities and concepts of civil society mentioned in the literature include: voluntariness, nongovernmental associations, healthy democracy, public sphere, exchange of opinions, political debate, self-organisation, self-reflection, non-violence, struggle for egalitarian diversity (Keane 2010; Kenny 2007; Salzman 2011; Sheldon 2001, 62f).

Salzman (2011, 199) mentions "environmental groups, bowling leagues, churches, political parties, neighbourhood associations, social networking Internet sites" as examples for civil society organisations. Keane (2010) adds charities, independent churches, and publishing houses as examples. In civil society theory, the concept of hegemony in particular has been used for stressing civil society's aspects of contradiction, power, counter-power, ideology, and its dialectical relation to the state and the economy (Anheier et al. 2010, 408ff). Such characterisations of civil society groups are merely enumerative, but lack a more systematic distinction that is based on a theoretical criterion.

Civil society is made up of the socio-political, the socio-economic, and the socio-cultural spheres. Claus Offe (1985) distinguishes between socio-political movements, which want to establish binding goals for a wider community and are recognised as legitimate, and socio-cultural movements, which want to establish goals, which are not binding for a wider community (retreat) and are considered as legitimate. Further forms of non-institutional action would be private crime (non-binding goals, illegitimate) and terrorism (binding goals, illegitimate). Offe's distinction between socio-political and socio-cultural movements has been reflected in Touraine's (1985) distinction between social movements and cultural movements. Table 2.1 summarizes the discussion. We add to this distinction one between socio-political and socio-economic movements.

The struggles of socio-economic movements are oriented on the production and distribution of material resources that are created and distributed in the economic system. They are focused on questions of the production, distribution, and redistribution of material resources. One modern socio-economic movement is the working-class movement that struggles for the betterment of living conditions as they are affected by working conditions and thereby opposes the economic interests of those who own capital and the means of production. In the history of the working-class movement, there have been fierce debates about the role of reforms and revolution. A more recent debate concerns the role and importance of non-wage workers in the working-class movement (Cleaver 2000). Another socio-economic movement is the environmental movement that struggles for the preservation and sustainable treatment of humans' external nature (the environment). Whereas the working-class movement is oriented on relationships between organised groups of human beings (classes) with definite interests, the ecological movement is oriented on the relationship between human beings and their natural environment. Both relations (human-human, human-nature) are at the heart of the economy and interact with each other.

Socio-political movements are movements that struggle for the recognition of collective identities of certain groups in society via demands on the state. They are oriented on struggles that relate e.g. to gender, sexual orientation, ethnicity and origin, age, neighbourhood, peace, or disability. Examples are the feminist movement, the gay-rights movement, the anti-racist movement, the youth movement, the peace movement, the anti-penitentiary movement, the anti-psychiatry movement, etc. Their common characteristic is that their struggles are oriented on recognising specific groups of people as having specific rights, ways of life, or identities. So for example the peace and human rights movement struggles for the recognition of the basic right of all humans to exist free from the threat of being killed or coerced by violence. As another example, racist movements struggle for recognising specific groups (like white people) as either superior and other groups as inferior or so culturally or biologically different that they need to be separated.

Socio-cultural movements are groups of people that have shared interests and practices relating to ways of organising your private life. Examples include friendship networks, neighbourhood networks, churches, sports groups, fan communities, etc.

Figure 2.5 visualises a model of modern society. The model is grounded in the social theory insight that the relationship between structures and actors is dialectical and that both levels continuously create each other. Modern society is made up of the dialectically mediated realms of the state, the economy, and culture. The civil sphere (civil society) is an intermediate realm, in which socio-political, socio-economic, and socio-cultural groups, structures, and practices establish interfaces between the three spheres. The state therefore is not the same as civil society, but is rather made up of coercive state apparatuses and state-controlled forms of economic (e.g. nationalized industries) and cultural (e.g. state schools and universities) institutions.

TABLE 2.1 A typology of different forms of non–institutional action (adapted from: Offe 1985)

	Civil society	
Goals	*Recognised as legitimate*	*Illegitimate*
Binding for a wider community	Socio-political and socio-economic movements (= Political public sphere) 1) NGOs: more hierarchical, formal, lobbying 2) Social movements: grassroots, informal, protest	Terrorism
Non-binding for a wider community	Socio-cultural movements (= Civic cultures) consensus, shared interests and values, affinity Examples: friendship networks, neighbourhoods, work networks, churches, sects, sports teams, fan communities, professional organisations/associations	Crime

The modern economy is the capitalistic way of organising production, distribution, and consumption, i.e. it is a system that is based on the accumulation of money capital by the sale of commodities that are produced by workers who are compelled to sell their labour power as a commodity to owners of capital and means of production, who thereby gain the right to exploit labour for a specific time period. The modern political system is a bureaucratic state system, in which liberal parliamentary democracy (including political parties, elections, parliamentary procedures), legal guarantees of bourgeois freedoms (freedoms of speech, assembly, association, the press, movement, ownership, belief and thought, opinion, and expression), and the monopolisation of the means of violence by coercive state apparatuses guarantee the reproduction of the existing social order. Besides the capitalist economy and the state, modern society also consists of the cultural sphere that can be divided into a private and a public culture. Modern culture is a sphere of the accumulation of definition power through which dominant meanings and worldviews are created, diffused, constituted, reproduced, and challenged.

Hannah Arendt stresses that the private sphere is a realm of modern society that functions as "a sphere of intimacy" (Arendt 1958, 38) and includes family life as well as emotional and sexual relationships. Habermas adds to this analysis that consumption plays a central role in the private sphere: "On the other hand, the family now evolved even more into a consumer of income and leisure time, into the recipient of publicly guaranteed compensations and support services. Private autonomy was maintained not so much in functions of control as in functions of consumption" (Habermas 1989a, 156). He furthermore points out that the private sphere is the realm of leisure activities: "Leisure behavior supplies the key to the floodlit privacy of the new sphere, to the externalization of what is declared

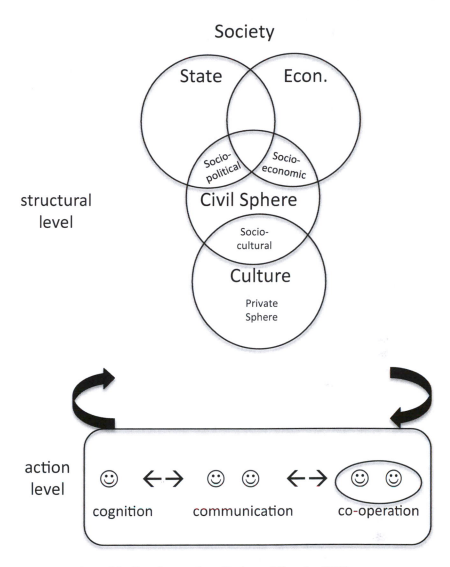

FIGURE 2.5 A model of modern society (Fuchs and Trottier 2013)

to be the inner life" (Habermas 1989a, 159). In other words, one can say that the role of the private sphere in capitalism as a sphere of individual leisure and consumption that Habermas identifies is that it guarantees the reproduction of labour power so that the latter remains vital, productive, and exploitable.

But there are also social forms of organising leisure and consumption, as e.g. fan communities, amateur sports clubs, churches, etc. This means that both individual and social forms of organising everyday life exist. Together they form the sphere of culture understood as the realm in which mundane everyday life is organised, and meaning is given to the world. The basic role of culture in society is that it guarantees the reproduction of the human body and mind, which includes on the one hand activities like sports, sexuality, health and social care, and on the other hand activities like education, knowledge production (e.g. in universities), art, literature, etc. If these activities are organised on an individual basis, then they take place in the private sphere; if they are organised on a social basis outside of the home and the family, then they take place in the socio-cultural sphere. According to Habermas (1989a), the realms of the systems of the economy and the state on the one hand and the lifeworld (culture, in our model) on the other are mediated by what he terms the public sphere or civil society.

In dominative societies, the hegemonic block of the dominant economic class in interaction with political and ideological groups tries to maintain economic, political, and cultural hegemony. It uses different forms of violence for doing so. Based on the works of Johan Galtung (1990), violence can be defined as "avoidable insults to basic human needs, and more generally to life, lowering the real level of needs satisfaction below what is potentially possible" (Galtung 1990, 292). Violence can according to Galtung (1990) be divided into three principal forms: direct violence (through physical intervention; an event), structural violence (through state or organisational mandate; a process), and cultural violence (dehumanising or otherwise exclusionary representations; an invariance). These forms operate through the denial of four basic needs: survival needs (through killing and exploitation), well-being needs (through maiming, sanctions, and exploitation), identity needs (through desocialisation, resocialisation, and segmentation), and freedom needs (through repression, detention, expulsion, marginalisation, and fragmentation) (Galtung 1990). Repressive state apparatuses try to monopolise the exercise of direct violence through the police, the military, secret services, and the prison system. The main forms of modern structural violence are commodity markets, labour markets, and the law. Cultural violence is the construction and diffusion of ideologies.

2.5. A Typology of the Dimensions of Working Conditions

A suitable starting point for a systematic model of different dimensions of working conditions is the circuit of capital accumulation as it has been described by Karl Marx (1867, 248–253; 1885, 109). According to Marx, capital accumulation in a first stage requires the investment of capital in order to buy what is necessary for producing commodities, i.e. the productive forces: labour time of workers (L or variable capital) on the one hand, and working equipment like machines and raw materials (MoP or constant capital) on the other hand (Marx 1885/1992, 110). Thus, money (M) is used in order to buy labour power as well as machines and resources as commodities (C) that then in a second stage enter the labour process and produce (P) a new commodity (C') (Marx 1885, 118). This new commodity (C') contains more value than the sum of its parts, i.e. surplus-value. This surplus-value needs to be realised and turned into more money (M') by selling the commodity in the market (Marx 1885/1992, 125). The circuit of capital accumulation can thus be described with the following formula:

$$M \rightarrow C \ldots P \ldots C' \rightarrow M' \text{ (Marx 1885, 110).}$$

According to Marx, surplus-value can only be generated due to the specific qualities of labour-power as a commodity. Marx argued that labour power is the only commodity "whose use-value possesses the peculiar property of being a source of value, whose actual consumption is therefore itself an objectification of labour, hence a creation of value" (Marx 1867, 270).

Labour is thus essential to the process of capital accumulation. The model in Figure 2.5 takes the labour process as its point of departure for identifying different dimensions that shape working conditions (Sandoval 2013). Its purpose is to provide comprehensive guidelines that can be applied for systematically studying working conditions in different sectors (for a systematic study of corporate irresponsibility of working and production conditions in eight companies in the media industries see Sandoval 2014).

The model pictured in Figure 2.6 identifies five areas that shape working conditions throughout the capital accumulation process: means of production, labour, relations of production, the production process, and the outcome

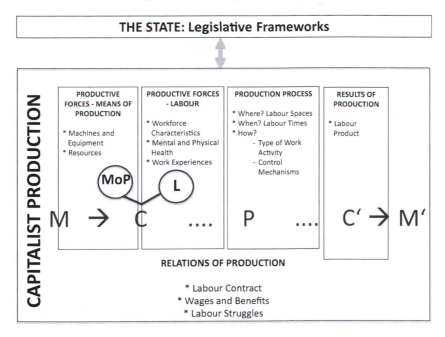

FIGURE 2.6 Dimensions of working conditions

of production. Furthermore this model includes the state's impact on working conditions through labour legislation.

Productive Forces—Means of Production: Means of production include *machines and equipment* on the one hand and *resources* that are needed for production on the other hand. The question whether workers operate big machines, work at the assembly line, use mobile devices such as laptops, handle potentially hazardous substances, use high-tech equipment, traditional tools, or no technology at all etc. shapes the experience of work and has a strong impact on work processes and working conditions.

Productive Forces—Labour: The subjects of the labour process are workers themselves. One dimension that impacts work in a certain sector is the question how the *workforce* is composed in terms of gender, ethnic background, age, education levels etc. Another question concerns worker *health and safety* and how it is affected by the means of production, the relations of production, the labour process, and labour law. Apart from outside impacts on the worker, an important factor is how workers themselves *experience* their working conditions.

Relations of Production: Within capitalist relations of production, capitalists buy labour power as a commodity. Thereby a relation between capital and labour is established. The purchase of labour power is expressed through *wages*. Wages are the primary means of subsistence for workers and the reason why they enter a wage labour relation. The level of wages thus is a central element of working conditions. *Labour contracts* specify the conditions under which capital and labour enter this relation, including working hours, wages, work roles and responsibilities etc. The content of this contract is subject to negotiations and often *struggles between capital and labour*. The relation between capital and labour is thus established through a *wage relation* and formally enacted by a *labour contract* that is subject to negotiations and *struggles*. These three dimensions of the relation between capital and labour set the framework for the capitalist labour process.

Production process: Assessing working conditions furthermore requires looking at the specifics of the actual production process. A first factor in this context is its *spatial location*. Whether it is attached to a certain place or is location independent, whether it takes place in a factory, an office building, or outdoors etc. are important questions. A second factor relates to the *temporal dimension of work*. Relevant questions concern the amount of regular working hours and overtime, work rhythms, the flexibility or rigidity of working hours, the relation between work time and free time etc. Finally working conditions are essentially shaped by how the production process is executed. This includes on the one hand the question which *types of work activity* are performed. The activities can range from intellectual work, to physical work, to service work, from skilled to unskilled work, from creative work to monotonous and standardised work tasks, etc. On the other hand another aspect of the production process is how it is *controlled and managed*. Different management styles can range from strict control of worker behaviour and the labour process to high degrees of autonomy, self-management, participatory management etc.

Space, time, activity, and *control* are essential qualities of the production process and therefore need to be considered when studying working conditions.

Product: Throughout the production process workers put their time, effort, and energy into producing a certain *product*. This actual outcome of production and how it relates back to the worker thus needs to be considered for understanding work in a certain sector.

The state: Finally the state has an impact on working conditions through enacting *labour laws* that regulate minimum wages, maximum working hours, social security, safety standards etc.

Table 2.2 summarises the dimensions of working conditions that we described above.

TABLE 2.2 Dimensions of working conditions

Productive forces— Means of production	Machines and equipment	Which technology is being used during the production process?
	Resources	What resources are used during the production process?
Productive forces— Labour	Workforce characteristics	What are important characteristics of the workforce for example in terms of age, gender, ethnic background etc.?
	Mental and physical health	How do the employed means of production and the labour process impact workers' mental and physical health?
	Work experiences	How do workers experience their working conditions?
Relations of production	Labour contracts	Which type of contracts do workers receive? What do they regulate?
	Wages and benefits	How high/low are wage levels? What other material benefits for workers are there?
	Labour struggles	How do workers organise and engage in negotiations with capital and what is the role of worker protests?
Production process	Labour spaces	Where does the production process take place?
	Labour times	How many working hours are common within a certain sector, how are they enforced, and how is the relationship between work and free time?
	Work activity	Which type of mental and/or physical activity are workers performing?
	Control mechanism	Which type of mechanisms are in place that control the behaviour of workers?
Results of production	Labour product	Which kinds of products or services are being produced?
The state	Labour law	Which regulations regarding minimum wages, maximum working hours, safety, social security etc. are in place and how are they enforced?

2.6. Why the Notion of Anti-Work Is Mistaken and Why We Need to Repeat William Morris and Herbert Marcuse Today

Some scholars and activists argue that work is inherently toil and alienated, and that it is therefore something that needs to be abolished. We want to show why this anti-work philosophy is mistaken.

A *first* common strategy is that anti-work theorists define work as identical with labour and do not further explore categorical differentiations and reasons why there may be two words for related, but at the same time different, phenomena in the English language and other languages. So for example André Gorz (1982, 1) writes that work "came into being at the same time as capitalists and proletarians. It means an activity carried out: for someone else; in return for a wage; according to forms and time schedules laid down by the person paying the wage; and for a purpose not chosen by the worker". Kathi Weeks (2011, 14) uses the terms *labour* and *work* interchangeably for "productive cooperation organized around, but not necessarily confined to, the privileged model of waged labor". Bob Black (1996) defines work as "forced labor, that is, compulsory production". Such definitions (a) leave unclear how human activities that in all types of society are necessary for the existence of humans and society should be termed, (b) why exactly labour and work should be equated, and why in many languages two words exist for characterising productive or creative human activity.

Toni Negri argues that in Marx's *Grundrisse*, work is a specifically capitalist concept:

> In the *Grundrisse*, work appears as immediately abstract labor. We can only understand it and integrate it within theory at this level. Work is abstract in so far as it is only immediately perceptible at the level of the social relations of production. Thus we can only define work on the basis of the relations of exchange and of the capitalist structure of production. We can find no concept of work in Marx that is not that of waged work, of work that is socially necessary to the reproduction of capital, thus no concept of any work to restore, to liberate, to sublimate, only a concept and a reality to suppress.
>
> *Negri 1991, 10*

In the *Grundrisse*, Marx (1857/58, 611) says that labour as "slave-labour, serf-labour, and wage-labour, [. . .] always appears as repulsive, always as *external forced labour*; and not-labour, by contrast, as 'freedom and happiness'". In a free society "labour becomes attractive work, the individual's self-realization". Such work would be social, scientific, or general (Marx 1857/58, 612), which means that for Marx work in communism produces knowledge and social relations. The quotation shows that contrary to Negri's claim, Marx advances a non-capitalist concept of work in the *Grundrisse*.

Also in other of Marx's major writings, work is not confined to capitalism. In *Capital, Volume I*, work is defined as "a condition of human existence which is independent of all forms of society; it is an eternal natural necessity which mediates the metabolism between man and nature, and therefore human life itself" (Marx 1867, 133). Work is "purposeful activity aimed at the production of use-values", "it is common to all forms of society in which human beings live" (Marx 1867, 290).

By the notion of species-being, Marx (1844, 74) in the *Economic and Philosophic Manuscripts* means that humans are practical beings that by the interaction of their activities and ideas change the world. "[L]ife-activity"—"productive life itself"—is a *means* of satisfying a need", "free, conscious activity is man's species character" (Marx 1844, 75). Man "produces even when he is free from physical need and only truly produces in freedom therefrom" (Marx 1844, 75). For Marx, work is a creative human activity conducted in society: "what I create from myself I create for society, conscious of myself as a social being".[1]

In the *Manuscripts*, Marx also uses the German term *Werktätigkeit* for describing human species-being, which expresses that humans in their practices create works (*Werk* = a work, *Tätigkeit* = practice, *Werktätigkeit* = practices that create works):

> Eben in der Bearbeitung der gegenständlichen Welt bewährt sich der Mensch daher erst wirklich als ein *Gattungswesen*. Diese Produktion ist *sein* werktätiges Gattungsleben. Durch sie erscheint die Natur als sein Werk und seine Wirklichkeit. Der Gegenstand der Arbeit ist daher die *Vergegenständlichung des Gattungslebens des Menschen:* indem er sich nicht nur wie im Bewußtsein intellektuell, sondern werktätig, wirklich verdoppelt und sich selbst daher in einer von ihm geschaffnen Welt anschaut.
>
> *Marx 1844 [German], 517*

This passage has been translated into English the following way:

> It is just in the working-up of the objective world, therefore, that man first really proves himself to be a species being. This production is his active species life. Through and because of this production, nature appears as his work and his reality. The object of labour is, therefore, the *objectification of man's species life*: for he duplicates himself not only, as in consciousness, intellectually, but also actively, in reality, and therefore he contemplates himself in a world that he has created.
>
> *Marx 1844 [English], 76*

The adjective *werktätig* has here been twice translated with "active", which is not a very suitable translation and can easily mislead English-speaking readers: "Active species-being" can literally be better translated as "working species-being". Marx also writes that by this kind of species-being nature appears as man's *Werk* and *Wirklichkeit*, which is translated with "work" and "reality", a translation that does not capture the full meaning: Marx has here deliberately chosen the two words *Werk* and *Wirklichkeit* because they are connected: *Wirklichkeit* comes from the German term *wirken* that could be translated with "creative work" that transforms and has transformative effects on reality (*Wirklichkeit*). The term "work" stems from the German notions of *wirken* and *werken*: in their work humans transform reality—*das menschliche Werken wirkt in der Wirklichkeit* (Human work works on reality).

The idea that work is a practical human activity and in communism becomes a creative, self-determined activity of human life is a constant element of Marx's thoughts from his early to his late works. Not all Autonomist Marxists share the view that work should be conceptualised as necessarily coerced, alienated, and a capitalist concept. So for example John Holloway (1995, 171) argues with Marx that work is "the creative power of human practice". The "existence of work as value-producing labour [in capitalism] does nothing at all to change the all-constitutive power of work: since work is the only creative force in society (any society), it could not be otherwise" (Holloway 1995, 172). Holloway argues that the central insight of Marx's law of value is that human work is a form of empowerment against capital, the capacity of humans to become independent of capital: "behind all the forms of our powerlessness lies the one thing that makes us all-powerful: work. That is the first, obvious, and generally overlooked, meaning of the labour theory of value. It is a great chest-thumping cry: 'we humans, as workers, are all-powerful'" (Holloway 1995, 177).

An associated claim of the first type of argument brought forward against the concept of work is that the word "work" did not exist before capitalism (e.g. Cleaver 2002, 2003). Harry Cleaver (2000) elaborated an important political reading of Marx's *Capital*. The importance of it lies not only in the circumstance that it is a political interpretation, but also that it is a Hegelian reading of Marx, which is rather rare today in Marxism in general and Autonomist Marxism in particular but can, as Cleaver shows, help stress Marx's focus on capitalism's class relation between labour and capital and associated struggles. Cleaver seems to have revised his view on the questions how to define work and if there is work in a communist society: whereas in his works from 2002 and later he makes statements like "the liberation *of* work can come only with the liberation *from* work, that is, from the capitalist reduction of life to work" (Cleaver 2011, 61),[2] in the second edition of *Reading Capital Politically* published in 2000 that has been widely translated into languages such as German, Indian, Korean, Mexican, Polish, and Turkish, he uses the term "'unalienated' work" that he sees as "work as an activity which is not a function of domination", which involves "the elimination of the element of compulsion" (Cleaver 2000, 130).

Marx does not, as argued by Harry Cleaver, take a genuinely capitalist concept and project it forward and backward in history. He is rather aware that the German term *Werktätigkeit* is an anthropological feature of all societies and therefore characterises the human being as "werktätiges Gattungsleben" (Marx 1844, 517) = working species-being. Marx used a dialectic of the general and the concrete for thinking about capitalism and other types of societies: there are general characteristics that are common to all societies and specific historical features that these dimensions take on under specific historical conditions. By developing a critical theory of capitalism Marx not only uncovered this society's logic, but also showed how the logic of capital accumulation estranges human beings from society as such, which requires a concept of society in general that Marx developed in constant interaction with the categories that are specific for capitalism.

A *second* common argument of anti-work philosophy is to point out that something is wrong with Marx's concept of work, e.g. to claim that Marx fetishized productive work and had no sense for idleness (Black 1996) or that the "real Marx" wanted to abolish work along with capitalism (Negri 1991). No matter what the specific claim is, the overall line of argument is that there is something wrong with Marx's concept of work and that only a certain idea, book, or interpretation of this concept is the right one and that other original Marxian writings on work have to be refuted.

Kathi Weeks (2011) makes in this respect a prototypical argument by distinguishing between three Marxes:

- The productivist Marx of *Capital* and the *Communist Manifesto* who wants to have more work, sees sloth as a sin, and influenced Leninism's and Stalinism's work ethics (Weeks 2011, 82–85).
- The humanist Marx of the *Economic and Philosophic Manuscripts* and the *German Ideology* who wants to have better, non-alienated work and influenced humanist socialists such as Erich Fromm (Weeks 2011, 85–89).
- The "good" anti-work Marx of the *Grundrisse* who wants to abolish, refuse, reduce, and overcome work, cherishes idleness, and who influenced Negri and other Autonomist Marxists (Weeks 2011, 92–103).

Weeks, in a move remindful of Althusser's (1969), claims that Marx's works on work are inconsistent and that he changed his positions. We want to refute this myth of inconsistency that only helps conservative opponents of Marx to construct the argument that Marx was wrong.

A consistent theme in Marx's works is the stress on the role of industry and technology for reducing the working day, i.e. the hours of necessary work needed for the survival of humanity. Technology tends to create misery under capitalism, but can create new forms of well-rounded individuality in a free society. Already in the 1844 *Manuscripts*, Marx (1844, 110) points out that natural science and industry have "prepared human emancipation, however directly and much it had to consummate dehumanization". In the *German Ideology*'s Feuerbach chapter, Marx says that communism "presupposes the universal development of productive forces" (Marx and Engels 1845/46, 57) and that the developed productive forces enable a well-rounded individuality (53). Creative activities and the reduction of necessary working time are here two sides of one coin.

In the *Grundrisse*, Marx continued to stress this connection by pointing out:

> The less time the society requires to produce wheat, cattle etc., the more time it wins for other production, material or mental. Just as in the case of an individual, the multiplicity of its development, its enjoyment and its activity depends on economization of time. Economy of time, to this all economy ultimately reduces itself.
>
> *Marx 1857/58, 172f*

In a similar passage, he later in the book wrote: "The saving of labour time [is] equal to an increase of free time, i.e. time for the full development of the individual, which in turn reacts back upon the productive power of labour as itself the greatest productive power" (Marx 1857/58, 711).

Also in *Capital, Volume 1*, Marx stresses the connection of technological productivity, the reduction of necessary work time and creative work:

> The more the productivity of labour increases, the more the working day can be shortened, and the more the working day is shortened, the more the intensity of labour can increase. From the point of view of society the productivity of labour also grows when economies are made in its use. This implies not only economising on the means of production, but also avoiding all useless labour. The capitalist mode of production, while it enforces economy in each individual business, also begets, by its anarchic system of competition, the most outrageous squandering of labour-power and of the social means of production, not to mention the creation of a vast number of functions at present indispensable, but in themselves superfluous.
>
> The intensity and productivity of labour being given, the part of the social working day necessarily taken up with material production is shorter and, as a consequence, the time at society's disposal for the free intellectual and social activity of the individual is greater, in proportion as work is more and more evenly divided among all the able-bodied members of society, and a particular social stratum is more and more deprived of the ability to shift the burden of labour (which is a necessity imposed by nature) from its own shoulders to those of another social stratum. The absolute minimum limit to the shortening of the working day is, from this point of view, the universality [*Allgemeinheit*] of labour. In capitalist society, free time is produced for one class by the conversion of the whole lifetime of the masses into labour-time.
>
> *Marx 1867, 667*

Given that Marx consistently stresses throughout his works that there is a necessary connection between productivity, technology, the reduction of necessary work time, well-rounded individuality, and free creative work, it is infeasible to assume as Weeks and others do that he had an inconsistent concept of work. It is an artificial separation to argue that one has to choose between one of three Marxes, the ones demanding "more work, better work, and less work" (Weeks 2011, 104). It is rather a consistent theme in Marx's oeuvre that the technological increase of productivity intensifies (and to a certain degree also extends) work in capitalism (*more work* and exploitation in less time, *more work* as longer working hours), but has the potential to lessen necessary work for all (less work) in a post-capitalist society to a minimum so that *alternative forms of work* (better work) emerge that are non-coerced, go beyond necessity, and are an expression of well-rounded individuality and human creativity. Modern technology has a dialectical character in that it contains potentials for the abolition of labour and toil as well as the freeing up of human life so that there is time for creativity as well as a reality of intensified alienation, i.e. non-control of humans over their own lives. A free society sublates (*aufheben*) work: it *eliminates* its coerced, exploitative, and toilsome aspects, i.e. it eliminates labour, it *preserves* certain aspects of contemporary work organisation, such as the importance of technology for achieving high productivity, and it *uplifts* society and economy to a new level, on which human individuality is well-rounded and all humans are enabled to have the time and possibilities for creativity.

A *third* argument of anti-work philosophy is that Marx was a productivist, i.e. that he stressed the need for being productive in order for humans to exist, which has turned into an ideological socialist work ethic that wants to eternalise toil and hates idleness. Weeks (2011) claims that productivist elements can be found in Marx's *Communist Manifesto* and *Capital*. Part of this argument is the criticism of Soviet ideology's use of the claim that everyone has become a worker for legitimatising forced labour.

Harry Cleaver writes that the idea that in communism everyone is a worker is an "ideology that has justified the brutal socialist imposition of work" (Cleaver 2003, 56). Our argument is that not everyone becomes a worker in communism, but that everyone in every society is always a worker of the commons that are created and reproduced by all. So Soviet ideology got it wrong by arguing that work became liberated and everyone became a worker in the Soviet Union.

The stress on necessary toil in Soviet Marxism is no wonder given that the Soviet system was first a predominantly agricultural and later an industrialising society that assumed that it could catch up with and overhaul Western capitalist countries' productivity. Herbert Marcuse (1958) stresses that the Protestant labour ethic was both an element of the Soviet system and Western capitalism. In the Soviet system, "love for one's work" is per se one of the highest principles of Communist morality, and work per se is declared to be one of the most important factors in the building of moral qualities. [. . .] Many of the rules of conduct in school and home, at work and leisure, in private and in public, resemble so much their traditional Western counterparts at earlier stages that they have the sound of secular sermons documenting the "spirit of Protestant-capitalist ethics". They are not too far from Puritan exhortations to good business.

Marcuse 1958, 234, 242

The religious component of this ethic is evident in the philosophy of Christianity, where work has been a virtue, as expressed in Paul's ethics of labour: "The one who is unwilling to work shall not eat" (2 Thessalonians 3).

Paul's labour ethic was directly reflected in Soviet ideology, which renders Lenin and Stalin more religious than they are generally considered to be. Lenin (1917b, 342) wrote that "He who does not work shall not eat" is a "socialist principle". Stalin reflected this idea:

The basis of the relations of production under the socialist system, which so far has been established only in the U.S.S.R., is the social ownership of the means of production. Here there are no longer exploiters and exploited. The goods produced are distributed according to labour performed, on the principle: "He who does not work, neither shall he eat".

Stalin 1938

This principle was also written into Article 18 of the 1936 Constitution of the USSR: "The Russian Socialist Federative Soviet Republic declares labour to be the duty of all citizens of the Republic, and proclaims the slogan: 'He who does not work, neither shall he eat!'"[3]

These examples are indications that the Soviet system was based on coercive labour and a religious labour ideology that aimed at increasing productivity as quickly as possible. So it is definitely true that the Soviet system reproduced the repressive organisation of work characteristic for labour under capitalism. This does, however, not imply that the concept of work cannot obtain a meaning that is in line with Marx's vision of a non-repressive organisation of human activities that are expressions of well-rounded individuality under the conditions of the minimisation of necessary working time.

In *Capital, Volume 3*, Marx says that capitalism

creates the material means and the nucleus for a higher form of society, with a greater reduction of the overall time devoted to material labour. [. . .] The realm of freedom really begins only where labour determined by necessity and external expediency ends; it lies by its very nature beyond the sphere of material production proper. [. . .] The reduction of the working day is the basic prerequisite.

Marx 1894, 958f

Marx's theme of the realm of freedom beyond necessity has been reflected in Herbert Marcuse's works: He says that a free society must be a highly productive knowledge society where "the prevailing 'economics of time' (Bahro) can be overthrown" and there is "free, creative time as the time for life" (Marcuse 1979, 223). Technology "may one day help to shift the center of gravity from the necessities of material production to the arena of free human realization" (Marcuse 1941b, 63). Such a new society would be shaped by "the planned utilization of resources for the satisfaction of vital needs with a minimum of toil, the transformation of leisure into free time, the pacification of the struggle of existence" (Marcuse 1964, 252–253). Alienation could be overcome:

The technological processes of mechanization and standardization might release individual energy into a yet uncharted realm of freedom beyond necessity [. . .] the individual would be liberated from the work world's imposing upon him alien needs and alien possibilities. The individual would be free to exert autonomy over a life that would be his own.

Marcuse 1964, 2

Marcuse (1965, 22) says that in a free society there will be "the redefinition of work in terms of a free realization of human needs and facilities". Technique would then be art "as construction of the beautiful, not as beautiful objects or places but as the Form of a totality of life—society and nature" (Marcuse 1967a, 119). In a free society, society can become a work of art (Marcuse 1967b, 128).

Marcuse's themes have been anticipated by and reflected in the works of William Morris (1884b, 98) who questioned that "all work is useful". It is a conservative ideology to assume that "all labour is good in itself" (Morris 1884b, 98). There is work that is a curse and should be refused (Morris 1884b, 98). The conservative British government used the labour ethic as ideology against the unemployed. In April 2013, it introduced benefit caps that Work and Pensions Secretary Iain Duncan Smith justified by saying that they pose "a strong incentive for people to move into work".[4] It does not matter for the UK government which labour one has or how much one earns; the stress is only on the circumstance *that* one "is in work" so that one can be exploited by capital. Unnecessary, hard, and harmful labour has no moral right to exist. It should be abolished as soon as possible.

There is a lot of *unnecessary, useless labour* (a waste of human energy) and labour that can be automated. Unnecessary labour is work that is not needed for the survival of humankind. It includes for example labour that controls the work force and private property, such as managers, directors, chief executives, protective and security workers, employment agents; labour that secures the state's monopoly of violence, such as lawyers, judges, police inspectors, police officers, prison guards, soldiers; labour that organises the monetary economy, such as accountants, brokers, securities and finance dealers, insurance representatives, bank personnel, debt collectors, estate agents, cashiers, sales personnel, and vendors. A society that abolishes money and the private property of the means of production can abolish or drastically reduce a lot of these occupations because money then no longer mediates the economy, there are no longer any wage earners that need to be controlled and monitored, private property no longer needs to be secured and guarded, and property-related conflicts and crimes are likely to be reduced.

Useless labour is today accompanied by some useless forms of entertainment that should no longer exist in a free society, especially those that are directly about winning money, such as gambling, betting, and the lottery. Also other stupefying activities, such as reading tabloids and horoscopes, are likely to vanish because tabloids are an expression of a highly commercialised press and horoscopes a form of organised irrationality. This does not mean that useful forms of playful entertainment, such as music, films, non-competitive sports etc. should no longer exist in a free society, but that money-mediated and ideological culture is likely to cease to exist. Many forms of organised and administered sports reflect the ideologies of nationalism, patriarchy, racism, competition, and the fascist idealisation of bodily strength that implies an implicit disregard of the weak. The liberal standard argument against these thoughts is: Wait a minute, there are also female soccer teams, anti-nationalist and anti-racist soccer fan clubs, the Paralympic Games, etc. These phenomena are like light beer: they are created for consoling the critics, but those who take joy in ideological sports that they consider as the "real thing" covertly or overtly laugh about and make fun of those who watch female soccer or the Paralympic Games, which even more asserts the ideologies that the liberal phenomena are supposed to dampen. But what if administered competitive sports are inherently racist, fascist, patriarchal, and nationalist? We will have to reinvent sports in a new society.

Harmful labour is labour that harms the survival capacities of humans. It includes e.g. the killing conducted by soldiers, the operation of nuclear power plants and fossil-fuel power stations, all forms of work that involve health risks (such as coal mining that increases the lung cancer risk, labour conducted at toxic workplaces, etc.), the production of cars powered by fossil fuels, jobcentre staff responsible for sanctioning unemployed people, etc.

There is also *repetitive, hard, and physically exhausting labour* that can be reduced and minimized by labour-saving technologies. Examples are the labour of cleaners, waste workers, machine operators, assemblers, metal workers, builders, miners and quarry workers, agricultural workers, forestry workers, waiters and waitresses, housekeepers, mail carriers, warehouse workers, transport workers, secretaries, data entry operators, and call centre agents. Robots and automation can reduce the amount of repetitive, hard, and exhausting work in society.

It may, however, not be possible to entirely abolish such activities. The question of how work in a free society can be organised, well envisioned by imagining how the most degrading and disgusting work would be organised.

What happens to disgusting labour in a literal sense in a free society? Cleaning toilets is one of these forms of work. Who cleans the toilets in a free society? One possibility is to automate humans to such an extent that they no longer digest. Besides the question if this is technologically possible, the moral question is if it is desirable and what would happen if the human turned into a machine or semi-machine. Another possibility is to automate toilet cleaning. There are constant advances in the development of toilet-cleaning robots (TCRs). Self-cleaning toilet seats are an early version of the automation of toilet cleaning. The iRobot Scooba is a floor-washing robot that can also clean the floor around toilets, i.e. those parts of bathrooms that are especially prone to be urinated on by men and women who prefer to stand or squat instead of sit and tend to miss the bowl while urinating. In the case of the not uncommon phenomenon of really dirty public toilets, this tendency reinforces itself because understandably nobody wants to sit down on or touch a dirty toilet lid and therefore many people stand or squat in public toilets, which due to aiming inaccuracies just intensifies the problem of disgusting toilets that one set out to avoid. In 2007 a consortium of robotics companies developed a TCR in Japan.[5]

Imagine a world where TCRs clean all public and private toilets. One may say that this is a stupid thought experiment, that public toilets are sometimes so dirty because people express the way they feel about their alienation in society in the way they deal with their own excrement in public toilets, that therefore people will keep public toilets much cleaner in a free society, etc. All of this is, however, highly speculative and the problem of a public toilet is that, given that so many people frequent it, the likelihood that one person unintentionally or deliberately floats it or pollutes it is quite high. We therefore can never guarantee that public toilets are kept clean.

So let us imagine a world of toilets managed by TCRs, in which the occupation of the human toilet cleaner is abolished. Robots are complex systems that function based on algorithms and cannot work based on reason. Therefore they will always be prone to failure, not be able to clean some toilets, have technical problems, mistake toilets with other objects, etc. So somebody has to develop, maintain, and repair TCRs. The problem of development could be solved once TCRs are at a high technological level and can be automatically manufactured by hardware printers. But of course somebody needs to develop and maintain hardware printers up to the point where universal hardware printers can print themselves, which just requires maintenance work. If TCRs fail, then somebody has to clean the toilets. Imagine a public toilet at a heavily frequented public train station, where the TCRs are out of operation for two weeks due to a technical failure. Either nobody cleans the toilets, which may result in overflowing and really disgusting toilets that can no longer be used, requiring people to urinate and defecate in public, which spreads diseases and attracts vermin. Or everyone thoroughly cleans the toilet after s/he has used it. Or toilet-cleaning work is distributed among all when TCRs fail. Or voluntary workers take over the TCRs' role for a limited time. The example wants to show that human work can be largely, but never fully, automated because high-tech machines are complex and failure-prone. The reason is that machines other than humans do not have reason, morals, and anticipatory thinking.

Creative work is work in which humans reflect a lot and envision by anticipatory reflection how parts of the world could look, be organised, and be changed. Such work tends to be gratifying. It includes the work of e.g. engineers, architects, librarians, authors, artists, composers, journalists, sculptors, painters, musicians, singers, choreographers, dancers, actors, film directors, decorators, designers, and gardeners. Creative work can make the world a nicer and more beautiful place. Reducing the necessary working time enlarges the potential time for creative work. A free society can also abolish the division of labour so that everyone is enabled to become a creative worker as s/he pleases. William Morris (1884b, 87) stresses the importance that work is pleasurable and that workers enjoy "hope of rest, hope of product, hope of pleasure in the work itself; and hope of these also in some abundance and of good quality". The precondition for these hopes to become reality is that "class robbery is abolished" (Morris 1884b, 99) and that a "Society of Equality" (Morris 1893, 265) is established. Morris imagined a post-capitalist condition, in which labour-saving technology reduces hard labour and humans are enabled to engage in creative and artistic work, by which they create "ornaments of life" (Morris 1884b, 116) as popular art (Morris 1884b, 113) and "a beautiful world to live in" (Morris 1885, 25).

Creativity could then become a

> pleasure which is unknown at present to the workers, and which even for the classes of ease and leisure only exists in a miserably corrupted and degraded form. I mean the practice of the fine arts: people living under the conditions of life above-mentioned, having manual skill, technical and general education, and leisure to use these advantages, are quite sure to develop a love of art, that is to say, a sense of beauty and an interest in life, which, in the long run must stimulate them to the desire for artistic creation, the satisfaction of which is of all pleasures the greatest.
>
> *Morris 1884c, 2*

Some or many "would find themselves impelled towards the creation of beauty [. . .] our factory which is externally beautiful, will not be inside like a clean jail or workhouse; the architecture will come inside in the form of such ornament as may be suitable to the special circumstances" (Morris 1884c, 2).

> One's imagination is inclined fairly to run riot over the picture of beauty and pleasure offered by the thought of skilful co-operative gardening for

beauty's sake, which beauty would by no means exclude the raising of useful produce for the sake of livelihood. [. . .] So in brief, our buildings will be beautiful with their own beauty of simplicity as workshops, not bedizened with tomfoolery as some are now, which do not any the more for that, hide their repulsiveness.

Morris 1884a

Some socialists have characterized Morris as romantic idealist, moralist, utopian, anarchist, and sentimentalist. Karl Kautsky was the first who in 1884 characterised Morris as "sentimental socialist" (Hampton 2008), a judgement that was repeated by Engels (1886b) in a letter to Laura Lafargue, Karl Marx's daughter. Engels also wrote that Morris is "a sentimental dreamer pure and simple, the personification of good will with so good an opinion of itself that it turns into ill will if ever there's a question of learning anything, has been taken in by the catchword 'Revolution' and fallen victim to the anarchists" (Engels 1886a, 471). Engels was convinced that socialism has to be scientific instead of utopian, which means that revolution and communism will with necessity like a natural law develop out of the contradictions of capitalism. We today know that history has falsified this assumption. Just as Morris's contemporaries vituperated him as idealist utopian, some of Herbert Marcuse's contemporaries conducted the same ideological operation by saying that Marcuse was a technological utopian (e.g. Habermas 1969). Edward P. Thompson argued in his 1976 postscript to his book *William Morris: Romantic to Revolutionary* that "Engels's disdain for Morris exemplifies the narrowing orthodoxy of those years, a narrowing noted not only in his own writings but in the Marxist tradition more generally" (Thompson 2011, 786). This tendency would have been characterised by "determinism and positivism" (Thompson 2011, 786). Morris in contrast stands for Thompson (2011) for an agency-based Marxism that doubts determinism and evolutionism (795) and vindicates concrete utopias as political force (792–793). For Thompson (2011), Morris is "our greatest diagnostician of alienation" (801) and stands for a Marxism that acknowledges both the importance and interaction of the economy on the one hand and morality and culture on the other hand (804), helps "people to find out their wants, to encourage them to want more, to challenge them to want differently, and to envisage a society of the future in which people, freed at last of necessity, might choose between different wants" (806), and asks the question "How Shall We Live Then?" (809). Peter Linebaugh (2011, viii) adds to this assessment that one important aspect of Morris is that he was a green communist who demanded to unwaste nature and work. Thompson (1994, 75) says that Morris and Marx complement each other and allow us to see that economic "relationships are at the same time moral relationships, relations of production are at the same time relations between people, of oppression or of co-operation: and there is a moral logic as well as an economic logic, which derives from these relationships".

William Morris and Herbert Marcuse not only share the political conviction that a free society beyond the realm of necessity is possible, but also that labour-saving technology can in such a framework abolish necessary labour and toil and that this framework can enable creative work and the becoming-art of the economy. It is no wonder that functionalists have dismissed their humanist Marxism, which just shows that their perspectives are much needed. The alternative to anti-work philosophy is not Stalinist labour fetishism, but the abolition of unnecessary and harmful work, the reduction of hard work and the enablement of creative work, the becoming-art of work, and the becoming-art of society.

The introduced anti-work approaches do not much consider the question if there are qualities that characterise all societies and all economies and how these qualities can best be termed. They construct critiques of capitalism without a theory of society. Some of them engage with the question of how a concept that characterises alternatives to work in a free society should be termed: suggestions are *anti-work*, *post-work*, *life*, *self-determined activity*, *self-valorisation* and *self-constitution*. Anti-work and post-work do not name a specific form of activity, but rather define themselves by what they are opposed to and what they refuse (anti-work) or by a future point of time (post-work). They do not have a vision of how work can be organised in a free society. Life, self-determined activity, and self-constitution are concepts that are too general for characterising work in a free society. Also a virus is a form of life, but we do not say that it works on the body when infecting or killing a human being. Self-determined activities exist not only in a free society, but also to a certain extent today. Not all forms of self-determined and self-constituted activities are equivalents of work. Sleeping is an activity that is needed for constantly reconstituting the mind and the body; it is self-constitution and self-reproduction, but different from work. The decision to go out and take a walk or to stay indoors and sleep is a relatively self-determined activity, but not work. Work creates novelty in the world that satisfies some human needs.

Now you can say that dreaming satisfies the human need to rest and produces a dream and that tooth brushing and showering satisfy the human need of cleanliness, so why are these activities, but not human work? It is certainly work of the human brain as an organ, but not work of human beings as interaction of body and mind or a social interaction because it does not have broader social effects in human groups. Humans not only produce and create for themselves, they do so for others, and in a true society do so to help and benefit not only themselves, but society at large. Human work is a social relationship, it is oriented towards others not just towards oneself. Work does in reality not occur in isolation. The life of Robinson Crusoe on an island would due to social isolation and lack of biological reproduction soon come to an end. Marx (1857/58, 83) criticized Adam Smith and David Ricardo for taking the "individual and isolated hunter and fisherman" as "point of departure" in the analysis of material production. The point of departure for the analysis of the economy should in contrast be "[i]ndividuals producing in society" (Marx 1857/58, 83).

It is also doubtful that self-valorisation is a better term than work for characterising the creation of goods and relations that satisfy human needs in a free society.

Marx (1867) titled chapter 7 of *Capital, Volume 1* "The Labour Process and the Valorization Process". The work process creates use-values (Marx 1867, 302) and this process is in capitalism connected to the "process of valorization", which is "the capitalist form of the production of commodities" (Marx 1867, 304) and in which surplus-value is generated that "results only from a quantitative excess of labour" (Marx 1867, 305). Marx describes that capital is a dynamic process and that in this process the exploitation of labour fosters the accumulation of capital. Capitalism is like a value-generating machine built on and driven by the exploitation of labour:

> By turning his money into commodities which serve as the building mate-
> rials for a new product, and as factors in the labour process, by incorporat-
> ing living labour into their lifeless objectivity, the capitalist simultaneously
> transforms value, i.e. past labour in its objectified and lifeless form, into
> capital, value which can perform its own valorisation process, an animated
> monster which begins to "work", "as if its body were by love possessed".
>
> *Marx 1867, 302*

Capital is self-valorising value. Negri opposes the concept of capital's self-valorisation to worker self-valorisation (Negri 1991, 148). Self-valorisation means "independence of the worker-subject" (Negri 1991, 135), "non-work" (149). He argues that it starts with the refusal of work in capitalism and comes to full effect in communism (Negri 1991, 148). Michael Ryan in the introduction to the English translation of Negri's (1991) *Marx beyond Marx* says Negri understands self-valorisation as "working for oneself as a class, asserting one's own needs as primary to capital's need for value" (Negri 1991, xxx). Harry Cleaver (1992, 129) defines it as "a process of valorisation which is autonomous from capitalist valorisation—a self-defining, self-determining process which goes beyond the mere resistance to capitalist valorisation to a positive project of self-constitution" that constitutes a "working class for-itself".

The basic idea that Negri expresses is the way that Marx imagined work in a free society—a creative process controlled by the immediate producers, who no longer work for others, but control their work, working time, and produce for society as a whole and therefore for themselves. Given that Marx saw the concept of valorisation deeply entrenched with capital accumulation, it is not self-evident that this concept can be rescued by prefixing "self" and used for signifying a process of liberation and a status of emancipation. By abolishing capitalism and establishing a free society, the revolutionary class in a movement of universality not only abolishes itself and capital and thereby all classes, it also abolishes valorisation. The term *self-valorisation* can easily be understood or mistaken as meaning the continuation of capital accumulation with workers as shareholders or collective capitalists and the maintenance of the wage, money, and commodity system. So although the content of Negri's self-valorisation concept expresses important transformations of work in a free society, the very term is confusing and easily creates the impression of signifying not the abolishment, but the mere transformation of capitalism. Substituting the term *non-alienated work* for self-valorisation is not an advantage, but rather complicates the terminology of Marxist theory.

Terms such as *anti-work*, *zerowork*, and *post-work* are unlikely to convince or mobilise the overall majority of people to struggle against capital and their own labour. Such terms may have an appeal for a limited group of anarchists and autonomists, but the majority of people seem way too much acquainted with the idea that work is not just a burden, but has positive qualities. Abolishing and refusing labour and capitalism may be easier to advance not by slogans such as the "refusal of work", but the "refusal of toil", the "reduction of unnecessary, burdensome and harmful work", and the enablement of the "creativity of all".

The World Values Survey (WVS) is an opinion poll conducted in more than 50 countries. It focuses on human attitudes towards a variety of normative questions that concern contemporary societies. Like many surveys, it surely has its own biases, but as long as a worldwide critical worker's inquiry is not available, it may give us a glimpse of how the working population thinks about its work. The WVS provides indications that only a minority of people in the world seem to agree with an anti-work perspective that celebrates idleness. In the World Values Survey 2005–2009, 62.1 per cent of the respondents said that work is very important in life, 27.6 per cent important, 6.0 per cent not very important, and 2.7 per cent not at all (N = 80,950). Of all respondents 54.9 per cent say it would be a bad thing if in the future less importance is placed on work (N = 82,734). These values are certainly based on an authoritarian work ethic. This work ethic is, however, not limited to wage workers, but extends to retired people, house workers, students, and the unemployed: 73.7 per cent of the respondents strongly agree or agree that "Work is a duty towards society" (N = 68,276). The share is 70.6 per cent for full-time employees (N = 22,356), 68.7 per cent for part-time employees (N = 4,297), 78.6 per cent for the self-employed (N = 8,661), 76.7 per cent for the retired (N = 8,617), 76.3 per cent for house workers (N = 8,307), 71.9 per cent for students (N = 5,211), and 71.7 per cent for the unemployed (N = 6,680). Of the unemployed respondents 70.5 per cent say that work is very important in life and 21.8 per cent that it is important (N = 7,751). Of the unemployed 53.6 per cent say that would be is a bad thing if work becomes less important in the future (N = 8,029).

These choices are certainly influenced by the circumstance that most people in capitalism need to earn wages in order to survive. This is reflected in that 34.9 per cent of the respondents say that a good income is the most important aspect of a job, 33.8 per cent say a safe job with no risk, 10.1 per cent working with people you like, and 19.2 per cent doing an important job (N = 76,997). It is interesting to see that for agricultural workers (37.7 per cent, n = 3,739) the most important characteristic is safety, for unskilled manual workers (39.6 per cent, N = 5,230) and semi-skilled manual workers (39.6. per cent, N = 4,625) a good income, whereas for professional workers who all tend to be knowledge workers the most important characteristic of work is doing an important job (30.6 per cent,

N = 6,059). This means that the focus on working for survival seems to be strong in the morals of those whose work involves physical toil or repetitiveness, whereas the focus shifts to a stress of an important content of work in the case of skilled knowledge work. Non-supervisory office workers (N = 6,176) such as secretaries have an intermediary position: more than manual workers but less than professional knowledge workers they stress safety (35.3%), income (30.8 per cent) and importance of the work (20.9 per cent).

Given that the work and labour ethic is so widespread, calling for destroying and refusing work may not be a viable strategy for many and calling for anti-work politics is likely to always remain a form of minority politics. Even those who are unemployed, conduct burdensome physical labour, or are precarious workers cherish something about work. In a different societal framework, the work and labour ethic is likely to change, but the political question is how one comes from here to there and what slogans work best in political mobilisations. Struggles for self-determined, self-controlled creative work that can freely be exercised by all in a highly productive society that abolishes toil, compulsion, necessity, wages, money, commodities, and capital may be easier to achieve and mobilise than struggles that mobilise under the slogans of anti-work, zerowork, and the refusal of work that communicate negativity without a positive vision, a negation without a determinate negation, and idleness without possibilities for social interaction and self-fulfilling creativity.

In Europe, especially young people are facing unemployment and precarious labour. There is a generation of dissatisfied young people, many of whom are no longer willing to accept the system. They are highly educated, skilled, and creative and often do not have opportunities to practice the work they are interested in it because they cannot find enough payment for it. Yet they are ready to fight for a different world and many of them already do so in movements such as Occupy, 15-M, or the Indignant Citizens Movement. They do not struggle against practicing the creative work capacities they have acquired; they rather struggle against bad working conditions and dull, useless labour that allows them no expression of their creativity and is a waste of human energy. Empirical studies show that creative workers often love the content and possibilities for interaction, self-expression, and creativity of their work and hate the precarious conditions under which they are often compelled to perform this work such as low income, long working hours followed by periods without work, insecurity, the individualisation of risk, and the difficulty of combining labour and family (Gill 2002, 2006, Hesmondhalgh and Baker 2011). Abolishing their work is not an option for these young people. They want to be creative workers, but what hinders them is capitalism. A free society must be a highly productive society and, as Marx knew, the technical development of the productive forces increases the role of knowledge work in society. If one thinks of call-centre agents trying to sell commodities over the phone, then it becomes clear that not all knowledge work is self-fulfilling and an expression of creativity. A feasible political strategy is to call for the abolishment of unnecessary labour such as the one conducted by call centre sales agents, the abolishment of precarious working conditions, and the enablement of creative work for all in a society that minimises necessary work time.

The slogan of the refusal of work in general does not speak to those who consider themselves to be creative workers, love the content of their work, but hate the precarious conditions under which this work is organised as labour.

There is work that produces commons that cannot be automated if we want to preserve a humane character of society: education, health care, care of the weak, and the ill. A free society will have to involve activities of teachers, doctors, nursing professionals, care workers, and institutions such as schools and hospitals. The authoritarian character of these institutions that today often makes them prison-like will have to be transformed, but the work of supporting learning and helping the weak and ill will still be needed. They will have a transformed character, but education and care are necessary for human survival. Silvia Federici argues in this context:

> One crucial reason for creating collective forms of living is that the reproduction of human beings is the most labour-intensive work on earth, and to a large extent it is work that is irreducible to mechanization. We cannot mechanize childcare or the care of the ill, or the psychological work necessary to reintegrate our physical and emotional balance. Despite the efforts that futuristic industrialists are making, we cannot robotize "care" except at terrible cost for the people involved. No one will accept "nursebots" as care givers, especially for children and the ill.
>
> *Federici 2012, 145f*

2.7. Conclusion

In this chapter, we have introduced a cultural-materialist approach for theorising cultural work and cultural labour. Many approaches are idealist in that they define concepts such as digital labour, virtual work, online work, cyberwork, immaterial labour, knowledge labour, creative work, cultural labour, communicative labour, information(al) work, digital craft, service work, prosumption, consumption work, audience labour, playbour, etc. only as an externalisation of human ideas that are objictified in contents and thereby neglect that this labour is based on and only possible because there is a global division of labour, in which many different forms of labour are conducted under specific modes of production. We have used Raymond Williams's framework of cultural materialism to argue that we should overcome cultural idealism and analyse cultural labour and cultural work based on the framework of cultural materialism.

We have introduced specific concepts for a materialist theory of culture: cultural work, cultural labour, physical cultural work, information work, modes of production, productive forces, relations of production. We argue for avoiding particularistic analyses that focus only on single elements of single production processes and for conducting holistic analyses that focus on the totality of elements and networks that determine and shape cultural work and cultural labour. The toolkit for the analysis of working conditions that we introduced allows analysing the totality of elements of the labour process. Cultural labour analysis should also look at how one specific form of cultural labour that is analysed is connected to and articulated with other forms of labour that express certain organisational forms of the productive forces and the relations of production. Cultural work is appealing because it is inherently connected to creativity, an essential feature capacity of all human beings. A free society is not an anti-work or zero-work society, but one in which useless and harmful labour are abolished and repetitive, hard, and physically exhausting labour automated, and necessary work minimised so that a realm of free creative work of all emerges and is enabled. William Morris and Herbert Marcuse's concepts of work remind us of these potentials for re-organising the world of work.

Cultural labour analysis can only interpret the cultural world; the point is to change it. Change can only be good change if it is informed change. Critical theory can inform potential and actual struggles for a better world. Everyday working realities of different people and in different parts of the world look so heterogeneous, different, and unconnected that it is often difficult to see what they have in common. Cultural materialism as critical political economy of culture can help to identify and make visible the common and different experiences of suffering and enjoyment, pleasure and pain, security and insecurity, alienation and appropriation, exploitation and resistance, creativity and toil. It is in this respect a cultural sociology of critique. But it is at the same time also a political philosophy and a critical cultural sociology that helps identifying and clarifying foundations and germinate forms of a better future and grounding judgements about what is good and bad in the context of culture. Cultural materialism therefore takes on the role of a critical sociology of critique that is both at once a critical sociology and a sociology of critique (Boltanski and Honneth 2009). It analyses the reality of life under capitalism, contributing intellectually to questioning this mode of human existence in order to show that there is and to help realise life beyond capitalism.

Notes

1 http://www.marxists.org/archive/marx/works/1844/epm/3rd.htm.
2 A similar formulation can be found in Gorz's work, who says it is necessary to free the working class "from work" (Gorz 1982, 2).
3 http://www.departments.bucknell.edu/russian/const/18cons01.html.
4 BBC *Online*, Iain Duncan Smith criticised over benefit cap figures. http://www.bbc.co.uk/news/uk-politics-22462265. 9 May 2013.
5 http://inventorspot.com/articles/cute_cleaning_robot_cleans_toile_8541.

3

COMMUNICATION, IDEOLOGY, AND LABOUR

3.1. Introduction

The relationship of work and ideology is a largely unclarified issue in Marxist theory. There are on the one hand critical discourse analysts who analyse ideology as texts, without tending to think about the circumstance that ideology is produced by people working in specific contexts under specific conditions (in marketing and PR agencies, consultancies, media organisations, press agencies, etc.). On the other hand, the sociology of cultural labour tends to analyse working conditions of cultural workers without thinking about the ideological effects that many cultural products tend to have under capitalist conditions, how ideology influences work, and the economy in general. It is therefore important to theorise the relationship of work on the one hand and culture and ideology on the other hand. This chapter wants to contribute to this task.

In critical discourse analysis, the discussion of the relationship of work/labour and language/ideology is conspicuous by its absence. So for example in Norman Fairclough's (2010) 592-page book *Critical Discourse Analysis*, the terms *labour* and *work* are hardly used and if so then predominantly not for signifying work and labour processes, but New Labour. There are no chapters dedicated to the relationship of labour and ideology, work and language. A similar assessment can be made of Fairclough's (1995) book *Media Discourse*, Teun van Dijk's (1998) *Ideology: A Multidisciplinary Approach*, *Discourse & Power* (2008), *Society and Discourse* (2009), the collection *Discourse Studies: A Multidisciplinary Introduction* (van Dijk 2011), or the methods book *Methods of Critical Discourse Analysis* (Wodak and Meyer 2009). Questions relating to the labour of producing ideologies, the role and relationship of language/ideology and work/labour in society, are largely absent in and a blindspot of critical discourse analysis. It tends to neglect basic assumptions of cultural materialism (Williams 1977). Although it is materialist in its basic critique of capitalism, it has thus far not much engaged with the relationship of language and work.

Section 3.2 discusses examples of a work/culture-dualism (Habermas, Holzkamp). Based on a reading of Ferruccio Rossi-Landi's critical semiotics, section 3.3 argues for understanding communication as work. Section 3.4 based on these foundations draws a distinction between ideological labour and critical work. Section 3.5 draws some conclusions.

3.2. Work/Communication-Dualism: Hegel, Jürgen Habermas, and Klaus Holzkamp on Communication and Work

Habermas's theory of communicative action makes a sharp distinction between on the one hand purposive (instrumental, strategic) action that is orientated on success and on the other hand communicative action that is orientated on reaching understanding (Habermas 1984, 285–286). Work is for Habermas always an instrumental, strategic, and purposive form of action, whereas communication's goal is to reach understanding. Habermas just like Holzkamp therefore separates work and communication. This separation goes back to Hegel's philosophy.

In the article *Arbeit und Interaktion (Work and Interaction)*, Habermas (1968) argues that Hegel (1803/1804, 1805/1806) in his Jena lectures on the philosophy of spirit argued that work and interaction are two ways that human beings relate to the world, organise the relationship between subject and object, and thereby constitute their self-conscious minds.

Habermas (1968) argues that Hegel would have after his Jena time (1801–1807) given up the concept of the dialectic of work and interaction because he became convinced that nature and work are just attributes of spirit and can therefore be reduced to the dialectical development of spirit. Marx in contrast would have reduced communicative action to instrumental action (Habermas 1968, 45). In the *Encyclopaedia of the Philosophical Sciences in Outline. Part 3: The Philosophy of Spirit*, work and interaction are treated separately and only very briefly. Hegel mentions language as part of the discussion of psychology. This discussion forms the third part of the book's first part that focuses on the subjective spirit. The first aspect of psychology is for Hegel the theoretical mind that consists of a) intelligent perception, b) mental idea, and c) thinking. Speech is for Hegel an aspect of the mental idea's dimension of imagination:

> The vocal note which receives further articulation to express specific ideas—speech and, its system, language—gives to sensations, intuitions, conceptions, a second and higher existence than they naturally possess—invests them with the right of existence in the ideational realm. Language here comes under discussion only in the special aspect of a product of intelligence for manifesting its ideas in an external medium.
>
> *Hegel 1830, §459*

Hegel analyses aspects of language such as sounds, symbols, categories, letters, vocals, consonants, different types of language, etc. But he does not mention the important role of language in establishing and maintaining social relations, work, and thereby society.

Hegel discusses work as part of the objective spirit's dimension of ethics. Besides the family and the state, civil society is for Hegel one of the three parts of ethics. Labour is for Hegel the crucial aspect of the system of wants: It is "the ever-continued production of fresh means of exchange by the exchangers" so that "the labour of all facilitates satisfaction of wants" (Hegel 1830, §524). Hegel discusses the division of labour, labour's need for education and technical skills, and three estates (the natural estate, the reflected estate, the thinking estate). But he does not mention the role of communication and language in the organisation of work and the production of knowledge and communication as a specific form of work. So in Hegel's later works such as the *Encyclopaedia*, the two realms of communication and work are entirely separated.

As pointed out by Habermas, Hegel's (1803/1804, 1805/1806) Jena system focuses more on work and language than his later works. In the *Philosophy of the Spirit* (Hegel 1803/1804, 185–232), Hegel argues that human reason produces the spirit that expresses itself as memory and language and is practically expressed in the form of work (197). So the connection of work and language is for Hegel that they are both utterances of the human spirit. Hegel says that the spirit of a people is an "active substance" (224). It would create works (224). One of the works of a people would be language (226), another one work and property (227). Hegel stresses that both language and work do have a general character: they connect single individuals (227, 229). Language would be the existence of consciousness (200, 208). Hegel grounds foundations of semiotics by arguing that in language one finds symbols that signify something outside of it (201).

Hegel argues that work is a specific form of the spirit—an expression of human drives (210–211). Tools would be means for humans to obtain the end of satisfying desires. Labour would be the middle of desire and a resulting object (211). In the practical work process, the tool would be the middle of the subject and the object (211). The satisfaction of needs would be a "general dependence of all on all" (229). The machine would be a tool that humans use for minimising the value of goods: "the more machines mediate work, the less value it has" (228). "But in the same proportion as the produced quantity increases, the value of labour decreases" (230). The result would be dead labour, "machine labour" (230) and the dullness of factory labour (230). Value would be the "identity in the thing" (Hegel 1805/1806, 207–208). "The general is the value" (Hegel 1805/1806, 208). Exchange would be the movement of the thing (Hegel 1805/1806, 208).

It here becomes evident how much Hegel's philosophy has influenced Marx's labour theory of value: In the passages just mentioned, Hegel grounds what Marx (1867) later described as a dialectical triad of use-value, value, and exchange-value. "Since the magnitude of the value of a commodity represents nothing but the quantity of labour embodied in it, it follows that all commodities, when taken in certain proportions, must be equal in value" (Marx 1867, 136). Abstract labour is for Marx that kind of labour which makes the privately spent use-value producing labour comparable. Abstract labour describes a specific quality of a capitalist mode of production. Marx says: "Equality in the full sense between different kinds of labour can be arrived at only if we abstract from their real inequality, if we reduce them to the characteristic they have in common, that of being the expenditure of human labour-power, of human labour in the abstract" (Marx 1867, 166). Abstract human labour is the substance of value; it is a common characteristic of commodities. Abstract human labour creates the value of a commodity, i.e. it is the performance of the (average) labour in a certain time span that is needed for producing a commodity. Marx's basic idea is that different forms of labour are distinguished by the fact that they create different goods and services—computers, television sets, cars, yoghurt, tables, etc. But what the computer, the TV, the car, the yoghurt, and the table have in common is that they are all goods that contain an abstract quanta of human work that can be measured as the average number of hours it takes to produce such goods.

Hegel grounded a phenomenology of work and communication and pointed out that both have in common that they are general qualities and products of human social activity—although they are for him two separate domains of society. Communication and culture are, however, also specific results of information work. And communication is the crucial social feature of work organisation. One could go one step further and say that communication is an essential human use-value and therefore a form of work. So communication is work and work always involves communication.

Habermas (1968), based on Hegel's Jena system, argues that consciousness and the mind would be media of communication. The difference between work and interaction would be that the first is a form of strategic action and the second oriented on understanding. Strategic action would make decisions without trying to reach understanding with others (Habermas 1968, 22). Both work and interaction would constitute the external nature of humans, their relational being. In work, there is a relation to nature organised by tools. In communication, there is a relation to other humans organised by language and its symbols. Work and interaction could not be reduced to each other (Habermas 1968, 3), but they would be dialectically connected: "But now also instrumental action, as soon as it enters the category of the actual spirit in the form of societal work, is embedded into a network of interactions and is therefore itself dependent on the communicative boundary conditions of every possible cooperation" (Habermas 1968, 32, translation from German).

In the *Theory of Communicative Action*, Habermas (1984, 1987) formalised the earlier drawn distinction between work and interaction in his own theory in the form of a distinction between instrumental-strategic rationality and communicative rationality. Habermas understands rationality as "problem-solving action" (Habermas 1984, 12). He introduces a typology of action, in which he differentiates action types based on action situations (non-social or social) and action orientation (oriented to success, oriented to reaching understanding). This results in the distinction between instrumental action, strategic action, and communicative action. Instrumental and strategic action are oriented on success and driven by "egocentric calculations of success" (Habermas 1984, 286). Instrumental action means that an actor identifies and uses means in order to achieve ends and maximise his/her benefits (Habermas 1984, 285, 85). Strategic action is instrumental action in a social situation with rational opponents so that the task is to beat the opponent or be more successful than him/her (Habermas 1984, 285).

In contrast, in communicative action the action situation is social and the orientation is "reaching understanding" (Habermas 1984, 286). "In communicative action participants are not primarily oriented to their own individual successes; they pursue their individual goals under the condition that they can harmonize their plans of action on the basis of common situation definitions" (Habermas 1984, 286). "The actors seek to reach an understanding about the action situation and their plans of action in order to coordinate their actions by way of agreement. The central concept of *interpretation* refers in the first instance to negotiating definitions of the situation which admit of consensus. [. . .] language is given a prominent place in this model" (Habermas 1984, 86). Reaching understanding in communicative action would require the three validity claims of truth, rightness, and truthfulness (Habermas 1984, 99). Habermas's distinction between instrumental and communicative action is reflected in his distinction between systems and the lifeworld. He locates work/labour in the interchange relationship between the economic system and the private sphere that is part of the lifeworld (Habermas 1987, 320). This relationship would be determined by the systemic steering media of money and power (exchange of money in the form of the wage for the control of labour power). Habermas (1976, 151) argues that work and language were necessary preconditions for the emergence of humans and society. Reconstructing historical materialism would require separating "the level of communicative action from the level of instrumental and strategic actions that are united in societal cooperation" (Habermas 1976, 160, translation from German to English). Historical progress would only be possible by developing the forms of social integration and the productive forces (Habermas 1976, 194).

Habermas consistently used the distinction between communication and work that he took from Hegel's Jena philosophy for creating a theory of modern society. Communication and work represent for him two different logics of society, an emancipatory and an instrumental one. He is critical of money and power's colonisation of lifeworld communication (Habermas 1987) and so stresses the importance of defending communication against instrumental logic. Habermas's political imperative is definitely laudable because it stresses that there is a society beyond capitalism and that a true society is not steered by capital and domination. But the question is if it is feasible to dualistically separate communication and work—an approach that Habermas characterises as "media dualism" (Habermas 1987, 281). There are several theoretical limits of Habermas's work/communication dualism:

- In a general sense, we can say that reaching communicative understanding and any form of communication is a form of instrumental action: the means of language are used for achieving the goal of relating oneself to other humans and reaching a joint understanding of the world.
- Communication in modern society is not an immune sphere: Ideologies are forms of communication and language that are highly instrumental. Ideologies instrumentalise language and meanings for justifying exploitation and domination. Communication thereby becomes an instrument of domination. Within communication studies, a specific field called strategic communication has developed. It studies how communication can be used for influencing and persuading specific audiences of particular purposes, especially in marketing and politics (see Hülsmann and Pfeffermann 2011; Paul 2011). Strategic communication is just another term for propaganda that serves capitalist and bureaucratic purposes. So communication is not immune from the logic of instrumentalising humans and speech for domination, but can serve quite different purposes.
- Work not only serves strategic-instrumental purposes, but can be quite altruistic and motivated by helping others and fostering the common good that benefits all. Marx was convinced that an entire society can be built on the logic of common goods. Limiting the notion of work to strategic-instrumental action deprives theory of a vocabulary for conceptualising social activities that produce use-values in a society based on solidarity, common goods, and voluntary work.

What distinguishes humans from animals is that they have a complex form of verbal language and communication, and have self-consciousness, morals, and anticipatory thought. But how did these capacities historically emerge? Klaus Holzkamp's (1985) critical psychology has engaged thoroughly with this question. Holzkamp (1985, 113–114) argues that communication is an optical and acoustical bidirectional/dialogical/reciprocal relationship between organisms, in which information is exchanged and social meaning is given to signals and symbols. Understood in this way, communication is not specific to humans, but can also be found in the animal world, where animals communicate for purposes such as procreation, breeding, hunting, defending their territory, warning each other, etc.

Historically, practical knowledge of how to manage reality had to be fixed and organised in some form, which required cooperative work between humans on the one hand and the need to communicate and store experiences on the other hand (Holzkamp 1985, 177, 211f). Holzkamp (1985, 162–206) describes four steps in the emergence of human society, language, and communication:

1   *Upright posture and the hand*: Subhuman hominids' swinging from tree to tree resulted over tens of thousands of years in the capacity to erect the body. This enabled the transformation of two of the four feet into hands and the development of optical observation capacities. Using the hands resulted in the capacity to actively manipulate the environment with the help of tools.

2   *Learning and relational, anticipatory thinking*: The transformation of forests into steppes and savannahs required upright posture for survival. As the hominids could no longer escape their enemies by climbing up trees and food had to be obtained on the ground, they developed tools for defence, hunting, and the collection and processing of plants. Over a period of 15 million years, bipedalism and evolutionary requirements resulted in a tremendous growth of brain volume. The use of more complex tools and the increased brain volume resulted in new learning capacities that allowed anticipating future events, observing consequences of one's actions, and relational thinking. Information processing increasingly allowed "storing and recalling relationship between one's own activities and the effects evoked by specific 'means'" (Holzkamp 1985, 166, translation from German to English).

3   *The reversal of means and ends*: Hominids no longer spontaneously built and used tools for satisfying immediate ends, but generalised the production of tools as means in case that they need to use them for obtaining specific ends. "The accordingly made stick [. . .] so no longer serves as a means for obtaining a specific fruit, but as *means for the generalized aim of obtaining fruits*" (Holzkamp 1985, 173, translation from German to English). The emergence of this generalised tool-making was connected to the emergence of provisioning and supply planning within collectives.

4   *Societal-historical development*: The social and collective production and use of tools resulted in a major dominance shift from phylogenetic to societal-historical development. Societal structures emerged that included the anticipation of future states and their management by planning the provision of means of subsistence and the development of specific tools. The specific novel quality in the societal mode of existence was the "planned anticipation of future actual situations and the generalized control of reality by the provision of means for their management" (Holzkamp 1985, 177, translation from German to English), the "conscious, precautionary provision of common living conditions by collective work" (Holzkamp 1985, 184, translation from German to English).

5   Holzkamp (1985, 224) assumes that verbal communication emerged in the development between the first qualitative dominance shift (the reversal of means and ends) and the second one (the emergence of societal-historical development): co-operative work in close range would have required coordination activities, and as the eyes and vision would have been used for constantly monitoring the work process and the hands and the body for

changing the objects of work, the use of the mouth for coordinating work would have been a logical step (Holzkamp 1985, 224). The development of speech that uses categories for signifying specific parts of reality would have been a practical requirement of the cooperative work process (Holzkamp 1985, 226–229). Concept formation would have happened in a practical manner. The emerging phonetic concepts would have been practical concepts that described tools, objects, and products. So for example "the planning and coordination of activities in the production of horizontally standing and flat boards, i.e. 'tables', requires a concept of 'horizontal' and one of 'flat'" (Holzkamp 1985, 227).

The development of learning capacities and anticipatory thinking together with verbal communication would have enabled humans to speak about relations and circumstances even if they were not immediately present (Holzkamp 1985, 228). As co-operative work became ever more complex and ever more transcended spatial and temporal distances, it was necessary to find trans-individual forms of communication and information transmission. So whereas the organisation of co-operative work required the development of human speech, the increasing spatio-temporal distantiation of the co-operative work process required forms of mediated communication, which historically resulted in the development of writing and painting as means for preserving, storing, and communicating information (Holzkamp 1985, 230–231).

Holzkamp explains in a logically consistent and convincing manner how the development of society, work, speech, and communication co-evolved in a dialectical manner. He grounds his approach in Marx's theory. Marx argued that the mind is "'burdened' with matter, which here makes its appearance in the form of agitated layers of air, sounds, in short, of language" (Marx and Engels 1845/46, 49). Marx stresses the material dimensions of the mind and language: the human being, the brain, the air that transports sound.

> Language is as old as consciousness, language *is* practical, real consciousness that exists for other men as well, and only therefore does it also exist for me; language, like consciousness, only arises from the need, the necessity of intercourse with other men. Where there exists a relationship, it exists for me; the animal does not "*relate*" itself to anything, it does not "*relate*" itself at all.
>
> *Marx and Engels 1845/46, 49*

For Marx, language and consciousness are "a social production" and remain so "as long as men exist at all" (Marx and Engels 1845/46, 50). By saying that language is practical and social, Marx means that it has historically arisen in the course of the organisation of economic production that became a social process. Holzkamp reflects this insight by arguing that communication and language emerged from the need of practical knowledge in the work process that became ever more complex and thereby a co-operative and social process.

Work is for Holzkamp a category of the theory of society that captures "the objective-economic aspects of the production and reproduction of societal life" (Holzkamp 1985, 234, translation from German to English). Work is "collective objectified transformation of nature and the control of natural forces for the pre-cautionary disposal over the common living conditions" (Holzkamp 1985, 176f, translation from German to English). He uses in contrast the notion of activity for characterising individual behaviour, "individual life activities" of humans that organise the "maintenance/development of his/her individual existence" (Holzkamp 1985, 234, translation from German to English). Activities would include psychological processes and the individual contributions to societal production and reproduction by work—"the work activities as psychological aspect of societal work" (Holzkamp 1985, 234, translation from German). Meanings would be developed in society and influence individual activities (Holzkamp 1985, 234).

Holzkamp argues that individual behaviour and psychological processes are human activities, whereas the co-operative organisation of the production of goods and services that sustain human existence, processes that are never possible by single individuals, by changing, transforming, and organising nature are work processes. He sees a dialectic between human individuals and collective co-operation in work processes.

Holzkamp in drawing the distinction between work and activity makes the basic mistake to assume that work is only a human collaborative transformation of natural resources so that goods and services (use-values) emerge that satisfy human needs. Holzkamp's approach here resembles Habermas's theory of communicative action that makes a sharp distinction between on the one hand purposive (instrumental, strategic) action that is orientated on success and on the other hand communicative action that is orientated on reaching understanding (Habermas 1984, 285f). Work is for Habermas always an instrumental, strategic, and purposive form of action, whereas communication's goal is to create understanding. Both Habermas and Holzkamp separate work and communication.

3.3. Communication as a Form of Work

Most Marxist approaches that have given attention to the communication process at a theoretical level have focused on the communicative character of work, but have neglected the question if communication is work. A few exceptions can be found in the political economy of communication-approach, such as the works by Wulf Hund (1976), Hund and Kirchhoff-Hund (1980), and Dan Schiller (1996). These authors have stressed the importance of not separating work and communication.

Stuart Hall's chapter "The Work of Representation" in the collected volume *Representation: Cultural Representations and Signifying Practices* (Hall 1997) promises due to its title insights into how meaning-making, and therefore also communication and language, and work are related. Hall uses some promising formulations: "Representation is a practice, a kind of 'work', which uses material objects and effects" (Hall 1997, 25–26). "Meaning is produced by the practice, the 'work', of representation. It is constructed through signifying—i.e. meaning-producing—practices" (Hall 1997, 28). Hall, however, not only puts work into inverted commas, but also does not further engage with the question of how to define work and labour, what their specific qualities are, what kind of work the work of representation and meaning-making actually is, and how this work's dimensions (such as labour-power, means of production, objects of works, use-values) look like. He rather focuses on the question "How does representation work?" (Hall 1997, 16) by engaging with the theories of Ferdinand de Saussure, Roland Barthes, and Michel Foucault. A discussion of Marx and Marxist semioticians such as Ferruccio Rossi-Landi could have informed the question, at which Hall hints in the chapter's title, but he does not deal with in detail. Hall is in this chapter also rather distant from Raymond Williams's cultural materialism. He for example says that "it is not the material world which conveys meaning: it is the language system or whatever system we are using to represent our concepts" (Hall 1997, 25). He also writes that "*meaning* depends, not on the material quality of the sign, but on its *symbolic function*" (Hall 1997, 26).

The problem is that Hall takes a constructionist approach (see Hall 1997, 5–6), in which culture is "as important as the economic or material 'base'" (Hall 1997, 6). Such formulations imply that the material and the symbolic as well as the economy and culture are in the last instance separate, although they are equally important and articulated. By articulation, Hall understands the "form of the connection that can make a unity of two or more different or distinct elements, under certain conditions. It is a linkage which is not necessary, determined, or absolute and essential for all time; rather it is a linkage whose conditions of existence or emergence need to be located in the contingencies of circumstance" (du Gay et al. 1997, 3). For Raymond Williams, culture is in contrast to Hall fully material and grounded inside the economy: cultural work produces meanings and representations that have emergent qualities that take effect in society as a whole. A dialectic is, in contrast to an articulation, not a simple connection of two separate entities, but rather a contradiction in which two moments overgrasp into each other so that they are mutually part of each other, but at the same time also non-identical and separate. Constructionism leads Hall's (1997) chapter too far away from a cultural-materialist approach, although single formulations indicate that just as representation, culture, and social meaning work in society, also humans in society perform *cultural work* when producing representations, culture, and meanings.

Jim McGuigan and Marie Moran (2014, 177) point out that Stuart Hall focuses on "how ideas can 'become' a material force", which reveals "a conception of social reality which distinguishes sharply between the 'cultural' realm of ideas, languages, values and beliefs, and the material world, thereby rendering sensible the very question of how ideas previously non-material – can *become* material and exert a causal force". For Raymond Williams, in contrast to Hall, such a question is not meaningful because for him culture is "material from the outset" (McGuigan and Moran 2014, 177).

Hall's non-dialectical, dualist version of constructionism in *Representation* differs widely from his study (Hall 1974/2003) of Marx's dialectical method in the 1857 *Introduction to the Grundrisse* (Marx 1857/58, 81–111), where he interprets Marx's dialectic of production, distribution, and consumption. Hall says that the dialectic for Marx is not just an "immediate identity" (Hall 1974/2003, 122), but at the same time also a "mediation" (122), "mutual dependence" (122, 124); and "an *internal connection* between two sides" (124), in which each moment of a dialectic is constituted by creating the other and thereby creating itself as the other and completing its own re-creation. The dialectic is a "differentiated totality" (127), "a *differentiated unity*" (127). Applying these insights to the relationship of economy and culture/work and communication/labour and ideology means that these moments are not just related and connected differences, but rather that culture is at the same time economic and non-economic, constituted by cultural work and taking on emergent qualities (social meanings) that shape the economy and society at large. Culture is at the same time part of the economy and non-part, economy and non-economy, constituted by the economy and constituting the economy. The differentiated and mutually constituted unity of culture and the economy has, as all dialectical totalities, a ground: the common ground of culture and the economy is that they are both material human-societal systems. In *Representation*, Hall falls behind his own reading of Marx.[1]

Colin Sparks presents in an analysis of Hall's relationship to Marxism: Hall in the 1970s engaged with structural Marxism and then was undergoing a "slow movement away from any self-identification with marxism" (Sparks 1996, 88). Two years before his death, Stuart Hall called for a return of Marx to cultural studies:

> It is not that Marxism is not around. [. . .] A Marxist tradition of critical thinking is absent [. . .] in Cultural Studies [. . .] And that's a real weakness. That's one of the reasons why I'd say we're not in a very good position. [. . .] I want to re-engage the same kind of issues. This is what Cultural Studies was in the beginning.[2]

When thinking about culture and economy, then we should bear in mind Stuart Hall's self-reflective and self-critical insight that Marx matters, which also encompasses that the Marxian dialectic matters.

If cultural production in specific work processes creates symbols that have meaning in society, then the communication of such meanings via language and media must also be a work process. An approach that helps to conceptualise communication as work is Ferruccio Rossi-Landi's (1977, 1983) Marxist semiotics. For him, language and communication are work that produce words, sentences, interconnected sentences, arguments, speeches, essays, lectures, books, codes, artworks, literature, science, groups, civilisation, and the linguistic world as totality (Rossi-Landi 1983, 133–136). As "words and messages do not exist in nature" (Rossi-Landi 1983, 36), they must be the products of human work that generates use-values. They are use-values because they satisfy the human needs of expression, communication, and social relations (Rossi-Landi 1983, 37). "Like the other products of human work, words, expressions and messages have a use-value or utility insofar as they satisfy needs, in this case, the basic needs for expression and communication with all the changing stratifications that have historically grown up around them" (Rossi-Landi 1983, 50).

Rossi-Landi (1983, 47) argues that language is a material instrument that is constant capital and that linguistic labour power is variable capital. A linguistic community would be a "huge market in which words, expressions and messages circulate as commodities" (Rossi-Landi 1983, 49). Words would have exchange value because in language they stand in relation to others' words, whereas messages would have exchange value in the exchange of information between humans (Rossi-Landi 1983, 49). Rossi-Landi (1983) conceptualises the linguistic value and exchange value of expressions by saying that Marx's logic of x commodity A = y commodity B has in language a homology when one expression's meaning is compared to another, for example: "art is an institution" and art "is a particular theoretical moment of the Spirit" (Rossi-Landi 1983, 61).

Rossi-Landi's approach is important, especially because he interprets human communication processes as work and in this context uses Marx's general notion of work. But it has limits in that it uses the terms *linguistic capital*, *linguistic market*, and *linguistic value* just like *linguistic work* as anthropological concepts. Whereas work is for Marx a general concept characteristic for all societies, capital, markets, and value are not anthropological features of humans and society, but rather historical features of specific class societies. A homology of language with capital, markets, and value therefore naturalises and essentialises historical categories. The logical consequence is that capital, markets, and values appear to be characteristics of all societies in Rossi-Landi's approach. Rossi-Landi's approach is feasible where he argues that language is work, but it fails when he argues that language is a form of trade, in which we can find capital, exchange-value, and markets.

Although linguistic products in capitalist societies or other societies that use markets as economic distribution mechanisms can be traded as commodities, this does not imply that language is always a commodity that is exchanged on markets. A market is a mechanism of exclusion in that it gives you only access to a good or service if you in return provide a good or service that is considered to have equal value. In everyday life, many communications do not assume the logic of getting something in return whose value can be quantified. Mothers and fathers talk a lot to their babies out of altruism and love, but do not expect the babies to return words and sentences that are equally meaningful. In fact, the babies would not be able to learn to speak if their parents applied the logic of markets, commodities, and exchange value because the adults then would not speak very much to them. Language and our brains are in general not constant capital, but rather a means of linguistic production—instruments of linguistic work. Human beings and their languaging-capacity and -activity are not variable capital, but rather they are the subjects of linguistic work. It is only in capitalism and other market-based societies that linguistic products can turn into capital and commodities, brains and language into constant capital, and linguistic work capacity into variable capital. Under such circumstances, linguistic products such as books are the expenditure of specific hours of labour power. When the book is sold, one can only read it if one pays a specific price for it (except if illegal copies are distributed).

Charles Sanders Peirce (1955) has in contrast to Ferdinand de Saussure's dualogical semiology created a trialogic version of semiotics. He has in this context coined the notion of semiosis, by which he means "an action, or influence, which is, or involves, a cooperation of *three* subjects, such as a sign, its objects, and its interpretant [. . .] this tri-relative influence not being in any way resolvable into actions between pairs" (Peirce 1955, 282). Peirce (1955, 99) calls the sign also *representamen*. A sign "is something which stands to somebody for something in some respect or capacity" (Peirce 1955, 99). "A *Sign*, or *Representamen*, is a First which stands in such a genuine triadic relation to a Second, called its *Object*, as to be capable of determining a Third, called its *Interpretant*, to assume the same triadic relation to its Object in which it stands itself to the same Object" (Peirce 1955, 99f). The Object is "[t]hat thing which causes a sign", it is "the 'real'", "the *existent* object". The Interpretant is the "effect of the sign", "the proper significate outcome of a sign" (Peirce 1955, 275).

An information process is according to Peirce a triadic relationship, in which an object is represented as a sign and produces certain mental effects that we term "interpretation". Semiosis is the process O—S—M, in which objects O are signified by signs S that are interpreted in the form of meanings M. Semiosis is not a static process, but continuous and dynamic because existing meanings are the starting point for new thought and communication processes through which meanings are produced and differentiated. There is a logical correspondence between Hegel's dialectical logic and Peirce's semiotic logic.

Semiosis is a dialectical process in the sense that a Something (an object) and an Other (a Representamen) refer to each other in such a way that a new meaningful sign system emerges that is again a new Something in the social world that enters the cultural process of interpretation. Peirce describes an endless process of the emergence of interpretants. This process is one of dialectical sublation (*Aufhebung*). This can be seen for example by the fact that Peirce made one definition of semiosis in direct analogy to Hegel's definition of the dialectical process. Peirce says that a sign is "anything which determines something else (its interpretant) to refer to an object to which itself refers (its object) in the same way, the interpretant becoming in turn a sign, and so on ad infinitum [. . .] If the series of successive interpretants comes to an end, the sign is thereby rendered imperfect at least" (Peirce 1958, 303).

Hegel has outlined that Identity and Difference and the One and the Many are dialectically connected. A thing is identical with itself, a reflection-into-self (A = A) (Hegel 1830, §113). "Essence is pure identity and inward shine only because it is negativity relating itself to itself, and hence by being self-repulsion from itself; thus it contains the determination of distinction essentially" (Hegel 1830, §116). A thing is only what it is in difference to other things; it is also reflection-into-other. But a thing is not only identical with itself and different from other things, there is also a unity of a thing and other things on a higher level. Hegel calls this unity the *Ground*. "*Ground* is the unity of identity and distinction; the truth of what distinction and identity have shown themselves to be, the inward reflection which is just as much reflection-in to-another and vice versa" (Hegel 1830, §121). Something is only what it is in its relationship to another, but by the negation of the negation this something incorporates the other into itself. The dialectical movement involves two moments that negate each other, a Something and an Other. As a result of the negation of the negation, "Something becomes an other; this other is itself something, so it likewise becomes an other, and so on *ad infinitum*" (Hegel 1830, §93). Being-for-self or the negation of the negation means that something becomes an Other, but this again is a new something that is opposed to an Other and as a synthesis results again in an Other and therefore it "follows that something in its passage into other only joins with itself" it is *self-related* (Hegel 1830, §95). In becoming there are two moments (Hegel 1812, 21.93–21.96): coming-to-be and ceasing-to-be. By sublation, i.e. negation of the negation, being passes over into nothing, it ceases to be, but something new shows up, is coming to be. What is sublated (*aufgehoben*) on the one hand ceases to be and is put to an end, but on the other hand is preserved and maintained (Hegel 1812, 11.245).

Hegel's crucial formulation is that "Something becomes an other; this other is itself something, so it likewise becomes an other, and so on *ad infinitum*" (Hegel 1830, §93). Peirce took up Hegel's formulation and applied it to information processes by saying that "anything which determines something else (its interpretant) to refer to an object to which itself refers (its object) in the same way, the interpretant becoming in turn a sign, and so on ad infinitum" (Peirce 1958, 303).

Semiosis as dialectical process takes place both in individual cognition and communication and thereby connects individual and social human existence. It operates as a threefold, nested, emergent, and interconnected process (see Figure 3.1):

1 *Individual semiosis* is a mental thought process—cognition—in which an individual interprets the world by mentally representing parts of reality by

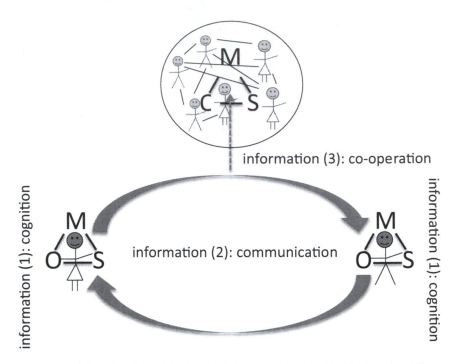

FIGURE 3.1 The tripleC model of semiosis/information (see Hofkirchner 2013 for foundations of the tripleC theory)

signs in his/her imagination and creating meanings that interpret the objects and signs.

2   Individual semiosis enables and constrains and is enabled and constrained, i.e. conditions and is conditioned, by *social semiosis*: human social relations are communicative relationships, in which humans use language, i.e. systems of grammatically connected signs that form words and sentences and are expressed in spoken, written, bodily, or visual forms, so that meaning is mutually communicated. One individual A communicates parts of the meanings s/he gives to the world to another individual B who communicates meanings that s/he gives to the world back to A. Social semiosis means that the meanings of at least two humans are changed by communication processes. These changes of meanings can be more or less substantial. In some cases qualitatively new interpretations, values, or knowledge are created; in other cases the communicated information is recognised and interpreted, but makes no profound changes. Individual semiosis emerges from humans' interactions with the natural and social environment and enables social semiosis. Cognition is conditioned by communication, which in turn conditions cognition.

3   Many communications are ephemeral and do not bring about more substantial structural changes in society. Some communications and social relations, however, are transformative, i.e. they result in societal changes, such as the formation of a new social system, the differentiation of an existing social system, the emergence of new rules or resources. In such cases, social semiosis becomes *structural/societal semiosis*: communication turns in co-operation/collaboration, in which several humans act together in such a way that new structures emerge or existing ones are transformed. Communication conditions co-operation and co-operation conditions communication.

In the tripleC model of information (Fuchs and Hofkirchner 2005; Hofkirchner 2013), cognition conditions and is conditioned by communication that conditions and is conditioned by co-operation. Semiosis has an individual, a social, and a societal level. It is a dialectical information process that is organised as a dialectic of dialectics: the semiosis of cognition mutually interacts with the semiosis of communication in human practices and relations, from which the semiosis of society that transforms social structures can emerge.

Information processes do not stand outside of matter and do not form a second substance besides or related to matter. Information—the semiosis of semioses and the dialectic of dialectics of cognition, communication, and co-operation—is material itself, has the potential to transform structures. On the cognitive and communicative level of the individual and social relations, semiosis transforms cognitive structures, i.e. patterns of established meanings of individuals, to which new meanings are added. On the co-operative level of society, semiosis reproduces and/or transforms structures of society, such as rules, resources, dominant and hegemonic social values, organisations, institutions, etc. Reproduction and transformation take place within the economic, the political, and the cultural system through communicative and collaborative work processes. Semiosis and structuration cannot be opposed because individual and social semiosis reproduces and changes individual autopoietic structures of human cognition, whereas societal semiosis reproduces and changes structures in the economic, the political, and the cultural systems of society.

Structures are routinised and regularised social relations between humans that are relatively constant in space-time. They do not occur spontaneously once, but are repeated forms of action that repeatedly take place in specific spaces at specific times. Structures are created and re-created by human practices that in turn are conditioned by existing and emerging structures. This insight of the dialectic of structures and practices has not only been formulated in the late twentieth century by social theorists such as Anthony Giddens (Fuchs 2003b), Pierre Bourdieu (Fuchs 2003a), Roy Bhaskar (Fuchs and Hofkirchner 2009), and Margaret Archer (Fuchs and Hofkirchner 2009), but much earlier by Karl Marx (see Fuchs 2008) when he argued that "just as society itself produces man as man, so is society produced by him" (Marx 1844, 104). This dialectic is visualised in Figure 3.2 (see Fuchs 2008, 52).

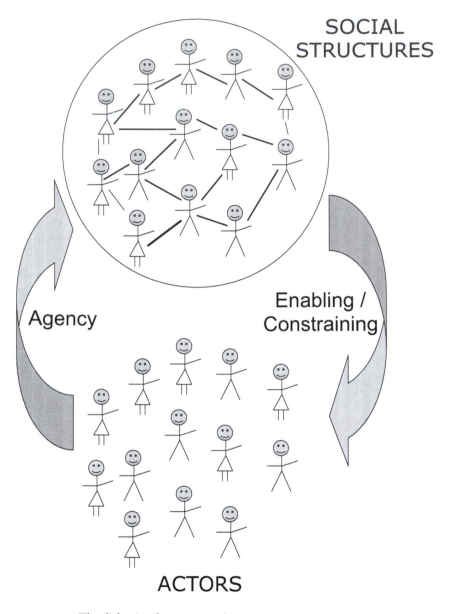

SOCIAL
STRUCTURES

Agency

Enabling /
Constraining

ACTORS

FIGURE 3.2 The dialectic of structure and agency as a constitutive, reproductive, and transformative feature of society

Marx's dialectic of structure and agency was reformulated by several contemporary social theorists. For Anthony Giddens, "the structural properties of social systems are both medium and outcome of the practices they recursively organise" (Giddens 1984, 25). They both enable and constrain actions (Giddens 1984, 26). Pierre Bourdieu argues that there is a dialectical relationship between the objective structures and the cognitive and motivating structures which they produce and which tend to reproduce them, [. . .] these objective structures are themselves products of historical practices and are constantly reproduced and transformed by historical practices whose productive principle is itself the product of the structures which it consequently tends to reproduce.

Bourdieu 1977, 83

In his Transformative Model of Social Activity, Roy Bhaskar introduces the notion of the "dialectics of structure and agency": "social structure is a necessary condition for, and medium of, intentional agency, which is in turn a necessary condition for the reproduction or transformation of social forms" (Bhaskar 2008, 144). Margaret Archer distinguishes between "people's emergent properties" (PEPs), "structural emergent properties" (SEPs), and "cultural emergent properties" (CEPs). Her approach of social realism is based on the "dialectical relationship between personal and social identities" (Archer 2002, 18), "a synthesis such that both personal and social identities are emergent and distinct, although they contributed to one another's emergence and distinctiveness" (Archer 2002, 18). Bhaskar and Archer understand society as the permanent emergence of structures based on human identity and activity.

In the individual's interaction with its physical and informational, i.e. material, environment, humans reproduce and transform cognitive and bodily, i.e. human structures. If a person reads a book, s/he transforms its cognitive structures. If s/he walks to the bus station, s/he transforms its bodily structures. Body and mind are in this process structurally connected: humans think while and for moving their bodies; bodily movement is enabled by cognition and transports a human physically through space-time so that s/he can make new experiences that enable the emergence of new cognitive patterns—specific relationships between neurons and neural networks in the human brain. Communication is the way for humans to engage in, create, and maintain social relations. Social relations become crystallised and objectified in social structures that are organised continuously in space-time, in modern society for example in the form of commodities, money, markets, laws, or dominant ideologies. Establishing, reproducing, and changing crystallised and objectified social structures takes place in and through communication. Communication thereby becomes co-operation, a process in which humans communicate in productive and transformative ways that bring about structural changes of social systems and society. New structures are introduced or existing ones are reproduced. Communication is a necessary and always-present feature of structuration that operates at the level of interacting human actors. It is a structure-producing and structure-reproducing feature of society. Semiosis is constitutive of structuration just like structuration is one of the features of semiosis. In social relations, also artefacts such as production technologies, communication technologies, buildings, infrastructures etc. play a role. Nature and natural resources transformed into use-values shape and are shaped by social relations. Co-operation processes continuously produce and reproduce specific economic, political, and cultural structures in society: use-values, collective decisions, and collective definitions of reality (e.g. norms and values, reputation, ideologies, worldviews, belief systems, morals etc.). Such structures can only come into existence in and through the interaction of cognitive, communicative, and collaborative semiosis and enable and constrain these processes. Just like social relations involve the interconnection of bodily movements and thought patterns, social structures are interconnections of physical artefacts and information.

Each social structure contains specific amounts of qualitatively different types of artefacts and information. The ideological structure of a religion is for example based on the combination of collective moral values (such as the belief in God, the Holy Ghost, redemption, conservative sexual morals etc.); regularised practices, in which humans conduct their bodies and minds in specific ways under specific space-time constellations (e.g. praying every Sunday similar prayers in a specific church); buildings (such as churches); artefacts (such as bibles, crucifixes, holy pictures etc.); social roles (such as pastors and believers), and so on.

Jessop and Oosterlynck (2008) as well as Sum and Jessop (2013, 184–185) argue that discourses are undergoing *variation*, but for society to exist particular discourses get *selected* and *privileged* in order to be *retained* and *reinforced* over space-time. Sum and Jessop (2013, chapter 5) have generalised this approach for arguing that society undergoes the variation, selection, and retention of structures, discourses, technologies, and actions. These four levels are, however, again not separate. Humans constantly move and relate to nature and other humans; they are relational beings. Society gets produced and reproduced through this constant dialectical-human movement. In this movement humans continuously breathe, live, think, communicate, and co-create structures. In their social relations, which are communicative encounters of human beings, their bodies and brains, mediated by language-use, humans variegate, select, and retain specific individual thoughts, individual actions, social communications, social relations, and structures so that society and social systems are co-produced, co-reproduced, co-dissolved, co-constituted, co-re-constituted, etc.

Individuals, social systems, and society are complex, dynamic systems (Fuchs 2008) that undergo constant changes at specific levels of organisation. Continuity at one level can only be achieved through constant change at the underlying levels. Change does not always reach up to all levels of organisation of society and nature; it is, however, always a potential that needs to be actualised through productive interactions of elements. Society is characterised by the fact that humans can anticipate in their mind and discussions how society could be changed, what it could and should look like. Humans are self-conscious, social, societal, anticipatory, thinking, judging, and moral beings. They can *work* towards changes based on their own specific human qualities. Not all transformations are equally substantial: they take place at different levels of organisation. Human agency constantly absents absences (Bhaskar 2008), i.e. it creates novelty and thereby negates that which exists by negating contradictions in a productive manner. Roy Bhaskar (2008, 5, 55, 377) has distinguished between real negation ≥ transformative negation ≥ radical negation in order to stress the non-deterministic and complex character of sublation (*Aufhebung*), i.e. dialectical transformations. Not all negations of negations are at the fundamental level, there are also partial sublations that are transformative, but not radical. The emergence of transnational informational capitalism is a transformational sublation, but not a radical one. Transformations can be fundamental, superficial, intermediate, full, partial, large, small, distantiation without transformation, etc.

How is semiosis (the information dialectic of cognition, communication, and co-operation) related to work? Rossi-Landi conceptualises the work process that he parallelises with the communication process as a dialectic of material, operations (instruments, worker, working operations), and product (see Withalm 2006). He thereby, however, relates two objects and not the human subject (its work, mental and physical work capacity and labour power) and the objects of work to each other so that his system is not a subject-object-dialectic. Language is the result of human activities over many generations. Words are not natural objects, but are produced by humans together in their culture. As information is produced by humans it is the product of human work. Hands, head, ears, mouth—body and brain—work together in order to enable speech. Work has a dual character, physical and social dimensions. Thinking and speaking that result in the production of information and symbols form the physical aspect, human relations the social dimension of communication.

Information can be conceived as a threefold process of cognition, communication, and co-operation (Fuchs and Hofkirchner 2005). Table 3.1. gives an

TABLE 3.1 The subject, object, and subject-object of cognitive, communicative, and co-operative work

	Subject	*Object of work*	*Instruments of work*	*Product of work*
Cognition = human brain work	Human being	Experiences	Brain	Thoughts, cognitive patterns, ideas
Communication = human group work	Group of humans	Thoughts	Brain, mouth, ears	Meaning
Co-operation = collaborative human group work	Group of humans	Meaning	Brain, mouth, ears, body	Information product with shared and co-created meaning

overview of the dimensions of the cognitive, communicative, and co-operative dimensions of information work (Fuchs and Sevignani 2013).

Figure 3.3 shows that these three processes are connected dialectically and form together the process of information work. Each of the three behaviours—cognition, communication, and co-operation—is a work process: cognition is work of the human brain, communication work of human groups, and co-operative work of human groups. Communication is based on cognition and uses the products of cognition—ideas—as its object of work. Co-operation is based on communication and uses the products of communication—meanings—as object of work. Information is a work process, in which cognitive work creates ideas, communicative work creates meanings, and co-operative work co-creates information products that have shared and co-created meanings. Information is a dialectical process of human work, in which cognition, communication, and cooperation are dialectically connected. Each of these three processes forms a work process that has its own subject-object-dialectic in itself.

Using the Hegel-Marxist triangle model of the work process, one can argue that the development that Marx points out on behalf of the notion of the general intellect can be formalised as follows: S-O>SO .. S-SO>SSO .. S-SSO>SSSO and so forth. The object position of a dialectical work triangle starts with the result, the subject-object of a previous triangle and so on. The advantage of this kind of thinking is that the reference to an object and ultimately nature never gets completely lost in the theory. Hence a dualism between subject and object, e.g. communication and work, is prevented. Dialectical thinking is capable of providing an integrative theory of human activity.

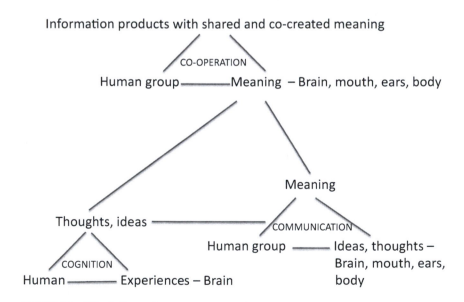

FIGURE 3.3 The information process as work process

An example: A person likes reading books about gardening and builds up a sophisticated knowledge of how to create and maintain a good-looking garden by reading more and more books and applying this knowledge in his/her garden. The created knowledge is a use-value in the sense that it helps him/her organise her/his own garden in a nice-looking manner. S/he meets another person, who has comparable knowledge. They start exchanging ideas on gardening. In this communication process, the shared knowledge of one person forms an object that is interpreted by the other person so that meaning, i.e. an interpretation of parts of the world, is formed. The process also works vice-versa. As a result, meanings are created as use-values on both sides; each person understands something about the other. After continuous conversations and mutual learning, the two hobby gardeners decide to write a book about gardening. They develop new ideas by discussing and bring their experiences together, whereby synergies, new experiences, and new gardening methods emerge. In the book, they describe these new methods that they have tried in practice in a jointly run garden. The representations of the joint experiences and of the co-created methods in the form of a book are a use-value not just for the two, but for others too.

Work requires information processes, and information creation is itself a work process. This model allows a non-dualistic solution to the question of how work and information/interaction are connected. It avoids separations between nature/culture, work/interaction, base/superstructure, but rather argues that information has its own economy—it is work that creates specific use-values. These use-values are individual in character only at the level of cognition—the human thinks and develops new ideas—whereas they have a direct social character at the level of communication and co-operation. But humans do not exist as monads; the objects of cognitive work stem to a large degree from society itself. To interpret the information creation process as work is not philosophical idealism because idealism sees spirit as an independently existing entity that is not connected to human labour. Ideas, meanings, and co-created information products are objects of labour that reflect society in complex ways.

Every work process requires cognition, communication, and co-operation as tools of production. Therefore the physical production of goods in manufacturing as well as agricultural work and mining are never separate from information processes. This aspect has been stressed in many Marxist analyses of the connection of communication and work. In these production forms, information is not a product, but a means of production. Work requires information. The other way round, information is also work: there is an informational mode of production that has grown in size in the twentieth century (in terms of the population active in it and share of the overall created value in the economy): it focuses on the production of informational goods and services. It is this kind of production that is the main focus of our attention in this chapter. Work requires information and communication. But at the same time, it is important to give attention to information and communication as forms of work.

The production of information is work. But society and the economy cannot be reduced to information, language, and communication. Pan-informational concepts of society that reduce all human existence to information are just like reductionist approaches that ignore information and culture. Work is always an economic process that produces physical and/or informational results. Information is grounded in work and the economy, but at the same time has emergent qualities in that it communicates meanings in society, which makes it a specifically cultural resource.

3.4. Ideological Labour and Critical Work

Ferruccio Rossi-Landi (1977) questions the assumption that language is always a common good that cannot be a private property. He introduces in this context the notion of linguistic private property, by which he means that a ruling class possesses "control over the emission and circulation of the verbal and non-verbal messages which are constitutive of a given community" (Rossi-Landi 1977, 191). Rossi-Landi (1983, 170–171) argues that the ruling class has linguistic private property over a) codes, modalities of codification, b) channels used for the circulation of messages, and c) modalities of decoding and interpretation. "The ruling class increases the redundance of the messages which confirm its own position and attacks with noise, or if necessary with disturbance, the codification and circulation of messages which could instead invalidate it" (Rossi-Landi 1983, 171). Communications are means for making information public and giving humans a voice that is heard by others and has the potential to influence what is happening in society. Communication power means the capacity to communicate information in society in a public manner so that it is recognized by others and has transformative effects on society.

Communications can have different ownership forms. Graham Murdock (2011, 18) argues that the three possibilities are ownership by capital (the commodity form of communications), the state (the public service form of communications), and civil society (communications as gifts/commons). Information, language, and communications can in the commodity form—what Rossi-Landi calls linguistic private property—take on two basic types (Doyle 2013, 13; Murdock 2011, 16; Napoli 2009, 163–167):

1 audiences as commodities in advertising-financed cultural capital accumulation regimes
2 content as commodity in cultural sales models.

In addition, the commodity form 3) also enters culture as ideologies that justify commodity culture (Murdock 2011, 20).

The logic of cultural commodities and private ownership of communications tends to generate large communication power inequalities so that a few people and organisations—the corporate media and their owners—have a lot of power to communicate, whereas others can communicate, but are more unlikely to be heard. Public service and alternative media are attempts to overcome this limit, but they are within a capitalist society facing specific antagonisms and problems.

Ruling groups and classes aim at controlling cultural production and dissemination tools (media) as well as the contents that are spread. This process tends to be contradictory and is not automatically successful. Nonetheless it is a general tendency in heteronomous societies that ruling classes engage in the production and dissemination of ideologies. Cultural work thereby becomes ideological work and media content becomes ideological content. But what is an ideology? And what is ideological work?

Terry Eagleton (1991, 28–31) has noted six core understandings of the concept of ideology:

a) The "general material process of production of ideas, beliefs and values in social life" (28).

b) Ideas coherently "symbolize the conditions and life-experiences of a specific group or class" (29).

c) The "promotion and legitimatization of the interests of a group or class in the face of opposing interests" (29).

d) The "promotion and legitimatization" (29) of the interests of a dominant social group in order to "unify a social formation" (30).

e) Ideas and beliefs that "help to legitimate the interests of a ruling group or class by distortion and dissimulation" (30).

f) "[F]alse or deceptive beliefs" arising from the "material structure of society as a whole" (30).

We can think about Eagleton's (1991) six concepts as variously interlinked levels of ideology. The differentiation between levels allows us also to see that false consciousness is not a necessary element of ideology; it may be just one outcome of ideological strategies, but can also be resisted (although there is no automatism of resistance and the means for producing hegemonic ideology and counter-hegemony are unequally distributed). Ideology is not necessarily a state of consciousness of dominated groups. It can be, but it is more a process, in which dominant groups communicate dominant ideas, to which others react in certain ways or do not react. Dominant ideas impact the culture of the dominant itself (e.g. neoliberal work norms—the new spirit of networked capitalism—that impact not only the behaviour of workers, but also managers).

Norman Fairclough (2010, 73) distinguishes between critical and descriptive concepts of ideology. Critical concepts would see ideology "as one modality of power, a modality which constitutes and sustains relations of power through producing consent or at least acquiescence, power through hegemony rather than power through violence and force" (Fairclough 2010, 73). Ideologies "are representations which contribute to the constitution, reproduction, and transformation of social relations of power and domination" (Fairclough 2010, 73).

For Fairclough (2010, 40–43) institutions are speech communities, in which ideological contradictions tend to be crystallised in the form of a dominant ideology and one or several competing dominated ideologies. Ideology tries to naturalize and disguise phenomena and to present them as natural, automatised, and common sense (Fairclough 2010, 67). Fairclough considers discourses, understood as "language use conceived as social practice" (Fairclough 2010, 95) and a way "of signifying experience from a particular perspective" (Fairclough 2010, 96), as ideological if there is "a relation between their meanings (ways of representing) and social relations of power" (Fairclough 2010, 79). We can say that in Fairclough's terminology, critical ideology concepts are Eagleton's versions c)–f).

Assume that there is a government that passes a law that outlaws Holocaust denial and justifies this with the argument that the Shoah should not be repeated and that state power should therefore guarantee that fascist and racist ideologies are contained. So if the dominant power is anti-fascist and anti-racist in character, then the question that arises is if ideas of this dominant power should also be characterised as ideology or if in this case merely fascism and racism shall be termed ideologies. Definitions a)–d) in the context of the example case see both fascism and anti-fascism as ideologies, whereas e) and f) would limit the use of the term *ideology* to fascist thought and practices.

On the one hand Gramsci uses the notion of ideology in an all-too-general sense as meaning the "superstructure of a particular structure and [. . .] the arbitrary elucubrations of particular individuals" (Gramsci 1988, 199). Georg Lukács (1986, 397) argues in this context that Gramsci shows the individual and social meaning of the term *ideology*, but also criticizes that individual thoughts cannot be considered as ideologies because ideas must take on a societal role in order to be effective.

But on the other hand Gramsci introduces the notion of the common sense for characterising "a conception of the world mechanically imposed by the external environment" (Gramsci 1988, 325). The counter-hegemonic move is

> to work out consciously and critically one's own conception of the world and thus, in connection with the labours of one's own brain, choose one's sphere of activity, take an active part in the creation of the history of the world, be one's own guide, refusing to accept passively and supinely from outside the moulding of one's personality.
>
> *(Gramsci 1988, 325).*

Common sense is a "conception of the world" that "is not critical and coherent but disjointed and episodic" (Gramsci 1988, 325). It is "fragmentary, incoherent and inconsequential" (Gramsci 1988, 343).

A critical concept of ideology requires a normative distinction between true and false beliefs and practices. It understands ideology as thoughts, practices, ideas, words, concepts, phrases, sentences, texts, belief systems, meanings, representations, artefacts, institutions, systems, or combinations thereof that represent and justify one group's or individual's power, domination, or exploitation of other groups or individuals by misrepresenting, one-dimensionally presenting, or distorting reality in symbolic representations. Domination means in this context that there is a system that enables one human side to gain advantages at the expense of others and to sustain this condition. It is a routinised and institutionalised form of asymmetric power, in which one side has the opportunity to shape and control societal structures (such as the production and control of wealth, political decision-making, public discussions, ideas, norms, rules, values), whereas others do not have these opportunities and are facing disadvantages or exclusion from the opportunities of others. Exploitation is a specific form of domination, in which an exploiting class derives wealth advantages at the expense of an exploiting class by controlling economic resources and means of coercion in such a way that the exploited class is forced to produce new use-values that the exploiting class controls. Ideology presupposes "societal structures, in which different groups and conflicting interests act and strive to impose their interest onto the total of society as its general interest. To put it shortly: The emergence and diffusion of ideologies appears as the general characteristic of class societies" (Lukács 1986, 405, translation from German).

Marx described the naturalising dimension of ideology by arguing that "in all ideology men and their circumstances appear upside-down as in a camera obscura" (Marx and Engels 1845/46, 42). Ideology is therefore for Marx "an inverted consciousness of the world" and functions as the "opium of the people" (Marx 1843b, 250). In *Capital*, Marx generalised his criticism of religion as ideology and characterised modern ideology as fetishist thought: The "fetishism peculiar to the capitalist mode of production [. . .] consists in regarding economic categories, such as being a commodity or productive labour, as qualities inherent in the material incarnations of these formal determinations or categories" (Marx 1867, 1046). Ideology presents social relations that are always historical, i.e. have a start and an end, as "socio-natural properties of [. . .] things" (Marx 1867, 165).

False consciousness "by-passes the essence of the evolution of society and fails to pinpoint it and express it adequately" (Lukács 1971, 50). "On the other hand, we may see the same consciousness as something which fails *subjectively* to reach its self-appointed goals, while furthering and realising the *objective* aims of society of which it is ignorant and which it did not choose" (Lukács 1971, 50). False consciousness is reified: For Lukács, reification means that humans are treated like things or relegated to the status of things. He said that the effect of reification on consciousness is that some humans perceive reality differently from how it is actually. Reification means "that a relation between people takes on the character of a thing and thus acquires 'phantom objectivity', an autonomy that seems so strictly rational and all-embracing as to conceal every trace of its fundamental nature: the relation between people" (Lukács 1971, 83).

Whereas for Gramsci, common sense is not false consciousness, but thought that is taken over from an external source without a lot of reflection, Lukács uses the notion of false consciousness for characterising knowledge and communications that are ideological and therefore bound up with the ideas of the ruling class and the whole worldview it creates and diffuses. Gramsci stresses that resisting forces must try to influence common sense, whereas Lukács stresses the need to create and diffuse the truth and overcome false consciousness. Whereas Gramsci sees ideology as the realm of struggle, Lukács (1986, 399) stresses that ideology is a means of social struggles that can make struggles conscious and fight them out (Lukács 1986, 404) in order to overcome ideology. For Gramsci, ideology is more continuous and essential, whereas for Lukács it is discontinuous and historical. If ideology is everywhere anytime, then it cannot be a critical-theoretical concept, but is rather relegated to the status of an anthropological-theoretical concept.

Lukács's concept of ideology allows going beyond a populist notion of ideology that sees everything that the masses collectively do and say as necessarily positive. It goes beyond "the naïve description of what men *in fact* thought, felt and wanted" and infers "the thoughts and feelings which men would have if they were *able* to assess" the whole of society "and the interests arising from it [. . .] That is to say, it would be possible to infer the thoughts and feelings appropriate to their objective situation" (Lukács 1986, 51).

Lukács has a Hegelian notion of ideology that sees ideologies as practices and communications that present phenomena that exist (existence) in a way that is different to their actual essence (how they really are) so that existence appears different from how it is in order to justify domination. One can say based on Hegel, in ideologies the "immediate being of things is here represented as a sort of rind or curtain behind which the essence is concealed" (Hegel 1830, §112). The essence is the foundational and grounding dimension of things. If there are ideologies, "when we say further that all things have an essence, what we mean is that they are not truly what they immediately show themselves to be" (Hegel 1830, §112). In contrast, truth for Hegel means "the agreement of a content with itself" (Hegel 1830, §24: addition 2). An ideology separates a phenomenon's ground and essence from its appearance; it makes part of reality appear different from its ground and thereby distorts reality. It constructs a false representation of reality. Critical knowledge in contrast to ideologies deconstructs false knowledge-representations of reality in order to uncover and communicate truths (how reality actually is and should be).

Lukács has strongly influenced ideology critique (such as the Frankfurt School's version of it) that can be contrasted to ideology theories. Horkheimer and Adorno have defended a critical concept of ideology against Karl Mannheim's general concept (Adorno 1955; Horkheimer 1930). Adorno has described ideology in a Lukácsian sense as "a consciousness which is objectively necessary and yet at the same time false, as the intertwining of truth and falsehood" (Adorno 1954, 189). Ideology "is *justification*":

> It presupposes the experience of a societal condition which has already become problematic and therefore requires a defense just as much as does the idea of justice itself, which would not exist without such necessity for apologetics and which has as its model the exchange of things which are comparable.
>
> *Adorno 1954, 189–190*

From the existence of ideology in class society follows for the Frankfurt School the necessity of the critique of ideology, which these thinkers define as "the confrontation of ideology with its own truth" (Adorno 1954, 190). The critique of ideology "is the negation defined in the Hegelian sense, the confrontation of the spiritual with its realization, and has as its presupposition the distinction of the truth or falsity of the judgment just as much as the requirement for truth in that which is criticized" (Adorno 1954, 191).

Ideology is a semiotic level of domination and exploitation—it practices the production and spread of information and meanings in the form of ideas, belief systems, artefacts, systems, and institutions so that domination and exploitation are justified or naturalised. Sum and Jessop (2013, 164) importantly point out that "[n]ot all semiosis is ideological even if all semiosis is selective". Ideology is "a *contingent* feature of culture and discourse that gets naturalised, articulated, selected and sedimented in the (re)making of social relations" (Sum and Jessop 2013, 172).

Ideology is a special form of individual, social, and societal semiosis that is embedded into structures of domination and aims at justifying, naturalising, upholding, defending, and containing actual or potential resistance against specific forms of domination. It aims at making a broader public believe that society or a social system in its dominative or exploitative status should remain unchanged and is good, fair, free, or just the way it is. This goal is associated with the task of spreading information that tries to convince subordinated individuals and groups not to work for transformations or to support forces and ideas that question the status quo.

A critical concept of ideology assumes a realist epistemology: by practicing critical thinking we are able to perceive and deconstruct ideologies that misrepresent reality and make false claims that do not correspond to reality in their task of constituting, maintaining, reproducing, and deepening domination and exploitation. Ideologies are both social and individual, structures and practices, orders and events. They take on routinised, crystallised, and objectified forms represented by groups and individuals, rules/resources/artefacts/systems/institutions and social and collective actions, continuous and spontaneous forms of existence. Ideology is a dialectic process that connects these different levels of ideological organisation. Racism is for example an ideology represented by specific groups (e.g. neo-Nazis), structures (such as immigration laws), and orders (such as National Socialism) that shapes and is shaped by and gets reproduced in and through specific individuals (and their thoughts and practices) such as concrete Nazis, collective practices such as police violence and deportation practices, and events such as the pogroms that took place in the German Reich in the night from 9 to 10 November 1938. Ideological groups, structures, and orders condition, enable, and constrain, and are produced and reproduced by ideological practices and events. Ideologies are to specific degrees hegemonic, but are often contradicted internally and potentially also externally by forces that oppose, challenge, and struggle against them. If a dominant group is split up into competing factions that have an overall common interest but have issues they internally struggle over, then the dominant ideology is often a compromise or outcome of internal contradictions. The actual policies of coalition governments whose participating parties represent different groups in society (e.g. large industrialists on the one hand and small and medium enterprises on the other hand) tend to only represent the individual party lines to specific degrees and are outcomes of negotiations.

If language use and communication are work processes, then a specific subset of language use and communication is ideological in character and a specific other subset is critical in character. Ideologies are the outcome of ideological work, critical knowledge the outcome of critical cultural work.

Ideologies have specific structures. Teun van Dijk (1998, chapter 5; 2011, 386, 395–396) classifies the structure of ideologies the following way:

- Membership, identity: Who are we? Where are we from? What do we look like? Who can become a member of our group?
- Activities: What do we do? What is expected of us? Why are we here?
- Goals: Why do we do this? What do we want to realise?
- Values/norms: What are our main values? How do we evaluate ourselves and others? What should (not) be done?
- Position and group-relations: What is our social position? Who are our enemies, our opponents? Who are like us, and who are different?
- Resources: What are the essential social resources that our group has or needs to have?

The production, reproduction, and diffusion of an ideology is work that defines the membership, identity, activities, goals, values and norms, positions and resources of a dominant or exploitative group in relation to a dominated or exploited group in such a way that the power of the first is with specific definition strategies that create particular meanings legitimatised, naturalised, and presented as unproblematic. The structure of an ideology can be explained as a dialectical information process: it defines individual dimensions of a group, system, or human being, the being-in-itself of the ideology: identity, membership, activities, norms, values, goals, controlled resources. Then it relates this being-in-itself in a specific manner to a dominated group's being-in-itself (its identity, membership, activities, norms, values, goals, resources) and defines this relationship (being-for-another) in such a way that the dominant group's being-in-itself is justified and the dominated group's being-in-itself presented as inferior, but an inferiority that is necessary and justified. Ideology suggests that this relationship of two phenomena or groups should be resolved in a specific manner by taking specific measures that change reality in specific ways so that the asymmetric power relation between dominant group and the dominated group is maintained. This fusion and resolution is then an ideological being-in-and-for-itself. So ideology defines individual existences, relates them, and suggests how this relationship should be shaped and changed. So a racist ideology describes a) a national group and a group of immigrants, b) a specific relationship between them by claiming e.g. that immigrants are criminals, do not work, speak different languages, have different customs etc. and thereby negatively impact the lives of the national group, and suggests c) specific measures, such as the deportation of immigrants. Ideological work conducts the definition of ideological identities (ideological being-in-itself), relations (ideological being-for-another), and measures (ideological being-in-and-for-itself); the diffusion of these definitions into society; the crystallisation of these ideologies in groups, institutions, structures, and orders; and the maintenance and reproduction of ideology on all of these levels.

Ideological work employs different ways of how in the second step of the definition process the relation between the dominant group and the dominated group is described. Teun van Dijk (2011, 397–398; 1998, 267) has logically formalised possible arguments in the Ideological Square Model. The model contains logical arguments of how ideologies justify dominative relationships. In reality, a concrete ideology often combines several of these logical possibilities that entail positive self-presentation and negative other-presentation. So ideology defines in-groups and out-groups and uses various ideological strategies:

1   To express/emphasise information that is positive about Us,
2   To express/emphasise information that is negative about Them,
3   To suppress/de-emphasise information that is positive about Them,
4   To suppress/de-emphasise information that is negative about Us.

Klaus Holzkamp (1985, 364, translation from German to English) stresses that ideology works by an "identification of general interests and partial interests" for the "perpetuation of the existing relations". Dominated and dominating individuals always have the possibility and therefore freedom to break through existing ideologies in order to think and act differently. This does not, however, automatically happen and in dominative relationships many "individuals by managing their everyday life in which they realize conditioned possibilities of action, relations and thought, reproduce *with their own existence simultaneously bourgeois class relations* as unquestioned precondition" (Holzkamp 1985, 364, translation from German to English). In ideologies, "*possibilities for action and thought that are determined by heteronomous constraints* appear as the *only 'thinkable' possibilities* for the creation of the conditions required to secure and unfold existence in 'freedom and equality'" (Holzkamp 1985, 365, translation from German to English). Holzkamp stresses that dominated groups' and individuals' reproduction of ideologies is grounded in existential fears and risks. Available ideologies, worldviews, and power constellations condition individuals' specific worldviews and actions and the actuality of realising alternative thoughts and actions that are always possible. If one thinks through Holzkamp's argument then it becomes evident that the major fear that keeps people who are dominated from resisting or trying to organise resistance or joining resistance movements is the fear of death and related to it the fear of violence and torture and the experience of these negative realities not just for oneself, but for one's friends and family. Humans do not by nature subject themselves voluntarily to domination, rather their existential fears and needs for security, harmony, recognition, and community are under conditions of domination often channelled into acceptance of one's own domination and exercise of domination against weaker groups and individuals (Holzkamp-Osterkamp 1983).

Many critical theories and analyses of discourse and ideologies in an idealistic manner focus on the level of texts and structures of ideologies and ignore the work of producing and reproducing ideologies. One needs to shed light on how ideologies operate and what their consequences are just like one needs to analyse who produces ideologies, under which circumstances, and with which motivations, goals, and intentions. Ideology critique requires analysis of ideology structures and the work of ideology production just like the analysis of work requires an analysis of the structures and conditions of work, including the ideologies that shape workplaces and work cultures.

Table 3.2 gives an overview of various cultural workers in various dimensions of society. They all produce knowledge that is either ideological or critical. In heteronomous/class societies, ideological workers are almost found with certainty. They dominate specific fields and the resources within these fields. Critical workers produce critical knowledge that challenges ideologies. In heteronomous/class societies such work is always a potential, but not necessarily and not automatically an actuality because critique requires resources that are not so easy to mobilise and often controlled by those ruling the societal field(s).

The hegemony of ideologies and ideological workers can be challenged by counter-hegemonic work. Gramsci (1988, 58) says in this context that making a revolution needs "intense labour of criticism". In such cases, there is the possibility for cultural class struggles, in which critical cultural workers oppose and struggle against ideological workers. In such cases, critical workers—those producing critiques as discursive knowledge in semiotic processes—create and diffuse socialism, equality, and participation, unity in diversity, dialectic, love, care, Progressivism, critical knowledge, or understanding in order to challenge the ideologies created, diffused, and reproduced by ideological workers, such as liberalism, inequality and domination, nationalism, one-dimensionality, hate, sexism, conservatism, administrative knowledge, and racism. Cultural struggles' emergence and outcomes are never determined, but highly uncertain. Ideological work and critical work are highly fluid, dynamic, and entangled. Whereas one article in a newspaper may be ideological, another may be critical. But in general there is a tendency of institutional clustering so that ideologies and critique become crystallised in institutions that continuously create, diffuse, and reproduce certain ideologies or critiques. Such institutions have internal contradictions

TABLE 3.2 Workers, ideologies, and worldviews in various fields of society

Realm of society	Ideological work	Critical work
Economy	Management gurus, consultants, managers: capitalist and liberal ideologies	Activists, unions, social movements, consumer protection groups, critical intellectuals: socialist worldviews critical of capitalism
Politics: government, parliament	Dominant or oppositional parties and politicians: political ideologies of inequality, domination, and repression/violence	Critical parties, politicians, intellectuals: political worldviews of equality, participation, and peace
Politics: civil society	Repressive social movements, NGOs, and activists: political ideologies of inequality, domination, and repression/violence	Emancipatory social movements, NGOs, and activists: worldviews of equality, participation, and peace
International relations	Nationalists: nationalist ideology	Anti-nationalists: global unity in diversity
News media	Uncritical journalists: one-dimensional, biased reports	Critical journalists: critical, engaging reports
Entertainment	Actors, entertainers, directors, artists: tabloidised, one-dimensional culture	Actors, entertainers, directors, artists: engaging, dialectical culture
Personal and gender relations	Hellbenders: hate, sexism	Altruists: love, care, solidarity
Belief systems, ethics, philosophy, and religion	Demagogues: Conservatism	Public intellectuals: Progressivism
Science and education	Administrative scholars and teachers: administrative knowledge	Critical scholars and teachers: critical knowledge
Intercultural relations	Racists, divisionists: racism	Universalists: intercultural understanding

(between dominant factions and their ideologies, between dominant and subordinate groups and their discourses) and external ones (between different institutions, institutions and other institutions, systems and groups in society etc.).

Culture and politics are the realms where consent to domination is established, but they are also the terrain where counter-hegemony that questions and resists domination can be established. A "crisis of the ruling class's hegemony" occurs when this class has failed on some major political undertaking [. . .] for which it has requested, or forcibly extracted, the consent of the broad masses (war, for example), or because huge masses [. . .] have passed suddenly from a state of political passivity to a certain activity, and put forward demands which taken together, albeit not organically formulated, add up to a revolution.

Gramsci 1988, 218

The result is a crisis of authority and the state. The "immediate situation becomes delicate and dangerous, because the field is open for violent solutions, for the activities of unknown forces, represented by charismatic 'men of destiny'" (Gramsci 1988, 218).

Subordinated groups and individuals do not necessarily develop critical or false consciousness. Ideology is a process with uncertain outcomes. Given the power of dominant groups and the relative powerlessness of dominated groups, the average likelihood of critical consciousness tends to be lower than that of critical consciousness, unless dominated groups and individuals empower themselves and learn to see through ideologies, to question them and to struggle against them. Dominant classes and groups always try to impose their ideologies on subordinated people. The dominated answer to this ideological communication process in a positive (affirmation, hegemony), negative (critique, counter-hegemony), or mixed way. As ideologists speak to individuals through ideology, those addressed tend to react and to communicate back in specific ways that are not determined.

The existence of ideologies created and diffused by ideological workers on behalf of a dominant group is independent of the question of how people react to ideologies. There are different possibilities, either that they are conscious or unconscious that an ideology is an ideology or a mixed form, either that they follow, partly follow, question, or resist ideologies. In the first German edition of *Capital, Volume 1*, Marx discussed the fetishism of commodities by saying that ideology is based on the logic "they do not know it, but they do it".[3] In the most widely used contemporary English version, the translation is: "They do this without being aware of it" (Marx 1867, 166-167). Slavoj Žižek (1989, 25) suggests based on Peter Sloterdijk that today the cynical subject bases its action on the logic "they know very well what they are doing, but still, they are doing it". In capitalism, the social relationship between capital and labour and between different forms of labour that are necessary for the production and exchange of commodities is "concealed by the *objectified* form".[4] The consumer buys a specific commodity for a sum of money and only sees money and the commodity, but does not see how in commodity exchange various forms of abstract labour that are embedded into class relations are equated with each other. Labour remains hidden behind the commodity. "So just *what* a value is does not stand written on its forehead. In order to relate their products to one another as commodities, men are compelled to equate their various labours to abstract human labour."[5]

Žižek argues that humans partly know about the falseness of ideology, but follow it because they derive a surplus of enjoyment from it. Ideology is always false in that it contains dominant ideas aimed at justifying dominative reality. How human subjects react to ideology has to do with their subjectivity, i.e. their knowing and their doing in relation to ideology. Table 3.3 shows 16 logic combinations of how humans can react to ideology. The way Žižek describes ideology is just one of 16 possibilities of how humans can react to ideologies. They partly or entirely reproduce ideologies in their actions in the eight possibilities of the first two columns. They do not follow or struggle against ideologies in the eight possibilities displayed in the third and fourth columns. The 16 logical possibilities have different likelihoods based on specific power structures. It is for example quite unlikely that people resist an ideology by accident, although they are unconscious of it, whereas it is much more likely that they are consciously aware and opposed to it when resisting it.

The production of ideologies and critiques requires workers who create the specific ideational content. To make and re-make ideologies and critiques that challenge them is not just a knowledge production process, but requires multiple associated work processes within institutions and social systems. Take for example a school: there are teachers and pupils who engage in learning, which manifests, creates, reproduces, challenges, and critiques ideologies to specific degrees. But work processes that are associated and necessary for enabling learning in schools are cleaners' maintenance of the school building; policy makers', consultants', and experts' design of the curriculum; food personnel's preparation of food in the cafeteria, etc. In order to understand the production of ideologies and critiques one therefore needs to consider the broader institutional foundations and contexts. This means that for analysing work that creates ideologies and

TABLE 3.3 A typology of subjective reactions to ideology

Action → Knowledge	Following an ideology	Following parts of an ideology	Not following an ideology	Resisting an ideology
Unconscious of an ideology	They do not know it, but they do it.	They do not know it, but they partly do it.	They do not know it, and they do not do it.	They do not know it, and they resist it.
Conscious of an ideology	They know it, but still, they are doing it.	They know it, and they partly do it	They know it, and they do not do it.	They know it, and they resist it.
Partly conscious of an ideology	They partly know it, but still, they are doing it.	They partly know it, and they partly do it.	They partly know it, and they do not do it.	They partly know it, and they resist it.
Critically conscious of an ideology	They oppose it, and they do it.	They oppose it, and they partly do (not) do it.	They oppose it, and they do not do it.	They oppose it, and they resist it.

critiques one should avoid cultural idealism and take, as suggested by Raymond Williams, a cultural materialist position that sees the embeddedness of culture, ideology, and knowledge in different forms of work (information work, service work, physical work, etc.).

3.5. Conclusion

I have argued that Marxist theory has too often treated the relationship of work on the one hand and culture, communication, language, and ideology on the other hand in a dualistic manner. Based on Raymond Williams and Ferruccio Rossi-Landi's works, I have argued for a cultural materialist approach that sees culture as work that produces symbols and meaning as specific use-values and communication as a work process that circulates symbols and meanings in society. Ideology based on these theoretical assumptions can be considered as a form of labour conducted by ideological workers that aims at legitimating the interests of dominant groups and classes. Critical work in contrast challenges ideological work, but is at the same time in capitalism often confronted with an unequal distribution of resources that enable critical work.

A theory of culture, communication, and ideology is a dialectical tool of theorising, understanding, and helping to inspire struggles against capitalism. It stands in solidarity with those who work towards overcoming class societies along with all ideological labour that legitimate these structures.

Part I has outlined theoretical foundations of a materialist and dialectical understanding of culture and the economy by focusing on the relationship between culture and labour as well as between communication, ideology, and labour. Parts II and III are applications of these foundations to social media. Cultural and economic processes happen in and are bound to space and time. Using reputation-building and social connections on social media is a time-consuming process. On targeted-advertising-financed social media, usage is furthermore a value-generating labour process. Therefore issues of labour time matter for understanding social media. Part II focuses on this dimension. Social media are in principle also not bound to certain geographical limits, although language features of platforms can constrain usage to specific parts of the world. So some Chinese platforms like the social networking site Renren can in principle be accessed everywhere in the world, but the Chinese interface tends to constrain usage to China and Chinese speakers. Social media are to specific degrees accessed from mobile phones, tablets, and laptops so that social and mobile media tend to converge. Social media not only transcends spatial boundaries in terms of transnational contacts, but its usage also blurs spatial boundaries and the production of information and communications technology is based on an international division of digital labour. Part III focuses on spatial aspects of social media, especially the role of China in the global political economy of social media.

Notes

1 Aspects of agency—labour, work, and class struggle—are rather missing and subordinate in Hall's 1974 interpretation of Marx's *Introduction to the Grundrisse*. Hall analyses structures of production, distribution, and consumption that are overdetermined by production. He explicitly acknowledges Louis Althusser's influence on the arguments (Hall 1974/2003, 128, 130). Although Hall gives a structuralist Althusserian interpretation of Marx that tends to underplay the role of agency, class struggle, and work, there is no doubt that it is dialectical, albeit structurally dialectical and not a meta-dialectic of a structural dialectic and an agency dialectic.

2 Stuart Hall interviewed by Sut Jhally, London, August 30, 2012. http://vimeo. com/53879491.

3 http://www.marxists.org/archive/marx/works/1867-c1/commodity.htm. German original: „Sie wissen das nicht, aber sie thun es" (Marx 1980, 38).

4 http://www.marxists.org/archive/marx/works/1867-c1/commodity.htm; for the German original see Marx 1980, 38.

5 http://www.marxists.org/archive/marx/works/1867-c1/commodity.htm. German original: „Es steht daher dem Werth nicht auf der Stirn geschrieben, was er ist. Um ihre Produkte auf einander als Waaren zu beziehn, sind die Menschen gezwungen, ihre verschiednen Arbeiten abstract menschlicher Arbeit gleichzusetzen" (Marx 1980, 38).

PART II

Social Media's Cultural Political Economy of Time

4

SOCIAL MEDIA AND LABOUR TIME

4.1. Introduction

The terms *social media* and *web 2.0* were established around 2005 in order to characterise World Wide Web (WWW) platforms like social networking sites (e.g. Facebook, LinkedIn), blogs (e.g. Wordpress), wikis (e.g. Wikipedia), microblogs (e.g. Twitter, Weibo), and user-generated content-sharing sites (e.g. YouTube). Such platforms include for example Facebook, YouTube, Wikipedia, Blogspot, Twitter, LinkedIn, Wordpress, VKontakte, Weibo, Tumblr, Pinterest, xvideos, FC2, and xHamster. Although there are very different forms of sociality and all media involve some form of sociality, the online platforms that today are referred to as social media[1] have in common that they make intensive use of contributions from (content) producing consumers—"prosumers". In this context, the notion of "digital labour" (Burston, Dyer-Witheford, and Hearn 2010; Scholz 2013) has emerged. It is especially used for social media activities on for-profit platforms.

In 2012, users spent 175 million hours per day and 63.875 billion hours per year on Facebook.[2] Given that in 2012, there were around 1 billion Facebook users in the world,[3] the average Facebook user spent 65 hours per year and 18 minutes per day on the platform. The notion of digital labour signifies that the time spent on Facebook and other corporate platforms is not simple consumption or leisure time, but productive time that generates economic value.

Marx saw the importance of time as a resource in capitalism and wrote that under this regime of the organisation of life and society, time "is everything, man is nothing; he is, at the most, time's carcass. Quality no longer matters. Quantity alone decides everything; hour for hour, day for day" (Marx 1847, 47). The emergence of social media is an expression of the changes between labour time and leisure time that have been conceptualised with terms such as *digital labour, prosumption, consumption labour,* and *play labour.* The task of this chapter is to discuss how corporate social media are related to the capitalist organisation of time and changes this organisation is undergoing. For doing so, the chapter employs social theory for discussing the relationship of time and matter (section 2), the role of time in capitalist society (section 3), and the capitalist economy (section 4). The resulting theoretical conceptualisations are used in section 5 for discussing social media usage in the context of changing modes of the organisation of time.

4.2. Time and Matter

Kant (1781/1922, 15) argued that objects "are given to us through our sensibility" and that sensibility requires a priori existences, especially space and time. In space, the "form, size and relative position" of objects is fixed (18). "All phenomena may vanish, but time itself [. . .] cannot be done away with" (24–25). "Time is the formal condition, *a priori,* of all phenomena whatsoever. Space, as the pure form of all external intuition, is a condition, *a priori,* of external phenomena only" (27). For Hegel, space is nature's "abstract generality of its self-externality, its unmediated indifference" (Hegel 1817, §197). It "is a mere form, i.e., an abstraction, that of immediate externality" (Hegel 1817, §197). Space is connected to time: "In time, it is said, everything arises and passes away, or rather, there appears precisely the abstraction of arising and falling away" (Hegel 1817, §201). Time and space are "the medium and outcome of one another" (Castree 2009, 52).

Space and time are aspects of the organisation of matter. The social organisation of space and time changes historically and based on the organisational forms of society. Time has to do with the changes that specific forms of matter are undergoing. It is the form of existence of matter. Matter is not static, but dynamic, which means that it changes its form. This means on the one hand that over a long period of time, one form of matter can give rise to a new one in the process of evolution. On the other hand each being that exists is also differentiating its form. In inanimate objects such as stones, this change is slower than in living beings, but nonetheless takes place through nature's processes. Living beings are cell-based organisms and these cells reproduce and differentiate themselves. In a society, the actions and interactions of humans bring about changes of structures that condition further actions and interactions. If one fixes one condition of a structure and then waits and again fixes another condition of the structure, then changes are observable. This change is an indication that the structure develops in time. Time is the development of the existence of being from one condition to the next. This means that time is the duration of processes. It is the sequence of events that form a process. It is irreversible, which means that when a form of being has reached a certain condition at a point of time, its structure cannot be exactly reverted to the condition it had at a previous point of time.

Matter is dynamic: it continuously changes and this change exists in time. Forms of matter have a beginning and an end. Matter as the totality of forms of matter is endless because it is the basic process substance of the world. It is the only form of existence that is so abstract and universal that it does not have a beginning and an end. This implies also that time is eternal: "Time itself is eternal, for it is neither just any time, nor the moment now, but time as time is its concept" (Hegel 1817, §201). Time is an ordering and directedness of existence into past, present, and future: "The dimensions of time, the present, future, and past, are only that which is becoming and its dissolution into the differences of being as the transition into nothingness, and of Nothingness as the transition into being" (Hegel 1817, §202).

The German Marxist philosopher Hans Heinz Holz (2005) formulates the dialectic of matter by saying that things exist both next-to-one-another (*Nebeneinander*) and after-one-another (*Nacheinander*): "Like time is the after-one-another of contents, space is the next-to-one-another of things" (Holz 2005, 170).[4] Matter has forms that exist next to one another in space, which means that one thing requires another to exist and vice versa. The content of matter is a sequence of events, in which things develop, i.e. one event follows another and one thing passes into another. Matter is the dialectical unity of the spatial next-to-one-another and the temporal after-one-another. For Hegel, matter is the dynamic dialectical unity of space and time: "This disappearance and regeneration of space in time and of time in space is motion; a becoming, which, however, is itself just as much immediately the identically existing unity of both, or matter." (Hegel 1817, §203). The "transition from ideality to reality, from abstraction to concrete existence, in this case from space and time to reality" appears as matter (Hegel 1817, §203).

Space, time, and matter are connected to the dialectic of being and nothing that constitutes becoming: "the truth of being and of nothing alike is the unity of the both of them: this unity is becoming. [. . .] being is the passage into nothing and [. . .] nothing is the passing into being" (Hegel 1830, §88). Development of matter means that a new thing emerges from old things so that something new comes into existence and the old existence ceases to exist in its specific form, although it continues to exist in sublated form in the new existence. The dialectic of being and nothing drives the development of matter as dynamic process: "Something becomes an other, but the other is itself a something, so it likewise becomes an other, and so on ad infinitum" (Hegel 1830, §93).

Matter is the self-creating, self-producing, and self-reproducing process-substance of the world. One can for each form of matter ask when its start and end of existence is. But for matter itself one cannot ask when it started to exist because something cannot emerge out of nothing. This assumption distinguishes a materialist worldview from religious ideology that believes in godly creation. There must always already be something. Before and after a specific form of matter there is always another form of matter. This means that matter as a whole is endless and does not have a beginning and an end.

Anthony Giddens has stressed, based on Torsten Hägerstrand's time-geography, that human actions and interactions are situated in space and time and that "social systems are constituted across time-space" (Giddens 1984, 110). Hägerstrand argues that humans repeat routine activities and in doing so meet at specific time-space locations he called stations (homes, streets, workplaces, etc.). Giddens (1984, 119) says that time-space is regionalised in everyday life. Henri Lefebvre (2004) writes that temporal structures in nature, culture, and society have rhythms: repetitions in time and space that involve measures, identity, but also unforeseeable novelty and difference. Rhythms would be induced by days and nights, seasons, waves and tides, but they would also be present in the media (e.g. light programmes in the morning, evening news followed by entertainment, etc.), in music and everyday life.

Theodor W. Adorno (1998, 218f) argues that that the way time is experienced is related to the structure of labour and the organisation of society. Time cannot be experienced independently, but "only in the configuration with its specific historical-societal moments" (Adorno 1998, 219). Ernst Bloch (1963, 129) says that time perception is organised in such a way that "an animate hour flies like an arrow, an odd one creeps on; in memory in contrast the animate hours or a 'big' day extend tremendously, whereas whole months of dullness shrink in memory to disappearance". Time is the mode of change of being. Human time is for Ernst Bloch (1975, 107) the "progression space to the possibly good". It is certainly true that a better order of things is always a possibility, but at the same time always a worse order, the possibly bad, is also a possibility. Bloch's concept of history is too optimistic: human time is at the same time a potential progression space to a good or better society and a potential regression space to a bad or worse society. Bloch (1975, 107) says that time is for Marx the "space of history". Given that the "history of all hithero existing society is the history of class struggle" (Marx and Engels 1848, 35) and that "men make their own history [. . .] under circumstances directly encountered, given and transmitted from the past" (Marx 1851/52, 92), the results of the temporal development of society are not predetermined, but depend on many factors (such as the distribution of power, strategic alliances in struggles, the mobilisation of resources in struggles, etc.). Time as political space of history has potentials for the good and the bad. It is a political space of possibilities and a potential or actual space of struggles.

4.3. Time and Capitalist Society

Pierre Bourdieu (1986a, 1986b) has generalised the concepts of capital and accumulation and describes capitalism as a class system based on the accumulation of economic, political, and cultural capital. Jürgen Habermas (1987) uses the distinction between the systems of the economy and the state and the lifeworld for critically analysing how the instrumental logic of capital accumulation and administrative state bureaucracy colonises lifeworld communication and how social movements struggle against the colonisation of the lifeworld for a communicative rationality. Anthony Giddens (1984) argues that there are economic, political, legal, and symbolic institutions in society. Bourdieu and Habermas make a distinction between political, economic, and cultural dimensions of society. If one combines political and legal institutions as interacting dimensions of the political system, then the same distinction of three dimensions of society can be found in Giddens's works. Distinguishing the political, economic, and cultural system as three dimensions of society is therefore feasible.

John B. Thompson (1995) discerns four forms of power: economic, political, coercive, and symbolic power. It is, however, not clear why he reduces the notions of violence and coercion to one dimension of power. Johan Galtung (1990) in contrast argues that there is not just direct violence (through physical intervention; an event), but also structural and ideological violence. Different forms of violence can be exerted in order to accumulate different forms of power. In modern society, economic, political, and cultural power can be accumulated and tend to be asymmetrically distributed. Table 4.1 gives an overview of these three forms of power that are based on the threefold distinction of three dimensions of society.

What is capitalism? Is it a mode of economic production or a form of the organisation of society? For Marx (1867), capital is self-expanding value and accumulation is its inherent feature. Capital needs to permanently increase; otherwise companies, branches, industries, or entire economies enter phases of crisis. Capitalism is therefore a dynamic and inherently expansive system, which has implications for the exploitation of nature, centralisation, concentration, uneven

TABLE 4.1 Three forms of power

Dimension of society	Definition of power	Structures of power in modern society
Economy	Control of use-values and resources that are produced, distributed, and consumed.	Control of money and capital.
Politics	Influence on collective decisions that determine aspects of the lives of humans in certain communities and social systems.	Control of governments, bureaucratic state institutions, parliament, military, police, parties, lobby groups, civil society groups, etc.
Culture	Definition of moral values and meaning that shape what is considered as important, reputable, and worthy in society.	Control of structures that define meaning and moral values in society (e.g. universities, religious groups, intellectual circles, opinion making groups, etc.).

development, imperialism, military conflicts, the creation of milieus of unpaid and highly exploited labour, the destruction of nature and the depletion of natural resources, etc. "The employment of surplus-value as capital, or its reconversion into capital, is called accumulation of capital" (Marx 1867, 725). The capitalist

> shares with the miser an absolute drive towards self-enrichment. But what appears in the miser as the mania of an individual is in the capitalist the effect of a social mechanism in which he is merely a cog. Moreover, the development of capitalist production makes it necessary constantly to increase the amount of capital laid out in a given industrial undertaking, and competition subordinates every individual capitalist to the immanent laws of capitalist production, as external and coercive laws. It compels him to keep extending his capital, so as to preserve it, and he can only extend it by means of progressive accumulation.
>
> *Marx 1867, 739*

Capitalism is a form of society that is grounded in and driven by the accumulation of capital and power.

Money capital is besides decision-making power and definition power one specific form of power. All three forms of power can be accumulated. The drive to accumulate is in contemporary society not limited to monetary power. We also find the accumulation imperative in the accumulation of political decision power and the accumulation of cultural distinction, reputation, and definition power. Capitalism is not a purely economic system, but rather a society, in which the subsystems are driven by the accumulation imperative. Accumulation logic is multidimensional and shapes the modern economy, politics, culture, private life, everyday life, and the modern humans' relationship to nature. The subsystems of modern society have their own specific forms of the accumulation logic, which means that they all have their own specific economies of production, circulation, and distribution of power. Power takes on economic, political, and cultural forms. The accumulation of power by the one results in disadvantages for others: exploitation, oppression, and inequality. The logic of accumulation that is inscribed into modern society brings about fundamental inequalities. Capitalism is not only a society that is based on the logic of accumulation, but a society that features fundamental inequalities and power asymmetries. One of the important achievements of Marx is that he has uncovered the logic of accumulation immanent in capitalism and pointed out the *immanent* inequalities that this logic produces.

How is the modern logic of accumulation related to time? Historically, cyclical concepts of variable time determined by the rhythms of nature (tides, day and night, the seasons, length of the day, etc.) have dominated agricultural societies, whereas the linearity of clock time measured in constant temporal units (seconds, minutes, hours, days, weeks, months, years) is a more recent phenomenon.

Postone (1993, 200f) distinguishes in this context between concrete and abstract time: in concrete time, time is a dependent variable determined by events. So for example in Europe, it was common until the fourteenth century that an hour had a different length depending on the season. Abstract time is independent of external events and consists of uniform segments that do not change, but are fixed. Abstract time is uniform, constant, continuous, homogenous, invariable, commensurable, and interchangeable. This concept was introduced in Western Europe in the fourteenth century. Abstract time is clock time. It can be measured with modern mechanical or digital clocks.

In the fourteenth-century Western European cloth industry, work was conducted in workshops owned and controlled by master weavers who hired workers and bought wool from cloth merchants, to whom they also sold the final products. "The organizing principle, in other words, was an early form of the capital-wage relationship. [. . .] Implicit in this form of production is the importance of productivity" (Postone 1993, 210). One introduced work bells that rang for indicating the start and end of the working day as well as breaks. They helped to discipline, organise, and control the workers' activities. The concern about productivity necessitated the measurement of output per unit of time, which in turn required abstract time. The mechanical watch and clock towers thereby obtained a specific social role in the economy. By "the end of the fourteenth century the sixty-minute hour was firmly established in the major urbanized areas of Western Europe, replacing the day as the fundamental unit of labor time" (Postone 1993, 212). Measuring labour time became a crucial aspect of capital accumulation because capitalists strived to minimise the work time for a single commodity by speeding up production in order to increase profits. Acceleration is an imperative fundamentally built into capitalism.

Social time in modern society is connected to "use and use-value on the one hand, and exchange and exchange-value on the other. On the one hand it is sold and on the other hand it is lived" (Lefebvre 2004, 74). This differentiation results in modern society in the rhythm of working time and free time typical of everyday life. "Mature industrial societies of all varieties are marked by time-thrift and by a clear demarcation between 'work' and 'life'" (Thompson 1967, 93). So capitalism has brought about a fundamental organisation of space and time: the zoning into homes, where leisure time and reproduction takes place, and the workplace, factory, and office, where wage labour takes place: "The development of modern capitalism [. . .] brings about a differentiation between the home and the workplace" (Giddens 1984, 122). "In modern societies, for the majority of males at least, the home and workplace form the two main centres in which the day's activities tend to be concentrated" (Giddens 1984, 131). This spatial differentiation is also a temporal one: employees spend parts of the day in the workplace, parts at home, and parts on the move from their homes to the workplace and back. "The buying and selling of time, as labour time, is surely one of the most distinctive features of modern capitalism. [. . .] The commodification of time, geared to the mechanisms of industrial production, breaks down the differentiation of city and countryside characteristic of class-divided societies" (Giddens 1984, 144).

Giddens (1984) sees the importance of the commodification of labour time and the economic organisation of time in modern society, but he underestimates the role of the economy of time and the temporality of the economy: capital accumulation is a permanent organisation and re-organisation of time. Corporations have to accumulate even more capital in order to exist. Therefore they strive to increase productivity and decrease wage and investment costs in order to produce as many commodities per unit of time as possible. Time in capitalism has its specific economy: it is a precious and scarce resource that in the form of labour time organises the economy. Accumulation is the need to increase productivity and to possess more capital at moment 2 than at moment 1. It is a specific temporality of the capitalist economy. Therefore Marx stressed the importance of the economy of time:

> The less time the society requires to produce wheat, cattle etc., the more time it wins for other production, material or mental. Just as in the case of an individual, the multiplicity of its development, its enjoyment and its activity depends on economization of time. Economy of time, to this all economy ultimately reduces itself.
>
> *Marx 1857/58, 172–173*

The temporality of the capitalist economy also shapes modern society at large. Modernity is not just based on the accumulation of money capital, but also on the accumulation of decision power as well as definition- and meaning-making power. This results in a multidimensional class society, in which economic, political, and cultural elites control economic, political, and cultural power, which allows them to accumulate even more power in time so that power at moment x + 1 tends to increase in comparison to moment x. Accumulation is organised in time and is a specific organisation of power in time. But accumulation is not smooth: it is threatened by social struggles and economic, political, and ideological crises that can interrupt or break down the reproduction of accumulation so that there is not an increase of the dominant class's power at moment x + 1. Accumulation is a mode of the organisation of the economy of time that is not limited to the system of production, but in a broader understanding of the term *economy* shapes all systems and dimensions that constitute modern society.

Hartmut Rosa (2005, 2012) has elaborated a critical theory of modernity that like Jürgen Habermas's and Axel Honneth's approaches shares the critical theory framework, but does not see the concepts of communication or recognition as foundational categories; it rather stresses that modernity is acceleration. The acceleration of a) technology, b) social change, and the c) tempo of life would be three dimensions of the acceleration of modernity that are driven by a) economic accumulation, b) functional differentiation, and c) cultural survival. The three forms of acceleration would intensify themselves in a cycle of acceleration.

In the capitalist economy, time is an inbuilt feature of accumulation: the need to accumulate more capital can be achieved by lengthening the working day, by increasing productivity (which requires permanent innovations that bring about more productive technologies)—which means decreasing production time—by decreasing the circulation and distribution time of commodities, by decreasing the life-span of commodities and increasing the subjective desire for new commodities. In addition, the credit and loan market, the stock market, and financial derivatives operate with time as the crucial category: money is exchanged with an entitlement to payments made in the future (future profits in the case of stocks, company credits and derivatives; future wages in the case of consumer credits and loans). The result is an economic acceleration logic that aims at the production, circulation, and consumption of ever more commodities in ever less time.

Modern politics tend to have to act in a reactive manner to the dynamics of the global economy. Corporations are political actors themselves. They exert pressure on governments that have to worry about tax incomes and employment. Governments facing the threat of losing investments in their countries may implement company-friendly measures that deregulate markets and the welfare state and benefit companies at the expense of working conditions. Politics is also influenced by the logic of commerce and corporate mass media that focuses on sensationalism, short statements, and advertising. Time for deliberation therefore tends to get lost and decisions tend to be made quickly, with short-term perspectives and without long and thorough deliberation. The result is a political acceleration logic that aims at taking and managing even more decisions in ever-shorter time.

In modern culture and everyday life, one finds a culture of speed shaped by the pressure for permanent activities, starting things that cannot get done due to lack of time, organised and commodified deceleration, high-performance sports and hobbies, fast food and fast life, short-lived consumer goods and technologies that require frequent updates and have short physical and moral depreciation times. The result is a cultural acceleration logic that aims at the production and management of ever more experiences in ever less time. Rosa (2005) argues that the culture of speed is also driven by human fears of death that in modern society result in "panic flight reactions" (Rosa 2005, 288) so that there is an "increase and intensification of experience episodes per unit of time" (Rosa 2005, 289). There is, however, also a specific capitalist form of the acceleration of culture: advertising and consumer culture can artificially create and accelerate the creation of new consumption needs.

All three logics are based on the principle of accumulating more (economic, political, and cultural) power in less time. There is an inherent connection between accumulation of economic, political, and cultural power and the logic of speed that accelerates human activities in modern society. Figure 4.1 visualises the logic of speed in modern society: acceleration is based on the economic principle "time is money", the political principle "time is strength and power", and the cultural principle "life/time is short". This results in the drive to accumulate ever more economic, political, and cultural power in ever less time, i.e. to speed up the accumulation of power in order to destroy other competitors.

The three logics all result in relatively autonomous acceleration processes that are connected to each other. There are three interconnections:

- Economy ⇔ politics: An acceleration of money accumulation tends to require politics to react to these changes with more and faster-taken decisions for more areas of life. These accelerated decisions in return shape and enable the acceleration of the capitalist economy.
- Politics ⇔ culture: The acceleration of culture, i.e. the intensification of experiences, makes society and everyday life more complex, which in turn requires more and more quickly taken political decisions that regulate this complexity. Faster-taken decisions in politics bring about a need of people in everyday life to confront bureaucracy and its decision in even more situations.
- Economy ⇔ culture: The acceleration of the economy results in more and more quickly produced commodities. This drives the extension and intensification of commodity- and consumer-culture. Individuals are hailed to consume even more commodities and to select from an increased offer of commodities. The differentiation and speed up of human experiences drives commodity production because capitalist companies are interested in commodifying human experiences and to offer commodities that fit the organisation of everyday life.

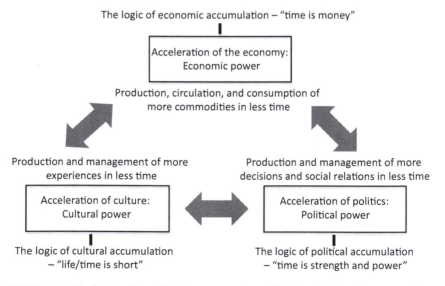

The logic of economic accumulation – "time is money"

Acceleration of the economy:
Economic power

Production, circulation, and consumption of
more commodities in less time

Production and management of more
experiences in less time

Acceleration of culture:
Cultural power

Production and management of more
decisions and social relations in less time

Acceleration of politics:
Political power

The logic of cultural accumulation
– "life/time is short"

The logic of political accumulation
– "time is strength and power"

FIGURE 4.1 The logic of speed in the economic, political, and cultural systems of modern society (based on: Rosa 2005, 2012)

Modernity is on the one hand adverse to idleness, rest, calmness, silence, slowness, and detachment. On the other hand, there can be attempts to slow down modernity. John Urry (1994, see also Lash and Urry 1994, chapter 9) argues in this context that disorganised capitalism on the one hand advances instantaneous time that focuses on acceleration in the form of e.g. the media, leisure, transport, tourism, travelling, and on the other hand glacial time that is oriented on long time periods and timelessness in the form of e.g. the environmental movement, museums, nostalgia, concerns for sustainability, heritage sites, areas of conservation (e.g. natural parks). The speed-up induced by capitalism can result in counter-attempts to install historicity, preservation, and a sense for permanence into society.

4.4. Time and the Capitalist Economy

The capitalist economy is based on the formula $M \rightarrow C .. P .. C' \rightarrow M'$: money is invested for buying commodities (labour power, means of production), and labour produces (P) a new commodity C' that is sold on the market to create a money sum M' that is larger than the initially invested capital M (Marx 1885).

The circulation time of capital is the time that it takes to buy investment goods, produce a new commodity, and sell it (Marx 1885, chapter 5). It is the time of one cycle of capital accumulation. It is the sum of the production time and circulation time (Marx 1885, chapter 5). In chapter 7 of *Capital, Volume II*, Marx (1885) says that capitalism has "been characterized by continuous efforts to shorten turnover times, thereby speeding up social processes while reducing the time horizons of meaningful decision-making" (Harvey 1990, 229).

Figure 4.2 outlines a model that visualises the relationship of time and capitalism. The single elements of the model will now be briefly explained.

Labour time is a crucial variable of capitalism:

> Just as motion is measured by time, so is labour measured by *labour time*. [. . .] Labour time is measured in terms of the natural units of time, i.e. hours, days, weeks, etc. Labour time is the living state of the existence of labour [. . .] it is the living quantitative aspect of labour as well as its inherent measure. [. . .] Regarded as exchange values all commodities are merely definite quantities of *congealed labour time*.
>
> *Marx 1859, 271f*

The capitalist economy is driven by the need to accumulate ever more capital. Methods for achieving this are the increase of productivity, i.e. the production of more in less time, and the lengthening of the working day. Labour time is on the one hand exerted in the production of commodities and on the other hand in the reproduction of labour power. *Reproductive labour time* is the time exerted in activities that re-create labour power. Labour time as a result is highly gendered

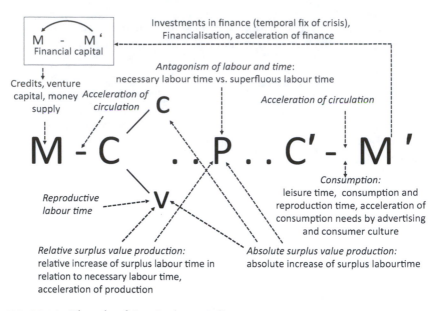

FIGURE 4.2 The role of time in the capitalist economy

in modern society: women tend to have little leisure time because they tend to have to take care of the household, children, and the family.

The history of capitalism is a history of the struggle over time, expressed in the earliest stage of capitalist development as a struggle over the duration of the working day. As "the new time-discipline is imposed, so the workers begin to fight, not against time, but about it" (Thompson 1967, 85). What interests capital "is purely and simply the maximum of labour-power that can be set in motion in a working day" (Marx 1867, 376). "The establishment of a normal working day is the result of centuries of struggle between the capitalist and the worker" (Marx 1867, 382). The normal working day is "the product of a protracted and more or less concealed civil war between the capitalist class and the working class" (Marx 1867, 412). The lengthening of the working day that Marx terms the method of *absolute surplus value production* reaches the physical and psychological limits of the human body. Therefore capital also employs the strategy of increasing productivity, i.e. the number of produced commodities per unit of labour time, for accumulating more profit. *Relative surplus-value production* is mainly achieved by the mechanisation and technification of production. Relative surplus value production means

> raising the productivity of the worker, and thereby enabling him to pro-
> duce more in a given time with the same expenditure of labour. [. . .]
> It imposes on the worker an increased expenditure of labour within a
> time which remains constant, a heightened tension of labour-power, and

a closer filling-up of the pores of the working day, i.e. a condensation of labour, to a degree which can only be attained within the limits of the shortened working day. This compression of a greater mass of labour into a given period now counts for what it really is, namely an increase in the quantity of labour.

Marx 1867, 534

Postone (1993, 193) observes that "[c]hanges in average productivity do not change the total value created in equal periods of time". If in 1970 100,000 people had worked 4 million hours a week and produced 4 million commodities in this period, and the productivity doubled in 1990 and the number of workers remained constant, then the number of hours worked per week was still 4 million. Some companies acquired the new level of productivity in 1990, whereas others still worked based on the old level of productivity. The first produced x commodities per hour, the second just half: x / 2. Both, however, had to pay the same number of workers. The first company produced in line with the new socially necessary work time needed for the production of a commodity, the second at a level higher than this. The first company at first has extra profits. The second company has to sell its commodities at the same level as the first company, which means that it makes less profit. It will either have to adopt the new level of higher productivity or is facing the threat of bankruptcy. The new level of productivity will assert itself as a new norm and change capitalism's standards of temporality: abstract time changes in the sense that the amount of units produced per hour increases. One hour of labour produces more units than previously.

> Increased productivity increases the amount of value produced per unit of time—until this productivity becomes generalized; at that point the magnitude of value yielded in that time period, because of its abstract and general temporal determination, falls back to its previous level. This results in a new determination of the social labor hour and a new base level of productivity. What emerges, then, is a dialectic of transformation and reconstitution: the socially general levels of productivity and the quantitative determinations of socially necessary labour time change, yet these changes reconstitute the point of departure, that is, the social labour hour and the base level of productivity.
>
> *Postone 1993, 289–290*

The dialectic of labour and time in capitalism is a dialectic of the transformation of labour time standards and the reconstitution of the new standards as the norm of production. There is a dialectic of abstract and concrete time in capitalism: one hour of labour is always a constant expenditure of human energy during 60 minutes. But the amount of units produced during these 60 minutes varies depending on the level of productivity and the speed of work. Concrete time is historical and variable, abstract labour is invariable. Concrete time is associated with concrete labour, abstract time with abstract labour. Abstract labour creates value: one hour of labour is always 60 minutes long and an expenditure of the combination of human physical and mental energy for 60 minutes. Concrete labour produces use-values in their physical and symbolic dimension of existence. Given the dialectic of labour and time, the abstract labour of one hour historically tends to be associated with an increase of the amount of use-values generated by concrete labour during this one hour.

The consequences of the dialectic of labour and time are the increased technisation of production and a progressively increasing importance of knowledge work in production. Marx (1857/58, 706) has described the rise of a knowledge economy with the concept of the "General Intellect".

The contradiction of labour and time constitutive for capitalism results in the situation that productivity increases so that toil can potentially come to an end and creative work that creates common goods becomes a potential for all, but the need to accumulate capital and private property relations posit alienated work as standard. Capitalism produces potentials and germ-forms of communism and at the same time intensifies exploitation of labour in order to create ever more profit during one hour of labour.

> Capital itself is the moving contradiction, [in] that it presses to reduce labour time to a minimum, while it posits labour time, on the other side, as sole measure and source of wealth. Hence it diminishes labour time in the necessary form so as to increase it in the superfluous form; hence posits the superfluous in growing measure as a condition—question of life or death—for the necessary.
>
> *Marx 1857/58, 706*

Acceleration not only affects the production, circulation, and consumption of commodities, but also finance, i.e. the production and circulation of money. Bank accounts, bank transfers, credit and debit cards, electronic payments, and finance markets that use networked and algorithmic trading are some examples for the acceleration of finance. For Marx (1894, 471, 515), all banking capital is based on the formula M (money)—M' (more money). Consumer credits, mortgages, stock, bonds, and derivatives are all based on this financial type of accumulation. Financial capital does not itself produce profit: it is only an entitlement to payments that are made in the future and derive from profits or wages (the latter for example in the case of consumer credits). Marx therefore characterises financial capital as *fictitious capital* (Marx 1894, 596). Financial investments in stocks and financial derivatives are transformed into operative capital, but they are not capital themselves, only ownership titles to a part of surplus-value that is expected to be produced in the future. "All these securities actually represent nothing but accumulated claims, legal titles, to future production" (Marx 1894, 599). If the company collapses or has falling profit rates, then the invested money is not paid back, the investors lose money. The value of shares is therefore speculative and not connected to the actual profits of the company, but only to expectations about future profits that determine buying and selling decisions of stock investors. Fictitious capital is an attempt to overcome problems of accumulation by a temporal fix (Harvey 1990; Castree 2009). Information and communications technology (ICT)–supported high-speed and high-risk global financial instruments have been embedded into a temporal contradiction between short-term financial gains and long-term profits that erupted in the global capitalist crisis that started in 2007/8 (Hope 2011).

4.5. Social Media and Changing Capitalist Times

Marx stresses the importance of communication technologies in speeding up capitalism and globalising production: "the creation of the physical conditions of exchange—of the means of communication and transport—the annihilation of space by time—becomes an extraordinary necessity for it" (Marx 1857/58, 524). Technology enables the reduction of the production and circulation time of capital. Communication technologies enable the temporal and spatial distanciation and re-embedding of communication, which allows the speed-up of accumulation. Increasing productivity by relative surplus-value production reduces production time and thereby also the circulation time of capital. The phenomenon that capitalism needs to continuously speed up production, circulation, and consumption has been reflected in the contexts of contemporary capitalism, networked computer technologies, and the mass media with the help of concepts such as time-space-compression (Harvey 1990), time-space distanciation (Giddens 1990), polar inertia (Virilio 1999), timeless time (Castells 1996), fast capitalism (Agger 2004), and instantaneous time (Urry 1994).

Hartmut Rosa (2005, 269) argues that the rise of flexible production, the deregulation of labour, just-in-time production, and project-based work in the knowledge industries influence the dedifferentiation of working time and leisure time. The combination of neoliberalism, the capitalist knowledge economy, digital media, and networked production not only results in a flexible regime of accumulation (Harvey 1990), but also in flexible humans (Sennett 1998) that have to work intensively for long hours and are as a result of a new spirit of capitalism that is expressed in management ideologies expected to love and show passion for their companies and to fully identify with their goals (Boltanski and Chiapello 2005), but are facing precarious working conditions with high insecurity, uncertainty, and unsafety (Bauman 2000/2012).

A specific way of increasing profits is to transform paid into unpaid labour time. Unpaid labour time has traditionally been present in the household, where houseworkers in social, emotional, affective, and physical labour reproduce labour power. Under neoliberalism and the flexible regime of accumulation, wage labour in the form of precarious labour has become more like housework—unsecure, unpaid, or badly paid. But in the realm of cultural consumption, unpaid labour has increasingly also become (just like wage labour) commodity producing. The examples of fast food restaurants, IKEA furniture assembled at home, and self-service gas stations show that prosumption (consumption that is productive and creating economic value and commodities) is not entirely new. The rise of the Internet and social media has amplified and extended this tendency. This emergence has intensified the historical trend that the boundaries between play and labour, work time and leisure time, production and consumption, the factory and the household, public and private life tend to blur. Toffler (1980) introduced in this context the notion of a prosumer economy. Ritzer and Jurgenson (2010) have spoken of the emergence of a prosumer capitalism and the need for a sociology of prosumption. Fuchs (2010) has, based on Smythe's (1977) notion of audience labour, introduced the notions of Internet- and social media-prosumer labour. Ursula Huws (2003) speaks of consumption work that is enabled by ICTs. Bruns (2008) introduced the concept of the produser (= producer and user). Kücklich (2005) was the first to speak of the emergence of playbour (play labour). Mark Deuze (2007) argues based on Zygmunt Bauman (2000/2012) that media work has become liquid. The neoliberal and flexible current form of modernisation means "liquefaction, melting and smelting" (Bauman 2000/2012, x). Although the circumstance that digital media are made out of minerals that are often extracted under slavery-like conditions, create a lot of eWaste, and are assembled under conditions of almost military discipline and control shows that we do not undergo a transition from a solid, heavy modernity to a more fluid, light modernity, as Bauman (2000/2012) claims. The liquefaction of boundaries seems to be a crucial quality of contemporary capitalism that shapes digital media. Marx and Engels's (1848, 38) insights that capitalism sweeps away all "fixed, fast-frozen relations" and "all new-formed ones become antiquated before they can ossify" so that all "that is solid melts into air" shape social media in the twenty-first century.

On social media, users create and reproduce content, profiles that contain personal data, social relations, affects, communications, and communities. Many corporate social media, such as Facebook, Twitter, YouTube, Weibo, Foursquare, LinkedIn, or Pinterest, use targeted advertising as their capital accumulation model. In this model, all online activities on a specific platform and on connected platforms are stored, assessed, and commodified. So users not only produce the just mentioned use-values, but also a data commodity that stores data about these use-values and is sold to advertising clients, who in return get access to the users' profiles, where they present advertisements tailored to user interests. Users are productive consumers who produce commodities and profit—their user labour is exploited. But this exploitation does not feel like toil; it is rather more like play and takes place during leisure time outside of wage labour—it is unpaid labour and play labour. As a consequence, labour time is extended to leisure time and leisure time becomes labour time. Ben Agger (2011) has introduced in this context the notion of iTime that features constant availability, the compulsion to connect, mobile time, the extension of working time into private time, iPhones and laptops as mobile work places and factories, the commodification of connection and Internet traffic, as well as the emergence of new potentials for an alternative "slowmodernity". iTime can be seen as a specific stage of what Robert Hassan (2003, 2012) terms "network time", a regime of time that in its specific capitalist organisation is connected to a pragmatic logic that fosters inconsiderateness, instrumentality, competition, temporal cognitive dissonance, and chronic distraction.

These transformations of society do not bring about an end of the capitalist time regime that separates leisure time and labour time, but rather signify an attempt to minimise leisure time by turning it into labour time. This circumstance shows how important it is for capital to increase unpaid labour time (surplus labour time) in absolute and relative terms. Corporate social media usage constitutes absolute surplus-value production in the sense that the time spent per day on average under the logic of capital and commodification increases absolutely. Mario Tronti (1962) speaks in this context of the social factory and Antonio Negri (1971, 1982) of the social worker: surplus-value production and surplus labour time extend beyond the factory and beyond paid labour time into the home, urban spaces, and leisure time. The crowdsourcing of paid labour to unpaid digital labour does not, as claimed by management gurus and consultants, bring about a "trend toward greater democratization in commerce" (Howe 2008, 14), but rather the intensification of exploitation.

Facebook is a paradigmatic expression of contemporary forms of acceleration in culture, politics, and the economy. It is a space for the accumulation of friends and the presentation of the self to others. Facebook's accumulation and presentation logic makes it necessary to manage ever more experiences in the same space. It *speeds up culture*. There are more and more potential impressions to be experienced that can only be managed by spending more time on the platform, dividing one's attention among more profiles and groups and trying to communicate with more users simultaneously. Facebook and social media are used in more and more companies and organisations for advertising, public relations, customer relations, and internal communication. The result is a convergence of labour so that knowledge workers have to take on additional tasks and become in addition to their regular profession also social media professionals. This can easily result in longer work times and/or the speed-up of work in order to manage the plethora of tasks. More and more companies invest capital in targeted advertisements on corporate social media. Targeted online advertising is a method of relative surplus-value production in advertising: At one point in time, the advertisers show not only one advertisement to the audience as in non-targeted advertising, but they show different advertisements to different user groups depending on the monitoring, assessment, and comparison of the users' interests and online behaviour. Corporate social media *speed up capital accumulation*. They are complex global spaces that bring about a lot of problems and new questions in terms of privacy, data protection, jurisdiction, labour, crime, policing, etc. The dynamic change of the Internet requires politics to react to these developments quickly, which creates a demand for *the speed up of politics*.

After the Internet economy's crisis in 2000, new confidence needed to be restored in order to attract venture capital investments. The notions of web 2.0 and social media created the impressions that newer platforms are radically new and promise huge economic returns. Web 2.0 and social media are therefore also marketing ideologies aiming at attracting venture capital investments for newly founded Internet companies.

Figure 4.3 shows the development of global advertising revenues in recent years. In 2007, Internet advertising accounted for 8.7 per cent of the global advertising revenues of the media. In 2011 this share had risen to 16.1 per cent, which is nearly a doubling. Radio, magazines, newspapers, and outdoor advertising had negative annual growth rates, with print industries having dramatic declines of more than 6 per cent per year, which has not only reduced profits, but also increased layoffs. Cinema and television had modest annual growth rates in the years 2007–2011.

The total surveillance in targeted online advertising promises more effective and efficient advertising, which may be one of the reasons why in situations of crisis advertisers tend to invest more into forms of advertisement that they perceive to be more effective and efficient. The global capitalist crisis that started in 2008 seems to have resulted in an accelerated shift of advertising investment from print to targeted online advertising on social media. It is, however, unclear if high targeting of advertising results in more commodity sales because it is not

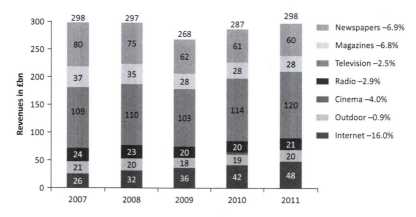

FIGURE 4.3   Global Advertising Revenue, by Medium 2007–2011

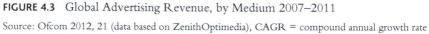

Source: Ofcom 2012, 21 (data based on ZenithOptimedia), CAGR = compound annual growth rate

self-evident that the presentation of targeted ads results a) in clicks on these ads and b) in purchases after users have been redirected to the advertisers' web-pages. The promise of high returns has also resulted in high financial invest-ments in social media corporations such as Google and Facebook. Such platforms are therefore spaces of financialisation and fictitious capital formation: the high investments operate with options on future profits that have not yet been cre-ated. If it turns out that social media returns are not as high as expected, this can result in a) the withdrawal of financial capital investments and b) the decrease of advertising investments in social media. The ultimate effect would then be the burst of a new financial bubble and possibly the next financial crisis.

For Marx, exploitation is the dominant class's appropriation of the dominated class's unpaid labour time. Marx distinguishes between two levels of analysis: values and prices. At the level of value, he speaks of labour time and at the level of prices of money. In the capital accumulation process $M \rightarrow C .. P .. C' \rightarrow M'$, capital transforms its form: it is first money M that is used for buying commodities C (labour power, means of production). We are here at the level of prices, where the capitalist uses money and buys commodities for a specific monetary price. Capital then leaves the circulation process and enters the production process P, where labour creates something new with the help of machines and raw materi-als. In the production process, only value counts: the capitalist wants to make the workers produce as many commodities in as little time as possible. Capitalist pro-duction is therefore an economy of time. When the new commodities C' are sold on the market, time also plays a role because capital wants to speed up the sale and distribution of commodities, but here we are at a level where labour values are transformed into money via sales. If value is all about labour time, does Marx's labour theory of value play any role on corporate social media such as Facebook?

In a debate between Arvidsson and me about the digital labour theory of value, Arvidsson argued that Marx's theory is outdated and cannot be used for understanding social media (Arvidsson and Colleoni 2012; Fuchs 2010, 2012a, 2012b; for a discussion of the labour theory of value and social media see also: Fuchs 2014a, chapter 11). Arvidsson does not conceive value in terms of labour time, but as value understood as "the ability to create the kinds of affectively significant relations" (Arvidsson 2005, 270). He assumes that everything in the contemporary economy has become affective and he argues that the law of value does not apply to "immaterial/intangible wealth" because this form of wealth would be produced in co-operation and its value would be determined by affects and intersubjective judgments so that an "affect-based law of value" (Arvidsson and Colleoni 2012, 142) would have emerged. On corporate social media, the "time spent online viewing or interacting with a particular site is not the critical parameter for defining or measuring value in the online advertising environ-ment"; rather "affective engagements" and "user affect" (e.g. measured by social buttons, sentiment analysis, network analysis) would be the "source of value" (Arvidsson and Colleoni 2012, 144). Given that Marx's labour theory of value is a theory of the role of time in capitalism, Arvidsson's argument is nothing more than the claim that time has become an irrelevant factor in capitalism with the rise of social media.

Facebook constantly monitors interests, usage behaviour, browsing behaviour, demographic data, user-generated content, social relations, etc. These are individual, affective, social, economic, political, and cultural data about users. The more profile, browsing, communication, behavioural, and content data s/he generates, the more data is offered as a commodity to advertising clients. Exploitation happens in this commodification and production process, whereas the data commodities are offered for sale to advertising clients after the production/exploitation process. The more time a user spends online, the more data is available about him/her that can potentially be sold and the more advertisements can be presented to him/her. Not all online time is automatically commodified, but as a tendency commodification is a process that tries to ever more expand itself, which can, but is not automatically resisted. Time therefore plays a crucial role on corporate social media. Users employ social media because they strive to a certain degree for achieving what Bourdieu (1986a, 1986b) terms "social capital" (the accumulation of social relations), "cultural capital" (the accumulation of qualification, education, knowledge), and "symbolic capital" (the accumulation of reputation). The time that users spend on commercial social media platforms for generating social, cultural, and symbolic capital is in the process of prosumer commodification transformed into economic capital. Labour time on commercial social media is the conversion of Bourdieuian social, cultural, and symbolic capital into Marxian value and economic capital.

Arvidsson and Colleoni (2012) ignore that the labour that generates content, affects, likes, social relations, networks, etc. is organised in time and space. Facebook usage time is productive labour time. All hours spent online by users of Facebook, Google, and comparable corporate social media constitute work time, in which data commodities are generated, and potential time for profit realisation. Arvidsson ignores the material realities and power of actual capital accumulation by substituting a materialistic concept of value and labour by a subjectivistic, idealistic concept of value. He replaces the economic concept of value by a moral one. This move is not a generalisation of the value concept, but a subjectification of value that corresponds to neo-classical economic theories that question Marx's concept of value as substance that is constituted as societal phenomenon in the production process. Arvidsson eliminates the notion of time from the explanation of value generation on corporate social media and thereby ignores that time is a crucial variable in any capitalist production process because "time is money" in any capitalist economy, hence also in the corporate social media economy.

Value on Facebook means the average time that users spend on the platform. The law of value on Facebook means that the more time a certain group spends on the platform, the more valuable the corresponding data commodity gets. A group that on average spends a lot of minutes per day on Facebook (e.g. the group of those aged 15–25) compared to another group (e.g. the group of those aged 75–85) constitutes a more valuable data commodity because a) it has a higher average labour/online time per day that generates more data that can be sold and b) it spends more time online, during which targeted ads are presented to this group.

Figure 4.4 visualises some details of Facebook's capital accumulation process.

Fixed constant capital (e.g. buildings, machines) is capital that the capitalist acquires and fixes in the production process for a longer time period (Marx 1885, chapter 8). Circulating constant capital is in contrast a raw material that is immediately used up in production and must be renewed (Marx 1885, chapter 8). Facebook's paid employees (v1) produce the software platform that enters the production process as fixed capital that the users employ in order to create data (profile data, communication data, content, social network data, browsing behaviour data). Whenever a user (= unpaid worker, v2) is online on Facebook, s/he transfers parts of the value of the platform and of the value of his/her existing personal data to a data commodity and s/he creates new value in the form of newly spent online time that creates additional data that enters the data commodity C′ in the form of stored data. The users' labour (= online activity) creates the value (the total time spent online by the user) and the commodity's new content (the newly generated and stored data). The whole commodity becomes part of Facebook's fixed capital that is reinvested in the production process: the existing

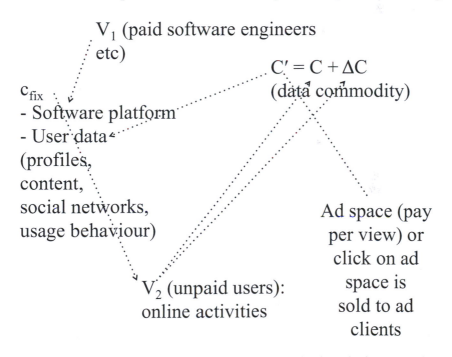

FIGURE 4.4 The commodity production process on Facebook (and other targeted advertising-based corporate social media)

data is used for organising the user's Facebook profile and is re-used in the creation of an updated user profile. The user's profile is stored in a database and updated by the user whenever s/he logs into Facebook or whenever s/he visits a website that is connected to Facebook.

An advertising client selects a specific number of users when setting up targeted ads on Facebook. The client buys specific portions of the screen display of specific users that only exist while the user is on Facebook, which means that the user generates these spaces by his online behaviour and the data s/he generates and has previously generated. This means that users produce advertising spaces themselves. These spaces are either sold as commodity when the users click on them (pay per click) or when they are online (pay per view). They, however, are commodities in the moment that they are generated, i.e. the moment a targeted ad is algorithmically generated and visualised on the screen. In the pay-per-click mode, the question is if this commodity can be sold or not, i.e. in which share of the presentations users click on ads. What is the value of a single ad space? It is the average number of minutes that a specific user group spends on Facebook divided by the average number of targeted ads that is presented to them during this time period. Facebook's ad clients fill the ads with their use-value promises that want to convince users to buy specific commodities. This means that the labour Facebook users perform enters the capital accumulation process of other companies in the realm of circulation, where commodities C' are transformed into money capital M' ($C'-M'$). Facebook users' labour is an online equivalent of transport work—their online activities help transporting use-value promises to themselves. Marx considered transport workers as productive circulation workers. Facebook users are productive online circulation workers who organise the communication of advertising ideologies on the Internet.

Sut Jhally (1987, 78) argues that "reorganizing the watching audience in terms of demographics" is a form of relative surplus-value production. One can interpret targeted Internet advertising as a form of relative surplus-value production: At one point in time, the advertisers show not only one advertisement to the audience as in non-targeted advertising, but they show different advertisements to different user groups depending on the monitoring, assessment, and comparison of the users' interests and online behaviour. On traditional forms of television, all watchers see the same advertisements at the same time. In targeted online advertising, advertising companies can present different ads at the same time. The efficiency of advertising is increased: the advertisers can show more advertisements that are likely to fit the interests of consumers in the same time period as in non-targeted advertising. Partly the advertising company's wage labourers and partly the Internet users, whose user-generated data and transaction data are utilised, produce the profit generated from these advertisements. The more targeted advertisements there are, the more likely it is that users recognise ads and click on them. Individual targeting and the splitting up of the screen for presenting multiple ads allows to present and sell many ads at one point of time.

The users' click-and-buy process is the advertising company's surplus-value realisation process, in which surplus-value is transformed into monetary profit. Targeted advertising allows Internet companies to present not just one advertisement at one point in time to users, but rather numerous advertisements so that there is the production of more total advertising time that presents commodities to users. Relative surplus-value production means that more surplus-value is generated in the same time period as earlier. Targeted online advertising is more productive than non-targeted online advertising because it allows presenting more ads in the same time period. These ads contain more surplus-value than the non-targeted ads, i.e. more unpaid labour time of the advertising company's paid employees and of users, who generate user-generated content and transaction data.

The preceding arguments aimed to show that time is a crucial category in corporate social media's capital accumulation process and that the law of value and the labour theory of value therefore fully apply to this realm.

4.5. Conclusion

Time is an important phenomenon that grounds the existence of the world, society, and capitalist society. It has objective and subjective, absolute and relative, natural and social, abstract and concrete aspects. Modern society is based on the imperative to accumulate economic, political, and cultural capital. The historically dominant form of modernity is therefore not just a capitalist economy, but a capitalist society. The accumulation imperative is connected to an acceleration imperative that makes the economy, politics, and culture accumulate even more power in even less time.

Time is an important dimension of the capitalist economy:

1   Capitalists try to reduce the turnover time (circulation time, production time) of capital in order to increase profits.
2   They try to increase unpaid labour time (surplus labour time) by absolute and relative surplus-value production so that capitalism means a struggle over time.
3   Capitalism sets up a specific relationship between labour time and leisure time.
4   Labour is enabled and reproduced by the reproductive labour time expended in the household and public and common services organised collectively in society.
5   Advertising and consumer culture accelerate the creation of artificial consumption needs.
6   Forms of fictitious capital (e.g. credits, loans, derivatives, stocks, bonds, mortgages) are ownership titles to a part of surplus-value that one expects to produce in the future.

Corporate social media are connected to all five dimensions of time in capitalism:

1 Social media play a role in the acceleration of the economy, politics, and culture.
2 The emergence of crowdsourcing, play labour, and prosumption extends the working day to leisure time. This absolute surplus-value production is complemented by relative surplus-value production, in which more advertisements and more targeted ads are presented at the same time by making use of personalised advertising and economic surveillance.
3 Social media are an expression of the circumstance that the factory and the worker have become social and diffused into all realms of society. Exploitation has in capitalism always been extended into the household in the form of reproductive labour. Digital labour on social media means that yet more time that is spent outside of the paid work conducted in factories and offices is becoming exploited. The amount and the intensity of the exploitation of unpaid labour have increased.
4 Targeted online advertising tries to make users consume more commodities by presenting personalised ads to them.
5 Corporate social media are based on fictitious capital investments that hope that targeted advertising will result in high future profits. The actual success rate of targeted advertising in making users buy more commodities is, however, unknown, which makes social media highly prone to financial crisis.

Corporate social media prosumption is a form of continuous primitive accumulation of capital that turns non-commodified leisure time into productive labour time that generates value and profit for capital. It is a form of accumulation by dispossession (Harvey 2005), in which consumption and leisure time become spaces of accumulation. Marx showed that the capitalist development of the productive forces increases disposable time: "The whole development of wealth rests on the creation of disposable time. The relation of necessary labour time to the superfluous (such it is, initially, from the standpoint of necessary labour) changes with the different stages in the development of the productive forces" (Marx 1857/58, 398).

The emergence of social media is an expression of the tendency of capitalism to increase disposable time. Such media are expressions of a high level of the development of the productive forces that could enable the creation of a society, in which "labour in the direct form has ceased to be the great well-spring of wealth, labour time ceases and must cease to be its measure, and hence exchange value [must cease to be the measure] of use value" (Marx 1857/58, 705). The reduction of necessary labour "then corresponds to the artistic, scientific etc. development of the individuals in the time set free, and with the means created, for all of them" (Marx 1857/58, 706).

Realising this potential requires, however, that "production based on exchange value breaks down" (Marx 1857/58, 705). Capitalism tries to resist its own explosion. Turning leisure time into labour time is one attempt at prolonging capitalism and the contradiction between time and capitalism. More disposable time means more time for consumption, creativity, and leisure, to which capital is connected because commodity consumption is necessary for the reproduction of capital and is also part of labour powers reproduction time. What is relatively new is that consumption time becomes production time. Capital tries to commodify disposable time, which explains the emergence of play labour, digital labour, and prosumption. The cause is the imperialistic tendency of capitalism: "But its tendency always, on the one side, to create disposable time, on the other, to convert it into surplus labour" (Marx 1857/58, 708). The emergence of social media is an expression of the contradiction between time and capitalism. These media posit new surplus labour under capitalist conditions and are at the same time germ forms of a society, in which necessary labour time is minimised, surplus labour time abolished, and creative activities shape human lifetime.

Notes

1 Social media at the level of the productive forces advance sharing, collaborative work, communication, and community maintenance. This sociality is, however, not matched at the level of the relations of production, where these platforms are privately owned (Hassan 2012).
2 http://www.zdnet.com/blog/facebook/10–5-billion-minutes-spent-on-facebook-daily-excluding-mobile/11034.
3 http://www.internetworldstats.com/stats1.htm (accessed on April 13, 2013): On December 31, 2012, there were an estimated 975,943,960 Facebook users.
4 Translation from German: „Wie die Zeit das Nacheinander der auftretenden Inhalte ist, so der Raum das Nebeneinander der Dinge."

5

SOCIAL MEDIA AND PRODUCTIVE LABOUR

5.1. Introduction

The world's largest online companies—Google and Facebook—are highly profitable. Facebook's profits were US$1.5 billion in 2013 (SEC Filings, form 10-K, January 31, 2014). Google's profits were US$12.9 billion in the same time period (SEC Filings, form 10-K, annual report 2013).

The emergence of such online platforms has intensified the historical trend that boundaries between play and labour, work time and leisure time, production and consumption, the factory and the household, public and private life tend to blur. Based on Zygmunt Bauman's (2005, 2011) concepts of liquid life and liquid world, we can say that social media are liquid media—they tend to make boundaries liquid. Considering corporate social media's economy, the question arises who creates the economic value that manifests itself in Google and Facebook's profits. Toffler (1980) introduced the notion of a prosumer economy. Ritzer and Jurgenson (2010) have in the context of social media spoken of the emergence of prosumer capitalism and the need for a sociology of prosumption. Fuchs (2010) has analysed the Internet prosumer and her/his labour. Huws (2003, 2012) discusses the consumption work enabled by information and communications technologies (ICTs). Bruns (2008) introduced the concept of the produser (= producer and user). Kücklich (2005) was the first to speak of the emergence of playbour (play labour). Mark Deuze (2007) argues based on Zygmunt Bauman that media work has become liquid. These contributions point towards actual changes in the economy and culture that, as the examples of fast food restaurants, IKEA furniture assembled at home, and self-service gas stations show, are not new, but have been amplified and extended by the rise of digital and social media.

The concept of digital labour has in this context emerged for stressing Internet prosumers' value-generating role (for overviews see: Burston et al. 2010; Scholz

2013; Fuchs 2014a, 2014b). The basic argument is that Internet usage is a new form of labour conducted beyond factory and office boundaries in a playful manner and that online companies appropriate this labour and make profit out of it. In this context the question has arisen if Marx's labour theory of value can help us understand digital labour and the class relation it is part of. Whereas some have, based on Dallas Smythe's (1977) notions of audience labour and audience commodification (for a discussion see Fuchs 2012a) or Sut Jhally's (1987) concept of the work of watching (see Andrejevic 2007, 2012), stressed that social media profits emerge from digital labour time, others have challenged the relevance of Marx and the labour theory of value, which has resulted in a sustained debate about the role of Marx for understanding digital media (see Arvidsson and Colleoni 2012; Arvidsson 2013; Fuchs 2012b, 2014a, 2014b).

A vivid Marxist debate has emerged about which of Marx's concepts can best be used for explaining and understanding the political economy of digital media. I have in this context suggested the importance of the concepts of surplus-value and the law of value (see Fuchs 2014a for Marxist theory of digital labour). Others have suggested using Marx's notion of rent for conceptualising value processes on corporate social media (Böhm et al. 2012; Caraway 2011; Huws 2014; Pasquinelli 2010; Rigi and Prey 2015).[1] These debates and contributions show that there is a vivid theoretical engagement with Marx among digital media scholars, that Marx matters for understanding digital media and that his works are not outdated.

A number of approaches (see for example: Bolaño and Vieira 2014; Carchedi 2014; Comor 2014; Foley 2013; Huws 2014; Reveley 2013; Rigi and Prey 2015; Robinson 2015) argue that users' digital labour on Facebook and other corporate social media is not exploited but is part of the sphere of circulation of capital that only realises, but does not create, value and/or that users' activities are one or several of the following: unproductive, no labour at all, less productive, a consumption of value generated by paid employees in sectors and companies that advertise on social media, the realisation of value generated by paid employees of social media corporations, or an expression of a system where what appears as profits are rents derived from advertisers' profits. These opinions are not new, but just a reformulation of Lebowitz's (1986) criticism of Smythe in the age of social media.

Rather absent from the digital labour debate has been a theoretical engagement with Marx's notions of productive and unproductive labour. This chapter engages with two of Marx's concepts that he especially worked out in *Capital, Volumes 2* and *3* (Marx 1885, 1894): productive labour and rent. The chapter's task is to give an overview of Marx's notions of productive labour and rent and to discuss their relevance for understanding value-generation on digital media. For Marx, productive labour is labour that creates surplus-value in capitalism. This concept is therefore one of the core notions for understanding whom capital exploits. It is a complex and multidimensional notion. The rent-concept is primarily covered in *Capital, Volume 3* (Marx 1894). Section 2 of this chapter discusses how Marx defined productive labour. As this is one of Marx's most multi-layered concepts, gaining an understanding requires a quite close reading and discussion of specific passages in the *Grundrisse, Capital*, and the *Theories of Surplus-Value*. Section 3 discusses the application of the concepts of productive labour to corporate social media such as Facebook. Facebook will in this section be used as shorthand for corporate social media that use targeted advertising as capital accumulation model. The section discusses the relationships and connections of corporate social media to the larger capitalist economy. Section 4 discusses the concept of rent in the context of digital media. Section 5 considers approaches in the digital labour debate that conceive productive labour as wage labour. Section 6 points out the political and ideological implications of theorising digital labour. Section 7 draws conclusions.

Before starting the discussion of productive labour, we need to set the context and have a look at Marx's value concept (5.1.2), which requires us to understand Hegel's notion of potentiality and actuality, essence and existence (5.1.1).

5.1.1. Hegel's Dialectic of Possibilities and Actuality

For Hegel (1830, §92), possibility (the potential) is an aspect of being-there: "But this alterability of being-there appears in our representation as a mere possibility, whose realisation is not grounded within being-there itself. In fact, however, self-alteration is involved in the concept of being-there, and is only the manifestation of what being-there is in-itself." What actually exists has a potential for being-there in the world. Outer reality has an inner potential and essence (Hegel 1830, §140). For example, humans acting in an altruistic manner must have the very concepts of and potentials for morality, aid, and welfare as part of their inner world.

Possibility is an aspect of actuality. Hegel says about actuality:

> As identity in general it is, first, possibility-the inward reflection that is posited as the abstract and unessential essentiality, in contrast to the concrete unity of the actual. Possibility is what is essential to reality, but in such a way that it is at the same time only possibility. [. . .] Possibility is indeed the empty abstraction of inward reflection—what was earlier called the inner, except that now it is determined as sublated, merely posited, external inwardness; and so it is certainly now also posited as a mere modality, as an inadequate abstraction, or taken more concretely, as belonging only to subjective thinking.
>
> *1830, §143*

The actual is an outer that is grounded in inner potentials; it is the dialectic of the inner and the outer. All outer actuality has its inner potentials and inner potentials can be realised as actuality. The dialectic of the inner and the outer also means that actuality can always change. There is always a potential for change:

> But, in fact, any such immediate actuality contains within it the germ of something else altogether. Initially, this other is just something possible; but this form then sublates and translates itself into actuality. The new actuality that emerges in this way is the specific inwardness of the immediate actuality, which the new actuality uses up. So what comes to be is quite another shape of things, and yet it is not another one either.
>
> *Hegel 1830, addition to §146*

Dialectical movement means that actuality as outer reality reverts back to inner potentials so that one potential or some of these potentials are actualised. The sublation of actuality is the negation of the contradiction (negative relation) between actuality and possibility so that new qualities that constitute a new actuality emerge.

But dialectical movement from possibility to actuality and from actuality back to possibility into a new actuality is in society no automatism of history, but requires activity: "This self-movement of the form is activity, activation of the matter [itself], as the real ground, which sublates itself into actuality, and the activation of the contingent actuality, i.e., of the conditions: their inward reflection and their self-sublation into another actuality, the actuality of the matter" (Hegel 1830, §147).

Necessity is the unity of the possible and the actual (§147): It starts with accidental, dispersed circumstances (addition to §147). These conditions are for the single individual relatively accidental, a form of chance which s/he is facing. But "we also have the consciousness of our freedom" (addition to §147). Activity is the sublation of the process that translates the accidental conditions into actual matter (§148). There are presupposed, contingent, passive conditions that are a mere potential—"material for the matter" (§148). Matter is a posited external existence that has emerged from conditions and is a "thing in question", i.e. an actuality that can change and has the potential for change. Activity "is the movement of translating the conditions into the matter, and the latter into the former as the side of existence; more precisely [it is the movement] to make the matter [itself] go forth from the conditions, in which it is implicitly present, and to give existence to the matter by sublating the existence that the conditions have" (§148). Necessity is for Hegel the dialectical unity of conditions, matter, and activity, in which activity transforms matter into new matter by realising potentials into new actual matter. Necessity is a unity of chance and actuality (§147).

Herbert Marcuse summarises Hegel's dialectic of potentiality and actuality and the dialectic of chance and necessity:

> The content of a given reality bears the seed of its transformation into a new form, and its transformation is a "process of necessity", in the sense

that it is the sole way in which a contingent real becomes actual. The dialectical interpretation of actuality does away with the traditional opposition between contingency, possibility, and necessity, and integrates them all as moments of one comprehensive process. Necessity presupposes a reality that is contingent, that is, one which in its prevailing form holds possibilities that are not realized. Necessity is the process in which that contingent reality attains its adequate form. Hegel calls this the process of actuality. [...]

We have mentioned that Hegel did not declare that reality is rational (or reasonable), but reserved this attribute for a definite form of reality, namely, actuality. And the reality that is actual is the one wherein the discrepancy between the possible and the real has been overcome. Its fruition occurs through a process of change, with the given reality advancing in accordance with the possibilities manifest in it. Since the new is therefore the freed truth of the old, actuality is the "simple positive unity" of those elements that had existed in disunity within the old; it is the unity of the possible and the real, which in the process of transformation "returns only to itself." [...]

A reality is actual if it is preserved and perpetuated through the absolute negation of all contingencies, in other words, if all its various forms and stages are but the lucid manifestation of its true content. In such a reality, the opposition between contingency and necessity has been overcome. Its process is *of necessity*, because it follows the inherent law of its own nature and remains in all conditions the same. At the same time, this necessity is *freedom* because the process is not determined from outside, by external forces, but, in a strict sense, is a self-development; all conditions are grasped and "posited" by the developing real itself. Actuality thus is the title for the final unity of being that is no longer subject to change, because it exercises autonomous power over all change—not simple identity but "self-identity".

Marcuse 1941a, 153–154

Natural things exist relatively accidentally in the world. Human activity has the freedom to connect mere accidental things into a new whole, to organise the sublation of actuality into new actuality by bringing conditions and potentials together into new matter and a new actuality. Necessity (*Notwendigkeit*) is therefore for Hegel not the mechanic determination of history, but rather the freedom of humans to act and change the world, the need (*Not*) to turn (*wenden*). The German term for necessity—*Notwendigkeit*—implies activity: *Not zu wenden* (the need to turn).

5.1.2. Marx's Concept of Value

Guglielmo Carchedi (2012) applies Hegel's dialectic of potentiality and actuality for interpreting Marx's labour theory of value. He bases his interpretation of Marx on the Hegelian insight that "social phenomena are always both realized and potential" (Carchedi 2012, 4). He argues that individual value is potential social value (5) and social value is potential money-value (8).

The outputs of a production and accumulation process—accumulated capital as monetary exchange-value and commodities as fixed and circulating constant capital—form the input for a new cycle of capital accumulation $M \rightarrow C .. P .. C' \rightarrow M'$. Monetary value is therefore potential value in a new cycle of accumulation (Carchedi 2012, 105–106). Abstract labour that is expended in the production process is "value in formation, potential embodied value". Once production is finished, the produced commodity contains specific quanta of abstract labour that are embodied or contained value or "potential realized value" (121). "When the commodity is sold, the value embodied in it becomes *realized value*" that takes on money-form" (121). Finally, the "realized value (price) of the output becomes the non-realised value, or value contained, or potential realized value of the same commodity as an input of the following period" (122).

Carchedi (2012) considers the production process as value's formation process and the circulation process as value's realisation and embodiment process. He has like some other Marxist authors the tendency to separate production and circulation by arguing that many circulation activities do not create new use-values and are therefore unproductive. Therefore he considers sales and advertising as unproductive. The sales and advertising process is a use-value for capital because it helps capital to satisfy its need to accumulate capital by exchanging other use-values for money. One could say that to a specific extent the sales and advertising process is also an ideological use-value for users that tries to make commodities interesting to them and communicates price information to them. In processes of prosumption, consumers are producers of use-values that are sold as commodities so that the separation between production and consumption cannot be clearly drawn.

Abstract human labour is the substance of value; it is a common characteristic of commodities. Value is a "social system, which is common" to all commodities, "the common factor" in the exchange relation (Marx 1867, 128). Abstract labour creates the individual value of a commodity that exists, however, in relation to the average value in an industry and the whole economy. The magnitude of value is measured "by means of the quantity of the 'value-forming substance', the labour, contained in the article. This quantity is measured by its duration, and the labour-time is itself measured on the particular scale of hours, days, etc." (Marx 1867, 129). The individual commodity value is, as Carchedi says, potential social value: "The value of commodities as determined by labour time is only their *average value*" (Marx 1857/58, 137). "If we consider *commodities as values*, we consider them exclusively under the single aspect of *realized, fixed*, or, if you like, *crystallized social labour*" (Marx 1865). As social value, commodity-value is the average time that it takes to produce a commodity: "What exclusively determines the magnitude of the value of any article is therefore the amount of labour socially necessary, or the labour-time socially necessary for its production"

(Marx 1867, 129). "The value of commodities as determined by labour time is only their *average value*" (Marx 1857/58, 137).

> Socially necessary labour-time is the labour-time required to produce any use-value under the conditions of production normal for a given society and with the average degree of skill and intensity of labour prevalent in that society. [. . .] What exclusively determines the magnitude of the value of any article is therefore the amount of labour socially necessary, or the labour-time socially necessary for its production.
>
> *Marx 1867, 129*

Each commodity has an individual value (production time). What counts on the market and in the industry is, however, the average production time. On the market in one industry, the average labour times needed for producing similar commodities compete with each other. Socially necessary labour time is the average labour time that is needed in the entire economy for producing a commodity based on average skills and an average level of productivity. An individual capital has its own productivity, its workforce has a specific skill level, etc. So the average value of a commodity produced may deviate from the socially necessary labour required to produce the commodity on average in the entire industry.

Marx (1867) shows in the value form analysis that commodities attract and repulse each other. They repulse each other because they have different natural forms, qualities, materials, and use-values. They are many different commodities. But abstract labour equalises them in the production process and money (or another general equivalent) equalises them in the exchange process: They all contain quanta of human labour, and are therefore objectifications of value that is in the exchange process assessed as representation of equal human labour. Qualitative different commodities that repulse each other attract each other via a general equivalent in the exchange process. The general form of value constructs a unity of the diversity of commodities. Marx describes it as the form of value that is "common to all" commodities and that therefore is general in character (Marx 1867, 157).

The law of value has to do with the speed of production and the level of productivity: The higher the productivity used to create a commodity, the lower its value:

> In general, the greater the productivity of labour, the less the labour-time required to produce an article, the less the mass of labour crystallized in that article, and the less its value. Inversely, the less the productivity of labour, the greater the labour-time necessary to produce an article, and the greater its value. The value of a commodity, therefore, varies directly as the quantity, and inversely as the productivity, of the labour which finds its realization within the commodity.
>
> *Marx 1867, 131*

Value is the essence of a commodity. Expressed in another way one can also say that abstract labour is the essence of value. Exchange value is the form of the appearance of value. Money is a specific form of the appearance of value, the highest form of value. Exchange value is "the necessary mode of expression, or form of appearance, of value" (Marx 1867, 128). In exchange, concrete use values that satisfy human needs are set as equals. They are all different in that they satisfy different human needs, but setting them as equals (x commodity A = y commodity B; or: x commodity = a unit of money; y commodity B = a unit of money) abstracts from this difference and constructs an equality by establishing an exchange relationship between two quantities of different commodities. The equalised commodities are considered to represent the same amount of value. The exchange relationship that in capitalism is organised with the help of money, which acts as general equivalent of exchange, constructs a unity in diversity, a unity of the different commodities' use values. In the exchange process, commodities are reduced to that which they have in common—value.

"Price is the money-name of the labour objectified in a commodity" (Marx 1867, 195–196). A commodity expresses its value in the money price. Money is a measure of the value of a commodity. It is the most developed form of value. The money price is a specific monopolised form of the appearance of value that shapes exchange in capitalist society by acting as a generalised medium of exchange in (almost) all market relations in which commodities are exchanged. Money has a "social monopoly [. . .] to play the part of universal equivalent within the world of commodities" (Marx 1867, 162).

That two commodities have the same price does not mean that they necessarily have the same value, only that they are assessed as having the same value. Marx argues that value and price do not necessarily coincide. There can be incongruences and oscillations:

> The magnitude of the value of a commodity therefore expresses a necessary relation to social labour-time which is inherent in the process by which its value is created. With the transformation of the magnitude of value into the price this necessary relation appears as the exchange-ratio between a single commodity and the money commodity which exists outside it. This relation, however, may express both the magnitude of value of the commodity and the greater or lesser quantity of money for which it can be sold under the given circumstances. The possibility, therefore, of a quantitative incongruity between price and magnitude of value, i.e. the possibility that the price may diverge from the magnitude of value, is inherent in the price-form itself.
>
> *Marx 1867, 196*

Socially necessary labour time is "the centre of gravity around which price turns" (Marx 1894, 279). The commodities "whose individual value stands below the market price will realize an extra surplus-value or surplus profit, while those whose individual value stands above the market price will be unable to realize a part of the surplus-value which they contain" (Marx 1894, 279). "The market value is always different, is always below or above this average value of a commodity. [. . .] The price of a commodity constantly stands above or below the value of the commodity, and the value of the commodity itself exists only in this up-and-down movement of commodity prices" (Marx 1857/58, 137). "[T]he production price of a commodity is not at all identical with its value. [. . .] It has been shown that the production price of a commodity may stand above or below its value and coincides with it only in exceptional cases" (Marx 1894, 892). Expressed in Hegelian dialectical language, one can say that the price is a "constant negation of the negation, i.e. of itself as negation of real value" (Marx 1857/58, 137).

Abstract human labour is the substance of value; it is a common characteristic of commodities. The value of a commodity is the average labour time that is needed for producing it. Labour time is the measure of value. Value has both a substance and a magnitude and is in these characteristics connected to human labour and labour time. Abstract labour is the substance and essence of a commodity. Labour-time is the commodity's measure and magnitude. Money and exchange-value are forms of the appearance of value. A commodity's individual value is the potential of its social value. Individual labour time is the potential of the formation of the average (socially necessary) labour time that it takes to produce a commodity. Social value and socially necessary labour time are the foundation and potential of the appearance of value as exchange-value and money. This appearance takes place when the commodity is sold. The sold commodity and the realised money-capital are the potential of a new accumulation process, in which capital is re-invested and fixed capital is used as material input.

Let us construct an example and consider that there are three capitals (alternatively one could assume these are three different industries). The average production time of one commodity within one year is 20 minutes in company A, 60 minutes in company B, and 40 minutes in company C. The average socially necessary labour time is therefore 40 minutes. Company C produces its commodity at an individual value that corresponds to the social value, company A produces at an individual value below the social value, and company B at an individual value above the social value. Given that there is heavy competition, all three companies sell the commodity at the same average price of 60£ so that the average price is 60£.

We assume that all three companies sell the commodity on average at 60£, have the same constant capital costs of 10£, and have different average wage costs deriving from the different production times, which means that more labour is required in company B than in companies A and C.

The Monetary Expression of Labour Time (MELT) is the ratio of money to labour-time in the whole economy (Freeman 1998). It is an average measure that tells us how much monetary value is produced on average during one working

TABLE 5.1 An example with three capitals, m = minutes, MELT (Monetary expression of labour time) = 1.5£/h

Capital	Labour time (h)	c_i	v_i	$profit_i$	$price_i$	c_s	v_s	s_s	$price_s$	$profit_s$	V_s	Extra value
A	20m	10£	20£	30£	60£	6.67m	13.3m	0m	40m	20m	30£=20m	+20m (30£)
B	60m	10£	60£	−10£	60£	6.67m	40m	13.33m	40m	−6.67 m	90£=60m	−20m (−30£)
C	40m	10£	40£	10£	60£	6.67m	26.67m	6.67m	40m	6.67 m	60£=40m	0m (0£)
Average	40m	10£	40£	10£	60£							

hour. It is measured as money unit per hour (e.g. $£$/hour). A commodity's value can be defined in units of labour-time (hours) or money (monetary units). The MELT allows connecting the two measures. Constant capital and variable capital can, when known from obtained data based on the MELT, be transformed into the amounts of average labour-time units that they represent. The average monetary commodity value in our example is

$$V = c + v + p = 10£ + 40£ + 10£ = 60£.$$

This average commodity is produced in 40 minutes. The MELT is therefore:

$$MELT = 60£ / 40 \text{ minutes} = 1.5 \ £/\text{minute}.$$

Given the MELT, we can transform the constant and variable capitals into average social values measured in hours:

$$c_s(x) = c_i(x) / MELT \ [h]$$
$$v_s(x) = v_i(x) / MELT(t) \ [h]$$

These values are shown in Table 5.1 as c_s and v_s. In these transformations, the individual values that are the potential of social value that expresses itself in form of the MELT are provided as amounts of socially necessary labour time.

Total labour time is the sum of necessary labour time and surplus labour time. The first is in monetary terms represented by v, the second by s.

The surplus-value of the individual commodities can be measured as social value by subtracting the social values of the constant and variable capitals from the average working hours:

$$s_s(x) = h_i(x) - c_s(x) - v_s(x) \ [h]$$

The results of this calculation are in Table 5.1 shown in the column s_s.

As we have seen, Marx argues that prices do not necessarily correspond to values and that commodities can be sold at prices above or below their social value. Monetary value is the form of appearance of value, for which social value is a potential. The monetary price of a commodity represents a specific amount of social value:

$$price_s(x) = price_i(x) / MELT \ [h]$$

The three commodities in our example are all sold at a price of $60£$, which represents 40 minutes of socially necessary labour time.

The social value of each commodity expressed in monetary terms can be calculated as

$$V_s(x) = h_i(x) \times MELT \ [£]$$

It is $30£$ for commodity A, $90£$ for commodity B, and $60£$ for commodity C.

The price is in contrast 60£ for all three commodities, which means that commodity A was sold 30£ above its social value, commodity B 30£ below its social value, and commodity C at its social value. These profits/losses represent +20 minutes work time for commodity A, −20 minutes for commodity B, and 0 minutes for commodity C. Company A has achieved an extra surplus-value because it has high above-average productivity, whereas company B has made an extra loss because it produces below-average productivity and its commodities there have a value that stands above the average value. The commodities "whose individual value stands below the market price will realize an extra surplus-value or surplus profit, while those whose individual value stands above the market price will be unable to realize a part of the surplus-value which they contain" (Marx 1895, 279). One can add: The commodities whose individual value stands above the market price will realise an extra loss or deficit. Expressed in Hegelian dialectical language, one can say that the price is a "constant negation of the negation, i.e. of itself as negation of real value" (Marx 1857/58, 137)

5.2. Marx's Concept of Productive Labour

Marx has advanced three notions of productive labour that I term productive labour (1), (2), and (3).

5.2.1. Productive Labour (1): Work That Produces Use-Values

The first definition of productive labour is that all work that creates use-values is productive: "If we look at the whole process from the point of view of its result, the product, it is plain that both the instruments and the object of labour are means of production and that the labour itself is productive labour" (Marx 1867, 287).

Marx on the one hand uses this definition in *Capital, Volume 1,* as the first basic understanding of productive labour. At the same time he argues that it is insufficient and needs to be further developed. He polemicises against those who only use this definition and said that it is "nonsense" (Marx 1862/63, 158):

> According to Storch, the physician produces health (but also illness), professors and writers produce enlightenment (but also obscurantism), poets, painters, etc., produce good taste (but also bad taste), moralists, etc., produce morals, preachers religion, the sovereign's labour security, and so on (pp. 347–50). It can just as well be said that illness produces physicians, stupidity produces professors and writers, lack of taste poets and painters, immorality moralists, superstition preachers and general insecurity produces the sovereign.
>
> *Marx 1862/63, 286–287*

What the other economists advance against it is either horse-piss (for instance Storch, Senior even lousier etc.), namely that every action after all acts upon something, thus confusion of the product in its natural and in its economic sense; so that the pickpocket becomes a productive worker too, since he indirectly produces books on criminal law (this reasoning at least as correct as calling a judge a productive worker because he protects from theft). Or the modern economists have turned themselves into such sycophants of the bourgeois that they want to demonstrate to the latter that it is productive labour when somebody picks the lice out of his hair, or strokes his tail, because for example the latter activity will make his fat head—blockhead—clearer the next day in the office.

Marx 1857/58, 273

5.2.2. Productive Labour (2): Labour that Produces Capital and Surplus-Value for Accumulation

Marx's second definition includes various elements. Productive labour:

- directly produces surplus-value,
- there is a surplus-product, i.e. an unpaid part of the working day,
- it directly produces capital,
- it produces commodities,
- capital is accumulated based on the product and value the worker creates.

This understanding can be found in the *Grundrisse*, *Capital*, *Results of the Immediate Process of Production*, and *Theories of Surplus-Value*. Marx closely aligns this concept of productive labour with Adam Smith's definition: "A. Smith was essentially correct with his productive and unproductive labour" (Marx 1857/58, 273). For Marx, the second understanding of productive labour is a specific capitalist category:

within capitalist production there are always certain parts of the productive process that are carried out in a way typical of earlier modes of production, in which the relations of capital and wage-labour did not yet exist and where in consequence the capitalist concepts of productive and unproductive labour are quite inapplicable.

Marx 1867, 1042

Productive labour is merely an abbreviation for the entire complex of activities of labour and labour-power within the capitalist process of production.

Marx 1867, 1043

I will next discuss five characteristics of productive labour (2) in sections 2.2.1–2.2.5.

5.2.2.1. Productive Labour (2) Directly Produces Surplus-Value

The only use value, therefore, which can form the opposite pole to capital is labour (to be exact, value-creating, productive labour [. . .])

Marx 1857/58, 272

Hence only that labour can be productive which takes place in the kind of field where the natural force of the instrument of labour tangibly permits the labourer to produce more value than he consumes [. . .] only labour which creates surplus-value is productive.

Marx 1857/58, 328

Yet the concept of productive labour also becomes narrower. Capitalist production is not merely the production of commodities, it is, by its very essence, the production of surplus-value. The worker produces not for himself, but for capital. It is no longer sufficient, therefore, for him simply to produce. He must produce surplus-value. The only worker who is productive is one who produces surplus-value for the capitalist, or in other words contributes towards the self-valorisation of capital. [. . .] The concept of a productive worker therefore implies not merely a relation between the activity of work and its useful effect, between the worker and the product of his work, but also a specifically social relation of production, a relation with a historical origin which stamps the worker as capital's direct means of valorisation. To be a productive worker is therefore not a piece of luck, but a misfortune. In Volume 4 of this work, which deals with the history of the theory, we shall show that the classical political economists always made the production of surplus-value the distinguishing characteristic of the productive worker.

Marx 1867, 644

Since the immediate purpose and the authentic product of capitalist production is surplus-value, labour is only productive, and an exponent of labour-power is only a productive worker, if it or he creates surplus-value directly, i.e. the only productive labour is that which is directly consumed in the course of production for the valorization of capital.

Marx 1867, 1038

Labour is productive if it directly valorizes capital, or creates surplus-value. That is to say, it is productive if it is realized in a surplus-value without any equivalent for the worker, its creator; it must appear in surplus produce, i.e. an additional increment of a commodity on behalf of the monopolizer of the means of labour, the capitalist. Only the labour which posits the variable capital and hence the total capital as $C + \Delta C = C + \Delta v$ is productive.

It is therefore labour which directly serves capital as the agency of its self-valorization, as means for the production of surplus-value.

Marx 1867, 1038–1039

The worker who performs productive work is productive and the work he performs is productive if it directly creates surplus-value, i.e. if it valorizes capital.

Marx 1867, 1039

Now if labour is productive it is precisely as the agent that performs this surplus labour, as the result of the difference between the actual value of labour power and its valorization.

Marx 1867, 1056

Productive labour, in its meaning for capitalist production, is wage-labour which, exchanged against the variable part of capital (the part of the capital that is spent on wages), reproduces not only this part of the capital (or the value of its own labour-power), but in addition produces surplus-value for the capitalist. It is only thereby that commodity or money is transformed into capital, is produced as capital.

Marx 1862/63, 152

Only labour *which is directly transformed into capital is productive;* that is, only labour which makes variable capital a variable magnitude and consequently [makes the total capital C] equal to C + Δ. If the variable capital before its exchange with labour is equal to x, so that we have the equation y = x, then the labour which transforms x into x + h, and consequently out of y = x makes y' = x + h, is productive labour. This is the *first* point to be elucidated. [That is,] labour which produces surplus-value or serves capital as agency for the creation of surplus-value, and hence for manifesting itself as capital, as self-expanding value.

Marx 1862/63, 393

Productive labour is therefore labour which reproduces for the labourer only the previously determined value of his labour-power, but as an activity creating value increases the value of capital; in other words, which confronts the labourer himself with the values it has created in the form of capital.

Marx 1862/63, 397

5.2.2.2. In Productive Labour (2), There Is a Surplus-Product, i.e. an Unpaid Part of the Working Day

Productivity in the capitalist sense is based on relative productivity—that the worker not only replaces an old value, but creates a new one; that he materialises more labour-time in his product than is materialised in the product that keeps him in existence as a worker. It is this kind of productive wage-labour that is the basis for the existence of capital.

Marx 1862/63, 153

5.2.2.3. Productive Labour (2) Directly Produces Capital

[. . .] productive labour—that which produces capital [. . .]

Marx 1857/58, 304

Productive labour is only that which produces capital.

Marx 1857/58, 305

Labour becomes productive only by producing its own opposite.

Marx 1857/58, 305

Only such labour is productive as produces capital; hence that labour which does not do this, regardless of how useful it may be—it may just as well be harmful—is not productive for capitalization, is hence unproductive labour.

Marx 1857/58, 306

Only that wage-labour is productive which produces capital. (This is the same as saying that it reproduces on an enlarged scale the sum of value expended on it, or that it gives in return more labour than it receives in the form of wages. Consequently, only that labour-power is productive which produces a value greater than its own.)

Marx 1862/63, 152

5.2.2.4. Productive Labour (2) Produces Commodities

"Labour remains productive as long as it objectifies itself in commodities, as the unity of exchange-value and use-value. But the labour process is merely a means for the self-valorization of capital. Labour is productive, therefore, if it is converted into commodities, but when we consider the individual commodity we find that a certain proportion of it represents unpaid labour, and when we take the mass of commodities as a whole we find similarly that a certain proportion of that also represents unpaid labour. In short, it turns out to be a product that costs the capitalist nothing.

Marx 1867, 1039

It can then be said to be a characteristic of *productive labourers*, that is, labourers producing capital, that their labour realises itself in *commodities*, in material wealth.

Marx 1862/63, 410

5.2.2.5. In Productive Labour (2), Capital Is Accumulated Based on the Product and Value the Worker Creates

The production of commodities is not a sufficient condition for the definition of productive labour. For Marx, productive labour (2) is a category specific for capitalism. Commodities are not necessarily oriented on capital accumulation and also existed before capitalism. Therefore productive labour not only produces commodities, but commodities that contain surplus-value and foster the accumulation of capital:

> The distinction between productive and unproductive labour is vital for accumulation since only the exchange for productive labour can satisfy one of the conditions for the reconversion of surplus-value into capital.
>
> *Marx 1867, 1048*

5.2.2.6. Examples of Un/productive Labour (2)

Marx discusses many examples of un/productive labour (2). The first is physical labour:

> Labour as mere performance of services for the satisfaction of immediate needs has nothing whatever to do with capital, since that is not capital's concern. If a capitalist hires a woodcutter to chop wood to roast his mutton over, then not only does the woodcutter relate to the capitalist, but also the capitalist to the woodcutter, in the relation of simple exchange. The wood-cutter gives him his service, a use value, which does not increase capital; rather, capital consumes itself in it; and the capitalist gives him another commodity for it in the form of money.
>
> *Marx 1857/58, 272*

> For example, the workman employed by a piano maker is a productive labourer. His labour not only replaces the wages that he consumes, but in the product, the piano, the commodity which the piano maker sells, there is a surplus-value over and above the value of the wages. But assume on the contrary that I buy all the materials required for a piano (or for all it matters the labourer himself may possess them), and that instead of buying the piano in a shop I have it made for me in my house. The workman who makes the piano is now an unproductive labourer, because his labour is exchanged directly against my revenue.
>
> *Marx 1862/63, 160*

The second form of un/productive labour is information labour. Marx says that there are 2 forms of knowledge work:

1 "non-material production" (Marx 1867, 1047): "It results in commodities which exist separately from the producer, i.e. they can circulate in the interval between production and consumption as commodities, e.g. books, paintings and all products of art as distinct from the artistic achievement of the practising artist" (Marx 1867, 1049).

2 "The product is not separable from the act of producing" (Marx 1867, 1048).

Marx (1867, 1048–1049) saw the possibility of productive knowledge work, but stressed that it was limited at his time. Today both forms of knowledge work have become very important in advanced capitalist societies.

Informational labour sometimes produces non-material information products:

> For instance, Milton, who wrote *Paradise Lost*, was an unproductive worker. On the other hand, a writer who turns out work for his publisher in factory style is a productive worker.
>
> *Marx 1867, 1044*

> For example Milton, who wrote *Paradise Lost* for five pounds, was an *unproductive labourer*. On the other hand, the writer who turns out stuff for his publisher in factory style, is a *productive labourer*.
>
> *Marx 1862/63, 401*

> A writer is a productive labourer not in so far as he produces ideas, but in so far as he enriches the publisher who publishes his works, or if he is a wage-labourer for a capitalist.
>
> *Marx 1862/63, 158*

Other informational labour does not result in an externalised product:

> The same relation holds for all services which workers exchange directly for the money of other persons, and which are consumed by these persons. This is consumption of revenue, which, as such, always falls within simple circulation; it is not consumption of capital. Since one of the contracting parties does not confront the other as a capitalist, this performance of a service cannot fall under the category of productive labour. From whore to pope, there is a mass of such rabble. But the honest and "working" lumpenproletariat belongs here as well; e.g. the great mob of porters etc. who render service in seaport cities etc. He who represents money in this relation demands the service only for its use value, which immediately vanishes for him.
>
> *Marx 1857/58, 272*

Actors are productive workers, not in so far as they produce a play, but in so far as they increase their employer's wealth. But what sort of labour takes place, hence in what form labour materializes itself, is absolutely irrelevant for this relation.

Marx 1857/58, 328–329

An actor, for example, or even a clown, according to this definition, is a productive labourer if he works in the service of a capitalist (an entrepreneur) to whom he returns more labour than he receives from him in the form of wages; while a jobbing tailor who comes to the capitalist's house and patches his trousers for him, producing a mere use-value for him, is an unproductive labourer. The former's labour is exchanged with capital, the latter's with revenue. The former's labour produces a surplus-value; in the latter's, revenue is consumed.

Marx 1862/63, 157

If we may take an example from outside the sphere of material production, a schoolmaster is a productive worker when, in addition to belabouring the heads of his pupils, he works himself into the ground to enrich the owner of the school. That the latter has laid out his capital in a teaching factory, instead of a sausage factory, makes no difference to the relation.

Marx 1867, 644

A schoolmaster who instructs others is not a productive worker. But a schoolmaster who works for wages in an institution along with others, using his own labour to increase the money of the entrepreneur who owns the knowledge-mongering institution, is a productive worker.

Marx 1867, 1044

A singer who sings like a bird is an unproductive worker. If she sells her song for money, she is to that extent a wage-labourer or merchant. But if the same singer is engaged by an entrepreneur who makes her sing to make money, then she becomes a productive worker, since she produces capital directly.

Marx 1867, 1044

A singer who sells her song for her own account is an *unproductive labourer*. But the same singer commissioned by an entrepreneur to sing in order to make money for him is a *productive labourer;* for she produces capital.

Marx 1862/63, 401

The third kind of un/productive labour is service labour:

It is possible for work of one type (such as gardening, tailoring etc.) to be performed by the same working man either in the service of an industrial capitalist or on behalf of the immediate consumer. He is a wage-labourer or day labourer in either situation, only he is a productive worker in the one case and unproductive in the other, because in the one he produces capital and in the other not; because in the one case his work is a factor in the self-valorization process of capital and in the other it is not.

Marx 1867, 1045

For example, the cooks and waiters in a public hotel are productive labourers, in so far as their labour is transformed into capital for the proprietor of the hotel. These same persons are unproductive labourers as menial servants, inasmuch as I do not make capital out of their services, but spend revenue on them.

Marx 1862/63, 159

The fourth kind of un/productive labour is wage labour. There are passages where Marx argues that only wage workers who produce surplus-value and capital that is accumulated are productive labourers:

Every productive worker is a wage-labourer, but not every wage-labourer is a productive worker. Whenever labour is purchased to be consumed as a use-value, as a service and not to replace the value of variable capital with its own vitality and be incorporated into the capitalist process of production—whenever that happens, labour is not productive and the wage-labourer is no productive worker.

Marx 1867, 1041

Productive labour is exchanged directly for money as capital, i.e. for money which is intrinsically capital, which is destined to function as capital and which confronts labour-power as capital.

Marx 1867, 1043

The distinction between productive and unproductive labour depends merely on whether labour is exchanged for money as money or for money as capital.

Marx 1867, 1047

Productive labour, therefore, can be so described when it is directly exchanged for money as capital, or, which is only a more concise way of putting it, is exchanged directly for capital, that is, for money which in its essence is capital, which is destined to function as capital, or confronts labour-power as capital. The phrase: labour which is directly exchanged for capital, implies that labour is exchanged for money as capital and actually transforms it into capital.

Marx 1862/63, 396–397

The question that arises is if one needs to necessarily earn a wage to be a productive (2) worker. Most of Marx's definitions of productive labour (2) are much more general and include both paid and unpaid labour. The ones just mentioned focus, however, exclusively on wage labour. In contemporary capitalism there is a tendency that parts of wage labour are outsourced to unpaid prosumer labour. Examples are self-service gas stations, self-assembled IKEA furniture, fast-food restaurants where customers are their own waiters, and corporate social media usage. Unpaid labour here creates parts of the use-value and value of the commodity. These phenomena fall into Marx's more general definition of productive labour (2) and are not antithetical to the ones just mentioned if we assume that in these cases the wage is zero so that surplus labour time is 100 per cent of the total labour time. Capitalists have to structurally strive to reduce investment costs in order to maximise profits and to survive in competition. Therefore to reduce the wage costs to zero is the dream of all capitalists. It has come true in prosumer labour, a form of productive labour (2).

The examples in sections 2.2.6.1–2.2.6.3 show Marx's theoretical conviction that the content of labour is not decisive for determining if it is productive or not. Therefore agricultural, physical, service, and informational labour could either be organised as productive or unproductive labour. "From the foregoing it is evident that for labour to be designated productive, qualities are required which are utterly unconnected with the specific content of the labour, with its particular utility or the use-value in which it is objectified" (Marx 1867, 1044). Marx provides examples that show that service and knowledge workers can be productive workers. The decisive criterion is not if somebody ploughs, produces a car, sings, cleans, or creates software, it is rather if s/he does so under the coercive force of capitalism that enables capital accumulation and profit making.

5.2.3. Productive Labour (3): Labour of the Combined/ Collective Worker: Work that Contributes to the Production of Surplus-Value and Capital

Marx stresses that work is not an individual process. The more cooperative and networked work becomes, which is the consequence of the technification of capitalism and the rise of knowledge in production, the more relevant becomes Marx's third understanding of productive labour: productive labour as labour of the collective worker. Marx has set out this concept both in *Capital, Volume 1*, and the *Results of the Immediate Production Process*:

> The solitary man cannot operate upon nature without calling his own muscles into play under the control of his own brain. Just as head and hand belong together in the system of nature, so in the labour process mental and physical labour are united. Later on they become separate; and this separation develops into a hostile antagonism. The product is transformed

from the direct product of the individual producer into a social product, the joint product of a collective labourer, i.e. a combination of workers, each of whom stands at a different distance from the actual manipulation of the object of labour. With the progressive accentuation of the co-operative character of the labour process, there necessarily occurs a progressive extension of the concept of productive labour, and of the concept of the bearer of that labour, the productive worker. In order to work productively, it is no longer necessary for the individual himself to put his hand to the object; it is sufficient for him to be an organ of the collective labourer, and to perform any one of its subordinate functions. The definition of productive labour given above, the original definition, is derived from the nature of material production itself, and it remains correct for the collective labourer, considered as a whole. But it no longer holds good for each member taken individually.

Marx 1867, 643–644

First, with the development of the real subsumption of labour under capital, or the specifically capitalist mode of production, the real lever of the overall labour process is increasingly not the individual worker. Instead, labour-power socially combined and the various competing labour-powers which together form the entire production machine participate in very different ways in the immediate process of making commodities, or, more accurately in this context, creating the product. Some work better with their hands, others with their heads, one as a manager, engineer, technologist, etc., the other as overseer, the third as manual labourer or even drudge. An ever increasing number of types of labour are included in the immediate concept of productive labour, and those who perform it are classed as productive workers, workers directly exploited by capital and subordinated to its process of production and expansion. If we consider the aggregate worker, i.e. if we take all the members comprising the workshop together, then we see that their combined activity results materially in an aggregate product which is at the same time a quantity of goods. And here it is quite immaterial whether the job of a particular worker, who is merely a limb of this aggregate worker, is at a greater or smaller distance from the actual manual labour. But then: the activity of this aggregate labour-power is its immediate productive consumption by capital, i.e. it is the self-valorization process of capital, and hence, as we shall demonstrate, the immediate production of surplus-value, the immediate conversion of this latter into capital.

Marx 1867, 1039–1040

The question that arises is where the collective worker ends. The boundary could be drawn at the level of an individual factory, an industry, or society as a whole. The latter is stressed by autonomist Marxists who speak of the emergence of a social factory, a notion that was first introduced by Mario Tronti (1962).

The concept of the collective worker becomes ever more important with the development of fixed capital and productivity. With rising productivity, a growing "part of production time is sufficient for immediate production" (Marx 1857/58, 707). It therefore becomes possible for society "to employ this part for labour which is not immediately productive (within the material production process itself). This requires a certain level of productivity and of relative over-abundance, and, more specifically, a level directly related to the transformation of circulating capital into fixed capital" (Marx 1857/58, 707). Surplus labour can be used for the production of fixed capital and circulating capital, for example "to build railways, canals, aqueducts, telegraphs etc." (Marx 1857/58, 707).

The socialisation of labour that is expressed in the collective worker expresses itself in the antagonism of the productive forces and the relations of production that anticipates the emergence of communism, in which disposable time is the measure of wealth: Once the "mass of workers [...] appropriate their own surplus labour", "disposable time will grow for all. For real wealth is the developed productive power of all individuals. The measure of wealth is then not any longer, in any way, labour time, but rather disposable time" (Marx 1857/58, 708). Only human practice can realise the potential for communism. There is no automatism of history because capitalism's "tendency [is] always, on the one side, to create disposable time, on the other, to convert it into surplus labour" (Marx 1857/58, 708).

Marx's concept of productive labour (3)—formulations such as the one that in "order to work productively [...] it is sufficient [...] to be an organ of the collective labourer, and to perform any one of its subordinate functions" (Marx 1867, 643f)—and many formulations (though not all) that define productive labour (2)—for example: productive workers "produce surplus-value" (Marx 1867, 644), "only labour which creates surplus-value is productive" (Marx 1857/58, 328)—do not imply that only wage labour can be productive and that all labour in the realm of distribution is unproductive. There are, however, interpretations of Marx that do not take into account the level of productive labour (3) and that argue that only wage labour can be productive that is not situated in the realm of commodity distribution.

Productive labour

> is wage labour performed for (and under control of) capital, in the sphere of production, and directly producing commodities for sale at a profit. [...] All other types of labour are unproductive, for example, labour that is not hired by capital (e.g. the independent producers of commodities, the self-employed, and most government employees), labour that is not directly employed in production (such as managers or workers employed in exchange activities, including the retail and financial sectors, as well

as accountants, salespeople and cashiers, even if they are employed by industrial capital), and workers not producing commodities for sale (e.g. housemaids and other independent providers of personal services).

Fine and Saad-Filho 2010, 40–41

Wage labour employed by capital in commodity production for profit performs both concrete and abstract labour, and produces surplus-value. This type of labour is *productive* [. . .] In contrast, workers employed in circulation activities [. . .] are unproductive.

Saad-Filho 2002, 42

Ricardo Antunes (2013, 81) argues that "all productive workers are wage-earners and not all wage-earners are productive". Productive labour "directly produces surplus-value and directly participates in the process of capital-valorisation" (81). The "industrial proletariat" would be productive labour's "primary nucleus" (81). The proletariat/working class would, however, not be restricted to industrial workers, but also include "unproductive workers, those whose forms of labour are used as a service" (81), "wage-earners in the service sector" (82) who are "non-productive, anti-value generating" (81) and cause "false costs and useless expenses of production" (81). Furthermore also rural workers, precarious workers, part-time workers, and the unemployed would be part of the proletariat (82). There would today be a "greater interrelation, the greater interpenetration between productive and unproductive activities, between manufacturing and services, between performative acts of labour and conception, between production and scientific knowledge, that is rapidly growing in the world of capital and its productive system" (111). Service workers for Antunes "do not directly create value" and are part of a "field of unproductive labour" (193).

Guglielmo Carchedi (2012, 73–74) criticises Michael Heinrich's "monetary theory of value" for not seeing that value has a pre-monetary, substantial, material, physiological form that is realised in the exchange process. Carchedi says that labour "is productive of (surplus-) value if employed by capital and if it (as concrete labour) transforms existing use-values into new use-values" (190). The question if service work is productive would depend on if it transforms use-values (190). Productive labour would therefore include labour involved in the provision of utilities, transportation, the transmission of knowledge (postal services, telephone, telegraph), whereas financial services, tax collection, and the work of the army, the police, and other repressive apparatuses would be unproductive (190–191). Labour involved in exchange contributes "to the redistribution of value" and is for Carchedi "unproductive labour" because it would "deal with use-values without however changing them" (191). Knowledge production could be production, redistribution, or destruction of value (192). The purchase and sale of commodities would not create use-values and therefore be unproductive (221). Knowledge would be a "mental use-value" (221) and knowledge work productive if "performed by mental labourers for the capitalists," so that it produces "value and surplus-value as well" (221). Carchedi argues that free-lance labour is via contracts tied to capitalist companies and can therefore also be considered as productive labour (221) Any labour involved in control, finance, purchases and sales, and destruction would be unproductive (222). Activities creating free information and knowledge (e.g. parents' education of children) would increase productivity, but not increase value and would therefore be unproductive (224). Such work would form a "collective mental labourer", but would, however, create knowledge that "is produced outside capitalist relations" (233), "cannot produce value but [. . .] affects the production of value" (233). For Carchedi, "unproductive sectors" are "an inflated measure of the profits appropriated from the productive sectors" (103).

Facebook is a targeted advertising space that commodifies personal data. The users generate a use-value (personal data) for capital, but do not receive a wage. Without their activities Facebook could not make any profits. Approaches such as the ones by Fine, Saad-Filho, Antunes, and Carchedi have little to say about unpaid labour such as housework and users' labour on targeted-advertising-based corporate Internet platforms. Fine, Saad-Filho, and Antunes's strict limitation of productive labour to the realm of wage labour and the strict separation of distribution activities from productive labour cannot account for Marx's emphasis on the collective worker as productive worker that he not by accident made part of his most important work—*Capital, Volume I* (Marx 1867). These authors also cannot account for blurring boundaries between production, distribution, and consumption.

Carchedi does not strictly restrict productive labour to wage labour and includes freelancers as potentially productive workers. There is, however, also a clear focus on remunerated work in his approach. Collective mental labour outside of capitalist relations is seen as unproductive. It is, however, unclear what "outside of capitalist relations" means. Supposedly it means unremunerated labour for Carchedi. In another paper, Carchedi (2014) makes this assumption more explicit when writing that if people are "not employed by capital they are unproductive". In relation to commercial Internet platforms he says that users "are not exploited" and do "not produce value and surplus-value" since "the mental agent does not work for capital" (Carchedi 2014, 77).

Facebook users just like houseworkers create use-values that play crucial roles in capitalism's social relations that penetrate not just the factory and the office, but many parts of our lives. It is capital's dream and deep interest to not pay any wages in order to maximise profits. It can do so only by physical or ideological violence. To tie the notion of productive labour to a wage or remuneration underestimates the barbarity of capital by assuming that capital has to pay in order to have others create value. Capital is thereby presented as a relatively civilised force. Such approaches overlook that capital tries to decrease wage costs as much as possible, if possible to zero, in order to maximise profits.

The mentioned authors and others strictly separate production and distribution, use-value and exchange-value, value and money. Facebook data is, however, both use-value for users (the enablement of communication and social relations) and a use-value for capital (that enables targeted advertising space) that gains exchange-value when access to targeted ad space is exchanged for money. Such targeted ads help distribute and organise the exchange-process of commodities. A dualist approach classifies them therefore as unproductive circulation work. Distribution is, however, enabled by a connected process, where users produce and maintain data that is both a use-value for users and capital. Facebook challenges a strict separation of production and distribution and shows that specific labour involved in the distribution of specific commodities is at the same time productive labour. Facebook and comparable prosumption phenomena make value generation more complex because the realisation of value of specific capitals that advertise on Facebook, and therefore their circulation process, is connected to the generation and production of data use-values on Facebook for both users and capital.

Turning use-values effectively into money via exchange on markets requires the creation of use-value promises by advertising (that is a use-value for capital) and the labour of those who help to transport physical and ideational commodities and the advertising ideologies that give meanings to these commodities. Such labour activities include sales, transportation, marketing and PR campaigns, attention to ads, the generation of personal data that allows targeting ads, the maintenance of commercial media, etc. These forms of labour are all productive and crucial for the existence of capitalism. For Carchedi (2014, 75), advertising is "unproductive mental labour" that deals with use-values "without transforming them" and does not transform "use-values into new use-values". He ignores that the advertised meaning and brand ideology of a commodity is an inherent part of the use-value and that personal data is both a use-value in the form of sociality for users and a use-value that allows capital to target users. New data is grounded in and emerges through online activities from existing data and so contributes to the emergence of a new use-value from an already existing one. Carchedi (2014, 72) distinguishes between mental labourers who are "mental producers who use the Internet to work for capital" and mental agents who are not employed by capital, but "who use the Internet for other purposes (for recreation, education, research, etc.) while not working for capital, but in their own free time". The first are for him productive, the latter unproductive. He can, however, not explain the fact that Facebook's wage-workers do not create commodities, but that Facebook is nonetheless a profit-making company, and that non-wage workers on Facebook create a data commodity. If wage-work were a necessary condition for value and profit to exist, then Facebook would need to be able to make profit only by relying on its paid software developers independent from its users who create its main resource and commodity (personal data). This is, however, not the case.

5.2.4. Capital, Volume 2: Circulation Work and the Special Productive Role of Transport Workers

Marx discusses the role of circulation work in capitalism especially in *Capital, Volume 2*. Although circulation workers are part of the collective worker, Marx (1885, chapter 6) argues that many circulation workers—he discusses sales workers, book-keepers, and financial labour—do not contribute to the creation of use-value and value of the commodity, but only transform value from the commodity- into the money-form. He says that a lot of circulation labour cannot produce value, but surplus-value. This means that if a retail business employs sales workers and makes them work 8 hours a day, but pays them only an equivalent of 5 hours, it makes a surplus-value and profit from selling commodities to end-consumers. But Marx argues that the wages of sales workers and the profits of merchants are paid by the profits of industrial capital. Therefore sales labour would not be productive, but reduce the profits of industrial capital and consume its value.

Sales workers are for Marx circulation labour that "does not create value, but only mediates a change in the form of value" (Marx 1885, 208) and constitutes deduction of value created in production. "[C]irculation costs that proceed from the mere change in form of value, from circulation in its ideal sense, do not enter into the value of commodities. The portions of capital spent on them constitute mere deductions from the capital productively spent, as far as the capitalist is concerned" (Marx 1885, 214). This labour transforms "existing values from the commodity form into the money form" (Marx 1885, 216) and does not "operate on the use-value in which the commodity value exists. They are only concerned with its form" (Marx 1885, 216–217). "The use-value is not increased or raised" (Marx 1885, 217).

> It is not necessary to go into all the details of the costs of circulation here, such as packing, sorting, etc. The general law is that all circulation costs that arise simply from a change in form of the commodity cannot add any value to it. They are simply costs involved in realizing the value or transferring it from one form into another. The capital expended in these costs (including the labour it commands) belongs to the faux frais of capitalist production. The replacement of these costs must come from the surplus product, and from the standpoint of the capitalist class as a whole it forms a deduction of surplus-value or surplus product, in just the same way as the time that a worker needs to buy his means of subsistence is lost time for him.
>
> *Marx 1885, 225–226*

So the decisive question for Marx for deciding on the productivity of circulation labour is if the incurred costs enter the commodity value (Marx 1885, 222).

In *Capital, Volume 3*, Marx discusses commercial capital and argues that it is part of a realm that does not create value:

> Commercial capital is nothing more than capital functioning within the circulation sphere. The circulation process is one phase in the reproduction process as a whole. But in the process of circulation, no value is produced, and thus also no surplus-value. The same value simply undergoes changes of form. Nothing at all happens except the metamorphosis of commodities, which by its very nature has nothing to do with the creation or alteration of value. If a surplus-value is realized on the sale of the commodity produced, this is because it already existed in the commodity.
>
> *Marx 1894, 392*

But the sales process creates a use-value for capital that satisfies its need to sell commodities in order to accumulate.

Marx discusses a second type of circulation labour that he considers as productive. This labour arises "from production processes that are simply continued in the circulation sphere, and whose productive character is thus merely hidden by the circulation form" (Marx 1885, 214). It has "value-forming effect" and forms "an addition to the selling price of [. . .] commodities" (Marx 1885, 214). Marx discusses as examples the labour involved in stock formation and transport. This circulation labour is different for him because it has costs "that do enter into the value of the commodity to a certain extent, and thus make the commodities dearer" (Marx 1885, 216).

Marx characterises the transport and communication industry the following way:

> There are however particular branches of industry in which the product of the production process is not a new objective product, a commodity. The only one of these that is economically important is the communication industry, both the transport industry proper, for moving commodities and people, and the transmission of mere information—letters, telegrams, etc.
>
> *Marx 1885, 134*

> [What] the transport industry sells is the actual change of place itself.
>
> *Marx 1885, 135*

> [. . .] surplus-value created by the surplus labour of the workers occupied in the transport industry.
>
> *Marx 1885, 135*

The transport industry follows the formular M→C (Lp, Mp) .. P .. M. "it is the production process itself, and not a product separable from it, that is paid for and consumed" (Marx 1885, 135)

The change in use-value that the transportation and communication industry brings about is the change of location of commodities: "The productive capital invested in this industry thus adds value to the products transported, partly through the value carried over from the means of transport, partly through the value added by the work of transport" (Marx 1885, 226–227).

> The capitalist mode of production reduces the transport costs for the individual commodity by developing the means of transport and communication, as well as by concentrating transport—i.e. by increasing its scale.
>
> *Marx 1885, 228–229*

> The "circulating" of commodities, i.e. their actual course in space, can be resolved into the transport of commodities. The transport industry forms on the one hand an independent branch of production, and hence a particular sphere for the investment of productive capital. On the other hand it is distinguished by its appearance as the continuation of a production process within the circulation process and/or the circulation process.
>
> *Marx 1885, 229*

Having introduced the concepts of productive labour (1, 2, 3), I will next discuss the role of these notions for understanding value-creation on corporate social media such as Facebook, which requires connecting the economic processes on Facebook to the broader capitalist economy.

5.3. Facebook and Productive Labour in the Capitalist Economy as a Whole

5.3.1. Advertising and Capitalism

Information is not, as claimed by the liberal theory of public goods, a naturally public good (a good that is non-rivalrous in consumption and from whose use people cannot be excluded) because any good or service can, based on specific political economies, be turned into a private, public, or common good. But culture and information form a peculiar commodity that is not used up by consumption; can easily, quickly, and cheaply be copied and transported; can be consumed simultaneously by many people; has large initial production costs (sunk cost rule) but low to zero reproduction costs; can often only be sold when it becomes a "hit" as part of a broader portfolio (hit rule); can face the problem of Baumol's disease of how to increase productivity (productivity paradox); and has uncertain demand which causes high risks (nobody knows anything rule). Selling culture and media content is therefore uncertain, risky, and contradictory in that it faces the "free rider" problem. There have been various ways of trying to overcome these risks, such as artificial monopolies, intellectual property rights regulation, criminalisation, access controls, state patronage and subsidies—as well as advertising-based business models (Garnham 1979, 141–142). The importance of commercial, advertising-financed media in contemporary capitalism stands in the context of the contradictions of information as a commodity. The Internet is a contradictory space, where not just users who share copyrighted data stand in a contradiction with media content capital, but also different capital factions compete, for example media content capital that sells content as a commodity and online advertising capital that sells user data and provides access to platforms without fees.

The digital labour debate has been accompanied by a resurgent interest in Dallas Smythe's concept of audience labour and audience commodification (for a detailed discussion see Fuchs 2012a; Manzerolle and McGuigan 2014). The commercial, advertising-financed media would sell audience attention time as commodity to advertising clients (Smythe 1977). The commercial media system would thereby fulfil four purposes: the supply of consumers, the diffusion of the ideology of possessive individualism, the attempt to produce hegemony for specific state policies, the maintenance of commercial media as profitable enterprises (Smythe 1977, 4–5). Graham Murdock (1978) rightfully stressed that Smythe's model cannot be totalised because there are also public service media, alternative media, and non-advertising-financed capitalist media that sell content.

Figure 5.1 gives an overview of capital accumulation in the advertising-financed media industry. There are regular companies that accumulate capital by investing money M and selling commodities C′ so that a larger sum of money M′ is the outcome that is reinvested. Part of their investments are directly spent on

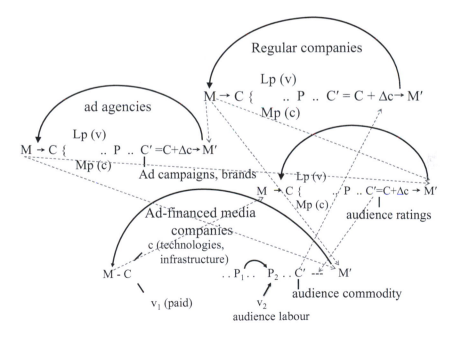

FIGURE 5.1   Capital accumulation in the advertising-financed media industry

purchasing audience ratings, ad campaigns, or ads in the media. This fuels separate capital accumulation cycles in the ratings industry, the ad agency industry, and the commercial advertising-financed media industry. The respective commodities of these industries are ad campaigns/brands, audiences, and audience ratings. Advertising agencies invest part of their money into ads run by commercial media in order to sell advertising campaigns. Ad-financed media companies sell their audiences as commodities to ad clients and purchase audience ratings in order to set prices for audiences. Most capitalist social media, such as Facebook, YouTube, and Twitter, are purely advertising financed. A crucial aspect of such commercial media is that they do not sell content or access as commodity, but rather tend to offer access without payment. Therefore in the case of Facebook, the platform P_1 is not a commodity, but rather a form of fixed capital that enters the production of the audience/prosumers commodity as means of production.

Mixed-media companies sell both audiences and contents. Examples are many newspapers and magazines. The structure of this industry is displayed in Figure 5.2. The difference to purely ad-financed media is that there is a dual form of the commodity: content (C'_1) and audiences (C'_2) are sold to different consumers: audiences and advertising clients.

The reputation of a commodity on the side of the customers depends on multiple factors such as the realities and structures of specific communities, fashion trends and styles, the dominant structures of feelings, morals and lifestyles of specific groups and classes at specific times, the positive or negative social

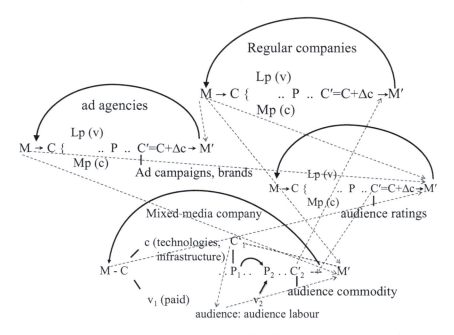

FIGURE 5.2 Capital accumulation in the mixed media industry

image of celebrities and other public figures who display specific commodities, the content of media reports about specific companies, the presence or absence of political campaigns against specific companies, the competition of lifestyles and status symbols between specific groups, etc. Commodity reputations on the side of consumers are the results of the complex interaction of antagonistic life realities, experiences, and structures of feelings of individuals, groups, and classes.

David Harvie (2005, 144) argues against the assumption that work conducted in circulation, advertising, and branding is unproductive:

> How do we understand the fact, for example, that a pair of Nike trainers costs four or more times as much as a physically similar "no logo" pair? If all the creative human activity involved in designing (beyond the physical design of the shoes) and marketing the Nike product is unproductive, adding nothing to the shoes' value, then the values of the Nike and "no logo" trainers will be similar. A significant divergence of price from value is the only result. How is this to be explained?

A company's investments in advertising and commodity reputation require specific working hours that are objectified in the commodity's value. They therefore tend to drive up commodity prices. The reputation of commodities on the consumers' side does not necessarily influence the commodity's price. Commodities with high consumer reputation do not necessarily have high prices, and the other way round.

Table 5.2 presents a list of the 25 companies with the highest reputation in 2013 combined with an analysis of the 10 most expensive consumer products in certain categories. Forbes's ranking of the World's Most Reputable Companies is based on a combination of consumers' trust, admiration, respect, and good feelings towards companies. A majority of customers of high-reputation companies is willing to buy the latter's products and to recommend these products to others.[2] For 22 of the 25 high-reputation companies price lists for specific product types were easily available from large-scale retailers. For each of the 22 companies I identified one popular product category. I then searched for the 10 most expensive products in this category and counted how many of these commodities were produced by the high-reputation company and how many by others. Only in 4 of 21 cases (19 per cent) was the high-reputation company also the one that provides the most expensive commodities, whereas in 17 cases (81 per cent) this was not the case. The data are an empirical indication that it is false to assume that an "affect-based law of value" (Arvidsson and Colleoni 2012, 142) has emerged and that value and the economy have become ethical (Arvidsson 2010). If this were the case then it would have to be a general tendency that prices are determined by reputation and that the most reputable company's commodities are the most expensive ones in specific product categories.

TABLE 5.2 The world's 25 most reputable companies and the role of their products in the sale of expensive commodities (data sources: Forbes List of the World's Most Reputable Companies 2013, various sales price lists accessed on June 4, 2013)

Rank	Company	Main Product	Price Source	Number of goods in the list of the 10 most expensive products	Leading provider of expensive products
1	BMW	Cars	parkers.co.uk:new cars	0	Jaguar (6)
2	Walt Disney	Films			
3	Rolex	Watches	amazon.co.uk:watches	0	Armand Nicolet (7)
4	Google	Advertisements			
5	Daimler	Cars	parkers.co.uk:new cars	0	Jaguar (6)
6	Sony	Consumer electronics	amazon.co.uk:digital cameras	0	Nikon (3)
7	Microsoft	Software	amazon.co.uk:business & office applications	8	Microsoft (8)
8	Canon	Cameras	amazon.co.uk:digital cameras	1	Nikon (3)
9	Nestlé	Food and drinks	Amazon.co.uk:coffee pod and capsule machines	1 (Nespresso = joint venture of Krups and Nestlé)	Grimac (5)
10	Lego	Toys	amazon.co.uk:toddler toys –bricks & blocks	0	6 (Weplay)
11	Intel	Processors	amazon.co.uk:processors	7	7 (Intel)
12	Apple	ICTs	argos.co.uk:laptops	10	10 (Apple)

No.	Company	Category	Website search	Count	Brand(s)
13	VW	Cars	parkers.co.uk:new cars	0	Jaguar (6)
14	Adidas	Shoes	amazon.co.uk:running shoes	1	MBT (6)
15	Johnson & Johnson	Medical and pharmaceutical equipment	amazon.co.uk:baby shampoos	1	Earth Mama (2)
16	Samsung	Consumer electronics	amazon.co.uk: digital cameras	0	Nikon (3)
17	L'Oréal	Cosmetics	amazon.co.uk:hair sprays & mists	0	Bumble and Bumble (2), Paul Mitchell (2)
18	Nike	Shoes	amazon.co.uk:running shoes	1	MBT (6)
19	Colgate–Palmolive	Household and personal products	Amazon.co.uk:toothpaste	1	Crest (6)
20	Philips Electronics	Electronics	Amazon.co.uk:electronic toothbrushes	3	Oral–B (7)
21	Michelin	Tyres	Amazon.co.uk:bike tubes	2	Continental (3)
22	Amazon	Retail			
23	Giorgio Armani Group	Clothes and beauty	Amazon.co.uk:eau de toilette	2	Creed (3)
24	IBM	ICT hardware and software			
25	Kellogg Company	Cereals and other food	Amazon.co.uk:cereal and fruit bars	10	Kellogg's (10)

Users and audiences work for commercial media companies. They are productive workers who are exploited by capitalist media organisations. The value-concept does not imply that values correspond to prices because values calculated in average working hours and prices calculated in monetary units are two different levels of analysis. In physical production, there is a logical tendency that products whose creation requires more working hours than others, i.e. products with higher value, are more expensive because wage and resource costs tend to be higher. A toothbrush tends to be much cheaper than a car because less working hours are needed for the production of the first. In advertising-financed media, two factors that can determine advertising prices are the number of hours worked by paid employees and the audience size. Commercial media can, but do not necessarily have to, follow the logic that they sell advertisements more expensive than others if they have higher advertising rates. It can be tested empirically whether this is the case or not. The model used is incomplete because audience size is only one aspect that influences the value of a commercial media commodity, whereas paid employees' average number of hours worked per unit of time is another one.

I gathered data on average audience size (readership) and advertising rates for one standard full-colour page during the week for all national UK daily newspapers (see Table 5.3).

Correlation analysis of advertising rates and average daily readers results in a Pearson $\rho = 0.52$ (correlation is significant at the 0.06 level, 1-tailed). There is a good correlation between the values. The probability that there is a chance correlation is 6 per cent, which is relatively small. So we can assume that there is an actual correlation. One obvious outlier is the *Financial Times* that has a small number of readers, but a high advertising rate, which is due to the fact that its readers are mainly managers who tend to have high incomes and are

TABLE 5.3 UK daily newspapers' advertising rates (one standard colour full-page advertising on weekdays) and average audience sizes (data sources: rate cards on the websites of national newspapers, National Readership Survey April 2012–March 2013)

Newspaper	Advertising rate (£)	Average daily readers (in 1000s)
The Sun	55,502	6,707
The Daily Mail	45,612	4,245
The Mirror	42,320	3,614
The Telegraph	46,000	1,352
The Times	27,195	1,300
Daily Star	23,765	1,279
Daily Express	31,500	1,157
The Guardian	18,000	1,027
The Independent	16,600	443
The Financial Times	58,600	312

therefore more likely to spend more money when making purchases. So there are indications that the business press does not follow the logic that larger audiences result in higher advertising rates. The number of business media tends to be strongly limited among the overall number of commercial media in a market, however. Therefore in spite of the business media outlier there is still a good and significant correlation between audience size and advertising prices in the studied example market. A study conducted by Robert Picard (2009) confirms this result. He conducted an analysis of the relationship of the circulation and advertising prices of a random sample of 160 daily newspapers. The study found that the average advertising price increases with higher circulation and that there is a significant correlation between the two variables.

5.3.2. Targeted Advertising and Prosumer Labour on the Internet

The Internet is both a machine and a medium, a tool of production and consumption of information in one. The consumer therefore tends to partly become a prosumer. Various political economies meet and collide online: the cultural economy that sells content and is facing various contradictions, the advertising economy that sells users' data, the access economy that sells access to platforms and information, the service economy that markets and sells non-digital goods and services online, various mixed models, and an alternative economy of the digital commons that challenges commodification.

Value's substance is labour. Labour-time is its measure. Companies use advertising in the circulation process for transforming commodities into money capital. For capital accumulation to work, the production and sale of commodities needs therefore to be connected to advertising labour that is organised in space and time.

Let us try to conduct some calculations for one of the largest information companies in the world—Facebook. In 2012, the social media company had 4,619 employees and 1.06 billion active users (Facebook SEC filings, form 10-K, 2012). In August 2012, Facebook users spent on average 7 hours and 46 minutes on the platform.[3] We can therefore calculate that an average user spent 93.2 hours per year on Facebook. In total this means 93.2 × 1.06 billion = 98.792 billion hours of annual Facebook usage time.

From Facebook's financial reports (SEC filings, form 10-K, 2012), we know the following data for 2012:

> Revenue: US$5.089 billion
> Profit before taxes: US$538 million
> Costs (constant and variable capital, share-based compensations): US$4.551 billion
> Share-based compensations: US$1.57 billion

According to data, the average working day of Facebook employees is 9–10 hours per day, so we can set it at 9.5.[4] This means that in total Facebook employees worked in 2012 around 10 million hours:

$$4619 \times 9.5 \times 5 \times 45 \text{ weeks} = 4{,}619 \times 2{,}137.5 \text{ hours} = 9{,}873{,}112.5 \text{ hours}$$

What do Facebook employees earn on average? Statistics from glassdoor.com allow an approximation. Glassdoor is a platform where employees report average salaries and review working conditions. The data in Table 5.4 is based on reports from N = 1,499 persons. Based on these data we can estimate that the salary of an average Facebook employee is US$120,675.

We can therefore approximate Facebook's total 2012 wage costs.
If there are 4,619 employees with an average salary of 120,675, then average 2012 wage costs are:

$$4{,}619 \text{ employees} \times US\$120{,}675 = US\$557{,}397{,}825$$

The data allow calculating the following shares:
Wage share (variable capital) in revenues: 11.0 per cent

Capital share in revenues (profit + constant capital + share-based compensation): 89.0 per cent

TABLE 5.4 An estimation of Facebook employees' average wages, N = 1,499. Data source: glassdoor.com (accessed on December 1, 2013)

Software engineer	US$117,652
Research scientist	US$128,996
Production engineer	US$126,565
Product designer	US$123,460
Operations engineer	US$98,789
Product manager	US$136,561
Software engineer	US$100,100
Technical programme manager	US$146,063
Data scientists	US$124,051
Engineering manager	US$155,724
Senior software engineer	US$147,144
User operations analyst	US$43,518
Software engineer	US$145,194
User interface engineer	US$115,299
Software engineering new grad	US$106,000
Database engineer	US$131,500
Applications operation engineer	US$104,852
Average	US$120,675

Profit share in revenues: 10.6 per cent
Shareholder compensation share in revenues: 34.5 per cent
Constant capital share in revenues: 43.9 per cent
Total working hours:
Employees: 9,873,112.5 hours
Users: 98.792 billion hours

Total: 9,873,112.5 + 98,792,000,000 = 98,801,873,112.5

Number of unpaid working hours:
89 per cent of employees' working hours were unpaid: 8,787,070.1 hours
100 per cent of users' working hours were unpaid: 98.792 billion hours

Total unpaid working hours: 98,792,000,000 + 8,787,070.1 =
98,800,787,070.1

Total paid working hours: 9,873,112.5 × 0.11 = 1,086,042.4
Rate of exploitation (Facebook 2012):

unpaid labour time / paid labour time = 98,800,787,070.1 hours /
1,086,042.4 = 90,973

The macro-economic wage share is the share of an economy's wage sum in the GDP. The macro-economic profit share is the share of the sum of an economy's profits in the GDP. We can approximate these shares the following way:

ws = net operating surplus (NOS) / GDP, ps = compensation of employees (COE) / GDP.

The US economy-wide profit share was 24.8 per cent in 2012 and the wage share 53.1 per cent (data source: AMECO). As shown, I estimated the company-level equivalents of the profit share and the wage share for Facebook: Facebook's wage share was 11.0 per cent in 2012, its profit share 45.1 per cent (calculated as the sum of actual profits and paid-out shareholder compensation). How can Facebook achieve such a high profit share? By keeping its wage costs low. Calculating exploitation at the level of prices only allows taking wage labour into account, not unpaid labour that also creates value. Therefore we need to calculate also at the level of labour time in order to grasp unpaid labour time of non-wage workers as source of value. What we can thereby see is that unpaid labour is a huge source of value on social media.

Whereas the capital accumulation mechanism in the traditional information economy that sells information or information technology as a commodity is to set the prices relatively high above values and investment costs, in the social media economy the basic strategy is to "crowdsource" value production to unpaid users.

Exploiting unpaid users allows keeping the relative wage costs way beyond the economy-wide wage share, which again allows achieving a high profit share of above 45.1 per cent. A company does not, however, need a capital growth of more than 40 per cent to operate and survive, so Facebook pays high compensations to its shareholders. The company's main shareholders are its directors, such as Mark Zuckerberg who in 2014 owned 74.3 per cent of Facebook's class B stock and held 55.2 per cent of the total voting power (SEC filings, proxy statement 2014). At age 30, he was in 2014 with a wealth of US$35.5 billion the world's 10th richest person (Forbes: The World's Billionaires 2014). The exploitation of users is at the heart of the growing wealth of Facebook. Crowdsourcing has not, as claimed by the inventor of this term, brought "greater democratization in commerce" (Howe 2008, 14), but is a capitalistically smart and perfidious mechanism of value-creation that intensifies exploitation.

Prosumer labour on social media differs in a number of respects from audience labour in broadcasting:

- *Creativity and social relations*: Broadcasting audiences produce meanings of programmes, whereas social media prosumers produce not just meanings, but also content, communications with other users, and social relations.
- *Surveillance*: Broadcasting requires audience measurements, which are approximations, in order to sell audiences as commodities. Social media corporations monitor, store, and assess all online activities of users on their platforms and also on other platforms. They have very detailed profiles of users' activities, interests, communications, and social relations. Constant real-time surveillance of users is an inherent feature of prosumer labour on capitalist social media. Personal data is sold as a commodity.
- *Targeted and personalised advertising*: Advertising on capitalist social media can therefore more easily target user interests and personalise ads, whereas this is more difficult in commercial broadcasting.
- *Algorithmic auctions*: Algorithms organise the pricing of the user data commodity in the form of auctions for online advertising spaces on the screens of a specific number of users. The ad prices on social media vary depending on the number of auctioneers, whereas the ad prices in newspapers and on radio and TV are set in a relatively fixed manner and are publicly advertised.

Corporate social media's capital accumulation cycle is connected to other realms of the economy: other capitalist companies, finance capital, rent-seeking, public services, common goods. Figure 5.3 visualises these connections.

The capital accumulation cycle of corporate social media such as Facebook is visualised in the lower section of Figure 5.3. It works the following way: Facebook has investment money M that it uses for buying constant capital c (technologies, infrastructure) and wage labour (v_1): The employees create a product P_1—the social media platform. This product is not a commodity—it is not

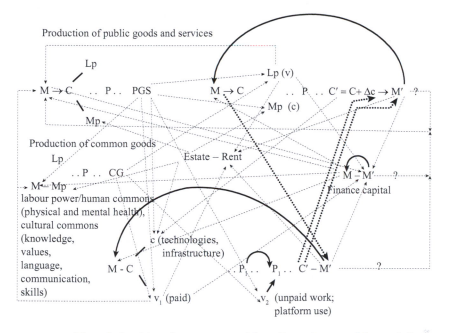

FIGURE 5.3   The relationships of corporate social media to the rest of the capitalist economy

sold to the users, but there is rather access without payments. So the commodity is something different: the users create based on access to P_1 new products P_2: profiles, communications, user-generated content, social relationships, and online behaviour. Data about these activities is sold as commodity C' in order to accumulate capital M' that is larger than the invested capital M.

Social media's capital accumulation is connected to other companies' capital accumulation processes. The latter are visualised in the upper right corner of Figure 5.3. They take on the form M→C (Lp, Mp) .. P .. C'→M': Invested capital M is used for buying commodities (labour power, means of production) that are used in the production process P for creating a new commodity C' that is sold at a price M' that allows making a monetary profit.

Banks and other financial institutions provide loans and credits to private households, the state, and capitalists as well as venture capital to capitalists. Its accumulation cycle is one where money M results in more money M' (M–M' in Figure 5.3) that stems from interests and dividends paid by companies and citizens. Marx considers the labour conducted by finance institutions' employees and managers as unproductive (2, 3). An indication of this circumstance is that companies that attract venture capital and high stock market values are extremely crisis-prone if they cannot achieve constant profit growth that satisfies the investors' expectations. Facebook and many other social media companies are public companies that aim to attract financial investments and have their shares valued on the stock market, which shows the immanent connection of these companies to the financial realm.

Private owners of real estate (built environments such as buildings, offices, flats, etc.; natural environments such as land, mines, forests, fields, parks, waters) rent these estates to companies, the state, and private households. They receive payments in return. These payments are called *rent*. The rent-seeking process is visualised as Estate-Rent in Figure 5.3. A rent is the monetary return that a tenant is paying for the temporal lease of a real estate that s/he does not own, but for which s/he during this time period purchases access and use rights. Leased property is produced once or exists as such in nature. It does not require constant expenditure and objectification of labour to guarantee its existence. Facebook and other social media companies have to rent offices and server storage spaces, for which they pay rent. One estimation from 2012 was that Facebook had 180,000 servers and Google more than a million.[5] These servers require a lot of space. Data centres and server farms are an important physical foundation of social media, which therefore is far from an "immaterial" phenomenon. Rent especially matters for corporate social media in the context of renting physical space.

Private households are the spheres of the reproduction of labour power. The household economy is visualised in Figure 5.3 as the sphere of production of common goods: Lp, M—Mp .. P .. CG. Continuous activities such as sleeping, communicating, emotional care, entertainment, leisure, rest, fun, family life, cooking, eating, sexuality, the education of kids, etc. regenerate labour power. The household has traditionally been a gendered space, where women conduct the largest part of reproductive labour. Reproductive labour tends to be unpaid. Households buy the means of reproductive labour (e.g. household appliances, houses, flats, apartments, private gardens, consumer goods, cars, etc.) by wages (dividends and profits in the case of shareholders and company owners) and/ or the state's public services (e.g. family allowance, old-age pension, social benefits, etc.). Reproductive labour produces human and cultural commons. Labour power is a human common that is permanently reproduced by the reproductive labour conducted in households. It guarantees humans' mental and physical health. Such labour is a basic service that the household supplies for capitalist companies. The household together with educational institutions develops and reproduces the cultural commons that consist of knowledge, values, language, communication, and skills. The cultural commons enter the capitalist production process in the form of educated, knowledgeable, skilful, moral, languaging, and intelligent humans that provide labour power for corporations. The production of the human and cultural commons is unpaid. It is an unpaid externality of the capitalist production process. Facebook's owners, managers, paid employees, and users reproduce their human lives by relying on reproductive labour.

The state organises the production of public services. The production of public goods and services is visualised in the upper left corner of Figure 5.3: M→C (Lp, Mp) .. P .. PGS.

The state obtains money in the form of tax payments. It purchases the labour power of public servants and other means of production as commodities. Public services are either provided without citizens having to pay for them or for a maintenance fee. The basic principle is that no monetary profit is derived from public goods and services, which allows broad access to these resources. Companies benefit from public goods and services such as education, research, transportation, health care, public service media, utilities, law enforcement, town planning, and waste management. Such services have nowadays often been privatised, but to the extent that they are public, private companies benefit from them because they can increase their profits by relying on cheap or free public services. The state finances public services by taxes. Most of these monetary inflows to the state are provided in the form of income taxes on wages, much less in the form of corporation taxes.

Table 5.5 provides empirical evidence that companies enabled by soft tax regulations in many countries pay little or no corporation taxes. ICT companies due to the global and often virtual nature of their business are especially prone to avoid paying taxes by channelling revenues and profits through subsidiaries located in tax havens. Amazon has 15,000 employees in the United Kingdom, but its headquarters are in Luxembourg, where it has just 500 employees.[6] In 2011, it generated revenues of £3.3 billion in the United Kingdom, but only paid £1.8 million corporation tax (0.05 per cent).[7] Facebook paid £238,000 corporation tax on a UK revenue of £175 million (0.1 per cent) in 2011.[8] Google has its headquarters in Dublin, but employs around 700 people in the United Kingdom.[9] Google's managing director for the United Kingdom and Ireland, Matt Brittin, admitted that this choice of location is due to the circumstance that the corporation tax is just 12.5 per cent in Ireland,[10] whereas in the United Kingdom it was 26 per cent in 2011.[11] Google had a UK turnover of £395 million in 2011, but only paid taxes of £6 million (1.5 per cent).[12] Given the phenomenon of tax avoidance and regimes of low or no corporation tax, I have marked the input flows from corporations to the state's public services in Figure 5.3 with question marks that signify the circumstance that neoliberal states and corporate practices are averse to the idea of corporation taxes. Facebook's employees and the mass of its users are everyday people who pay taxes for the organisation of public services. Facebook in contrast hardly pays taxes, but benefits from public services such as science, higher education, law enforcement, etc.

Marx could not analyse advertising because it was not a large-scale phenomenon in the nineteenth century. Its rise was connected to the emergence of the culture industry and consumer capitalism in the twentieth century.

Figure 5.4 visualises a part of Figure 5.3 in more detail, namely the economic relationships of Facebook and its advertising clients.

A commodity has use-value, value, exchange-value, and symbolic value. A company's production workers create the basic use-value that satisfies human needs. These activities take an average combined number of labour hours.

TABLE 5.5 Capital taxes, percentage of GDP at market prices, data source: AMECO

	2013	2007	2005	2000	1995	1990	1985	1980	1975	1970
Germany	0.2	0.2	0.2	0.1	0.1	0.1	0.1	0.1	0	0.1
Netherlands	0.3	0.3	0.3	0.4	0.3	0.2	0.2	0.2	0.2	0.2
Austria	0	0.1	0.1	0.1	0	0.1	0.1	0.1		
Portugal	0	0	0	0.1	0.1	0.1	0.2	0.1		
Finland	0.2	0.3	0.3	0.3	0.2	0.2	0.1	0.1	0.1	
United Kingdom	0.2	0.3	0.2	0.2	0.2	0.2	0.3	0.2	0.3	0.8
United States	0	0.2	0.3	0.4	0.3	0.3	0.2	0.3	0.4	0.5

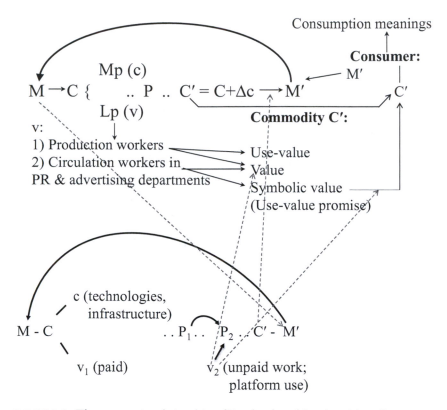

FIGURE 5.4   The economic relationship of Facebook and its advertising clients

Labour is the substance of value, labour time its measure and magnitude. In order to sell its commodity, a company tries to give positive meanings to it and to communicate these meanings to the public's members whom it tries to convince that this good or service can enhance their lives and that they should therefore buy this commodity and not a comparable one offered by another company. Most commodities have, independent from their physical or informational nature, a cultural component that is created by cultural labour. The cultural dimension of a commodity is necessarily ideological: it appeals to consumers' imagination and wants to make them connote positive images and feelings with the idea of consuming this commodity.

The creation of a commodity's symbolic ideology is a value-creating activity. The use-value of a commodity can be physical and/or informational: we have cars for satisfying the need of driving from A to B, we listen to music for satisfying our aesthetic desires, etc. The exchange-value of a commodity is the relationship in which it is exchanged with another commodity, normally money: x commodity A = y commodity B (money). Symbolic value establishes a link and mediates between use-value and exchange-value; it helps to accomplish the exchange in which consumers obtain use-values and capitalist money. Wolfgang Fritz Haug (1986) speaks in this context of the commodity's use-value promise: The sales and advertising ideology associated with a commodity promises specific positive life enhancement functions that the commodity brings with it and thereby conceals the commodity's exchange-value behind promises. The symbolic commodity ideology promises a use-value beyond actual consumption, an imaginary surplus and surplus enjoyment. These promises are detached from the actual use-value and are therefore a fictitious form of use-value. Capitalism's antagonism between use-value and exchange-value takes in the commodity aesthetic the form of a contradiction between use-value and appearances of use-value: as long as the consumer has not purchased a commodity, s/he can only imagine how using it actually is. Advertising makes use-values appear in specific forms and promises specific qualities—it communicates the commodity aesthetic. The commodity's appearance becomes more important than its being and is an instrument for capital accumulation. "The aesthetics of the commodity in its widest meaning—the sensual appearance and the conception of its use value—becomes detached from the object itself" (Haug 1986, 16–17).

David Harvie (2005, 153) argues that advertising "provides an individual capital with the use-value of easing the realisation of its commodities' values as money and profit". He adds that branding and advertising also "provide workers (as consumers) with use-values". Advertising and branding provide use-values for capital, i.e. an ideological service that bestows specific meanings to commodities that try to make them better saleable. For the consumer, these ideological and symbolic values are, however, not use-values itself, but only use-value promises—they promise specific positive qualities that consumers can attain by purchasing specific commodities.

Advertising is a commodity-fetishistic ideology (Marx 1867, chapter 1.4) that makes actual social relations that underlie commodities disappear behind ideological promises. Sut Jhally (2006) argues that in capitalism, the division of labour makes people work only on one part of the product and that the division between mental and physical labour lets us not understand commodities' origins.

"The social relations of production embedded in goods are systematically hidden from our eyes. The real meaning of goods, in fact, is *emptied* out in capitalist production and consumption" (Jhally 2006, 88). But advertising fills up this vacuum with ideology: "Production empties. Advertising fills" (Jhally 2006, 89). Advertising is so powerful because it tells stories and provides meanings about goods and the economy that are not presented in other forms. It uses various strategies for doing so, for example the strategy of black magic, in which "persons undergo sudden physical transformations" and "the commodity can be used to entrance and enrapture other people" (Jhally 2006, 91). "The real function of advertising is not to give people information but to make them feel good" (Jhally 2006). Advertising can therefore be seen as a secular form of religion and God. Advertising is a system of commodity fetishism: it promises satisfaction and happiness through the consumption of things (Jhally 2006, 102). Raymond Williams in this context described advertising as a magic system: "You do not only buy an object: you buy social respect, admiration, health, beauty, success, power to control your environment. The magic obscures the real sources of general satisfaction because their discovery would involve radical change in the whole common way of life" (Williams 1980/2005, 189).

Saying that the cultural labour of branding, public relations, and creating commodity advertisements creates symbolic value is not detached from the notion of economic value. Rather *value* here precisely means that for the creation of this symbolic dimension of the commodity, labour time is invested. It is therefore no wonder that almost all larger companies have their own public relations departments or outsource public relations and advertising to other companies. Paying the circulation workers employed in such departments or companies needs to be planned and calculated into the price of commodities.

Consumers give specific meanings to the commodities they buy and consume. They thereby construct consumption meaning and in doing so can react to use-value promises in different ways:

1   They can share these ideologies and buy the commodities because they hope the promise is an actual use value;
2   they can deconstruct the use-value promise as ideology and refuse to buy the commodity;
3   they can deconstruct the use-value, but nonetheless buy the commodity for other reasons.

For communicating commodity ideologies to consumers, companies need to buy advertisement spaces in commercial media. Commercial media link commodity ideologies to consumers; they "transport" ideologies to consumers, although it is unclear and not determined how the latter react and if the confrontation with commodity ideologies results in actual purchases. Facebook and other corporate social media are advertising companies that sell advertising space and user data as commodities to clients who want to present commodity ideologies to users and hope that the latter buy their commodities. Facebook has paid employees that organise the development, maintenance, and provision of its software platform. On December 31, 2012, Facebook had 4,619 paid employees.[13] But Facebook cannot sell advertising space without its users. Without them, it would be a dead platform that would immediately cease to exist. On June 3, 2013, 42.513 per cent of all Internet users had accessed Facebook within the preceding 3 months.[14] These were more than 1 billion people in the world.[15]

Are Facebook users productive workers? They are certainly not less important for Facebook's capital accumulation than its paid employees because without users Facebook would immediately stop making profits and producing commodities. Facebook's commodity is not its platform that can be used without charges. It rather sells advertising space in combination with access to users. An algorithm selects users and allows individually targeting ads based on keywords and search criteria that Facebook's clients identify. Facebook's commodity is a portion/space of a user's screen/profile that is filled with ad clients' commodity ideologies. The commodity is presented to users and sold to ad clients either when the ad is presented (pay-per-view) or when the ad is clicked (pay-per-click). The user gives attention to his/her profile, wall and other users' profiles and walls. For specific time periods parts of his/her screen are filled with advertising ideologies that are with the help of algorithms targeted to his/her interests. The prosumer commodity is an ad space that is highly targeted to user activities and interests. The users' constant online activity is necessary for running the targeting algorithms and for generating viewing possibilities and attention for ads. The ad space can therefore only exist based on user activities that are the labour that create the social media prosumer commodity.

Facebook clients run ads based on specific targeting criteria, e.g. 25- to 35-year-old men in the United States who are interested in literature and reading. What exactly is the commodity in this example? It is the ad space that is created on a specific 25- to 35-year-old man's screen interested in e.g. Shakespeare while he browses Facebook book pages or other pages. The ad is potentially presented to all Facebook users who fall into this category, which was 27,172,420 on June 3, 2013. What is the value of the single ad presented to a user? It is the average labour = usage time needed for the production of the ad presentation. Let's assume these 27,172,420 million users are on average 60 minutes per day on Facebook and in these 60 minutes 60 ads are presented to them on average. All time they spend online is used for generating targeted ads. It is labour time that generates targeted ad presentations. We can therefore say that the value of a single ad presented to a user is in the presented example 1 minute of labour/usage/prosumption time.

So Facebook usage is labour. But is it productive labour? We have seen that Marx sees transportation labour that moves a commodity in space-time from location A to location B, which takes a certain labour time x, as productive labour.

The value generated by transporting a commodity from A to B is therefore x hours. The symbolic ideology of a commodity first needs to be produced by special ad and public relations employees and is in a second step communicated to potential buyers. *Advertising therefore involves (informational) production and transportation labour.* Advertising production does not create a physical commodity, but an ideological dimension of a commodity—a use-value promise that is attached to a commodity as meaning. Advertising transport workers do not transport a commodity in physical space from A to B, but rather organise a communication space that allows advertisers to communicate their use-value promises to potential customers. Facebook's paid employees and users are therefore twenty-first-century equivalents of what Marx considered as transport workers in classical industry. They are productive workers whose activities are necessary for "transporting" use-value promises from companies to potential customers. Marx associated transport with communication when he wrote of the means of transport and communication. On Facebook and other social media platforms, transportation labour is communication labour.

Dallas W. Smythe argued that it is a specific feature of audience labour that audiences "work to market [. . .] things to themselves" (Smythe 1981, 4). Facebook users constantly work and constantly market things to themselves—they transport advertising ideologies (use-value promises). Their usage behaviour constantly generates data that is used for targeting ads. All Facebook usage is productive labour, with the exception of those cases where users block advertising with the help of ad block software. Facebook usage labour adds value to the commodity that is sold by Facebook's ad clients. Practically this means that a lot of companies want to advertise on Facebook and calculate social media advertising costs into their commodity prices. Nielsen (2013) conducted a survey among advertisers and advertising agencies: 75 per cent of the advertisers and 81 per cent of the agencies that participated in the survey indicated that they buy targeted ads on social media. This shows the importance of social media for advertising today.

The production workers of Facebook's clients produce use-value and value. Their PR and advertising employees (or the workers in the companies to which this labour is outsourced) produce value and use-value promises as symbolic value. Facebook's users produce value and communicate use-value promises to themselves. They are productive workers (1, 2, 3). That they create value means that their labour time objectifies itself in commodities: the ad clients' employees objectify their labour in the commodity that is marketed to Facebook users, whereas Facebook users objectify their labour in the prosumer commodity that is sold to Facebook's clients. User labour is thereby also objectified in the commodity that is marketed and potentially sold to users themselves.

The following table gives an overview of the validity of various dimensions of productive labour for different forms of labour. Note that productive labour (3) can be interpreted at different levels, for example the level of a company as indicated in the fourth column of Table 5.6 (in which case productive labour

[3] is identical with productive labour [2]), the level of a specific industry or the economy as a whole (as indicated by Table 5.6's fifth column). Productivity (3) also includes the housework economy and the public service economy that produce common and public goods that reproduce labour-power and form inputs and preconditions of capital accumulation.

The financial labour conducted in banks, stock market brokerage, and other financial organisations does not create use-values that satisfy humans' physical, mental, or social needs. If you take a loan by a bank, then you are not interested in the loan as such, but rather the things you can buy with it such as a house. The use-value you are interested in is the house. The loan only has an intermediated function, as a means to an end, not an end in itself. It is therefore not a use-value that satisfies human needs. Similarly the act of creating a house is productive (1), whereas renting it out does not create a new use-value, but financial revenue in the form of rent that the property owners extract from wages or profits.

TABLE 5.6 The application of Marx's concepts of productive labour (1, 2, 3) to various forms of production

Labour type	Productivity (1): production of use-values for consumers	Productivity (2): production of surplus-value, capital, and commodities in processes of capital accumulation	Productivity (3): collective labour that produces surplus-value, capital, and commodities	Productivity (3): collective labour that produces surplus-value, capital, and commodities in the economy
Housework	Yes	No	No	Yes
Public service work	Yes	No	No	Yes
Financial labour	No	No	No	Yes
Renting out estates	No	No	No	Yes
Paid work for producing a car or book as commodity	Yes	Yes	Yes	Yes
Unpaid Facebook usage	Yes	Yes	Yes	Yes
Working in a company's public relations and advertising department	Yes	Yes	Yes	Yes

People working in the advertising department of a dairy company do not create a physical use-value such as milk or butter, but an ideological use-value promise that helps sell milk or butter because their labour helps to create certain customers' impression that drinking a specific type of milk or eating a particular kind of butter makes them slim. They create a symbolic value, the image a company wants to give to its products. Apple computers and phones for example have the image of being used by intellectuals who have interesting jobs and lives. Advertisements attach these images to the commodity by e.g. communicating that Apple users "think different", by showing neon-coloured images of young stylish people with iPods, a relaxed young sunburnt man with an iPad, etc. Advertising space provided by Facebook is a use-value for capital that wants to sell commodities to consumers or improve its public reputation. People may not just buy Apple products because they think they are technically better than comparable products, but also to communicate that they are part of the group of intellectuals or young urban professionals. In this case the Apple product satisfies not only the need that one informs or entertains oneself or communicates with other people, but also the need to create a certain reputation of oneself, which is also a use-value. This means that the symbolic dimension of commodities can also be and for many people is a use-value. It does not matter if this use-value is purely ideological or not because use-value is not a moral but rather an analytical concept. Also an atom bomb has a use-value: it serves the desire of some people to kill a lot of other people. It is morally wrong to produce and use an atom bomb, but it nonetheless is a use-value.

Facebook usage produces a use-value for the users themselves: they can inform themselves, communicate with others, and form and maintain communities. Facebook usage is therefore cognitive, communicative, and collaborative work that is productive (1). At the same time the same activity produces a prosumer commodity that is sold to advertising clients; it is productive labour (2, 3). It thereby is labour that communicates a commodity's use-value promises to the users themselves. The circumstance that usage creates use-values that can be immediately consumed helps disguise that Facebook is an advertising company and that usage helps create surplus-value for Facebook as well as create and realise surplus-value for other companies.

Companies create an official image of a commodity that they communicate in public relation campaigns, advertisements, and the design and packaging of the commodity. The labour that goes into creating and communicating this brand image is productive labour (1, 2, 3).

> The purpose of branding [. . .] is to produce imagined, non-corporeal qualities of products and, as such, branding *does alter* the use-values of commodities. In fact, in terms of use-value, it is probably impossible to disentangle the product, in its tangible form, from the brand, i.e., to separate the corporeal and ethereal qualities of commodities.
>
> *Harvie 2005, 153*

All labour that goes into the creation and communication of advertising forms part of the commodity's value and is therefore in a certain manner reflected in the commodity's price. But commodities not only have official reputations represented by advertisements and companies' campaigns. They also have specific reputations on the side of consumers. Commodity reputation is a communication process: companies communicate certain images to customers who share or reject these meanings to specific extents or give different meanings to the commodities. The meanings that companies encode into commodities are not necessarily decoded the same way, although successful image campaigns result in decoding forms that positively correlate with the encoded meanings and make a lot of people buy the commodity.

Sabine Pfeiffer (2013) discusses value-generation and -realisation in the context of the World Wide Web (WWW). She introduces a taxonomy that distinguishes between value-generation online or offline, value-realisation online or offline, value-generation that utilises commons or commodities, and value-realisation that utilises commons or commodities. The model entails 16 different versions of combinations of value-generation and-realisation. It is an interesting approach in that it tries to classify different forms of online work. Value

> *creation* will be understood as the actual process of producing new values; that is, values that did not exist prior to their production-process, before the application of human labour. Value *realisation*, on the other hand, is the process by which the product that originated as part of value generation is valorised and successfully exchanged in the market for other money or other value.
>
> *Pfeiffer 2013, 20*

In the case of Facebook, products are first created online or offline as commodities and then sold online via advertising on Facebook. Understood as one entire production and sales product, Sabine Pfeiffer's model implies that only the labour that creates the advertised products is productive, whereas the labour involved in the organisation of advertising and commodity sales ("value realisation") is unproductive because realisation is analytically split off from value creation, which implies that value realisation cannot involve value creation. The typology cannot without logical inconsistency explain cases where value realisation for one production process is a value-creation process in another production process. In the case of Facebook, a second commodity different from the commodity sold via Facebook advertising is involved: the user and its data. This data (user-generated content, relationship data, profile data, meta-data) is generated in labour processes. Something new that did not exist before comes into being, which is according to Sabine Pfeiffer's own definition a form of value creation. This value is created and realised online and in a complex way connected to the realisation process of commodity circuits that originate outside of Facebook.

The model leaves unspecified interconnected forms where categories overlap. It leaves open if users working unpaid for Facebook and similar commercial platforms, paid advertising and public relations workers, journalists working for newspapers or magazines that are 100 per cent advertising-financed, etc. are productive workers who are exploited by capital or if, as a dichotomous distinction between value creation and value realisation implies, they in unproductive processes help realise profits but do not create value themselves.

This section has shown why unpaid user labour on corporate social media should be considered as productive labour (1, 2, 3) and how it is connected to the capitalist economy as a whole. A competing conception is to conceptualise Facebook as a rent-seeking organisation. The next section discusses Marx's concept of rent and why it cannot be meaningfully applied to Facebook.

5.4. Facebook and Rent

Understanding rent and if it is a concept that can be applied for understanding Facebook's political economy in a meaningful manner within a Marxist theory requires first to discuss how Marx defined rent (section 5.4.1). In a next step, I will show how the concept of rent has recently been applied for arguing that profit becomes rent (section 5.4.2). In a third step, I will argue that Facebook's political economy is not a form of rent seeking (section 5.4.3).

5.4.1. How Did Marx Conceive Rent?

A discussion of how Marx actually conceived rent is conspicuous by its absence in the works of many digital rent theorists and related approaches (such as Comor 2014, Huws 2014, Reveley 2013, and Rigi and Prey 2015).

Marx defines rent as a renter's payment of "a contractually fixed sum of money (just like the interest fixed for the borrower of money capital), for the permission to employ his capital in this particular field of production" (Marx 1894, 755). Rent could e.g. be paid for "agricultural land, building land, mines, fisheries, forests, etc." (Marx 1894, 755f). Landowners "capture part of the surplus-value produced in the economy" (Fine and Saad-Filho 2010, 134). For Marx, rent "can be understood only by examining the relationship between capital and land. Rent depends upon the production and appropriation of surplus-value through the intervention of landed property" (Fine and Saad-Filho 2010, 144). Rented property according to Marx typically enters the capitalist production process as fixed constant capital: "I have elsewhere used the expression 'la terre-capital' to denote capital incorporated into the earth in this way. This is one of the categories of fixed capital" (Marx 1894, 756). David Harvey (2006, 330) argues that rent "is simply a payment made to landlords for the right to use land and in appurtenances (the resources embedded within it, the buildings placed upon it and so on)". Rent is derived from charging money for the access to and use of property in land (landed property). Landed property can be provided by nature and propertied by legal measures (e.g. a waterfall or lake) or produced by humans (e.g. a building on a piece of land, an artificial lake). Investments into landed property can improve the productivity that the capital that rents the property achieves. Such investments are paid by part of the rent and allow charging higher rents in the future. Separate companies that e.g. construct houses or fertilise land can turn these activities into a profitable capitalist business. If land is traded as a commodity on the market then it becomes fictitious capital (Harvey 2006, 347) and its prices are prone to create financial bubbles, as the role of housing specula-tion in the 2008 crisis has shown.

For Marx (1894, 772), rented forms of property are "things that have no value in and of themselves" because they either are not "the product of labour, like land" or "cannot be reproduced by labour, such as antiques, works of art by cer-tain masters, etc.". Rent "is in no way determined by the action of its recipient" (Marx 1894, 775). Marx's theory of rent does not "in any way suggest that land or mineral deposits 'create' value" (Mandel 1990, 16). Marx uses the example of a waterfall: "The waterfall, like the earth in general and every natural force, has no value, since it represents no objectified labour and hence no price, this being in the normal case nothing but value expressed in money. Where there is no value, there is *eo ipso* nothing to be expressed in money. This price is nothing but capitalised rent" (Marx 1894, 787). "Value is labour. So surplus-value cannot be earth" (Marx 1894, 954). Given that renting does not create value, Marx argues that it consumes value that has been created by workers in capitalist production processes: "Just as the functioning capitalist pumps out surplus labour from the worker, and thus surplus-value and surplus product in the form of profit, so the landowner pumps out a part of this surplus-value or surplus profit in turn from the capitalist in the form of rent, according to the laws developed earlier" (Marx 1894, 959). Rent is a deduction from capital. "Landed property has nothing to do with the actual production process. Its role is limited to transferring a part of the surplus-value produced from capital's pocket into its own" (Marx 1894, 960). Land is "for the landowner a permanent magnet for attracting a part of the surplus-value pumped out by capital" (Marx 1894, 961). Renting would there-fore be unproductive: unproductive labour "is labour which is not exchanged with capital, but *directly* with revenue, that is, with wages or profit (including of course the various categories of those who share as co-partners in the capitalist's profit, such as interest and rent)" (Marx 1862/63, 157). Marx (1894, chapter 48) stresses in the trinity formula that the value created by workers that is transformed into capital consists of three parts: profits (including the interest paid to banks), wages, and rent. Parts of the value are transferred to rentiers and in return the capitalist obtains access to a property that s/he uses as fixed constant capital in the production process.

Rent requires a certain monopoly status of an owner over property. "Landed property presupposes that certain persons enjoy the monopoly of disposing of particular portions of the globe as exclusive spheres of their private will to the exclusion of all others" (Marx 1894, 752). The "monopoly to a piece of the earth enables the so-called landowner to extract a tribute, to put a price on it" (Marx 1894, 762). "All rent is based on the monopoly power of private owners of certain portions of the globe" (Harvey 2006, 349; Harvey 2001, 395) or "over certain assets" (Harvey 2012, 90). This on the one hand means the simple fact that every landed property has one specific owner. On the other hand it means that if a person controls a landed property with a specific quality, s/he can extract extremely high rents. If there is e.g. only one river running through a country and one person owns the river and all surrounding land, a company wanting to set up a hydroelectric power station depends on renting land from this person who can due to the monopoly ownership status charge an extremely high rent. Marx (1894, 908, 910) gives the example of a vineyard that due to its location is the only piece of land that is able to help create specific wine. In contrast if there are several rivers running through the country and there are multiple owners of the land next to the river and of usage rights of the river, the rentiers compete with each other for attracting renters. Harvey (2001, 395; 2012, 91) mentions the example of a unique work of art such as a Picasso or Rodin whose ownership can yield a monopoly rent when the artwork is leased to galleries, museums, and exhibitions. He also argues that cities such as Barcelona, Bilbao, London, Paris, or San Francisco try to extract monopoly rents by "city branding" that conveys the impression that these metropolises are culturally unique and authentic (Harvey 2001, 394–411; Harvey 2012, 103–109). Collective symbolic capital would thereby become the foundation for monopoly rents.

Leased property is a conservative type of property that does not need the constant influx of labour for its existence. Labour can from time to time improve the property, but a piece of land, a building, a Picasso picture, a vineyard, or a lake can also exist without constant labour inputs. A commodity in the capital accumulation process in contrast needs to be constantly re-produced by labour.

We can summarise the discussion by identifying four specific qualities of the renting process:

- A good that is rented out does not require constant production and reproduction. It can be rented out independent of labour because it does not objectify value.
- Capital accumulation requires the constant production of a commodity, surplus-value and a surplus product as well as the constant sale of this commodity at a price that is higher than the investment costs, whereas rent-seeking does not require productive labour. Rent is a transfer of parts of profits that realise the value created by workers in capital accumulation processes.
- Property that is rented out to capitalists primarily enters the capital accumulation process as fixed constant capital.

- Renting is the rentier's sale of landed property to a renter that enables the latter's temporary access to and usage of the property

5.4.2. The Becoming-Rent of Profit

It is not an accident that some scholars have recently suggested that Facebook is a rent-seeking organisation. The usage of the rent concept has been framed by a broader popularity of this concept in specific forms of Marxist theory, especially cognitive capitalism theory that argues that in contemporary capitalism due to the central role of cognitive labour in production (e.g. Moulier-Boutang 2012; Negri 2008; Vercellone 2007, 2010), profit tends to become rent.

Carlo Vercellone (2010) has formulated the idea of the becoming-rent of profit. He argues that "the existence of rent is based upon forms of property and positions of power that permit the creation of scarcity and the imposition of higher prices, justified by the cost of production. Scarcity is induced in most cases by institutional artefacts, as shown today by the policies of reinforcement of Intellectual Property Rights" (Vercellone 2010, 95). Rent would be exterior to production. Cognitive capitalism's (assumed) crisis of the law of value would make it impossible to compel capital to make the supply of specific goods rare and to extract rent from their lease.

Capitalists are driven by the need to increase productivity in order to be able to compete on the market. This means that there is a historical trend that productivity increases so that commodities are produced faster. As a result, they contain less value than before. At the same time, the value created by human labour is the precondition for monetary profit. Marx describes this simultaneous positing and elimination of value as an antagonism between necessary and superfluous labour, between living and dead labour, and between the relations of production and the productive forces. The result is that there is a tendency that machines substitute human labour. This circumstance can contribute to capitalist crises. We can therefore not say, as Vercellone and some other autonomists do, that the law of value is today in a crisis because of the rise of cognitive capitalism, but rather that the law of value is fundamentally an expression of capitalism's inherent crisis tendency.

Hardt and Negri (2009, 141) argue that whereas "profit is generated primarily through internal engagement in the production process, rent is generally conceived as an external mode of extraction". As the accumulation of capital would today strongly be based on cognitive, affective, and cooperative labour, "the exploitation of labor-power and the accumulation of surplus-value should be understood in terms of not profit but capitalist rent" (Hardt and Negri 2009, 141). There would be a "renewed primacy of rent" because "in the contemporary networks of bio-political production, the extraction of value from the common is increasingly accomplished without the capitalist intervening in its production" (Hardt and Negri 2009, 141).

Also Slavoj Žižek (2009, 138–148) has taken up Vercellone's argument: the struggle over intellectual property would be a good example for the becoming-rent of profit. In the realms of the WWW, intellectual property, software, and "immaterial" labour, "exploitation in the classical Marxist sense is no longer possible" (Žižek 2009, 145). Bill Gates would "collect rent for enabling people to participate in global networking" (Žižek 2010, 233).

> Let us take the case of Bill Gates: how did he become the richest man in the world? His wealth has nothing to do with the production costs of the products Microsoft is selling (one can even argue that Microsoft is paying its intellectual workers a relatively high salary), i.e., Gates's wealth is not the result of his success in producing good software for lower prices than his competitors, or in higher "exploitation" of his hired intellectual workers. If this were to be the case, Microsoft would have gone bankrupt long ago: people would have massively chosen programs like Linux which are free and, according to specialists, of better quality than Microsoft programs. Why, then, are millions still buying Microsoft? Because Microsoft imposed itself as an almost universal standard, (almost) monopolising the field, a kind of direct embodiment of the "general intellect". Gates became the richest man in a couple of decades through appropriating the rent for allowing millions of intellectual workers to participate in the form of the "general intellect" that he privatised and controls.
>
> *Žižek 2009, 146*

Profit stems from the exploitation of labour; rent stems from profits or wages, but not from exploitation. Profit can therefore not become identical with rent. George Caffentzis (2013) has formulated a critique of the assumption that profit today becomes rent: "The problem with the cognitive capitalist theorists is that they attribute the sources of revenues like profit and rent to the behavior of profit-making capitalists and to rentiers" (Caffentzis 2013, 120). Capitalists would therefore be conceived as productive workers, which would contradict Marx's theory and his basic assumption that only labour creates value and that capitalism is an exploitative system because capital does not produce, but rather appropriates, surplus-value.

Jeon (2010) and Fine, Jeon, and Gimm (2010) argue that cognitive capitalism theory's dismissal of Marx's labour theory of value and its embracement of the rent concept is based on a false interpretation that separates and does not see the connection of cognitive and physical dimensions of work. "Marx's value theory is degraded into execution-labour theory of value where no consideration of conception (or knowledge) is presented" (Jeon 2010, 100). The applicability of the value concept and its measurement would in this theory be confined to the appropriation of nature and industrial capitalism. Abstract labour would be reduced to a naturalistic concept that neglects the human energy expended in cognitive labour. Cognitive capitalism theory would therefore be a dualistic, non-dialectical theory that separates industrial labour/cognitive labour, consumption/production of value, repetition/creativity, and measurement by time/immeasurability (Jeon 2010, 103). In such a dualistic theory framework, rent is a category that substitutes value in the realm of knowledge production because value is seen as standing on just one side of a dual economy that has two disconnected parts. Cognitive capitalism theory reduces the analysis of information in the economy to a subjective side and neglects how subjective knowledge interacts with objectified forms of knowledge, such as information technologies (Fuchs 2009, 2011a, 2014a: chapter 5). Cognitive capitalism theory therefore is a subjective and reductionist version of information society theory (Fuchs 2009, 2011a, 2014a: chapter 5).

The discussion shows that rent is a contested concept in contemporary Marxist theory. I will next show why it is also contested in the digital labour debate.

5.4.3. Facebook as a Rent-Seeking Organisation?

Teixeira and Rotta (2012) introduce the notions of the knowledge-commodity and the knowledge-rent. They do not explain the political economy of corporate social media, but rather have the sale of knowledge in mind. They say that knowledge has no value, even though it is created by labour over a specific time-period: If "highly-skilled Microsoft employees spend three whole years developing a new operating system that even a child of 8 can easily copy, its value is nil. So even though large investments were necessary for the development of the software, the fact that the commodity can be duplicated without any further complication makes it valueless" (Teixeira and Rotta 2012, 454–455). Knowledge companies would therefore monopolise knowledge with the help of copyrights, patents, and intellectual property rights. Large amounts of labour would be employed in the first production of knowledge, but in copying de-facto no labour would be applied, which would make knowledge valueless. Similar to land and the ground-rent derived from renting it out, knowledge would be rented for specific periods, which would result in knowledge-rent. Land would not have value because it could not be reproduced by labour. The knowledge-commodity producing sector would absorb "surplus-value generated from productive activities" (Teixeira and Rotta 2012, 463). The authors therefore argue that knowledge-creation in capitalist knowledge companies is unproductive.

One problem of this approach is that it only discusses one form of commercial knowledge, where knowledge is rented out/sold, but generalises this form for the entire information economy that is presented as a rentier economy. There are, however, also other commodity forms in the information economy, such as the payment for subscriptions/access and the sale of audiences and user data as commodity.

Teixeira and Rotta (2012, 455) cite a supplementary passage from *Capital, Volume 3*, in which Marx (1894, 238) says that the "value of any commodity—and thus also of the commodities which capital consists of—is determined not by the necessary labour-time that it itself contains, but by the socially necessary labour-time required for its reproduction". Therefore they argue that software engineers at Microsoft work, but this work "is not considered to be 'labor time' according to Marx, mainly because they are producing the commodity, not *re*producing it" (Teixeira and Rotta 2012, 462). This supplement differs from passages in *Capital, Volume 1*, where Marx says e.g. that value is measured "by the labour-time socially required for its production" (Marx 1867, 434). The authors' definition taken for arguing that Microsoft workers are unproductive contrasts with Marx's more common definitions of value provided in *Capital, Volume 1*.

Teixeira and Rotta's account of knowledge is static. They present it as something that is just produced once and then is statically reproduced and rented out. Knowledge such as software is dynamic, however, and tends to be updated, renewed, re-worked, re-mixed, re-purposed, and combined with various services. There is also a difference between software that is sold for a one-time price or via licences that expire and must be updated after a year or another time period. A single-use 12-month licence for IBM Advanced SPSS Statistics cost £1,182 in 2014. By buying this licence you do not buy a static piece of knowledge, but also access to technological support services over 12 months and the access to software updates. IBM's software engineers do not stop coding after they have created one version of SPSS; they rather create one version after another and many smaller updates that licensed users can access. Furthermore technological and administrative support services are offered by IBM, which is also a concrete daily expenditure of labour time. Producing use-values that capitalists turn into profits by selling commodities is a sufficient condition for speaking of productive labour that capital exploits. But software engineers also *re*produce software code by the simple fact that they continue to write new code that improves and updates specific versions. The reproduction of software is the creation of a history of versions and updates. Software versions thereby becomes outdated and updated. If you want to today use MS Word 1.0 published in 1983 you will face problems because you either need the Xenix or MS-DOS operating systems that are no longer in use and you will also face file compatibility problems. If software were static and not a constantly updated dynamic commodity, then Microsoft would still sell MS Word 1.0, and IBM SPSS 1.0 that was released in 1968 when computers were large mainframes that looked like huge cupboards.

In the SPSS example, there is a base of software code that is often updated and reproduced into licensed copies stored on customers' computers. Furthermore, the license-fee-paying users get access to support services. Code and services form an integrated commodity. The coding and service labour necessary for the supply of SPSS account for a specific number of working hours h per year that IBM exploits. A specific number of copies c is sold over these 12 months. One can now on the one hand argue that the total knowledge and service base has the value h and that the total profit and price is not determined by h, but diverges from value. Or one can on the other hand argue that one copy bought during these 12 months has the average value of h / c hours and that this value does not determine the price, i.e. one cannot calculate the price of a copy if one knows the annual number of invested hours. There is indeed a divergence of value and price of knowledge commodities, but one does not need the rent concept for explaining this circumstance because Marx argued that there is "a quantitative incongruity between price and magnitude of value, i.e. the possibility that the price may diverge from the magnitude of value, is inherent in the price-form itself" (Marx 1867, 196).

Knowledge is a peculiar commodity that can quickly be copied and does not disappear by consumption, which does not, however, mean that its producers are unproductive. The software industry is an industry of a substantial size. It is odd to argue that the workers in it are unproductive and consume rather than produce value because this means that they are not exploited and are not relevant political subjects for making a revolution. This is an odd claim that sounds like only classical industrial wage workers in factories are productive, which is an old fashioned notion of class that does not help leftist movements to make concrete politics that improve the living conditions of workers. Software engineers and other knowledge workers tend to be highly exploited, especially because they conduct a lot of unpaid overtime. To exclude them from the proletariat is an idiosyncratic move. The notion of rent does not help us to advance a revolutionary theory of the information society.

Some scholars argue that licensed software or other licensed knowledge is not a commodity because it does not change ownership and can therefore not be re-sold. For Marx, the commodity is, however, just like money not specific for capitalism, rather "[i]n themselves, money and commodities are no more capital than the means of production and subsistence are. They need to be transformed into capital" (Marx 1867, 874). For a commodity to become capital it must be embedded into a capital of capital accumulation so that labour creates its value and it is sold in order to generate ever-more money. Marx also terms labour-power that is sold for wages on the labour market a commodity. Other than a slave, the wage-worker owns her/his labour power her-/himself; the capitalist gets control over it as a commodity that s/he can command and control over specific periods of time. This terminology shows that a commodity does not necessarily fully change ownership when it is sold. "In order to become a commodity, the product must be transferred to the other person, for whom it serves as a use-value, through the medium of exchange" (Marx 1867, 131). The transfer of use-value can mean full transfer of ownership or a temporal right to access and control a use-value. When discussing ground-rent, Marx says that ground-rent is the price of land "so that the earth is bought or sold just like any other commodity" (Marx 1867, 762). Land that is rented is a commodity just like labour-power or beer that is sold on the beer market. But it is a specific commodity that in capitalism if rented out to capitalists generates ground-rent and becomes fixed capital:

The presuppositions for the capitalist mode of production are, thus as follows: the actual cultivators are wage-labourers, employed by a capitalist, the farmer, who pursues agriculture simply as a particular field of exploitation of capital, as an investment of his capital in a particular sphere of production. At certain specified dates, e.g. annually, this farmer-capitalist pays the landowner, the proprietor of the land he exploits, a contractually fixed sum of money (just like the interest fixed for the borrower of money capital), for the permission to employ his capital in this particular field of production. This sum of money is known as ground-rent, irrespective of whether it is paid for agricultural land, building land, mines, fisheries, forests, etc. It is paid for the entire period for which the landowner has contractually rented the land to the farmer. Ground-rent is thus the form in which landed property is economically realized, valorized. We have together here, moreover, and confronting one another, all three classes that make up the framework of modern society—wage-labourer, industrial capitalist, landowner. Capital may be fixed in the earth, incorporated into it, both in a more transient way, as is the case with improvements of a chemical kind, application of fertilizer, etc., and more permanently, as with drainage ditches, the provision of irrigation, levelling of land, farm buildings, etc. I have elsewhere used the expression '*la terre-capital*' to denote capital incorporated into the earth in this way. This is one of the categories of fixed capital.

Marx 1867, 756

Land exists as part of nature, whereas licensed software must be produced by labour and is in most cases further developed and updated. Whereas land is a more conservative good, software is a dynamic good. If you own one acre of land and rent it out, it will yield a certain rent per year. During this one year, the land is detracted from the owners' use and he cannot put it to other purposes.

In contrast to a landowner, a capitalist beer brewery sells one bottle of beer and invests the profit in producing and trying to sell even more beer. In contrast to the piece of land, there is labour involved that again and again produces something new—beer. A software company can make use of different commodification strategies: it can sell software licenses for limited time periods, or for unlimited usage periods, or it can sell free software whose source code can be changed, re-used, and updated by the buyers. In any case, the software is a commodity and the capitalist software firm will continuously let workers engage in labour in order to further develop and update the software's quality so that its use-value changes qualitatively: new versions are generated that can again be sold in order to yield more profit. Just like in the case of the capitalist beer commodity and unlike in the case of the leased land, capitalist software companies make use of labour in order to produce something new that can be sold and re-sold. They exploit commodity-producing labour in order to accumulate capital. The decisive aspect of a capitalist software company is that it exploits labour in order to accumulate capital. A rentier in contrast does not exploit labour, although it sells and re-sells land as commodity for deriving rent.

Brett Caraway (2011) criticises Dallas Smythe by arguing that audiences are not workers and are not exploited, but that the transaction between media owners and advertisers is a renting process:

> The economic transaction described by Smythe is *rent*. The media owner rents the use of the medium to the industrial capitalist who is interested in gaining access to an audience. The rental may be either for time (broadcasting) or space (print). It is the job of the media owner to create an environment which is conducive to the formation of a particular audience. Speculation on the size and quality of the audience determines the rent charged to the advertiser. The media owner eats into the surplus-value generated by the future sales of the industrial capitalist's commodities. [. . .] *But does the audience work to create surplus-value by purchasing a commodity after being exposed to a commercial?* Instead it would seem to be the people who toil away in manufacturing, marketing and advertising departments who are responsible for the generation of surplus-value.
>
> *Caraway 2011, 701*

Some authors have applied the rent-argument to social media. Matteo Pasquinelli (2010, 296–297) argues that parasitic rent is a crucial dimension of the contemporary Internet:

> Technological rent is the rent applied on the ICT infrastructures when they established a monopoly on media, bandwidth, protocols, standards, software or virtual spaces (including the recent social networks: Myspace, Facebook, etc.). It is composed by different layers: from the materiality of hardware and electricity to the immateriality of the software running a server, a blog, a community. The technological rent is fed by general consumption and social communication, by P2P networks and the activism of Free Culture. [. . .] Similarly also attention economy can be described as an attention rent applied on the limited resource of the consumer time-space. In the society of the spectacle and pervasive media the attention economy is responsible for commodity valorisation to a great extent. The attention time of consumers is a like a scarce piece of land that is constantly disputed. In the end the technological rent is a large part of the metabolism sustaining the techno-parasite.

Steffen Böhm et al. (2012, 3) apply the concept of profit-becoming-rent to corporate social media and argue that "Facebook does not reap a profit merely from organising the paid labour of its relatively few employees (as labour process theory would suggest), but extracts a rent from the commons produced by the free labour of its users". Facebook would be able to extract rent "by its sheer ability to monopolise social interactions over the Internet. As Microsoft has monopolised PC computing through its proprietary software platform, Facebook has created an 'obligatory passage point' through which most people wanting to use the Internet need to go" (Böhm et al. 2012, 15).

Böhm et al. want to combine the logic of labour-exploitation with the logic of renting for explaining how Facebook operates. It remains unclear, however, how such a combination can be accomplished within a Marxist framework and what exactly is rented out to whom: Is it a rent for data, platform access, or advertising clients' access to users? In a blog post, Land and Böhm (2012) argue that it is a "rent on attention", which leaves the question how attention-renting can be combined in a Marxian framework with the assumption that the subjects of this attention are exploited and produce surplus-value.

One may agree or disagree on the feasibility of the rent concept for digital labour theory, which is more of a theoretical issue. But what one should, however, see and acknowledge is that Böhm et al.'s approach is important in that it challenges the neglect of aspects of a political economy of digital and social media in organisation studies and labour process theory and introduces issues of a Marxist political economy of communication and the Internet to these fields (Beverungen, Böhm and Land 2015). The authors furthermore show that Marxist organisation studies can fruitfully inform digital labour studies in respect to issues such as management, coercion, control, and the organisation of alternatives (Beverungen et al. 2015). The three authors are quite uniquely positioned to foster the discussion of digital labour from a Marxist perspective in the fields of organisation, management and business studies and to bring insights from Marxist organisation studies to the broader field of digital labour studies. They are therefore making a quite important contribution to the digital labour debate.

Ursula Huws (2014) argues that Facebook's profits are derived from rent. It would be rent because the workers who produce the commodities advertised on Facebook would create value that partly is transformed and transferred into Facebook's profits. Huws distinguishes four kinds of labour in capitalism: paid production work, unpaid consumption work, paid reproduction work, and unpaid reproduction work. The first two would be directly productive. Paid work that creates commodities would be the quintessential form of labour that forms the centre of capital accumulation. Huws argues that also consumption work is directly productive. At the same time she puts forward the argument that not Facebook users, but the ad clients' workers generate the value that underlies Facebook's profits:

> How can we understand the profits made by online social networking or search engine companies? [. . .] they derive from rent. [. . .] The value that accrues to the social networking and search engine sites does indeed

ultimately derive from surplus-value produced by labour. But this is the labour of the workers who produced the commodities that are advertised on these sites, not the labour of the people who use the sites.

Huws 2014, 89

This means that Huws does not consider users as consumption workers in her own theoretical distinction, but as unproductive consumers. She argues that paid workers employed by capitalists constitute "the quintessential form of labour" (Huws 2014, 83), labour "inside the knot" (Huws 2014, 84), the "centre of the know" (Huws 2014, 102), "the point of production: the point where workers have the power to challenge capital" (Huws 2014, 101f), "critical points [. . .] where workers' agency can be implemented to some effect" (Huws 2014, 101).

Ursula Huws opposes considering reproductive and consumption workers as equally important as wage labour employed directly by capital. Consumption work would be "outside the knot" because "it does not generate income directly for the worker" (Huws 2014, 96). The same could be said of reproductive labour. Underlying this view is the assumption that wageworkers directly employed by capital have the largest level of power for exerting pressure and resisting capital. Wageworkers according to this view are the "front-line adversary in the struggle between capital and labour" (Huws 2014, 84).

In the case of Facebook, there are besides user-workers also paid employees that produce and maintain the software platform, the servers storing data, public relations, etc. These workers are, however, much less powerful than the users: if they go on strike and leave the workplace, the platform is likely to be still online and to generate profit by selling targeted ads because the actual sales process is based on the data generated by users and auctions for ad space that are organised by an algorithm. If the *users* go on strike and stop using the platform, Facebook can no longer make any profits because no new data is generated and nobody watches and clicks on the targeted ads. On corporate social media, users have tremendous power to bring profit-making to an end, which shows that their consumption work is crucial in the process of value-generation.

Jakob Rigi and Robert Prey (2015) argue that there is no correspondence between the time users spend on social media and ad prices and that this "shows that social media users do not produce the value of ads. Social media, like mass media before it, extract rent in exchange for the lease of (virtual) space". Similarly to Pasquinelli and Huws, Rigi and Prey argue that the origin of this rent is surplus-value generated by people working for the companies that advertise on Facebook. On the one hand Rigi and Prey say that "social media exploits pro-sumers by expropriating the commons of content they produce", but on the other hand they argue that users "do not produce surplus-value", which means they are either unproductive workers or no workers at all, which also means they are unproductive. This statement is a contradictio-in-adjecto because exploitation always presupposes the existence of surplus-value and a surplus product that is created by a class and ex- and appropriated by the enemy class. Rigi in a comment on Land and Böhm's (2012) blogpost argues that Facebook does not exploit users, but "wage laborers worldwide".

Duncan K. Foley holds that the labour theory of value cannot be applied to culture and information. He argues that the "glamorous successes of the information economy are best understood as innovative [. . .] modes of surplus-value appropriation, not novel methods of value creation" (Foley 2013, 259). Productive labour would only take place "in the productive phase of the circuit of capital rather than in the realisation or financial phases" (Foley 2013, 261). Therefore finance, banking, renting, accounting, advertising, legal activities, and other activities would be unproductive. The growth of information and knowledge activities would "result in a reduction in surplus-value based incomes in the rest of the global economy" (Foley 2013, 264). Copyrighted songs or software would be rented to users like land. Corporate social networking sites would have a direct "connection to the global pool of surplus-value [. . .] in that the incomes supporting these activities come from advertisers who are willing to pay to divert spending toward themselves" (Foley 2013, 265).

Foley dismisses the whole realm of the information economy as unproductive. A rent is a payment from wages or profits for the usage of a dead thing such as a piece of land that does not have to be produced by living labour in order to be rented out. If an entity is rented by a business for economic purposes, it enters the capital accumulation process as fixed constant capital. If a worker in contrast rents an apartment or house, then it enters the reproduction of his/her labour power as an infrastructure, in which reproductive labour, family life, intimacy, and consumption take place. Information on social networking sites does not have the same status as a piece of land: human labour creates and updates it constantly, which enables its sale to targeted advertising clients. Advertising needs to be paid for as part of commodity prices. Ad departments that provide ad contents and users that provide targeting data and attention create targeted ads. Both activities are necessary forms of labour for the existence of such ads and their sale. They take place in space and time and thereby enable the accumulation of advertising capital and so have to be accounted for in a labour theory of value. As value is in substance labour and is measured by labour-time, advertising forms an important commodity-in-itself that as symbolic brand or ad ideology that hails the consumer becomes part of another commodity. Ads are thereby commodities-in-themselves and commodities-for-another-commodity.

Bruce Robinson (2015) argues that for Marx the realm of circulation involves unproductive labour and that therefore advertising is "part of the unproductive functions of selling and, whoever undertakes it, is paid out of value produced in productive functions" and that "no value-producing activity has to take place on Web 2.0 platforms for it to be possible for Google and Facebook to make the overwhelming bulk of their revenue". Robinson presents Marx's labour theory of value as homogenous and overlooks that there are at least three ways Marx uses the term *productive labour* and that the definitions are not always consistent and allow multiple interpretations. He takes one specific definition that excludes circulation from productive labour for granted and ignores that Marx considered transport labour as productive labour and that he also advanced the notion of the collective worker as productive worker. He gives an orthodox interpretation of Marx that believes in one true interpretation and does not see the complexities of Marx's writings.

César Bolaño and Eloy Vieira (2014) argue that Facebook users are unproductive and that "productive labour in SNSs is precisely the work done by employees, engineers, researchers and much other kind of professionals that produce statistics, interfaces and algorithms that make possible the constitution of the commodity audience". The difference to the just mentioned approaches is that Bolaño and Vieira put more weight on paid employees working for corporate social media.

Huws, Pasquinelli, Foley, Rigi and Prey, Robinson, and Bolaño and Vieira present a version of the Facebook rent argument, where users are in the last instance unproductive, although they attenuate this assessment by some contradictory formulations or concepts. Böhm et al. share the theoretical insight that Facebook users create surplus-value, are productive workers and exploited, but at the same time try to save the rent argument.

There are several reasons why I consider Facebook as a capitalist company and not a rentier, which also means that these are reasons why Facebook users are productive and exploited workers and not unproductive.

- A good that is rented out does not require constant production and reproduction; it can be rented out independently of labour because it does not objectify value:

  The owner of a picture, a piece of land, a lake, a building or a flat can rent out these properties independently of labour. S/he does not necessarily require labour for acquiring rent. Some goods that can be rented out can be turned into capital that is accumulated: the picture can be industrially reproduced and sold as commodity in order to accumulate ever more money. Facebook cannot make money if its users do not constantly use the platform and thereby produce data and attention. If all users quit Facebook, the company cannot make any profit. Without users' activities and online presence, Facebook cannot "rent out" anything in this case because it constantly requires the users' labour = usage activities in order to be able to sell something. Therefore Facebook does not rent out virtual space, but sells a commodity, in which users' attention and personal data is objectified. Users produce this commodity; Facebook exploits them and thereby accumulates capital. Facebook is not a rentier, but a capitalist company that exploits users.

- Capital accumulation requires the constant production of a commodity, surplus-value, and a surplus product as well as the constant sale of this commodity at a price that is higher than the investment costs, whereas rent-seeking does not require productive labour. Rent is a transfer of parts of profits that realise the value created by workers in capital accumulation processes:

Facebook invests money into production and constantly lets users produce data commodities in order to sell ever more advertisements and accumulate ever more capital. Facebook is first and foremost an advertising company: it lets its users produce ever more data and ever more commodities in order to accumulate ever more capital. Such a dynamic process of accumulation of use-values, surplus-labour, surplus-products, commodities, and money capital cannot be found in the case of a rentier. Facebook therefore is a capitalist company, not a rentier.

- Property that is rented out to capitalists primarily enters the capital accumulation process as fixed constant capital:

A company uses its leased building or piece of land/nature as a means of production that enters the capitalist production process that results in commodities. Facebook advertisements in contrast enter the capital accumulation cycle of other companies in the realm of circulation C'-M', where a specific commodity is sold. Facebook users are contemporary online equivalents of what Marx termed *transport workers*—their labour helps transporting use-value promises to themselves. Transport workers are productive workers who create surplus-value and are exploited.

- Renting is the rentier's sale of landed property to a renter that enables the latter's temporary access to and usage of the property:

I cannot resell my leased flat, garden, or car because the state's property laws guarantee the rentier's property rights and only provide a temporary usage right to me. I can therefore only use the leased properties as means of production if I start a business and cannot directly transform it into a commodity that I resell for accumulating capital. In contrast if I buy advertising space on Facebook, I own the content that I advertise. I can therefore start a business that accumulates capital by offering social media marketing to clients. I can sell the advertising spaces on Facebook, Twitter, Google, or YouTube that I acquire for this purpose to another person and can fill them with the content that the client provides to me in return for money s/he pays.

It is a tendency of capital that it tries to subsume all activities under it and to create ever more spheres of capital accumulation: "While capital struggles to subsume all of life under it, reducing all labours to value-producing, abstract (and hence productive) labour, the working class (or better, *humanity*) struggles to be *un*productive, to free its activities from value, to go *beyond value*" (Harvie 2005, 160–161). David Harvie understands "productive and unproductive labour as *opej* categories, as categories of struggle" (Harvie 2005, 160). Capital tries to make all work productive, i.e. to exploit it. This does not mean that it pays a wage; the existence and extension of prosumers' labour is an indication that unpaid work can be subsumed under capital and helps the latter to maximise profits. Commodification and capitalisation mean that capital tries to subsume ever more activities and realms of life under the law of value, i.e. to make humans work for a specific time in ways that favour capital's interests in accumulating profits. As value is measured in the form of labour-time, the capitalisation and commodification of society has resulted in "an immense battery of tests and examinations. [. . .] In more and more areas of life, economists, statisticians, bureaucrats, civil servants are struggling to devise and impose new metrics, frameworks by which performances can be judged and productivity measures" (Harvie 2005, 149, 151). We live in a society with all-present quantifications, evaluations, and performance metrics and measurements. The formation of corporate social media that use a targeted advertising-capital accumulation model is the attempt to make Internet use a productive (2, 3) and therefore exploited activity. It can only be resisted by making Internet use unproductive (2, 3), i.e. turning the Internet into a public and common good that guarantees the production and circulation of the communication commons independent of the commodity form and capital.

Figure 5.5 visualises some details of Facebook's capital accumulation process.

Fixed constant capital (e.g. buildings, machines) is capital that the capitalist acquires and fixes in the production process for a longer time period (Marx 1885, chapter 8). Circulating constant capital is in contrast a raw material

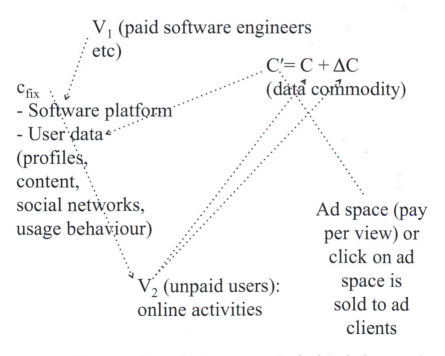

FIGURE 5.5   The commodity production process on Facebook (and other targeted advertising-based corporate social media)

that is immediately used up in production and must be renewed (Marx 1885, chapter 8). Facebook's paid employees (v1) produce the software platform that enters the production process as fixed capital that the users employ in order to create data (profile data, communication data, content, social network data, browsing behaviour data). Whenever a user (= unpaid worker, v2) is online on Facebook, s/he transfers parts of the value of the platform and of the value of his/her existing personal data to a data commodity and s/he creates new value in the form of newly spent online time that creates additional data that enters the data commodity C' in the form of stored data. The Facebook platform is a means of informational production—a fixed constant capital. It enables user labour that generates data. This data is stored and when a user accesses the platform, the stored data is used for generating the profile. So personal data as part of fixed constant capital remains fixed in the production process and enables user activity. The same data is also the starting point for the users' online activities on their profiles. They create new content based on existing content, contacts, and communications. Therefore personal data is simultaneously fixed constant capital and circulating constant capital—a means of production that enables information, communication, and networking and the resource based on and out of which user labour creates new data. On Facebook, circulating constant capital and fixed constant capital tend to converge.

The users' labour (= online activity) creates the value (the total time spent online by the user) and the new content (the newly generated and stored data) of the commodity. The whole commodity becomes part of Facebook's fixed capital that is reinvested in the production process: the existing data is used for organising the user's Facebook profile and is re-used in the creation of an updated user profile. The user's profile is stored in a database and updated by the user whenever s/he logs into Facebook or whenever s/he visits a website that is connected to Facebook.

An advertising client selects a specific number of users when setting up targeted ads on Facebook. The client buys specific portions of the screen display of specific users that only exist while the user is on Facebook, which means that the user generates these spaces by his/her online behaviour and the data s/he generates and has previously generated. Users produce advertising spaces themselves. These spaces are either sold as commodity when the users click on them (pay per click) or when they are online (pay per view). They are commodities in the moment that they are generated, i.e. the moment a targeted ad is algorithmically generated and visualised on the screen. In the pay-per-click mode, the question is if this commodity can be sold or not, i.e. to which degree/share of the presentations users click on ads. What is the value of a single ad space? It is the average number of minutes that a specific user group spends on Facebook divided by the average number of targeted ads that is presented to them during this time period. Facebook's ad clients fill the ads with their use-value promises that want to convince users to buy specific commodities. This means that the labour Facebook users perform enters the capital accumulation process of other companies in the realm of circulation, where commodities C′ are transformed into money capital M′ (C′-M′). Facebook users' labour is an online equivalent of transport work—their online activities help transport use-value promises to themselves. Marx considered transport workers as productive circulation workers. Facebook users are productive online circulation workers who organise the communication of advertising ideologies on the Internet.

5.5. Productive Labour as Wage Labour in the Digital Labour Debate

There are some scholars in the digital labour debate who argue that only wage labour is productive labour and that Facebook usage and other unpaid labour can therefore not be productive labour and a form of exploitation.

The argument itself is not new and was also directed against Dallas Smythe. Michael Lebowitz (1986, 165) argues that Smythe's approach is only a "Marxist-sounding communications theory". Marxism would assume that

> surplus-value in capitalism is generated in the direct process of production, the process where workers (having surrendered the property rights over the disposition of their labour-power) are *compelled* to work longer than is necessary to produce the equivalent of their wage. Perhaps it is for this reason that there is hesitation in accepting the conception that audiences work, are exploited, and produce surplus-value—in that it is a paradigm quite different to the Marxist paradigm.
>
> *Lebowitz 1986, 167*

Media capitalists would compete "for the expenditures of competing industrial capitalists" and help to "increase the commodity sales of industrial capitalists", and their profits would be "a share of the surplus-value of industrial capital" (Lebowitz 1986, 169). Smythe's audience commodity approach would advance an "entirely un-Marxian argument with un-Marxian conclusions" (Lebowitz 1986, 170). Richard Maxwell (1991, 40) argues that "Jhally and Livant misapplied certain propositions in the theory of value to a realm which may be relatively autonomous from the discipline of wage-labor" and that "wage-labor" is "the necessary element of labor control and exploitation in the trans-valuation of televiewing".

A specific version of the labour theory of value argues that only wage-workers in factories are productive workers, which implies that they are the only people exploited in capitalism and the only ones capable of making a revolution. Dallas Smythe wrote his *Blindspot* article also as a criticism of this approach that ignored aspects of communication. This is evident when he says that Baran and Sweezy in an idealist manner reduce advertising to a form of manipulation in the sales effort and when he criticises them for "rejecting expenses of circulation as unproductive of surplus" (Smythe 1977, 14). Baran and Sweezy developed a Keynesian theory that puts the main focus on monopolies rather than the exploitation of labour. Consequently, they reduce advertising to an unproductive attribute of monopoly—"the very offspring of monopoly capitalism" (Baran and Sweezy 1966, 122) that is one form of "surplus eaters" (127) and "merely a form of surplus absorption" (141). Smythe concluded that the "denial of the productivity of advertising is unnecessary and diversionary: a cul de sac derived from the pre-monopoly-capitalist stage of development, a dutiful but unsuccessful and inappropriate attempt at reconciliation with Capital" (Smythe 1977, 16).

In a criticism of "critical social media studies" that identifies me as main representative, James Reveley (2013) focuses on what he in the article's title terms "misuses of Marx". Reveley re-iterates Leibowitz's claims against Marx in the context of discussing my work. The key point that he stresses over and over again is that users are not exploited:

- "users of social media platforms are not exploited in the specifically Marxian sense" (Reveley 2013, 513).
- "I maintain that exploitation is unique to labor supplied under specifically capitalist conditions of production within the wage-relation" (Reveley 2013, 514).
- "the term exploitation should be reserved for labor supplied under specifically capitalist relations of production—namely, the sale of labor-power, the wage labor/capital nexus, and the anchoring of value creation within the capitalist labor process" (Reveley 2013, 525).
- "The error also risks obscuring the unique facets of worker exploitation within the wage relation's confines" (Reveley 2013, 531).

Reveley argues that social media only has secondary effects on labour power by increasing its skills, which could result in rising productivity that fosters capital accumulation and/or a resistant use of social media against the capitalist class. He uses a non-dialectical either/or logic and does not see that corporate social media's potential effects on labour-power do not logically exclude the possibility that users are exploited when using these tools. Corporate social media can enhance productivity that benefits capital, workers' skills of resistance, as well as the exploitation of unpaid labour at the same time.

Reveley totalises wage labour as the only realm of exploitation. The logical inference is that the unpaid labour of houseworkers or slaves is also not exploited. For Marx, the existence of surplus labour and a surplus product logically implies the existence of exploitation. Both exist in all cases, where individuals or groups stand in power relations to others, in which the dominated group creates a product or part of a product that it does not own itself, but that is owned by those for whom they produce. Exploitation means a more or less permanent separation and hierarchisation has taken place between producers and consumers, and that the latter can appropriate products and services of the former without themselves producing. [. . .] Exploitative social relations exist when non-producers are able to appropriate and consume (or invest) products and services of actual producers.

Mies 1986, 46

Marx (1857/1858b, 238) therefore says that in a class society, "labour will create alien property and property will command alien labour". Exploitation therefore exists not only if a wage-worker produces monetary profits for a capitalist: it also exists if a feudal worker produces 1,000 potatoes a week for his lord and 100 for himself; or a slave extracts 1 kilo of gold per week for a slave master; or a woman conducts 40 hours a week of cooking, child education, and laundry for a family, in which the husband contributes zero hours house work. In all these cases, a surplus-product and surplus-labour exist within class relations. Class relations are always relations of exploitation. Marx knew this circumstance very well and warned to conceive exploitation not just as a specifically capitalist phenomenon:

> Capital did not invent surplus labour. Wherever a part of society possesses the monopoly of the means of production, the worker, free or unfree, must add to the labour-time necessary for his own maintenance an extra quantity of labour-time in order to produce the means of subsistence for the owner of the means of production, whether this proprietor be an Athenian kaloz k'agadoz ['aristocrat'], an Etruscan theocrat, a civis romanus, a Norman baron, an American slave-owner, a Wallachian boyar, a modern landlord or a capitalist.
>
> *Marx 1867, 334–335*

Marx (1867, 675) defines the wage as "a certain quantity of money that is paid for a certain quantity of labour". Patriarchy, feudalism, and slavery are not over, but continue to exist within capitalism, where these forms of exploitation are mediated with wage labour and capitalists' monetary profits. Reveley is so much fixed on the wage labour–capital relation that he excludes the non-wage labour constituted in class relations from the category of exploitation. Consequently, houseworkers and slaves are for him not exploited.

Patriarchy and slavery are historical and contemporary realities of class society's history. Dominant classes try by all means to extract as much surplus-labour as possible that paying nothing at all by different means is a way of exploitation that they tend to foster. Forms of unpaid labour differ qualitatively: whereas slaves are threatened by being killed if they stop to work, houseworkers in patriarchal relations are partly coerced by physical violence and partly by affective commitments, and Facebook workers are coerced by the threat of missing social advantages (such as being invited to a friends' party) and monopoly power.[16]

Edward Comor (2014) makes an argument comparable to Reveley's: "For Marx, a fundamental condition for capital's ability to generate surplus-value is the worker's legally institutionalised freedom (i.e. her autonomy) to sell her labor power as a commodity in return for a wage" (Comor 2014, 248). Comor says that "abstract (waged) labor is crucial for the formal creation of value" (Comor 2014, 257) and that "surplus-value remains the outcome of capital's exploitation of waged labor" (Comor 2014, 258). He does not conceptualise exploitation beyond wage labour. Consequently, he never mentions the exploitation of houseworkers and other unpaid workers. A foundational assumption of Marxist feminism is that in capitalism there is the "*superexploitation* of non-wage labourers (women, colonies, peasants) upon which wage labour exploitation is possible" (Mies 1986, 48). Exploitation in the case of unpaid labour is appropriation "of the time and labour *necessary* for people's own survival or subsistence production. It is not compensated for by a wage, [. . .] but is mainly determined by force or coercive institutions" (Mies 1986, 48).

Comor writes that when I argue that Facebook users and other unpaid workers are super-exploited, I conflate knowledge work "with the formal economic process of exploiting wage workers" (Comor 2014, 249). I would conduct an analytical "totalisation of exploitative and value-creating relationships" (Comor 2014, 249). One can, however, turn this logic around and argue that the problem is not a "totalisation" that is grounded in assumptions made by Marxist feminism, but a reductionism that only accepts wage labour as a form of exploitation.

Comor (2014, 258) argues that the argument that considering only wage labour as productive is sexist and racist is "laudable but analytically weak" and is not "helpful in a debate concerning the economics of value and exploitation". The labour theory of value is, however, not a purely analytical tool for intellectual debates. For Marx, theory was an intellectual tool for political struggles. The labour theory of value wants to define who is exploited and who is not in order to identify actual or potential revolutionary subjects. Questions of unpaid labour, the unemployed, precarious workers, patriarchy, and racism matter for a labour theory of value in order to overcome a banal concept of the revolutionary class that focuses on Western, white, urban, male industrial workers.

"It is, in fact, the form in which labor power is used to produce other commodities that yields value and this form is comprehensible only through the use of money" (Comor 2014, 258). This formulation is crucial for Comor's approach. Consequently, he argues that "[u]nwaged concrete prosumer labor therefore cannot *itself* produce surplus-value and, as such, the digital prosumer's assumed economic exploitation also is false" (Comor 2014, 258). So Comor's logic is similar to Reveley's: only wage labour is productive labour and creates value and can be exploited by capital.

"Fuchs' modification of value theory has generated yet another version of idealism" because if "value is understood in the absence of its objectified (monetary) form (as in Fuchs and others), the value produced in capitalist political economies is devoid of a [. . .] form of value. In capitalism, for a commodity to have an objectively discernable value, the use of both labor power and money are required" (Comor 2014, 259). When Comor stresses over and over that "*only money concretely demonstrates and mediates the value process*" (Comor 2014, 257), then he does not seem to mean the triviality that capitalism is a system of exploitation that accumulates ever more money-capital and that accumulation of capital is therefore not only the accumulation of money and the on-going exploitation of (paid, unpaid and precarious) labour, but also the accumulation of money. It rather seems that he wants to express with different formulations that only wage labour produces value and is therefore the only form of productive and exploited labour in capitalism. But the exploitation of wage labour is in capitalism in general and due to outsourcing and crowdsourcing today in particular mediated with the exploitation of unpaid labour and with pre-capitalist modes of exploitation such as patriarchy and slavery.

Comor's internal logic of arguments is not very consistent. He says on the one hand that "the digital prosumer's assumed economic exploitation also is false" (Comor 2014, 258) and that unpaid prosumer labour "does not create surplus-value" (Comor 2014, 263). But on the other hand only three years earlier he wrote that "plugged-in, active prosumers [. . .] seems more likely to become, at the very least, the subject of ongoing exploitation" (Comor 2011, 322).

Comor is suspicious of everyone using the term *prosumption* and tends to lump the Tofflerites together with Marxist proponents of a digital labour theory of value. He says there is a "remarkable coming together of politically disparate analysts" and that "both mainstream and progressive theorists have arrived at similar conclusions regarding the primary agent of this new social order: the prosumers or co-creator" (Comor 2011, 316).

Self-service gas stations, McDonalds, and Ikea are examples that show that prosumption is neither necessarily informational nor that it is new. Social media prosumption, however, erects a real-time system of visibility of users' activities that enables Internet companies to constantly update the users' data in their databases. For doing so, they collect data about users internally on their platforms and externally from other spaces on the Internet. In the case of self-service gas stations, McDonalds, and Ikea, the consumer conducts parts of the service she bought herself (filling in gas, being the waiter, assembling furniture). Wage costs are thereby reduced. The extra-work is part of the commodity the user purchases for consumption. On Facebook, however, the consumers of the produced commodity are advertising clients. The user creates a commodity not for himself, but for advertisers who offer targeted ads to him/her in order to try to make him buy advertised commodities. So there is a difference between the mentioned examples and Facebook prosumption. Offline prosumption processes can only make use of limited consumer labour time, whereas online there is a surveillance system that renders almost all activities performed on a platform and beyond on the broader Internet visible, storable, commodifiable, and marketable. Whereas in Comor's (2014, 254) example of the US Pillsbury Bake-Off, users submit recipes that are then offered in the form of a book that helps marketing Pillsbury products, Pillsbury cannot or only to a limited extent get hold of information about what consumers cook at home from day to day. On Facebook in contrast all activities and interests about cooking and many other interests are profiled. Real-time personalised advertising thereby becomes possible.

All of these examples have in common that capitalists aim to reduce wage costs by outsourcing parts of or the full commodity production process to consumers in order to try to increase profits. Digital prosumption is neither entirely new nor entirely old. Prosumption has dialectically developed over time. There are dialectics of continuity and discontinuity of capitalism and technology.

Edward Comor (2014, 245–246, 263) makes a plea for "precision" and "rigour" in the digital labour debate. The question that arises is, however, if it is a precise and rigorous analysis to describe exploitation as a single relationship. Capitalism is a complex mode of production, in which capital organises exploitation in the form of relations to wage labour, non-wage labour, precarious labour, unpaid labour, pre-capitalist modes of production (such as patriarchy and slavery), agricultural/industrial/informational modes of the organisation of the productive forces, imperialism, a global division of labour etc. (Fuchs 2014a, 2014c).

5.6. Politics, Ideology, and Fetishism in the Context of Digital Labour

The distinction between productive and unproductive labour is not just an analytical but also a political tool that identifies important and unimportant actors in class struggles that can bring about transformations of society. The notion of unproductive labour carries the connotation that those who are signified as such are unimportant, peripheral, or even parasitic elements in political change processes that are necessary for overcoming capitalism.

Marxist feminists have long resisted the reduction of housework to peripheral, secondary, or unproductive activities. They have argued that reproductive work in capitalism is productive labour. A few examples shall illustrate this circumstance, although this chapter does not allow space for a detailed discussion. Mariarosa Dalla Costa and Selma James (1972, 30) challenged the orthodox Marxist assumption that reproductive work is "outside social productivity". In contrast a socialist feminist position would have to argue that "domestic work produces not merely use values, but is essential to the production of surplus-value" and that the "productivity of wage slavery" is "based on unwaged slavery" in the form of productive "social services which capitalist organization transforms into privatized activity, putting them on the backs of housewives" (Dalla Costa and James 1972, 31). Zillah Eisenstein (1979, 31) argues that the gender division of labour guarantees "a free labor pool" and "a cheap labor pool".

Maria Mies (1986, 37) says that women are exploited in a triple sense: "they are exploited [. . .] by men and they are exploited as housewives by capital. If they are wage-workers they are also exploited as wage-workers". Capitalist production would be based on the

> *superexploitation* of non-wage labourers (women, colonies, peasants) upon which wage labour exploitation then is possible. I define their exploitation as super-exploitation because it is not based on the appropriation (by the capitalist) of the time and labour over and above the "necessary" labour time, the *surplus* labour, but of the time and labour *necessary* for people's own survival or subsistence production. It is not compensated for by a wage.
>
> *Mies 1986, 48*

Mies also reminds us that female productivity is the precondition of male productivity in the sense that "women *at all times* will be the producers of new women and men, and [. . .] without this production all other forms and modes of production lose their sense" (Mies 1986, 58). Subsistence production would create the basic use-values for human survival—it would produce life itself. It would largely be women's non-wage labour that produces life and is thereby productive for capital (Mies 1986, 50). Leopoldina Fortunati (1995) argues that reproductive labour is productive because "it produces and reproduces the individual as a commodity" (70) by "producing and reproducing labor-power" (70) and "the use-value of labor-power" (69).

One should mention that a different version of Marxist feminism disagrees with the position just outlined and argues that capitalist patriarchy works by excluding women's reproductive labour from value generation and rendering it unproductive. Roswitha Scholz calls this the value-dissociation hypothesis (*Wertabspaltungsthese*). Abstract labour could only create value by dissociating a sphere of emotions, house work, and sensuality that is constructed as being typically female, rendered inferior, and excluded:

> The value-dissociation hypothesis claims [. . .] a "dissociation" of the feminine, housework etc. from value, abstract labour and the related forms of rationality that attributes specific qualities such as sensuality, emotionality etc. that are connoted as female to women; the man in contrast stands for intellectual power, strength of character, courage, etc. The man was under modern development equated with culture, the woman with nature.
>
> *Scholz 2000, 9, translation from German*[17]

The Endnotes Collective (2013) makes a comparable argument: The activity of turning the raw materials equivalent to the wage into labour-power takes place *in a separate sphere from the production and circulation of values*. These necessary non-labour activities do not produce value, not because of their concrete characteristics, but rather, because they take place in a sphere of the capitalist mode of production which is not directly mediated by the form of value. [. . .] There must be an exterior to value in order for value to exist. Similarly, for labour to exist and serve as the measure of value, there must be an exterior to labour (we will return to this in part two). While the autonomist feminists would conclude that every activity which reproduces labour-power produces value, we would say that, for labour-power to have a value, some of these activities have to be cut off or dissociated from the sphere of value production.

Both Scholz and the Endnotes Collective share with other Marxist feminists' the concern about capitalism's exploitation of women in reproductive labour. However, the political problem associated with this connection of reproductive labour to value as a dissociation is that it reproduces the dichotomies between productive and reproductive labour, paid and unpaid, public and private, sex and gender that capitalist patriarchy has constructed in order to control and legitimatise women's exploitation and domination.

Value is the average amount of time it takes to produce a commodity. Labour-power is a necessary constituent for the existence of value, the commodity, and profit. It does not simply exist, but needs to be permanently reproduced by reproductive labour. The average number of hours required for the reproduction of labour power must therefore be taken into account when calculating the value of a commodity. An example:

It takes on average 10 workers working each an hour to produce a car. We assume they have an average hourly wage of £10 and that the average profit that can be achieved per car is £900. The relationship of surplus to necessary labour is therefore 900 / 100 = 9. This means that unpaid labour is in this case nine times as large as paid labour. Going back from the price to the value level, this means that in the example only 6 minutes per hour are paid and 54 minutes are unpaid. Given the combined labour of 10 workers needed for the production of one car, we have a total of 540 minutes of unpaid labour for the production of one car. We also assume that they all have families, in which women are responsible for all the housework. This means that the capitalist not just consumes 540 minutes of unpaid labour for the production of one car, but also 10 times one hour = 10 hours of unpaid reproductive labour that constitutes and re-creates the labour power of the 10 workers. Therefore the total production time for one car is not 10 hours of working time, but 20 hours or 1,200 minutes. Out of these 1,200 minutes, only 60 minutes are paid working time, whereas 1,140 minutes are unpaid labour time of wageworkers and reproductive workers.

It could, however, be the case that in a household the total reproductive labour sustains not just one, but two or several wage workers. In this case the total number of reproductive labour hours needs to be divided by the number of wageworkers in the household.

Lebowitz's (1986) criticism of Smythe bases its argument on three specific assumptions:

1   That industrial capital is the central form of capital.
2   That only work performed under the command of industrial capital is productive labour and creates surplus-value.
3   That only wage labour can be exploited.

The immediate theoretical and political consequences of this logic of argumentation are the following:
1   Commercial media are subsumed to industrial capital.
2   Slaves, house workers, and other unpaid workers are not exploited.
3   The wage and non-wage labour performed under the command of media capital is unproductive. Media companies cannot exploit workers because they create products and services that are part of the circulation sphere of capitalism.

The political question that Lebowitz's argument poses is if one wants to share the implications of a wage-centric theory of value that unpaid workers cannot be exploited. For me, there is also a historical reason why I think one should not characterise Facebook users as unproductive or minor productive: Soviet Marxism. In the Soviet Union, the notions of productive and unproductive labour were at the heart of the calculation of national wealth. The Material Product System (MPS) was the Soviet equivalent of the Gross Domestic Product (GDP). The MPS was introduced under Stalin in the 1920s (Árvay 1994). It only considered physical work in agriculture, industry, construction, transport, supply, and trade as productive, whereas services, administration, public services, education, culture, and housework were seen as unproductive work that does not contribute to national income, but rather consumes it (Noah 1965). Women had especially high employment shares in medicine (physicians, nurses), schools, light industry (e.g. textiles), child-care, culture, retail, and catering (Katz 1997). The Soviet wage system privileged domains such as heavy industry, construction, energy, metalwork, and mining because the MPS considered them to contribute strongly to national wealth and productivity (Katz 1997). The feminised employment sectors just mentioned were seen as secondary and unproductive and thus had lower wage levels. A gender bias was "built into perceptions of productivity" (Katz 1997, 446). The gender division of labour and wages was "hidden behind a screen of officially proclaimed 'equal participation in the national economy'" (Katz 1997, 446). The reality was that "the Soviet wage-structure [. . .] was in itself male-biased" (Katz 1997, 446).

The notion of unproductive labour has historically been used for signifying reproductive work, service work, and feminised work as secondary and peripheral. It has thereby functioned as ideological support mechanism for the discrimination of women. This circumstance should caution us to be careful in whom one analytically characterises as "unproductive", i.e. not creating surplus-value in the capitalist production process.

One should not be mistaken by the application of the rent argument to Facebook and other corporate social media: speaking of Facebook as a rent-seeking organisation implies that its users are unproductive, that they do not create value and are unimportant in class struggles. Approaches that say that Facebook usage is unproductive because advertising is not part of the sphere of production, but located in the sphere of circulation, also imply that users' activities are parasitic and help eat up the surplus-value created by wage workers in other parts of the economy. Some try to combine the rent-argument with the assumption that Facebook users are exploited, but the two concepts of rent and exploitation go uneasily together.

Conceptualising somebody as unproductive is not just an analytical term; it is also a slur and quite emotive. Nobody wants to be called unproductive as it carries the connotation of being useless and parasitic. Saying that Facebook users do not create value and that Facebook is a rentier that consumes the value produced by wageworkers employed by other companies politically implies that users are unimportant in class struggles in the digital age. Wageworkers in the non-digital economy are seen as the true locus of power. Hence recommended political measures to be taken focus on how to organise these workers in unions, parties, or other organisations and struggles for higher wages and better wage labour conditions. Users and Facebook are seen as being outside the locus of class struggle or only as something that unions and parties can also use in wage labour struggles.

Capitalism is grounded in an antagonism between the commodity's value and exchange-value on the one side and value and use-value on the other side. Moishe Postone argues that in capitalism, value is "abstract, general, homogeneous", whereas use-value is "concrete, particular, material" (Postone 2003, 90). The commodity logic fetishises the concrete and veils value as an abstract social relation that underlies the commodity. In commodity fetishism, the abstract dimension (of e.g. money) appears as impersonal, immaterial, and rootless, whereas the concrete dimension (of a commodity) appears as a material thing without social relations (Postone 2003, 90–91). Both dimensions "appear to be natural rather than social. The abstract dimension appears in the form of abstract, universal, 'objective', natural laws; the concrete dimension appears as pure 'thingly' nature. That is, the social relations specific to capitalism do not appear to be social and historical at all" (Postone 2003, 91).

Postone (1980, 109) says that in the value form capitalism's "dialectical tension between value and use-value" is doubled in the appearance of money as abstract and the commodity as concrete. Capitalism requires for its existence both money and commodities, value and use-value, abstract and concrete labour. Money mediates commodity-exchange, so it cannot exist without the logic of commodities. Commodities are made for being exchanged. Money is the general equivalent of commodity exchange. So commodities cannot exist without exchange-value and a general equivalent. Another way of expressing the dialectic of commodity and money is to say that the sphere of commodity production exists in relation to the sphere of circulation and vice-versa. Commodity fetishism is a form of appearance, in which the abstract sociality of commodities is split off from its concreteness: only the immediate concrete (the good one consumes, the money one holds in the hand) is taken as reality. This immediate concrete obscures the existence of the more abstract, not directly visible social relations behind the immediate phenomena.

Postone says that in specific ideologies, the dual character of the commodity of use-value and value is

> "doubled" in the form of money (the manifest form of value) and the commodity (the manifest form of use-value). Although the commodity as a social form embodies both value and use-value, the effect of this externalization is that the commodity appears only as its use-value dimension, as purely material. Money, on the other hand, appears as the sole repository of value, as the source and locus of the purely abstract, rather than as the externalized manifest form of the value dimension of the commodity form itself.
>
> *Postone 2003, 91*

Postone argues that ideology often naturalises the commodity fetish. It would be based on the "notion that the concrete is 'natural'" and that the "natural" is "more 'essential' and closer to origins" (Postone 1980, 111). "Industrial capital then appears as the linear descendent of 'natural' artisanal labor", "industrial production" appears as "a purely material, creative process" (Postone 1980, 110). Ideology then separates industrial capital and industrial labour from the sphere of circulation, exchange, and money that is seen as "parasitic" (Postone 1980, 110). Such ideology is a one-sided "critique" of capitalism that sees the sphere of circulation as totality of capitalism, biologistically inscribes non-productivity into circulation and into capitalism, and excludes technology and industry—that are perceived as productive—from capitalism. In this ideology, capitalism "appeared to be only its manifest abstract dimension, which was in turn held responsible for the economic, social, and cultural changes associated with the rapid development of modern industrial capitalism" (Postone 2003, 93).

The negative changes, dislocations, and deterritorialisations associated with capitalism, such as urbanisation, proletarianisation, individualisation, technification, and detraditionalisation, are in commodity-fetishistic ideology identified with the abstract side of capitalism that is perceived as the powerful universality of capitalism, socialism, or some other phenomenon. "Capitalism appeared to be only in its manifest abstract dimension which, in turn, was responsible for the whole range of concrete social and cultural changes associated with the rapid development of modern industrial capitalism" (Postone 1980, 112).

Horkheimer and Adorno argue that "money and mind, the exponents of circulation, are [. . .] an image which power uses to perpetuate itself" (Horkheimer and Adorno 1944/2002, 141). Advertising is a creation and circulation of information associated with a commodity for assisting the realisation of money-profit. It gives mind and meaning to the commodity in order to help transforming it and bringing about its metamorphosis into money. In advertising, mind and money come together as exponents of circulation.

The two poles of the distinction between productive and unproductive labour can easily be associated with the dualities concrete/abstract, material/immaterial, use-value/exchange-value, and production/circulation. If labour that has an important role in the circulation and metamorphosis from commodities into money—such as audience or digital labour—is described as unproductive, then this is not just a normative statement about what one considers important and unimportant or not so important in class struggle. Denying that audience labour and digital labour are exploited is also a reduction of productivity to the concrete dimension of capitalism and labour—commodities that have a concrete use-value and labour that has a concrete result in the form of wages. An abstract dimension of capitalism and labour that is crucial for the existence of both is split-off and downgraded. The abstract dimensions are the commodities' abstract use-value promise, labour's abstraction from the wage and from the experience as labour that comes about when it blurs into the experience of fun and play.

The theoretical denial of digital labour's productivity is the ideological reflection of the inverse commodity fetishism (Fuchs and Sevignani 2013; Fuchs 2014a) characteristic for corporate social media: Digital labour on Facebook is abstract in that it is not tied to a wage and that the commodity status of data and Facebook's commodity form are not immediately visible to the user. The abstract status of labour and the commodity that cannot be directly experienced by the user is veiled by the pseudo-concreteness of free access to the platform, social benefits, and a playful atmosphere. Commodity fetishism appears in an inverse form (Fuchs and Sevignani 2013; Fuchs 2014a)—the gift and the social hide the actuality of exploitation and commodification. The denial of the reality of Facebook's abstractions is not just an ideology in theory, but also the fetish that enables social media companies' very capital accumulation model: Facebook creates the impression that users are free and not exploited and that the platform is a gift without commodity logic in order to maximise its users and profits. Hiding the commodity form behind the social and the gift is big business.

5.7. Conclusion

This chapter has questioned the division between informational/industrial labour, unproductive/productive labour, and production/circulation. Capitalism has differentiated itself and become more complex. The boundaries between established categories of industrial capitalism such as working time/leisure time, production/circulation/consumption, office and factory/home and private/public have become more porous/liquid. Capitalists aim at intensifying and extending exploitation by trying to make people work more hours and more intensively across the boundaries of the dualities characteristic for Fordist capitalism. This new development is neither total nor does it supplant capitalist exploitation or the existence of industrial and agricultural labour. But one has to recognise that more and more (especially younger) people work under liquefied conditions and that Marxist political economy therefore needs to take account of these developments.

David Harvey (2014, 114) writes in this context:

> In socialist theory, of course, it has traditionally been the industrial proletariat (the "productive" labourers) within the overall division of labour that has been favoured as the vanguard of revolutionary transformation. Bank clerks, domestic workers and street cleaners have never been thought of as revolutionary agents whereas miners, car workers, steelworkers and even schoolteachers have. Most of these dualisms turn out to be crude distinctions that have limited purchase in helping us to understand an increasingly complex and intricate world that is constantly subject to revolutionary transformation.

David Harvey has successfully fought against the exclusion of space, urban space, global space, and geography from radical and Marxist theory. After many decades, these dimensions have been recognised as having a quite crucial role in capitalism and society. They have, however, become a new orthodoxy. Still too often questions of communication are not taken serious in Marxist theory and are considered as being of secondary importance and as being superstructural. When I asked David Harvey as part of the audience discussion of his talk at the Dangerous Ideas for Dangerous Times Festival 2013 on June 1, 2013, in London, how his theory relates to communication and why communication is not a central aspect of his conceptualisation of space, he answered that the Arab Spring was not a Facebook revolution, but took place on the street and that there is too much hype about social media. In this instance he reproduced the dualistic logic that he criticises in the passage just cited: he considered communication and online space as secondary and reducible to the realms of urban space and offline political action. I am not trying to make the point that Facebook or Twitter were determinative in the Arab Spring, but rather that Marxist theorists are often too dismissive of communication and that we need to take it more into account and recognise communication as a crucial dimension of Marxist theory that is not less important than space and time. In society, humans work and communicate, and work by communicating and communicate by working, which takes a certain time and requires a spatial organisation. Time, space, and communication are foundationally connected and are the most important dimensions of the development process of matter in society. You are never too old to use social media, but it comes as no surprise that older radical theorists such as David Harvey, Slavoj Žižek, Jürgen Habermas, Terry Eagleton, or Noam Chomsky do not give a lot of attention to aspects of contemporary media and communications that they do not use a lot themselves. I am not trying to make the argument that digital, mobile, and social media and knowledge labour make everything new, or that they are forms of immaterial labour that constitute new communist potentials. I rather think that information, communication, and the Internet are important dimensions of contemporary capitalism that have an antagonistic character that oscillates between repressive actuality and immanent-transcendent potentials so that more attention needs to be given by Marxist scholarship and theory to these issues.

My argument in this chapter has been that the concept of rent is mistaken for understanding the political economy of Facebook and that Facebook users are productive transport workers who communicate advertising ideologies that make use-value promises. Their activities are productive labour (1, 2, 3). Politics for the digital age need to consider users as political subjects. Unions, organisations of the Left, and struggles are nothing that should be left to wageworkers, but need to be extended to digital media users. Pirate parties have understood this circumstance better than the orthodox wage labour fetishistic parts of the Left, but they have not well understood that the exploitation of digital labour is connected to the commodification of the commons that include the communication commons and that as a consequence Internet politics need to be connected to the critique of the political economy of capitalism as a whole. So whereas the orthodox part of the Left tends to dismiss users as politically unimportant and to neglect Internet politics, Pirate parties see users as the only political subjects.

The only feasible political way forward is to create unions and organisations of users that are connected and part of a broader political Left. For doing so, the orthodox part of the Left needs to overcome its ignorance of and technophobic biases against the Internet and users need to perceive themselves as being ripped off by Internet companies. We need social media unions and a fusion of Pirate parties and left-wing parties.

Some people argue that if wage-workers in classical industries go on strike, then society comes to a halt, whereas cultural workers cannot have the same effect, which would show that they are less productive, powerful, and important. Raymond Williams was once asked if he did not concede that a strike of novelists and people working for "television, radio and press [. . .] would not be comparable to major strikes in the docks, mines or power stations. The workers in these industries have the capacity to disrupt the whole fabric of social life, so decisive is the importance of their productive activity" (Williams 1979, 354). The question implies that cultural workers are rather unimportant and unproductive. Williams answered: "After all, stoppages of electrical power or oil would now make life impossible in the very short terms yet it is obvious enough historically that our society didn't possess them until recently, yet life could be sustained by other methods" (Williams 1979, 355). So Williams' argument is that given these activities are historical achievements of industrial societies and we know that life was possible without them, alternatives can be organised. He continued to say that if half the population were active and employed in producing and handling information, as is the case in many societies today, then "an information strike would call the maintenance of human life *in that social order* very quickly into question" (Williams 1979, 355). Williams rejects a separation of agricultural and industrial labour as primary, productive, and base on the one side and information work as secondary, unproductive, and superstructure on the other side. In contemporary societies both would be so important that workers going on strike could cause serious disruption.

That Facebook users are productive workers means that they have the power to bring corporate social media to a standstill. If users go on strike, then Facebook immediately loses money. If Facebook's wageworkers go on strike, the platform is still online and can be further operated for exploiting users. Users are economically powerful because they create economic value. Organising a collective Facebook strike or shifting to alternative non-commercial platforms is a refusal of digital labour. Besides unionisation and online strikes, also policy-oriented measures are feasible in order to strengthen the protection of users from capitalist exploitation. Ad block software is a tool that deactivates advertisements on the websites a user visits. It can either be used as add-on to web browsers or is automatically integrated. Using ad block software is digital class struggle: it disables Facebook and others' monetisation of personal data by blocking targeted ads. Think of a legal requirement that makes ad block the standard option in all web browsers: users would be empowered because commodification of data would not be the standard, but an opt-in chosen by the users if they turn off the ad blocker. A useful complementary legal measure is to require all Internet platforms to deactivate targeted and other forms of advertising and to make users opt-in if they want to enable such mechanisms.

Large-scale ad blockage has been discussed in the form of Do Not Track cookies. Do Not Track is a software mechanism that if activated tells websites not to collect and use users' personal data and thereby disables targeted advertising. The EU Article 29 Data Protection Working Party stresses:

> The WP 29 is aware of a number of different mechanisms which will allow users to provide meaningful consent for tracking their web surfing behaviour. One of the most promising initiatives regarding consent mechanisms is the work done by the W3C on the Do Not Track (DNT) protocol. [. . .] The WP 29 is of the opinion that a global DNT mechanism could be a very efficient way to deal with user consent for the tracking of their web surfing behaviour across different websites. [. . .] However, such consent can only be provided if users of all browsers have made an active and informed choice to allow or disallow the tracking. Such a choice could be offered in a manner similar to the browser selection tool in an operating

system. A second essential condition for DNT to meet the requirements of European data protection law is that a DNT-setting in a browser means that users should no longer be tracked, instead of just not being shown targeted advertisements. DNT should imply that no user data are collected, retained, processed and shared anymore, with the exception of information strictly necessary to provide the service explicitly requested by the subscriber or user. It must be clear that data from a user with an active DNT-setting cannot be used for purposes such as "market research" and "product development".[18]

One question about the Do Not Track protocol is if browsers should implement it as automatically activated or deactivated. If one assumes that users value being in control of their privacy settings, then a point can be made for an automatic activation in web browsers. Opt-in is also a stronger form of consent than opt-out. Opt-out assumes that users agree to certain data processing even if they do not really know about it. Opt-in on the other hand can better guarantee that consensus is explicit, unambiguous, and specific. Another issue is that the Do Not Track protocol sends information to websites that a user does not wish to be tracked. The technical task of not collecting and storing data about such a user is, however, accomplished by the website itself. If a website has commercial interest in targeting users with ads, one can imagine that it may not automatically be inclined to stop collecting data about users. Therefore if Do Not Track should have some effect, legal measures are needed that require all websites not to collect data about users for commercial purposes if they have the Do Not Track protocol activated. To enforce such a standard, adequate penalties may be needed.

In a poll conducted in 2011 in the United States, 81 per cent of the respondents said they wanted to add their names to Do Not Track lists.[19] In an Australian study conducted by the Personal Information Project, 95 per cent of the respondents agreed to the item that "there should be a law requiring Web sites and applications to provide a 'do-not-track' option that would prevent them from gathering information about people".[20] Hoofnagle et al.'s (2012) study showed that 66 per cent of the users in a survey (N = 1,203) said that they never or hardly ever found online ads useful. In a 2012 Pew Internet & American Life Project survey, 68 per cent of the respondents said they did not like targeted ads.[21]

Blocking advertisements is not popular everywhere, especially not in the advertising industry that with the help of targeted and behavioural advertising forms the heart of the commercial Internet. The Interactive Advertising Bureau is "comprised of more than 500 leading media and technology companies that are responsible for selling 86 per cent of online advertising in the United States" and "is dedicated to the growth of the interactive advertising marketplace, of interactive's share of total marketing spend, and of its members' share of total marketing spend".[22] Its CEO Randall Rothenberg said at the IAB 2012 Leadership Meeting:

Political activists have infiltrated a body called the World Wide Web Consortium (W3C). [. . .] And they are attempting to encode specific forms of Do Not Track technologies into browsers that will create a potential for the global blacklisting of specific of legitimate news, entertainment, and commerce sites. [. . .] powerful regulators inside the European Commission are recommending the passage of a "Right to Be Forgotten", that's what they call it—a "Right to Be Forgotten", which will require all owners of electronic databases of any sort to remove any information that consumers deem personal. [. . .] And if the EU passes it, it has impact on companies operating in America. [. . .] [This] can kill your company.[23]

The Digital Advertising Alliance argues that Do Not Track should be an opt-in mechanism because it hopes that users would then hardly use or overlook it. It masks this suggestion with the claim that it strengthens consumer privacy: "For this to be workable for the business community in a way that provides consumers with a choice but also allows responsible businesses to continue to act responsibly and benefit consumers, we'd want to make sure the setting is consistent and off by default"[24] (Stuart Ingis, Counsel for the Digital Advertising Alliance). The suggestion shows that progressive digital politics should argue for standard activation of Do Not Track in all web browsers.

The advertising industry is afraid of ad block software and similar mechanisms. This is an indication that struggles against the commercial character of media and culture need to see social media as a sphere of production, not just circulation. The commercial Internet is not just a sphere of commodity ideologies and sales; it is also a sphere of the exploitation of labour. Those who are concerned about workers' rights therefore need to take users' realities as exploited workers seriously. Exploitation is not tied to earning a wage, but extends into broad realms of society. Class struggles need to extend from factories and offices to Google, Facebook, and Twitter. The theory of digital labour is an ally of users, whereas the digital rent concept and related approaches are a slur that does not side with the interest of users and denigrates them as unproductive and unimportant in class struggles.

Part II of this book has looked at temporal aspects of social media's cultural political economy. In this context I have especially explored the concept of labour time. Users of corporate social media are workers whose labour is exploited. All usage time on platforms such as Facebook, Google, YouTube, Twitter, Pinterest, Instagram, Weibo, Renren, etc. is productive labour time that generates value. Capitalist Internet companies transform this value into monetary profits. Space-time is an integrated dimension of matter; matter is organised in space and time. Space evolves in time and time is organised in space. Social space can only be organised through human interactions. There is therefore an inherent interconnection of communication and social space. Whereas part II of this book has focused on temporal aspects, part III will outline spatial dimensions of social media's cultural political economy. Digital labour is organised in the form of an international division of digital labour (IDDL) that I analyse in chapter 6. China's economy has played an increasingly important role in global capitalism. In the Internet economy it becomes evident that Chinese platforms such as Baidu, QQ, Taobao, Sina, Hao123, Weibo, Tmall, Sohu, 360, 163, and Soso are among the world's most accessed WWW sites. Chapter 7 will analyse the role of Chinese social media in capitalism's global political economy, which also requires to outline how we can understand China's economy, the role of capitalism in China, and the connection of the Chinese economy to global capitalism.

Notes

1 Teixeira and Rotta (2012) introduce the notions of knowledge-commodities and knowledge-rent. Their typical examples concern the sale of knowledge, not social media.
2 http://www.forbes.com/sites/jacquelynsmith/2013/04/09/the-worlds-most-reputable-companies-2/ (accessed on June 5, 2013).
3 http://mashable.com/2011/09/30/wasting-time-on-facebook/ (accessed on January 7, 2014).
4 http://www.quora.com/Facebook-company/What-are-the-average-working-hours-per-day-for-a-Facebook-engineer (accessed on January 7, 2014).
5 http://gigaom.com/2012/08/13/facebooks-number-of-servers-soar-to-an-estimated-180k/ (accessed on June 3, 2013).
6 Ibid.
7 "Amazon: £7bn Sales, No UK Corporation Tax." *The Guardian Online.* April 4, 2012. http://www.guardian.co.uk/technology/2012/apr/04/amazon-british-operation-corporation-tax. "Google, Amazon, Starbucks: The Rise of 'Tax Sharing'". *BBC Online.* December 4, 2012. http://www.bbc.co.uk/news/magazine-20560359.
8 "Should We Boycott the Tax-Avoiding Companies?" *The Guardian Online.* Shortcuts Blog. October 17, 2012. http://www.guardian.co.uk/business/shortcuts/2012/oct/17/boycotting-tax-avoiding-companies.
9 "Google and Auditor Recalled by MPs to Answer Tax Questions." *The Guardian Online.* May 1, 2013. http://www.guardian.co.uk/technology/2013/may/01/google-parliament-tax-questions.
10 "Starbucks, Google and Amazon Grilled over Tax Avoidance." *BBC Online.* November 12, 2012. http://www.bbc.co.uk/news/business-20288077.
11 In the UK, the main rate of corporation tax that applies for profits exceeding £1,500,000 was reduced from 28 per cent in 2010 to 26 per cent in 2011, 24 per cent in 2012, 23 per cent in 2013, and 21 per cent in 2014.
12 Ibid.
13 Facebook Inc., SEC Filings, Form 10-K 2012, http://www.sec.gov/Archives/edgar/data/1326801/000132680113000003/fb-12312012x10k.htm.
14 Data source: http://www.alexa.com.
15 According to http://www.internetworldstats.com/stats.htm, the latest available world population count was 2,405,518,376 on June 3, 2013.
16 Reveley also argues that I am an imperialist: "Fuchs' assertion that social media users suffer unbridled exploitation necessarily results in overestimating the rate of exploita-

tion in the developed world relative to the underdeveloped world. [...] Oppositional political activities should prioritise the most exploitative sites of labor, so saying that social media users are infinitely exploited makes developed societies the locations where resistance to capitalism is most urgently needed. If anything, globalisation has heightened imperialism, so this results in a retrogressive, core country-centric style of radical politics. It is as distastefully imperialistic as the world system itself" (Reveley 2013, 524). In the book *Digital Labour and Karl Marx* (Fuchs 2014a, see also Fuchs 2014c), I have described how the digital media industry is entangled into a global network of exploited digital labour that includes mineral-mining slaves in Africa, Fordist assemblage workers, labour-aristocratic software engineers, precarious knowledge workers, unpaid users of corporate Internet platforms, and others. Digital capital exploits a unity of diverse forms of low-paid, relatively high-paid, precarious, and unpaid digital workers. Given the networked, complex, and global forms of the exploitation of digital labour, it would be short-sighted to focus the political struggle on one form of exploitation. In fact, the only feasible strategy is to question, challenge, and struggle against all forms of exploitation. I have never suggested that one should only focus on the struggle on one form of exploitation. All forms of unpaid labour are infinitely exploited. Marxist feminists expressed this circumstance by arguing that unpaid labour is "superexploitation of non-wage labourers" (Mies 1986, 48). Revelly wants to focus class struggle on one form of labour. His strategy is idealist and detached from the twenty-first century's reality. He does not want workers of the world to unite, but to keep separate, which legitimatises capitalism. If one follows Revelly's absurd logic that I am an imperialist, then according to the same logic he is a capitalist.

17 German original: „Die Wert-Abspaltungsthese behauptet nun [...] eine 'Abspaltung' des Weiblichen, der Hausarbeit etc. vom Wert, von der abstrakten Arbeit und den damit zusammenhängenden Rationalitätsformen, wobei bestimmte weiblich konnotierte Eigenschaften wie Sinnlichkeit, Emotionalität usw. der Frau zugeschrieben werden; der Mann hingegen steht etwa für Verstandeskraft, charakterliche Stärke, Mut usw. Der Mann wurde in der modernen Entwicklung mit Kultur, die Frau mit Natur gleichgesetzt" (Scholz 2000, 9).

18 http://ec.europa.eu/justice/data-protection/article-29/documentation/other-document/files/2012/20120301_reply_to_iab_easa_en.pdf.

19 http://thehill.com/blogs/hillicon-valley/technology/168871-survey-shows-consumers-want-government-to-protect-their-privacy-online.

20 http://cccs.uq.edu.au/documents/privacy-report.pdf.

21 http://marketingland.com/pew-survey-targeted-ads-negatively-7548.

22 http://www.iab.net/about_the_iab.

23 http://www.youtube.com/watch?v=ZTjsaJi-NMU&feature=youtu.be&t=28s.

24 http://www.adexchanger.com/online-advertising/industry-renews-plea-to-set-do-not-track-off-by-default/.

PART III
Social Media's Cultural Political Economy of Global Space

6

SOCIAL MEDIA'S INTERNATIONAL DIVISION OF DIGITAL LABOUR

6.1. Introduction

Muhanga is an enslaved miner in North Kivu (Democratic Republic of Congo). He extracts cassiterite, a mineral that is needed for the manufacturing of laptops and mobile phones:

> As you crawl through the tiny hole, using your arms and fingers to scratch, there's not enough space to dig properly and you get badly grazed all over. And then, when you do finally come back out with the cassiterite, the soldiers are waiting to grab it at gunpoint. Which means you have nothing to buy food with. So we're always hungry.

> *Finnwatch 2007, 20*

The Chinese engineer Lu assembles mobile phones at Shenzhen. He reports about overwork and exhaustion: "We produced the first generation iPad. We were busy throughout a 6-month period and had to work on Sundays. We only had a rest day every 13 days. And there was no overtime premium for weekends. Working for 12 hours a day really made me exhausted" (SACOM 2010, 7; for a critical analysis of Foxconn see also Sandoval 2013).

In Silicon Valley, the Cambodian ICT (information and communications technology) assembler Bopha has been exposed to toxic substances. He highlights, "I talked to my co-workers who felt the same way [that I did] but they never brought it up, out of fear of losing their job" (Pellow and Park 2002, 139).

Mohan, a project manager in the Indian software industry who is in his midthirties, explains, "Work takes a priority. [. . .] The area occupied by family and others keeps reducing" (D'Mello and Sahay 2007, 179). Bob, a software engineer at Google, explains that

> because of the large amounts of benefits (such as free foods) there seems to be an unsaid rule that employees are expected to work longer hours. Many people work more than 8 hours a day and then will be on email or work for a couple hours at home, at night as well (or on the weekends). It may be hard to perform extremely well with a good work/life balance. Advice to Senior Management—Give engineers more freedom to use 20% time to work on cool projects without the stress of having to do 120% work.

> *data source: www.glassdoor.com*

Ann, a web designer, writer, and illustrator, offers her services on the freelance market platform People Per Hour that mediates the creation and purchase of products and services that are not remunerated by worked hours, but by a fixed product price. She describes her work:

> My design styles are as broad as my client base, from typical hard hitting, sound, clear and concise business branding, to more stylised, and fluid hand drawn or illustrated work. I relish working to a deadline, and although I often work to very specific criteria, some clients are looking for a moment of inspiration, and that's where I excel. I'm always ready for a challenge, and providing the brief is concise and well-conceived I can produce work to a very tight schedule. If you are online, you will see amendments almost immediately!

> *data source: peopleperhour.com*

The working lives of Muhanga, Lu, Bopha, Mohan, Bob, and Ann seem completely different. Muhanga extracts minerals from nature. Lu and Bopha are industrial workers. Mohan, Bob, and Ann are information workers creating either software or designs. They work under different conditions, such as slavery, wage labour, or freelancing. Yet they have in common that their labour is in different ways related to the production and use of digital technologies and that ICT companies profit from it. In this chapter, I discuss the commonalities and differences of the working lives of workers like these by identifying different dimensions of digital labour.

If you look around the apartment, office, public space, or means of transportation in which you currently are, it is likely that you see at least one computer, laptop, or mobile phone that is connected to the Internet. And it is likely that this device has a label on it that says one of the following: Acer, Apple, Asus, BenQ, Compal, Dell, Fujitsu, Hewlett-Packard, HTC, Huawei, Lenovo, LG, Logic Instruments, Motorola, NEC, Nokia, MEDION, Panasonic, Quanta, Samsung,

Sony, Sony Ericsson, Toshiba, Wistron, Wortmann Terra, ZTE. When asked, "Where does your computer/phone come from? Who has produced it?", one may therefore be tempted to answer: "Well, it has been produced by the company X." The main information that the ICT user has about his/her device is from which retailer and company s/he bought it. But these companies are only those actors that sell these devices and own the profits made from these sales. The production process itself consists of multiple forms of labour that are invisible to the user. Yet without this labour ICTs would not exist because they are objectifications of complex human labour processes that are organised in an international division of digital labour (IDDL).

This chapter deals with the questions "Where does the laptop/computer/mobile phone come from? Who produces it? Which forms of labour are involved?". It analyses and theorises steps in the production processes of ICTs by discussing specific cases of ICT work: the extraction of minerals in African mines (section 3), ICT manufacturing and assemblage in China (section 4), software engineering in India (section 5), call centre service work (section 6), software engineering at Google in the context of Silicon Valley (section 7), the digital labour of Internet prosumers/users (section 8). The method of analysis that is employed consists of a presentation of existing empirical data and empirical research results that are theoretically interpreted. The theoretical framing is achieved by applying Karl Marx's theory of modes of production to the ICT industry. For doing this, foundations of this theory are introduced in section 2. The various forms of ICT labour that are needed so that the end user can connect to the Internet on his/her phone, PC, or laptop involve a multitude of labour forms, such as mineral extraction, hardware manufacturing and assemblage, software engineering, service work, and users' productive consumption. All of these labour forms are objectified in a single ICT device, which shows that ICTs have a complex spatial and temporal history of production that involves an IDDL, in which different forms of labour create the use-values needed for obtaining a computer or mobile phone. These different use-values created at different times in different places by different workers facing certain working conditions all work together and become objectified in single ICT devices. The bigger picture and theoretical results of the IDDL that involves an international division of labour and articulated modes and forces of production are presented in section 9.

Jairus Banaji (2011) stresses that Marx's theory of the mode of production shows that "capitalist relations of production are compatible with a wide variety of forms of labour, from chattel-slavery, sharecropping, or the domination of casual labour-markets, to the coerced wage labour peculiar to colonial regimes and, of course, 'free' wage labour" (Banaji 2011, 359). This chapter argues that Banaji's concept of the mode of production matters for understanding the digital media economy because in this economy a variety of modes of production and organisations of the productive forces (= variations within a specific mode of production) are articulated, including slavery in mineral extraction, military forms of Taylorist industrialism in hardware assemblage, an informational organisation of the productive forces of capitalism that articulates a highly paid knowledge labour aristocracy, precarious service workers as well as imperialistically exploited knowledge workers in developing countries, and industrial recycling and management of e-waste as well as highly hazardous informal physical e-waste labour. This chapter furthermore argues that the notion of the mode of production is much better suited for explaining the complexity and global/transnational dimension of digital labour than the rather bourgeois notion of the "global value chain".

6.2. Marx and Engels on Modes of Production

The approach taken in this chapter stands in the Marxist tradition that stresses class contradictions in the analysis of globalisation. It explores how the notion of the mode of production can be connected to the concept of the new international division of labour. Figure 6.1 gives an overview of dimensions of the relations of production and the productive forces.

The notion of the mode of production stresses a dialectical interconnection of on the one hand class relationships (relations of production) and on the other hand the forms of organisation of capital, labour, and technology (productive forces). The class relationship is a social relationship that determines who owns

Productive forces ⇔ Relations of production	
Subject, labour power: Means of subsistence/reproduction: individual, social, institutional	**Mode of ownership:** Labour power, means of production, products of work
	Mode of coercion None Physical violence Structural violence Ideological violence
Object, means of production Instruments of work: body, brain, tools, machines, space-time Objects of work: natural, industrial, informational resources	
	Mode of allocation/distribution To each according to his/her needs, exchange exchange for exchange-value, exchange for maximum exchange-value, Exchange for capital accumulation
Subject/object, products of work: Natural products Industrial products Informational products	
	Division of labour: Household, physical/mental, generalists/specialists global division of labour, politics

FIGURE 6.1   Dimensions of the productive forces and the relations of production

private property and has the power to make others produce surplus-value that they do not own and that is appropriated by private property owners. Class relationships involve an owning class and a non-owing class: the non-owning class is compelled to produce surplus value that is appropriated by the owning class.

The relations of production determine the *property relations* (who owns which share [full, some, none] of labour power, the means of production, products of labour), the mode of allocation and distribution of goods, the mode of coercion used for defending property relations, and the division of labour. Class relationships are forms of organisation of the relations of production, in which a dominant class controls the modes of ownership, distribution, and coercion for exploiting a subordinated class. In a classless society humans control ownership and distribution in common.

Every economy produces a certain amount of goods per year. Specific resources are invested and there is a specific output. If there is no contraction of the economy due to a crisis, then a surplus product is created, i.e. an excess over the initial resources. The property relations determine who owns the economy's initial resources and surplus. Table 6.2 (see further below) distinguishes modes of production (patriarchy, slavery, feudalism, capitalism, communism) based on various modes of ownership, i.e. property relations.

The *mode of coercion* takes on the form of physical violence (overseers, security forces, military), structural violence (markets, institutionalised wage labour contracts, legal protection of private property, etc.), and cultural violence (ideologies that present the existing order as the best possible or only possible order and try to deflect attention from the causes of societal problems by scapegoating, silencing, ignoring, ridiculing and other ideological strategies). In a free society no mode of coercion is needed.

The *mode of allocation and distribution* defines how products are distributed and allocated: In a communist society, each person gets whatever s/he requires to survive and satisfy human needs. In class societies, distribution is organised in the form of exchange: exchange means that one product is exchanged for another. If you have nothing to exchange because you own nothing, then you cannot get hold of other goods and services, except those that are not exchanged but provided for free. There are different forms how exchange can be organised: general exchange, exchange for exchange-value (x commodity A = y commodity B), exchange for maximum exchange-value, exchange for capital accumulation.

The *division of labour* defines who conducts which activities in the household, the economy, politics, and culture. Historically there has been a gender division of labour, a division between mental and physical work, a division into many different functions conducted by specialists, and an international division of labour that is due to the globalisation of production. Marx in contrast imagined a society of generalists that overcomes the divisions of labour so that society is based on well-rounded, universally active humans. Marx (1867, 334–334). Marx (1857/58, 238) says that in class society "labour will create alien property and property will command alien labour". The historical alternative is a communist society and mode of production, in which class relationships are dissolved and the surplus product and private property are owned and controlled in common.

The relations of production are dialectically connected to the system of the productive forces (see Figure 6.2): human subjects have labour power that in the labour process interacts with the means of production (object). The means of production consist of the object of labour (natural resources, raw materials) and the instruments of labour (technology). In the labour process, humans transform the object of labour (nature, culture) by making use of their labour power with the help of instruments of labour. The result is a product of labour, which is a Hegelian subject-object, or, as Marx says, a product, in which labour has become bound up in its object: labour is objectified in the product and the object is as a result transformed into a use value that serves human needs. The next figure summarises the dialectical subject-object process in the economy. The productive forces are a system, in which subjective productive forces (human labour power) make use of technical productive forces (part of the objective productive forces) in order to transform parts of the natural productive forces (which are also part of the objective productive forces) so that a labour product emerges. One goal of the development of the system of productive forces is to increase the productivity of labour, i.e. the output (amount of products) that labour generates per unit of time. Marx (1867, 431) spoke in this context of the development of the productive forces. Another goal of the development of the productive forces can be the enhancement of human self-development by reducing necessary labour time and hard work (toil).

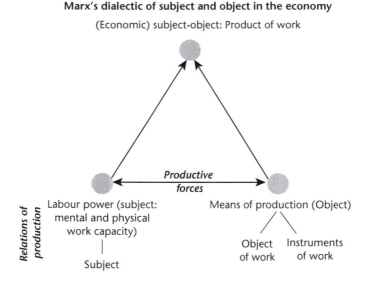

Marx's dialectic of subject and object in the economy

(Economic) subject-object: Product of work

Productive forces

Relations of production

Labour power (subject: mental and physical work capacity)

Subject

Means of production (Object)

Object of work   Instruments of work

FIGURE 6.2   The dialectical triangle of the work process: The system of productive forces—the labour process as dialectical subject-object

The instruments of work can be the human brain and body, mechanical tools, and complex machine systems. They also include specific organisations of space-time, i.e. locations of production that are operated at specific time periods. The most important aspect of time is the necessary work time that depends on the level of productivity. It is the work time that is needed per year for guaranteeing the survival of a society. The objects and products of work can be natural, industrial, or informational resources or a combination thereof.

The productive forces are a system of production that creates use-values. There are different modes of organisation of the productive forces, such as agricultural productive forces, industrial productive forces, and informational productive forces. Table 6.1 gives an overview.

Classical slavery, serfdom, and wage labour are three important historical forms of class relations that are at the heart of specific modes of production (Engels 1884). Marx and Engels argue that private property and slavery have their origin in the family: The first historical form of private property can be found in the patriarchal family (Marx and Engels 1845/46, 52). The family is a mode of production, in which labour power is no commodity but organised by personal and emotional relationships, which result in commitment including family work that is unremunerated and produces affects, social relations, and the reproduction of the human mind and body. It can therefore also be called reproductive work.

A wageworker's labour power has a price, its wage, whereas a slave's labour power does not have a price—it is not a commodity. However, the slave him-/herself has a price, which means that his/her entire human body and mind can be sold as a commodity from one slave owner to another, who then commands the entire life time of the slave (Marx 1857/58, 288–289). The slave in both ancient slavery and feudalism is treated like a thing and has the status of a thing (Marx 1857/58, 464f).

In the *Grundrisse*'s section "Forms Which Precede Capitalist Production" (Marx, 1857/58, 471–514) as well as in the *German Ideology*'s section "Feuerbach: Opposition of the Materialist and /Idealist Outlooks" (Marx and Engels 1845/46), Marx discusses the following modes of production:

TABLE 6.1 Three modes of organisation of the productive forces

Mode	Instruments of work	Objects of work	Products of work
Agricultural productive forces	Body, brain, tools, machines	Nature	Basic products
Industrial productive forces	Body, brain, tools, machines	Basic products, industrial products	Industrial products
Informational productive forces	Body, brain, tools, machines	Experiences, ideas	Informational products

1   The tribal community based on the patriarchal family;
2   Ancient communal property in cities (Rome, Greece);
3   Feudal production in the countryside;
4   Capitalism.

Table 6.2 provides a classification of modes of production based on the dominant forms of ownership (self-control, partly self-control and partly alien control, full alien control). But how are modes of production related to each other? In a historical way, where they supersede each other, or in a historical-logical way within a specific social formation that sublates older formations but encompasses older modes of production into itself? Jairus Banaji (2011) argues that Stalinism and vulgar Marxism have conceptualised the notion of the mode of production based on the assumption that a specific mode contains only one specific historical form of labour and surplus-value appropriation and eliminates previous modes so that history develops in the form of a linear evolution: slavery => feudalism => capitalism => communism. For example Althusser and Balibar (1970) argue that the historical development of society is non-dialectical and does not involve sublations, but rather transitions "from one mode of production to another" (Althusser and Balibar 1970, 307) so that one mode succeeds the other. This concept of history is one of the reasons why Edward P. Thompson (1978, 131) has characterised Althusser's approach as "Stalinism at the level of theory". The Stalinist "metaphysical-scholastic formalism" (Banaji 2011, 61) has been reproduced in liberal theory's assumption that there is an evolutionary historical development from the agricultural society to the industrial society to the information society so that each stage eliminates the previous one (as e.g. argued by Bell 1974 and Toffler 1980), which shows that in the realm of theory the liberals of today are contemporary Stalinists. According to Banaji, capitalism often intensified feudal or semi-feudal production relations. In parts of Europe and outside, feudalism would have only developed as a "commodity-producing enterprise" (Banaji 2011, 88). In the Islamic

TABLE 6.2 The main forms of ownership in various modes of production

	Owner of labour power	Owner of the means of production	Owner of the products of work
Patriarchy	Patriarch	Patriarch	Family
Slavery	Slavemaster	Slavemaster	Slavemaster
Feudalism	Partly self-control, partly lord	Partly self-control, partly lord	Partly self-control, partly lord
Capitalism	Worker	Capitalist	Capitalist
Communism	Self	All	Partly all, partly individual

world capitalism would have developed without slavery and feudalism (Banaji 2011, 6).

Banaji advances in contrast to formalist interpretations a complex reading of Marx's theory, in which a mode of production is "capable of subsuming often much earlier forms" (Banaji 2011, 1); "similar forms of labour-use can be found in very different modes of production" (6). Capitalism is "working through a *multiplicity* of forms of exploitation" (145) and is a combined form of development (358) that integrates "diverse forms of exploitation and ways of organising labour in its drive to produce surplus value" (359).

A mode of production is a unity of productive forces and relations of production (Marx and Engels 1845/46, 91). If these modes are based on classes as their relations of production, then they have specific contradictions that result in the sublation (*Aufhebung*) of one mode of production and the emergence of a new one. The emergence of a new mode of production does not necessarily abolish but rather sublates (*aufheben*) older modes of production. This means that history is for Marx a dialectical process precisely in Hegel's threefold meaning of the term *Aufhebung* (sublation): 1) uplifting, 2) elimination, 3) preservation:

1) There are new qualities of the economy,
2) the dominance of an older mode of production vanishes,
3) but this older mode continues to exist in the new mode in a specific form and relation to the new mode.

The rise of e.g. capitalism, however, did not bring an end to patriarchy, but the latter continued to exist in such a way that a specific household economy emerged that fulfils the role of the reproduction of modern labour power. A sublation can be more or less fundamental. A transition from capitalism to communism requires a fundamental elimination of capitalism; the question is, however, if this is immediately possible. Elimination and preservation can take place to differing degrees. A sublation is also no linear progression. It is always possible that relations that resemble earlier modes of organisation are created.

Capitalism is at the level of the relations of production organised around relations between capital owners on the one side and paid/unpaid labour and the unemployed on the other side. On the level of the productive forces, it has developed from industrial to informational productive forces. The informational productive forces do not eliminate, but sublate (*aufheben*) other productive forces (Adorno 1968/2003; Fuchs 2014a, chapter 5): in order for informational products to exist a lot of physical production is needed, which includes agricultural production, mining, and industrial production. The emergence of informational capitalism has not virtualised production or made it weightless or immaterial, but is grounded in physical production (Huws 1999; Maxwell and Miller 2012). Whereas capitalism is a mode of production, the terms *agricultural society*, *industrial society*, and *information society* characterise specific forms of the organisation of the productive forces (Fuchs 2014a, chapter 5; Adorno 1968/2003).

I suggest that the Marxist notion of the mode of production is a more useful concept for the analysis of digital labour than the one of the global value chain. Michael Porter (1985) introduced the notion of the value chain that he defined as "a collection of activities that are performed to design, produce, market, deliver and support its product" (Porter 1985, 36). The term *value chain* has become a popular category for analysing the organisation of capital, which is indicated by the circumstance that 11,682 articles indexed in the academic database Business Source Premier use the term in their abstracts (accessed on May 21, 2013). The term has also been used in mainstream media economics for analysing the value chains of traditional media and ICTs (see Zerdick et al. 2000, 126–135). The problem of the mainstream use of the concept of the value chain is that it focuses on the stages in commodity production and tends to neglect aspects of working conditions and class relations. Interestingly, also critical scholars have also used the affirmative notion of the global value chain (e.g. Huws 2008; Huws and Dahlmann 2010).

Critical scholars introduced the notion of the new international division of labour (NIDL; Fröbel et al. 1981) in the 1980s:

> The development of the world economy has increasingly created conditions (forcing the development of the new international division of labour) in which the survival of more and more companies can only be assured through the relocation of production to new industrial sites, where labour-power is cheap to buy, abundant and well-disciplined; in short, through the transnational reorganization of production.
>
> *Fröbel et al. 1981, 15*

A further development is that "commodity production is being increasingly subdivided into fragments which can be assigned to whichever part of the world can provide the most profitable combination of capital and labour" (Fröbel et al. 1981, 14). In critical media and cultural studies, Miller et al. (2004) have used this concept for explaining the international division of cultural labour (NICL). The concept of the NIDL has the advantage that it stresses the class relationship between capital and labour and how in processes of class struggle capital tries to increase profits by decreasing its overall wage costs via the global diffusion of the production process. It is also a concept that encompasses workers' struggles against the negative effects of capitalist restructuring.

Marx and Engels (1845/46) considered the division of labour not as a separate holistic concept, but discussed it as part of the notion of the mode of production. They especially gave focus to the division of labour between men and women in the household, citizens and slaves, the town and the country side, branches of the economy, labour in industry and commerce, intellectual and physical labour, and centres and colonies as sources of raw materials. The NIDL organises the labour process in space and time in such a way that specific components of the overall commodity are produced in specific spaces in the global economy and are reassembled in order to form a coherent whole that is sold as a commodity. It thereby can command labour on the whole globe and during the whole day. The NIDL is a global organisation level of the social relation between different forms of labour required in the production process.

The following sections will analyse various forms of exploitation in the global production of digital media and how they are related to specific modes of production and organisation forms of the productive forces.

6.3. Slave Mineral Workers and the IDDL

African countries (Democratic Republic of Congo [DRC], Ethiopia, Mozambique, Rwanda, South Africa, Zambia, Zimbabwe) are among the largest producers of minerals needed for ICTs, whereas they hardly range among important importing countries (Finnwatch 2007; SOMO 2007; U.S. Geological Survey Statistics 2012). This is an indication that the production and use of ICTs is based on a division of labour where Africa has the role as an important and relatively cheap source of natural resources (cheap because of highly exploited labour) that are further processed in non-African countries, especially China. In the IDDL, Africa is a highly exploited economic colony. And this colonial status is, as will be shown, based on the highly exploited work and slave work of Africans. Marx has argued that colonies are a form of primitive accumulation (Marx 1867, 916). The contemporary existence of economic colonies shows that primitive accumulation is a continuous process that capitalism uses for getting hold of resources and labour in a way that minimises investment costs by maximising exploitation. Whereas the minerals required for ICTs tend to be extracted in Africa and China, the smelting, refinement, and enrichment of them often takes place in Asian countries such as Thailand, Malaysia, China, and Indonesia that supply the electronics markets (Finnwatch 2007, 37).

In 2011, the DRC produced 53.0 per cent of the world's cobalt, 2.3 per cent of the world's tin (U.S. Geological Survey Statistics 2012), and around 10 per cent of the world's tantalum (Eichstaedt 2011, 140). The DRC is the world's largest producer of cobalt and a significant producer of coltan and tin. The demand of Western companies for cheap minerals has been an important driver of the violence, slavery, and exploitation in Eastern DRC. The DRC has since the 1990s been haunted by wars in which millions of people were killed. The poverty and violence the country experienced spurred conditions in which everyone did whatever was necessary in order to survive, which created conditions for the existence of modern forms of slavery. In the DRC, the mining that is relevant for the ICT industry involves tin-ore cassiterite, tantalum-ore coltan (that is by refinement transformed into the metal tantalum), wolframite, and gold (Finnwatch and Swedwatch 2010). These minerals are used as raw materials in the production of cell phones, laptops, light bulbs, and cars (Free the Slaves 2011). Many mines in the DRC are either controlled by armed government forces (Forces Armées de la République Démocratique du Congo, FARDC) or rebel armies.

Empirical research conducted for the Free the Slaves (2011) report focused on interviewing workers in the Bisie and Omate mines as well as mining workers in Walikale and Masisi (N = 742 interviews). The study found that slavery is widespread in the mining industry, including work in digging, sorting, transporting, and the sale of minerals as well as industries that provide services to miners, such as work as domestic servants, in pubs, and in the sex industry. Of the respondents in the Bisie mine (Free the Slaves 2001), where 80 per cent of the DRC's tin/cassiterite is mined (Eichstaedt 2011, 121), 40 per cent worked under conditions of slavery. This circumstance shows that the informational productive forces of capitalism that create digital media are to a certain extent coupled with the slave mode of production in developing countries in order to reduce labour costs and maximise profits.

Researchers documented forced labour, where the government-FARDC soldiers forced villagers to work in the Bisie mine without payment and under the threat of being killed if they flee. Also a system called *salongo* was documented, in which all mine workers on a particular day of the week have to work for one FARDC official (Free the Slaves 2011, 13). Marx (1861–63, 180–181, 212–215) described this system of corvée labour, in which the days worked for the lord create surplus labour and the other days form necessary labour time. Another system found in East DRC is that miners have to pay a weekly rent to mine controllers and the government in order to work in a specific mine (Nest 2011, 43). They extract tin and have to pay fees for mining, and leaving and entering the mine (in order to sell the extracted minerals), to the armed group that controls the mine. The imposed fees are so high that the workers cannot ever get out of the working relation in which they are trapped—they are slaves (Poulsen 2011). In the DRC's mining industry, both the classic form of slavery as well as feudal slavery based on rent and corvée slavery exist. In wage labour, the worker is double free, i.e. "free" to sell his/her labour power and "free" from the ownership of means of production and the products of labour, and sells her/his labour power as a commodity for the whole working week. In classic slavery, the slave is unfree and a property of the slave-owner for the entire working week. In the corvée system, the worker is a slave for part of the working week, whereas the other part of the week is free for other activities that are needed for earning a living. In the Free the Slaves (2011) study, a significant share of respondents was facing debt bondage slavery: money is borrowed at very high interest rates, which forces the debtors to work in a mine. There are fraud schemes that "make it impossible to pay off the debt" (Free the Slaves 2011, 14). Also peonage slavery was documented. In this form of slavery, a person is arrested under some charges that are mostly made up and then told that the sentence is that he must work in a mine. Of the interviewed children (N = 31) 89 per cent were living in and working under conditions of slavery. In the DRC, 75 per cent of the miners cannot cover basic needs with their wage (Finnwatch 2007, 29). In 2013, 29.8 million people lived in modern forms of slavery (Global Slavery Index 2013). Modern slavery includes slavery, debt bondage, forced marriage, sale and exploitation of children, forced labour, and human trafficking (ibid.).

The tragedy of the DRC is that a country that is rich in mineral resources has been the locus of one of the bloodiest conflicts in the world in the twentieth and twenty-first centuries and that this conflict has in the form of conflict minerals a connection to the West and the Western ICT industry. The DRC was in 2011 the least developed country in the world, had a very high inequality rate (Gini) of 44.4 per cent, 59.2 per cent of the population lived in extreme poverty (less than US$1.25 per day for survival), and the life expectancy was 45 years (UNHDR 2011). In 2014, the DRC was ranked 186 out of 187 countries in human development, 87.8% lived in extreme poverty on less than US$1.25 per day, and 38.8% of the population aged 15 or older were illiterate (data source: Human Development Indicators, http://hdr.undp.org/, accessed on October 26, 2014). War and neo-imperialist exploitation of labour and the country's resources that does not benefit local people, but primarily Western companies, have created the paradox typical for capitalism that one of world's countries that is richest in natural resources—45 per cent of the world's cobalt reserves, 25 per cent of the world's diamonds reserves (U.S. Geological Survey Statistics 2012) and according to estimates between 7–8 per cent (Nest 2011, 18–20) and 64 per cent (Gootnick 2008) of the world's coltan reserves are located in the DRC—is socially the world's poorest country.

6.4. Foxconn: ICT Assemblage in China

Hon Hai Precision (also known as Foxconn) is a Taiwanese company that was the 139th largest company in the world in 2014 (Forbes 2000, 2014 list). According to CNN Global 500 (2012), Foxconn is the fifth largest corporate employer in the world. In 2011, Foxconn had enlarged its Chinese workforce to a million, with a majority being young migrant workers who come from the countryside (SACOM 2011a). Foxconn assembles e.g. the iPad, iMac, iPhone, Kindle, and various consoles (by Sony, Nintendo, Microsoft). Its customers are Western companies such as Apple, Dell, HP, Motorola, Nokia, Sony, and Sony Ericsson (SACOM 2010, 4).

Seventeen Foxconn workers attempted suicide between January and August 2010. Students and Scholars against Corporate Misbehaviour (SACOM 2010) conducted a study, in which 100 Foxconn workers in Shenzen and Hangzhou were interviewed and observed. In June 2010, the basic wage of Foxconn Shenzen workers was CNY (Chinese yuan renminbi) 1,200 per month. SACOM (2010) calculated that the living wage that is needed for surviving should in Shenzen should be CNY 2,293. With more than 420,000 workers, Shenzen is Foxconn's largest factory (SACOM 2010, 10). In 2008, Foxconn Guanlan workers on average worked 120 hours overtime per month (SACOM 2010, 7). Tian Yu, a seventeen-year-old girl who survived an attempted suicide, reports that at Foxconn Longhua she had to work from 7 AM to 7 PM (Qiu 2010). SACOM (2010) also documented frequent work shift changes, regular working time of over 10 hours per day, a lack of breaks, monotonous work, physical harm caused by chemicals such as benzene or solder paste, lack of protective gear and equipment, forced use of students from vocational schools as interns (in agreement with the school boards) that conduct regular assembly work that does not help their studies, prison-like accommodations with 6–22 workers per room (SACOM 2011a: 18) who do not know each other in one dormitory, and yellow unions that are managed by company officials and whom the workers do not trust. SACOM (2011b) conducted interviews with 120 workers in Shenzen, Chengdu, and Chongdinq in order to test if, a year after the Foxconn suicides, the working conditions had changed. The bad working conditions documented in the previous study were confirmed. In 2012, SACOM (2012) conducted a follow-up study comprising 60 interviews with workers in Zhengzhou, which again confirmed the previous results. SACOM (2010) documented harsh management methods, including a lack of breaks; a prohibition that workers move, talk, or stretch their bodies; workers that had to stand during production; as well as punishments, beatings, and harassments by security guards. The Fair Labor Association (2012) conducted a survey with N = 35,166 respondents who are Foxconn employees in Chengdu, Guanlan, and Longhua. Of the respondents, 64.3 per cent think that their salaries do not cover their basic needs. Workers were asked what three things they would change if they had the chance to: salaries were the top priority, followed by benefits/allowances, food quality, and working hours. Only 22.1 per cent said that they are union members.

Of the respondents 72.2 per cent were migrant workers. According to official statistics, there were 252.78 million migrant workers in China in 2011, an increase of 4.4 per cent in comparison to 2010 (National Bureau of Statistics of China 2012). In 2013, the number increased to 268.94 million (National Bureau of Statistics of China 2014). Rural poverty is the basic reason for the Chinese young rural population to migrate to urban areas (Hong 2011, chapter 5; see also Qiu 2009, chapters 4 and 6). In the period 2001–2005, 40 million landless peasants were created by government appropriation of rural land, which further spurs migration into cities (Hong 2011, 204). What is happening to Chinese peasants is exactly what Marx (1867) described as the process of primitive accumulation that started in Europe in the fifteenth and sixteenth centuries: primitive accumulation creates an "incomparably larger proletariat by forcibly driving the peasantry from the land. [. . .] and by usurpation of the common lands" (Marx 1867, 878).

SACOM concluded: "In order to maximize productivity, workers at Foxconn are made to work like machines" (SACOM 2010, 10). Marx (1867) describes two methods of how capitalists can try to organise the working day in order to accumulate ever more profit. Absolute surplus-value production, which is characteristic for what he (Marx 1867, 1019–1023, 1025–1034) terms the formal subsumption of labour under capital, means that workers work more hours unpaid because the working day is prolonged. In relative surplus-value production that is characteristic for the real subsumption of labour under capital (Marx 1867, 1023–1025, 1034–1038), working time remains the same, but work becomes more productive and undergoes a speed-up so that more surplus value is produced in the same amount of time as before.

The analysed reports make clear that in Foxconn factories mainly absolute methods of surplus value production are used in order to increase profits: one finds in these factories unpaid overtime, hardly any breaks, long working days of up to 12 hours, working weeks with 6 working days, work without a day off for up to two weeks' time, etc. A certain wage is paid, but the management strategy is to in exchange try to press as many hours of work out of the workers as possible. The reports also show that absolute surplus-value production is to a certain, although lesser, degree combined with relative surplus-value production: the military system of worker surveillance and coercion that uses drill, control, and punishment aims at disciplining them in such a way that they not only work long hours without breaks, but also work in an intense manner, i.e. produce as many items per hour as possible. Foxconn is typical for the Chinese ICT industry, in which, as Yu Hong argues, the "FDI-driven and outward-looking mode of ICT development has created a new working-class stratum who are regionally clustered, largely peasant-based, semi-skilled, low-wage, irregularly employed, and mostly female manual workers" (Hong 2011, 113). Jack Qiu (2009, x) argues that China has "the largest exploited working class of the global information age".

6.5. Work in the Indian Software Industry

After the assassination of Indira Gandhi in 1984, Rajiv Gandhi became the new Indian prime minister and substituted the politics of techno-nationalism with politics that modernised and liberalised communications, which resulted in a deregulation of the computer industry and the focus on the attraction of foreign capital and export-orientation of the Indian ICT economy (Chakravartty 2004; Upadhya and Vasavi 2008). In the years 2000–2009, the export orientation of the Indian software industry has increased from roughly 50 per cent to more than 75 per cent (ICSSR 2012; NASSCOM 2012). In 2010, software services accounted for 54.4 per cent of all exported services in India (Government of India, Ministry of Finance 2011, 166). In 2011, this value increased to around 58 per cent (NASSCOM 2012). Although the Indian software industry has had a huge growth rate and a large share of exports in services, it in 2009 accounted for only 0.5 per cent of the total Indian labour force and in 2012 for 0.6 per cent (ICSSR 2012; NASSCOM 2012). This circumstance shows that given the fact that India is the second largest country in the world (following China), its mere size poses an attractive location for the outsourcing of ICT services for Western companies in order to increase profit rates by decreasing overall wage costs. The overall employment impact was nonetheless modest within the Indian economy. But the Indian software sector accounted according to estimations for 7.5 per cent of the Indian GDP in 2012 (NASSCOM 2012).

D'Costa (2002) argues that Indian software development is embedded into an uneven combined development of Indian capitalism that produces winners and losers and develops some regions, cities, and groups at the expense of others. Ilavarasan (2007) based on empirical research concludes that the Indian ICT workforce has large urban-rural and gender differences and that these differences contribute to uneven development in India. Commander et al. (2008) conducted a survey among 225 Indian and 60 US software firms. The average wages in Indian software companies were in this study 9.6 per cent of the wages in US software firms. "The single greatest motivation for considering India for offshoring from a developed country is lower labor costs" (Dossani and Kenney 2007, 777).

Ilavarasan (2007) conducted a survey (N = 114) as well as 62 interviews in two large Indian software companies that confirm the results of D'Mello and Sahay (2007). He found that most employees had flexible working times and often worked during the night; 56 per cent said that they also worked on holidays and 86 per cent that they were not paid for overtime. Actual working hours per week would be far more than the 40 hours that are formally required. Indian ICT workers are "'high tech' nomadic" workers (Upadhya and Vasavi 2008, 20). The phenomenon of "global body shopping" is a "uniquely Indian practice whereby an Indian-run consultancy (body shop) anywhere in the world recruits IT workers, in most cases from India, to be placed out as project-based labor with different clients" (Biao 2007, 4; see also Aneesh 2006). Indian ICT workers also perform support tasks for American companies while it is night in the United States and daytime in India (Aneesh 2006).

A neoliberal programme of liberalisation, deregulation, and privatisation has characterised India in the past decades. Arundhati Roy (2003) says in this context that India "is currently at the forefront of the corporate globalization project. [. . .] Corporatization and Privatization are being welcomed by the Government and the Indian elite". The software industry has in the neoliberal policy framework become a strategic focus of economic policy making in India; its deregulation, export-orientation, and attraction of foreign capital investments has created a specific case of capital accumulation in India.

Lenin (1917a) has characterised capital export as an important feature of imperialism: "Under modern capitalism, when monopolies prevail, the export of capital has become the typical feature" (Lenin 1917a, 215). The goal would be to achieve high profits by exporting capital to countries in which "capital is scarce, the price of land is relatively low, wages are low, raw materials are cheap" (Lenin 1917a, 216). Exploiting labour in colonies with high exploitation rates can be achieved by military means (annexation of a country) and/or by economic means. David Harvey (2005) characterises the contemporary new imperialism as a form of accumulation by dispossession. In the Indian software industry, the new imperialism takes on a specific economic form, in which foreign capital controls the industry, pays internationally comparatively low wages (which is supported by the deregulation of the sector), and thereby achieves high returns. Indian software engineers' wages are only a portion of the ones their US equivalents enjoy, which allows Western companies to maximise profits by outsourcing software engineering to India or temporarily employing Indians in the United States or other countries. The value created by Indian software engineers does to a large degree not stay in the country and does not benefit all, but rather is appropriated and owned by Western capital that accumulates capital by selling software that is based on the dispossession of the value created by Indian software engineers in such a way that high exploitation rates are given. The Indian software industry is part of a IDDL that is shaped by the new imperialism in such a form that there is a very high rate of exploitation so that value from India is exported to Western countries. As a result, there is an uneven global development in the ICT industry and the creation and amplification of uneven development within India. Marx wrote about India that the "aristocracy wanted to conquer it, the moneyocracy to plunder it, and the millocracy to undersell it" (Marx 1853, 218). Contemporary forms of neo-imperialism are still based on the exploitation of colonies: Western capital acts as "moneyocracy" that plunders India and other countries in the Global South. This plunder takes on specific form. The Indian software industry is a strategic industry in the new imperialistic IDDL. Just like Marx wrote in 1853 (Marx 1853, 221), also today the large share of Indians do "not reap the fruits of the new elements of [the information] society" that exist in India in the software sector.

6.6. Call Centre Work

The Global Call Center Project (http://www.ilr.cornell.edu/globalcallcenter/) is a research network that has studied call centre work in 20 countries. The project conducted a survey (Holman et al. 2007) that covered 2,500 call centres in 17 countries. Women accounted in total for 69 per cent of the employees. In coordinated economies, the median annual pay of a call centre agent was US$23,599, in liberal economies US$32,925, and in industrialising countries US$19,105. The median turnover rate of personnel was 20 per cent. Call centres extensively use call monitoring and software for call performance metrics (Holman et al. 2007, 9–10). The study found that 39 per cent of the analysed call centres have low to very low quality jobs that feature relatively low job discretion and relatively high performance monitoring. Another result was that 36 per cent of the employees have very low quality jobs, 67 per cent low to very low quality jobs, and only 14 per cent high or very high quality jobs. The Global Call Center Project in general found a high level of standardisation of call centre jobs, high performance monitoring, low level of employees' influence on decisions about the work process, low job quality, and a high rate of female employment.

Zillah Eisenstein (1979, 33) argues that the gender division of labour that shapes capitalist patriarchy assigns five types of labour to women: reproduction, child-rearing, maintenance of home, sexuality, and organisation of consumption. Call centre labour shows that the gender division of labour extends from the home into the capitalist workplace: in the home, women are compelled to take care of biological reproduction and child-rearing; in call centre work this role is reproduced because a patriarchal ideology is at play that sees women as being affective, social, friendly, and caring not just for children and the family in the home but also for customers on the phone. The activity of keeping constant order in the home gets reproduced in the call centre as assigning employees the task of keeping order in the customer database so that the clients keep on buying the offered commodities. In the household, patriarchy assigns women the role of organising consumption of the family—buying and preparing food, informing herself about new consumer goods that could improve family life, etc. In the call centre, workers are also in charge of organising consumption—they respond to the consumer needs of customers and have to try to help them fix problems that relate to consumption and improving the consumption experience. Last, but not least, sexual work and desire also gets reproduced from patriarchal relations to the call centre: talking to a woman at the customer service may more easily please male customers because it may invoke sexual desires. Just like the telecommunicated form of prostitution—paid phone sex—provides a sexual service to men, the female call centre agent provides services that may more easily please male customers if they are reminded of the submissive and sexual connotations of women that the phone carries in the culture of capitalist patriarchy. All five types of housework that Eisenstein distinguishes—reproduction, child rearing, maintenance of home, sexuality, organisation of consumption—get reproduced in the call centre. It is therefore no surprise that the majority of call centre agents are women: capitalism uses patriarchal ideologies, such as the identification of women with being social, caring, affective, sexual, relational, and communicative, for creating precarious employment relations. In call centres, like in the home, "the biological distinction male/female" is ideologically used "to distinguish social functions and individual power" (Eisenstein 1979, 17), and the position of employees "as paid workers is defined in terms of being a woman" (Eisenstein 1979, 30).

Like housework, call centre work relies on workers' temporal availability and flexibility defined by others: houseworkers often have to be available around the clock for children and the whole family, and call centres tend to be open 24 hours, which requires around-the-clock availability of the collective call centre worker. This can bring problems for health and family life. The call centre agent's work—insecure, precarious, stressful, standardised work that entails spatio-temporal flexibility requirements defined by capital's needs—has become the model for the creation of an entire economy of insecure and precarious jobs that especially affects and negatively impacts young people's lives. Cutting labour costs by casualisation is a form of absolute surplus-value production—the part of the day that produces surplus-value and profit is lengthened. Ideology defines women as working mothers in order to pay them less than men.

Call centre work is highly monitored and standardised—it is a kind of Taylorist white-collar work that blurs the boundaries between blue- and white-collar work. It could be called grey-collar work because grey is the colour that results from mixing blue and white. The standardisation and surveillance of work, accompanied by precarisation that puts workers under survival pressures, is a method of relative surplus value production—constant control and pressure is aimed at making workers' discipline their brains and bodies in such a form that they work more intensively, i.e. take care of more customers in less time and so increase productivity. Call centre work is like other work characterised both by the formal and the real subsumption of labour under capital: both methods of absolute surplus value production (cutting wage costs) and relative surplus value production (standardisation, surveillance, grey collar Taylorism) are used for advancing capital accumulation.

6.7. Software Engineering at Google and the Silicon Valley of Nightmares

Silicon Valley is the name for the area located in the Santa Clara Valley, south of San Francisco. The average wages of employees in the software industries in Silicon Valley were in 2011 between 2 (other computer-related services) and 5.6 times (Internet publishing and web search portals) as high as the general US wage average (data source: US Bureau of Labor Statistics: Quarterly Census of Employment and Wages).

What do working conditions look like in knowledge-intensive jobs, such as software engineering? To test this, we want to have a look at labour in one of Silicon Valley's most well-known companies, Google. In 2013 Google had a record profitable year: its profits were US$12.92 billion (Google SEC Filings: Annual Report 2013), the largest amount since the company's creation in 1998.

I analysed job reviews for Google that contained a job title related to the keyword "software". This resulted in a total of 307 postings from Glassdoor that were written between February 5, 2008, and December 15, 2012. In addition, I analysed a thread on reddit that asked people to report anonymously on working conditions at Google.[1] I searched for and analysed postings in which workers talked about working time issues. This resulted in a sample of 75 postings, 10 from the reddit thread and 65 from Glassdoor. Of that total, 58 postings mentioned negative aspects of working times at Google. The issue that all (100 per cent) of these 58 postings exclusively focused on in relation to working time were long working hours and a resulting bad work-life-balance. The picture that emerges from the analysis is that people tend to work long hours at Google. They feel that the nice working environment that features free food, sports facilities, restaurants, cafés, events, tech-talks, and other perks encourages employees to stay and work longer; that working long hours is not something that is formally dictated by the management but that it is rather built into the company culture so that there is a lot of competitive peer-pressure to work long hours; and that one tends not to have enough time to make use of the 20 per cent work that Google promises for one's own projects or has to add these hours to much more than 100 per cent of working time.

In the early times of capitalism that Marx describes in *Capital, Volume 1*, the lengthening of the working day was achieved by control, surveillance, disciplinary measures, and legitimation by state laws. The price was an increase of class struggles that pressed for reducing working hours. Google's main way of increasing surplus value production is also absolute surplus value production, i.e. the lengthening of the working day, but it takes a different approach: the coercion is ideological and social, built into the company's culture of fun, playbour (play labour), employee services, and peer pressure. The result is that the total average working time and unpaid working hours per employee tend to increase. Marx described this case as a specific method of absolute and relative surplus value production, in which the productivity and intensity of labour remain constant, whereas the length of the working day is variable (Marx 1867, 663).

In comparison to Californian semiconductor processors, who in 2012 on average earned US$36,584, and Californian electronic equipment assemblers, whose average wage was US$33,179 in 2012 (data source: State of California Employment Development Department), the average 2012 wage of a Google software engineer (US$112,915, data source: glassdoor.com, N = 2744, January 13, 2013) was respectively 3.1 times and 3.4 times higher. These data show that there is a significant wage gap in the ICT industry between assemblers and software engineers. There is high wage inequality between professionals, especially managers, on the one hand and manufacturing workers on the other hand (Benner 2002; Carnoy et al. 1997). Whereas white people constitute a large share of officials, managers, and professionals, especially Hispanic and Asian employees make up the large share of semi- and unskilled production and service workers in Silicon Valley (Benner 2002; Pellow and Park 2002). In 2012, a Californian systems software developer earned on average 3.5 times the salary of an electronic equipment assembler and 3.2 times the salary of a semiconductor processor (data source: State of California Employment Development Department). Pellow and Park (2002) have analysed the working conditions in Silicon Valley's ICT manufacturing industry. They show that the wealth of this industry and its beneficiaries is linked to the "hyperexploitation of undocumented and documented persons by employers" (Pellow and Park 2002, 6) and toxic workplaces that are highly gendered and racially structured. Toxic substances that have frequently been released into the workplace and contaminated the air, the soil, and drinking water have resulted in cancer, respiratory diseases, reproductive problems of women, miscarriages, and birth defects of babies.

There is a significant wage gap in the ICT industry between assemblers and software engineers. Both types of labour are exploited and necessary for capital accumulation in the ICT industry. Software engineers at Google (and other companies) form what Engels termed the "labour aristocracy": Engels describes that in 1885 in the United Kingdom, there were workers whose "state of misery and insecurity in which they live now is as low as ever", but there was also "an aristocracy among the working-class" (engineers, carpenters, joiners, bricklayers) that has "succeeded in enforcing for themselves a relatively comfortable position" (Engels 1892, 266). Also Lenin (1920), based on Engels, spoke of a labour aristocracy that consists of "workers-turned-bourgeois", "who are quite philistine in their mode of life, in the size of their earnings and in their entire outlook" and are "the real *agents of the bourgeoisie in the working-class* movement, the labour lieutenants of the capitalist class". Google workers in comparison to ICT manufacturers have much higher wages and privileges, which also means that they are more unlikely to resist, which is, as Engels describes, typical for the labour aristocracy: "they are very nice people indeed nowadays to deal with, for any sensible capitalist in particular and for the whole capitalist class in general" (Engels 1892, 266).

Slavoj Žižek (2012, 12) has inappropriately described the Occupy movement as salaried bourgeoisie that consists of "privileged workers who have guaranteed jobs" and are "driven by fear of losing their surplus wage" (Žižek 2012, 12). But what he really described in this passage, without knowing it, are Google professionals, who as a labour aristocracy have in comparison to ICT manufacturers relatively high wages. Marx grounded the notion of the surplus wage: In the *Grundrisse*, he describes conditions of production, such as a high demand of labour in one specific industry, in which certain workers gain "surplus wages" that represent a "small share of [. . .] surplus labour" (Marx 1857/58, 438). Martin Nicolaus therefore writes in the foreword that Marx shows that it is

> theoretically possible, quite apart from the question of the economic cycle, for one fraction of the working class (but not the whole) to receive, via the mechanisms of the distribution of profit among the different capitalists, 'an extremely small share of' the surplus value produced by themselves in the form of 'surplus wages'.
>
> *(Marx 1857/58, 48)*

If the ICT industry is seen as a combined industry and its profits as combined profits, highly paid software engineers and other highly paid knowledge workers have a wage that is higher by a certain surplus in contrast to poorly paid ICT assemblers. This relative surplus wage comes, however, at a price: long working hours, high stress, a relative high turnover of labour in the software industry, bad work-life balance, and the tendency to have no social life outside the company. Google's software engineers are a prototypical example of the knowledge labour aristocracy.

The term "labour aristocracy" is meant in an objective and not necessarily subjective sense: the Google labour aristocracy has relative surplus wages in relation to ICT manufacturing workers. Whether this status results in bourgeois consciousness that is quite homologous to the one of managers and owners or not can only be determined empirically. Google and similar knowledge companies totalise their employees' labour time to lifetime. They pay relatively high wages as incentives to exploit high volumes of unpaid labour time. The Google labour aristocracy shows the internal contradictions of the global working class. Dyer-Witheford and de Peuter (2009) have analysed such contradictions for the computer game industry whose existence depends on the labour of game designers, developers, testers, players, goldfarmers in China, coltan miners in Africa, and e-waste pickers.

Marx (1867, chapters 9, 18) argued that the rate of exploitation of workers can be calculated as e = profits / wages. It does not follow from the circumstance that software engineers tend to have higher wages than ICT assemblers that they are not or less exploited, because the rate of exploitation depends not just on the level of wages but also on the level of profits.

Silicon Valley is only the valley of dreams for some: it is the valley of dreams for the class made up of those who reap high profits in the ICT industry precisely because it is the valley of death for ICT manufacturing workers and the valley of stress for the labour aristocracy in software engineering. Silicon Valley is shaped by a geography of inequality, death, stress, and the destruction of nature and human livelihood that is the foundation of the capitalist ICT industry and its profits.

6.8. Digital Labour and Online Prosumption

Corporate social media (Facebook, YouTube, Twitter, Weibo, Blogspot, LinkedIn, etc.) have in common that they use a business model that is based on targeted advertising and that turns users' data (content, profiles, social networks, online behaviour) into a commodity. Commodities have producers who create them, otherwise they cannot exist. So if the commodity of the mentioned Internet platforms is user data, then the process of creating these data must be considered to be value-generating labour. This means that this type of Internet usage is productive consumption or prosumption in the sense that it creates value and a commodity that is sold. Dallas Smythe's concept of the audience commodity has been revived and transformed into the concept of the Internet prosumer commodity (Fuchs 2012a). Digital labour creates the Internet prosumer commodity that is sold by Internet platforms to advertising clients that in return present targeted ads to users.

Digital labour on "social media" resembles housework because it has no wages, is mainly conducted during spare time, has no trade union representation, and is difficult to perceive as being labour. Like housework it involves the "externalization, or ex-territorialization of costs which otherwise would have to be covered by the capitalists" (Mies 1986, 110). The term "crowdsourcing" (Howe 2008) expresses exactly this outsourcing process that helps capital to save labour costs. Like housework, digital labour is "a source of unchecked, unlimited exploitation" (Mies 1986, 16). Slaves are violently coerced with hands, whips, bullets—they are tortured, beaten, or killed if they refuse to work. The violence exercised against them is primarily physical in nature. Houseworkers are also partly physically coerced in cases of domestic violence. In addition, they are coerced by feelings of love, commitment, and responsibility that make them work for the family. The main coercion in patriarchal housework is conducted by affective feelings. In the case of the digital worker, coercion is mainly social in nature: large platforms such as Facebook have successfully monopolised the supply of certain services, such as online social networking, and have more than a billion users, which allows them to exercise a soft and almost invisible form of coercion, in which users are chained to commercial platforms because all of their friends and important contacts are there—they do not want to lose these contacts and therefore cannot simply leave these platforms.

In a passage in the *Grundrisse*, Marx (1857/58, 462) makes clear which elements of alienation there are in capitalism: the worker is alienated from: a) herself/himself because labour is controlled by capital, b) the material of labour, c) the object of labour, and d) the product of labour. These four elements of alienation can be related to the labour process that consists in a Hegelian sense of a subject, an object, and a subject-object. Alienation is alienation of the subject from itself (labour-power is put to use for and is controlled by capital), alienation from the object (the objects of labour and the instruments of labour), and the subject-object (the products of labour).

All workers that are exploited by capital are alienated from the products of their work. On corporate social media, alienation takes on a specific form: Users are objectively alienated because a) in relation to subjectivity, they are coerced by isolation and social disadvantage if they leave monopoly capital platforms (such as Facebook); b) in relation to the objects of labour, their human experiences come under the control of capital; c) in relation to the instruments of labour, it is not the users who own the platforms, but private companies that also commodify user data; and d) in the relation to the product of labour, the platform individually controls profit. These four forms of alienation constitute together capital's exploitation of digital labour on corporate social media.

Congolese miners, Foxconn workers, Indian and Californian software engineers, call centre workers, social media prosumers, and other digital workers are all alienated in the sense that they do not own the profits and products they produce. In the case of social media users, the situation is, however, somehow different: they create two different use-values by the same digital work: communication and public visibility, and the possibility that they are confronted with targeted ads. We can therefore speak of the double character of use-values on corporate social media: on the one hand, users produce use-values for themselves and others; they create a social relation between users and public visibility. On the other hand, users produce use-values for capital, i.e. targeted advertising space for the advertising industry. The dual character of the use-value makes the Facebook product a peculiar product: it serves users' own social needs and the commercial needs of advertisers. At the same time, the commercial use-value is first controlled by corporate platforms and enables the exchange value character and commodification of user data. There is also a specific form of coercion that takes on a social form: leaving a corporate platform is not so easy if one has many contacts there because one is facing the threat of less contacts and communicative impoverishment.

In the world of digital labour, the fetish character of the commodity takes on an inverted form. We can speak of an inverse fetish character of the social media commodity. The commodity character of Facebook data is hidden behind the social use-value of Facebook, i.e. the social relations and functions enabled by platform use. The inverse fetish of Facebook is typically expressed in statements like "Facebook does not exploit me because I benefit from it by connecting to other users." The object status of users, i.e. the fact that they serve the profit interests of Facebook, is hidden behind the social networking enabled by Facebook. The impression that Facebook only benefits users socially is one-sided because it forgets that this social benefit, the social relations and the obtained visibility, are at the heart of the commercial and corporate side of Facebook, its exchange-value and commodity dimension. Exchange-value gets hidden in use-value; the object side of Facebook hides itself in social relations. The object side of Facebook is grounded in social relations between Facebook, ad clients, and users: the exchange relation between Facebook and advertisers on the one hand and coupled to it the advertising relation between advertisers and users. Both relations are necessary in order to create profit for both Facebook and the advertisers. These commercial relations do not immediately present themselves to the users, who mainly see the relationships between themselves and other users. The commercial relations that constitute the commodity side of Facebook are hidden behind the social relations between users. Facebook takes advantage of its inverse fetish character by presenting itself as an organisation that is about sharing and social relations and not about profit.

6.9. Conclusion

The IDDL shows that various forms of labour that are characteristic of various stages of capitalism and capitalist and pre-capitalist modes of production interact so that different forms of separated and highly exploited forms of double free wage labour, unpaid "free" labour, casualised labour, and slave labour form a global network of exploited labour and a collective worker that creates value and profits for a variety of companies involved in the capitalist ICT industry. The IDDL shows that stages of capitalist development and historical modes of production (such as patriarchal housework, classical slavery, feudalism, capitalism in general) and modes of organisation of the productive forces (such as agriculture, industrialism, informationalism) are not simply successive stages of economic development, where one form substitutes an older one, but that they are all dialectically mediated. Capitalism has not destroyed the possibility of slavery: on the one hand slavery exists in a new form as wage slavery, and on the other hand possibilities for the existence of classical and feudal forms of slavery remain and, as the example of slavery in mining shows, exist today in a way that benefits Western ICT companies.

The earliest form of private property was constituted in the patriarchal family. The patriarchal mode of production and housework continue to exist in the IDDL in the form of casualised work of the "free" online workers of Google, Facebook, YouTube, Twitter, etc. and the highly controlled and exploited work of call centre agents and ICT manufacturers. Classical and feudal forms of slavery, in which workers are not double free, but rather the property of slave owners who physically coerce and almost limitlessly exploit them, persist in the extraction of conflict minerals that form the physical foundation of ICTs. Capitalism is based not only on capital accumulation, but also on double-free wage labour, which means that workers are by the threat of dying of hunger compelled to sell their labour power as commodity to capitalists, which alienates them from the process and the products of capitalist production and installs wage labour as specific form of exploitation of labour. Double-free wage labour takes on several specific forms in the IDDL. First, there are wageworkers who work under conditions that resemble the early stage of industrial capitalism. These are manufacturing and assemblage workers, who risk their health and lives at work. Their work is no fun at all. They are subject to high levels of control, workplace surveillance, and standardised work, which shows that Taylorist and Fordist factory work does not cease to exist but continues under new conditions in the information society. Also call centre agents are facing a kind of Taylorist work situation, with the difference that their labour is in contrast to ICT manufacturing and assemblage not primarily physical, but informational in nature in respect to the circumstance that their main activities are talking, convincing with affects, typing, using phone systems, and accessing databases. The IDDL also involves relatively new forms of wage labour that are forms of highly paid and highly stressful play work, as represented by the Google worker. Another important phenomenon are freelancers in the digital industries, who tend to have precarious working conditions.

Digital labour has thus far mainly been used as a term characterising unpaid labour conducted by social media users (see the contributions in Scholz 2013). We can conclude from the discussion in this chapter that social media prosumption is just one form of digital labour that is networked with and connected to other forms of digital labour that together constitute a global ecology of exploitation that enables the existence of digital media. It is time to broaden the meaning of the term *digital labour* to include all forms of paid and unpaid labour that are needed for existence, production, diffusion, and use of digital media. Digital labour is relational in a twofold sense: it is a relation between labour and capital and relational at the level of the global division of labour that is shaped by articulated modes of production, forms of the organisation of the productive forces, and variations of the dominant capitalist mode of production.

The realm of digital media is a specific subsystem of the cultural industries and of cultural labour. Digital labour is a specific form of cultural labour that has to do with the production and productive consumption of digital media. There are other forms of cultural labour that are non-digital. Think for example of a classical music or rock concert. But these forms of live entertainment that are specific types of cultural labour also do not exist independently from the digital realm: artists publish their recordings in digital format on iTunes, Spotify, and similar online platforms. Fans bring their mobile phones for taking pictures and recording concert excerpts that they share on social media platforms. There is little cultural labour that is fully independent from the digital realm today. The notion of digital work and digital labour wants to signify those forms of cultural labour that contribute to the existence of digital technologies and digital content. It is a specific form of cultural labour.

Given these preliminary assumptions about the work-labour distinction and cultural materialism, one can provide a definition of digital work and digital labour:

> Digital work is a specific form of work that makes use of the body, mind or machines or a combination of all or some of these elements as an instrument of work in order to organize nature, resources extracted from nature, or culture and human experiences, in such a way that digital media are produced and used. The products of digital work are depending on the type of work: minerals, components, digital media tools or digitally mediated symbolic representations, social relations, artefacts, social systems and communities. Digital work includes all activities that create use-values that are objectified in digital media technologies, contents and products generated by applying digital media.
>
> *Fuchs 2014a, 352*

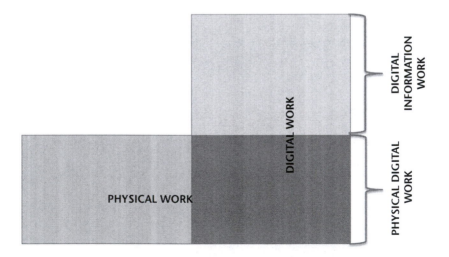

FIGURE 6.3 A stage model of digital work

Digital labour is alienated digital work: it is alienated from itself, from the instruments and objects of labour and from the products of labour. Alienation is alienation of the subject from itself (labour-power is put to use for and is controlled by capital), alienation from the object (the objects of labour and the instruments of labour) and the subject-object (the products of labour). Digital work and digital labour are broad categories that involve all activities in the production of digital media technologies and contents. This means that in the capitalist media industry, different forms of alienation and exploitation can be encountered. Examples are slave workers in mineral extraction, Taylorist hardware assemblers, software engineers, professional online content creators (e.g. online journalists), call centre agents and social media prosumers,

Fuchs 2014a, 351–352

The realm of digital media is a specific subsystem of the cultural industries and of cultural labour. Digital labour is a specific form of cultural labour that has to do with the production and productive consumption of digital media. There are other forms of cultural labour that are non-digital. Think for example of a classical music or rock concert. But these forms of live entertainment that are specific types of cultural labour also do not exist independently from the digital realm: Artists publish their recordings in digital format on iTunes, Spotify, and similar online platforms. Fans bring their mobile phones for taking pictures and recording concert excerpts that they share on social media platforms. There is little cultural labour that is fully independent from

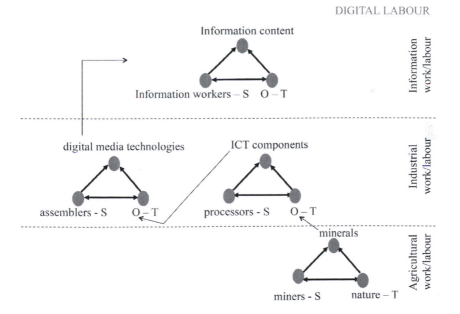

FIGURE 6.4 The complex network of cycles of digital labour

the digital realm today. The notion of digital work and digital labour wants to signify those forms of cultural labour that contribute to the existence of digital technologies and digital content. It is a specific form of cultural labour. Figure 2 applies the stage model of cultural work (see Figure 2.1 in chapter 2) to digital work.

Figure 6.4 shows a model of the major production processes that are involved in digital labour. Each production step/labour process involves human subjects (S) using technologies/instruments of labour (T) on objects of labour (O) so that a product emerges. The very foundation of digital labour is an agricultural labour cycle in which miners extract minerals. These minerals enter the next production process as objects so that processors based on them in physical labour processes create ICT components. These components enter the next labour cycle as objects: assemblage workers build digital media technologies and take ICT components as inputs. Processors and assemblers are industrial workers involved in digital production. The outcome of such labour are digital media technologies that enter various forms of information work as tools for the production, distribution, circulation, prosumption, and consumption of diverse types of information.

Digital labour is not a term that only describes the production of digital content. I rather use the term in a more general sense for the whole mode of digital production that contains a network of agricultural, industrial, and informational forms of work that enables the existence and usage of digital media. The subjects involved in the digital mode of production (S)—miners, processors, assemblers, information workers, and related workers—stand in specific relations of production that are either class relations or non-class relations. So what I designate as S in Figure 6.4 is actually a relationship S_1—S_2 between different subjects or subject groups. In contemporary capitalist society, most of these digital relations of production tend to be shaped by wage labour, slave labour, unpaid labour, precarious labour, and freelance labour. The political task is that people working under such class relations emancipate themselves so that a communist mode of production can emerge that contains a communist mode of digital production as well as non-digital communist modes of production.

What is the advantage of a broad concept of digital labour? For a revolution that overcomes capitalism and establishes a participatory democracy, workers of all lands have to unite globally. Digital workers are, however, most immediately confronted with the rule of specific transnational companies in a direct or indirect way. Transnational digital media companies make use of a global division of labour, which allows them to outsource labour and reduce labour costs. If workers involved in a division of labour that creates a specific product for a transnational corporation join forces and protest or strike together, they are more likely to make demands successfully because they can bring the entire interconnected chain of production to a standstill. A broad definition of digital labour stresses the need of workers who operate in the same division of labour to unite in order to challenge capitalist rule. Practically speaking this means that efforts of converging and transnational unions and labour movements should be strengthened and supported. Bringing together workers whose job contents are different, but whom the same transnational communication company exploits, can overcome

TABLE 6.3 Dimensions of working conditions

MODEL 2 (Figure 2.6, Table 2.2)		MODEL 1 (Figures 2.3, 6.2)
Productive forces—	Machines and equipment	Object: Instruments of labour
Means of production	Resources	Object: Object of labour
Productive	Workforce characteristics	Subject
forces—Labour	Mental and physical health	Subject
	Work experiences	Subject
Relations of production	Labour contracts	Subject-subject relationships: Relations of production
	Wages and benefits	Subject-subject relationships: Relations of production
	Labour struggles	Subject-subject relationships: Relations of production
Production process	Labour spaces	Object: Instruments of labour
	Labour times	Subject-subject relationships: Relations of production
	Work activity	Subject
	Control mechanism	Subject-subject relationships: Relations of production
Results of production	Labour product	Subject-object: Products of labour
The state	Labour law	Subject-subject relationships: Relations of production

the anonymity of the commodity fetish and the division of labour and be a foundation for workers' solidarity. The final step is that all workers of the world unite for a revolution against capitalism. A first step is, however, that workers exploited by the same company unite in order to challenge their immediate exploiters.

In chapter 2's section 4, we introduced a model of the work process in general (see Figures 2.3, 6.2). Section 2.5 presented a model for the analysis of working conditions in capitalism (Table 2.2, Figure 2.6). How are these two models connected? The first one is more general and presents typologies for all modes of production (patriarchy, slavery, feudalism, capitalism, communism) and productive forces (agricultural, industrial, informational). The second model shows dimension of labour within the capitalist mode of production. Table 6.3 shows how elements in model 1 (Figures 2.3, 6.2) correspond to elements in model 2 (Figure 2.6, Table 2.2).

We have developed a systematic digital labour analysis toolkit that helps to ask systematic questions about the involved labour processes. It can be applied to agricultural, industrial, and informational digital labour and combinations of these forms of work. Table 6.4 presents the digital labour analysis toolkit (first introduced in Fuchs and Sandoval 2014) that is based on the more general model introduced in Table 2.2 (the model in Table 2.2 was first introduced in Sandoval 2013).

Just as Raymond Williams (1977) stressed the need for cultural materialism, we need to stress the importance of a "digital materialism" in the digital labour debate. But one may interpose that miners or assemblers may not just produce minerals and components for digital media, but for many other products too. In such cases, their

TABLE 6.4 Digital labour analysis toolkit (source: Fuchs and Sandoval 2014)

Productive forces—Means of production	Machines and equipment	What technologies or combinations thereof are being used during the agricultural, industrial, and informational production process that create digital media and contents?	a) non-digital machines b) digital machines c) human brain d) human hands
	Resources	What resources or combinations thereof are used during the agricultural, industrial, and informational production processes of digital media and content?	a) physical resources: natural resources b) digital and mediated data/information c) human ideas d) physical resources: industrial resource
Productive forces—Labour	Workforce characteristics	What are important characteristics of the workforce in agricultural, industrial, and informational digital labour (for example in terms of age, gender, ethnic background etc.)?:	a) class b) gender b) age c) ethnicity d) abilities e) education, etc.
	Mental and physical health	How do the employed means of production and the labour process impact mental and physical health of agricultural, industrial, and informational digital workers?	a) mental health b) physical health
	Work experiences	How do agricultural, industrial, and informational digital workers experience their working conditions?	

Relations of production	Labour contracts	Are there labour contracts or not? In the case where there are labour contracts: Which type of contracts do digital workers receive, what do they regulate?	a) no contract, b) written/oral contract, c) part-time or full-time employment contract, d) permanent or temporary employment contract, e) employment or service contract, f) freelancer or employee, etc.
	Wages and benefits	Are there wages and specific benefits digital workers enjoy or not? In cases where there are wages and benefits: How high/low are wage levels and what are other material benefits for digital workers?	a) wage level b) included/excluded health benefits c) included/excluded retirement insurance (state/private/company/mixed insurance) d) included/excluded unemployment insurance e) included/excluded monetary and non-monetary perks, etc.
	Labour struggles	Is there the possibility that digital workers form associations (freedom of association)? If so, do such associations exist and what do they do? If so, how do digital workers organise and engage in negotiations with capital and what is the role of worker protests?	a) yellow unions, b) no worker associations, c) informal social networks, d) state-recognised trade unions, e) autonomous trade unions and social movements, f) self-managed companies, co-operatives, etc.

(continued)

TABLE 6.4 (Continued)

Production process	Labour spaces	In which space or combination of spaces does the production process take place?	a) natural (e.g. mines, parks, etc.) or human-built spaces (offices, factories, coffeehouses, homes, etc.) spaces, b) private, public, or semi-public spaces, c) digital or non-digital spaces, d) clear, fluid, or non-existing boundaries between working spaces and other spaces of human life, etc.
	Labour times	How many working hours are common within a certain sector, how are they enforced, and how is the relationship between work and free time?	a) legally unregulated or regulated working times, b) contractually unregulated or regulated working times, c) average amount of hours worked per week/month/year d) average amount of d1) paid and d2) unpaid overtime worked per week/month/year, e) clear, fluid, or non-existing boundaries between work time and free time, etc.
	Work activity	Which type of mental and/or physical activity or combinations thereof are digital workers performing?	a) physical work: agricultural work, b) physical work: industrial work, c) information work

Control mechanism	Are there forms of control that benefit others at the expense of workers? Which type of mechanisms are in place that control the behaviour of workers? Are there forms of control that control the controllers?	a) no control mechanism, b) self-control and/or control by others, c) social and/or technological control, d) social control by peers (peer control), e) social control by supervisors and managers, f) digital or non-digital technological control, g) surveillance of applicants, workplace, workforce, output, activities, property, consumers, prosumers, competitors, h) controls that are inherent to production technologies, controls that are external (i.e. separate control technologies), g) forms of counter-control (corporate watchdogs, workplace inspectors,
Results of production	Which kinds of products or services does digital labour produce?	a) digital or non-digital products, b) online or offline products, c) physical (agricultural, industrial) and/or informational and/or social (-service) product, etc.

(continued)

TABLE 6.4 (Continued)

The state	Labour legislation	Are there state laws that regulate work? Which regulations regarding minimum wages, maximum working hours, safety, social security, etc. are in place and how are they enforced?	a) Regulation and enforcement of work and service contracts, legal dispute resolution, b) Wage legislation: wage protections, minimum wage regulation, etc., c) Work time legislation: standard working times, maximum working hours, overtime regulations, annual leave, sabbatical leave, on-the-job-training times and further education, flexible working, termination of employment (protection from unfair dismissal, redundancy payments, etc.), etc., d) Health and safety legislation: work space regulations, work equipment and resources regulations, dangerous substances, protective gear, etc., e) Social security benefit legislation: parental leave, unemployment, pension, health care, etc., f) Employee representation and freedom of association, g) Taxation: corporation tax, income and wage tax, etc.

labour is not digital labour to a full degree, but to a specific relative percentage share that can be calculated on average for a specific period of analysis (such as one year).

The upper level of information work in Figure 6.4 can certainly not be ignored and is an important dimension of digital labour. Here we do not just find one form of information work, but a complex multitude of different types of information processing that relates to digital media in various ways.

Digital information labour can take on different forms. The information worker can have an online profile/website/blog etc. or not. Also the employer/contractor can have an online profile/website/blog etc. or not. The relationship between the two can be established and maintained primarily online (e.g. via platforms such as Amazon Mechanical Turk, oDesk, or PeoplePerHour), offline, or in a blended way. The technologies used for production always involve the brain because we talk about information work. But in addition also digital tools and/or non-digital tools can be used as means of production. The objects on which the labour is conducted can either be entirely digital, non-digital, or both digital and non-digital. The created products can be digital, non-digital, or a mix of both. Their distribution and consumption can take place online or offline. This means that there are eight dimensions of digital information labour that can have various characteristics. The number of logical forms of digital information labour can be calculated by multiplying various binominal coefficients:

$$\binom{2}{1} \times \binom{2}{1} \times \binom{3}{1} \times \binom{4}{1} \times \binom{3}{1} \times \binom{3}{1} \times \binom{2}{1} \times \binom{2}{1}$$

$$\binom{n}{k} = \frac{n!}{k! \times (n-k)!}$$

$$\binom{2}{1} = \frac{2!}{1! \times 1!} = 2$$

$$\binom{3}{1} = \frac{3!}{1! \times 2!} = 3$$

$$\binom{4}{1} = \frac{4!}{1! \times 3!} = 4$$

$$2 \times 2 \times 3 \times 4 \times 3 \times 3 \times 2 \times 2 = 1,728$$

So from a purely logical point of view, there are 1,728 different possible forms of digital information labour. Which of them occur in actual reality is an empirical question. These 1,728 possibilities represent the productive forces of digital information labour that are embedded into and interact with specific relations of production.

It is a theoretical question if all of these 1,728 forms of labour are digital labour or if only those that satisfy a minimum number of characteristics that are digital should be considered as digital labour. Or should all activities characterised by

TABLE 6.5 A typology of the digitalisation of information labour

Information worker	Employer, contractor	Relations of production	Technology	Objects	Products	Distribution	Consumption
1 Online	1 online	1 online	1 brain	1 digital	1 digital	1 online	1 digital
2 Offline	2 offline	2 offline	2 brain + digital technologies	2 non-digital	2 non-digital	2 offline	2 non-digital
		3 blended	3 brain + non-digital technologies	3 blended	3 blended		
			4 brain + digital technologies + non-digital technologies				

the typology that contain at least one dimension that is digital be considered as forms of digital labour? The typology shows in any case that it is possible to observe and with this typology characterise the digitalisation or informatisation of various dimensions of work, such as the way people look for jobs and employment, employers' search for labour power, the relations of production, the technological means of production, the used resources, the created products, forms of distribution, and forms of consumption. Rudi Schmiede (1996) uses the term "informatisation of work" for describing how information technologies shape the work process. He does not limit the term to the computerisation of work, but mentions other information technologies, such as the postal service, the telegraph, double bookkeeping, books of accounts, or file card systems (Schmiede 1996, 122). The computerisation or digitalisation of work is one specific form of the informatisation of work: digital media technologies shape various aspects of different forms of work. Schmiede says the fact that computer technologies enable the networking of information has resulted in a form of abstract societalisation (*Vergesellschaftung*) in capitalism: all forms of work could in principle be shaped and influenced by the networked computer so that "the informatisation of societal work opens access for the measure of value and valorisation to each individual work that is integrated into an in principle global information context" (Schmiede 1996, 125, translation from German[2]).

The characterisation of digital information work makes use of eight symbolic positions: each describes one dimension of digital information work according to Table 6.5. Each dimension's expression is defined according to the codes in Table 6.5. The typology in Table 6.5 describes various dimensions of the digitalisation or networked computerisation of labour. It is a theoretical question which of these forms of labour should be termed digital information labour and which ones should not.

Let us consider an example: a call centre worker conducting labour at a physical call centre where s/he meets colleagues and is supervised by a boss is like her employer primarily located offline. The class relation is primarily mediated offline. We assume that she calls people to try to convince them to participate in a phone survey. She uses her brain and digital technologies such as a networked computer database, a computer, and a digital phone as means of production and obtains phone numbers to call from a digital database (= object of production). She creates content (survey data) in a database, so the created product is digital. The final data is distributed to the call centre's client online in the form of a SPSS file that is consumed in digital format. So this form of call centre work is digital information work version number 22221111 (according to the classification in Table 6.5).

Another example: a blogger who generates postings for a newspaper's website and works from home. She conducts her work primarily online, i.e. she blogs on the Internet, and her employer's presence for her is its newspaper website. The communication between the blogger and the newspaper's online editor takes place primarily online, but from time to time there are real-life meetings in order to discuss the newspaper's online strategy. So the production relationship has a blended character. The blogger uses her brain and digital technologies such as a laptop connected to the Internet and a blogging platform, so the used technologies are a human brain and digital technologies. The objects of work are the blogger's experiences, opinions, and thoughts (non-digital information) and other online documents to which she links (digital), so the objects of work are blended. The product is a digital text that is distributed and consumed online in digital format. Using the typology in Table 6.5, we can characterise the blogger's work as an example of digital information work version number 11323111.

A third example: freelancers offering translation or copyediting services via a freelance platform such as peopleperhour.com. The information worker advertises her/his services online with help of the freelance platform. The contractor searches for freelancers in the online database of the platform. The class relationship is entirely organised online, it is unlikely that the contractor and the worker meet in person. The freelancer uses his/her brain and a computer as main production technologies and takes an existing digital document as input (object of work). The output has digital format, is distributed to the contractor online, and is read or published in digital format. Using the typology in Table 6.5, we can characterise the freelancer's work as an example of digital information work version number 11121111.

When analysing digital labour, one not just needs to characterise the digital productive forces, but also the relations of digital production. Marx pointed out that the piece wage is "the most fruitful source of reductions in wages, and of frauds committed by the capitalists" (Marx 1867, 694). On peopleperhour.com, it is only possible to pay for a full product, not per hour. It organises relations of exploitation that are grounded in the piece wage. The piece wage relationship is both a method of absolute and relative surplus value production: Workers may have to work long hours in order to achieve a minimum wage that guarantees their survival. This is especially the case with platforms such as peopleperhour or Amazon Mechanical Turk that are designed to crowdsource labour in order to reduce investment costs. At the same time the online freelancers will try to work as fast as possible because they do not have a guaranteed hourly wage. The result is that as a result of platforms such as peopleperhour, there is a tendency that there are fewer jobs and less payment.

Marx (1857/58, 305) discusses the role of the piano maker and the piano player in the world of music. Today, there are not just these two rules and cultural industries commodifying both activities, but there is also the separate labour of the composer. They all together form the cultural industry of music. There is an analogy between piano music and digital labour. Just like we find piano makers, music composers, and piano players in the music industry, we find labour involved in hardware production (makers), content and software production (composers), and productive users (prosumers, players, play labour) in the world of digital labour. In the realm of digital labour, we have to emphasise that practices are "from the beginning social and material" (Williams 1989, 206).

The world of digital media is shaped by a complex global articulation of various modes of production that together constitute the capitalist mode of creating and using digital media. The digital tools that we use for writing, reading, communicating, uploading, browsing, collaborating, chatting, befriending, or liking are embedded into a world of exploitation. Yet most of us cannot and do not want to imagine a world without digital media. So the alternative is not digital Luddism, but political praxis.

Notes

1 http://www.reddit.com/r/AskReddit/comments/clz1m/google_employees_on_reddit_fire_up_your_throwaway/ (accessed October 26, 2014).
2 „Allgemein gesagt, eröffnet die Informatisierung der gesellschaftlichen Arbeit dem Wert- und Verwertungsmaßstab den Zugriff auf jede einzelne Arbeit, die in einen prinzipiell globalen Inforamtionszusammenhang eingegliedert ist."

7

BAIDU, WEIBO, AND RENREN: THE GLOBAL POLITICAL ECONOMY OF SOCIAL MEDIA IN CHINA

7.1. Introduction

Six of the world's 20 most accessed WWW platforms are based in China: Baidu, QQ, Taobao, Sina, Hao123, and Weibo. Thirteen are US companies.[1] This circumstance is indicative for what some have termed the rise of China (Hsiao and Lin 2009; Li 2008b; Schmitt 2009). The four companies that operate the major six Chinese WWW platforms—Alibaba, Baidu, Sina, and Tencent—are all privately owned capitalist corporations listed on stock markets. They are therefore also symbols of China's economic transformation: The 1954 Chinese Constitution defined as "the main categories of ownership of means of production in the People's Republic of China": "state ownership, that is, ownership by the whole people; co-operative ownership, that is, collective ownership by the masses of working people; ownership by individual working people; and capitalist ownership" (article 5). Capitalist ownership was seen as transitory: the state would aim at "gradually replacing capitalist ownership with ownership by the whole people" (article 10).[2] In contrast, a 1998 amendment to China's 1982 Constitution defines capitalism as a compliment to socialism: "The State permits the private sector of the economy to exist and develop within the limits prescribed by law. The private sector of the economy is a complement to the socialist public economy" (Amendment 1).[3]

The Chinese Internet stands in the context of capitalism in China. The task of this chapter is to conduct a political-economic analysis of China's major social media platforms in the context of the Chinese economy's transformations. A critical political-economic analysis of the media focuses on aspects of commodification, ideology, and social struggles (Fuchs 2011a; Hardy 2014; Mosco 2009; Murdock and Gdding 2005). This multidimensional approach is grounded in

Karl Marx's (1867) approach. Marx stressed that capitalism is a) "an immense collection of commodities" (125) and b) that the commodity form is connected to ideological structures that present the world standing "on its head" (163), make reality's "content concealed within these [ideological] forms" (173–174), and present historical forms as "eternal natural form" (174). It also stresses that c) capitalism is "a struggle between collective capital, i.e. the class of capitalists, and collective labour, i.e. the working class" (345).

Given these three dimensions, for studying social media in the context of Chinese capitalism this chapter therefore analyses a) social media's capital and commodity form in China (section 3), b) social media ideologies associated with Chinese social media capital (section 4), and c) Chinese working-class struggles' implications for social media (section 5). Search engines, microblogs, and social networking sites are three important forms of contemporary social media (Fuchs 2014b). In Western countries, Google, Twitter, and Facebook are the major representatives of these three kinds of platforms. The methodological approach taken in this chapter compares the political economy of the major Chinese search engine Baidu to Google, the political economy of the major Chinese microblog Sina Weibo to Twitter, and the political economy of the major Chinese social networking site Renren to Facebook. These analyses are contextualised by an analysis of transformations of the Chinese economy (section 2).

7.2. The Development of the Chinese Economy

7.2.1. Data on the Chinese Economy

Table 7.1 shows that what some call the rise of China (Hsiao and Lin 2009; Li 2008b; Schmitt 2009) has to do with the circumstance that China has since the 1980s increased its share in the global GDP from around 5 per cent to more than 17 per cent. According to other data, China's share of the worldwide GDP (PPP) was 15.98 per cent in 2014 and projected to be 17.88 per cent in 2018, whereas the United States' share was 19.11 per cent in 2014 and projected to be 18.60 per cent in 2018 (data source: IMF World Economic Outlook Database). China and the United States were the only two countries with shares above 10 per cent. The European Union's share was 18.29 per cent in 2014 and projected to be 16.75 per cent in 2018.

Figure 7.1 shows that China has since the early 1990s continuously had high annual GDP growth rates varying between 7 per cent and 15 per cent. The OECD countries, the European Union, and the United States could in the same period never reach such high growth rates, have had fluctuating economic performances, and were much harder hit by the crisis that started in 2008 than China. Peter Nolan (2012) cautions to be careful about the interpretation of such data. China's national income per person would only be a fraction of that of the European Union and North America, income inequality would be high, and the

TABLE 7.1 Percentage share of selected countries and regions in world GDP, data source: Agnus Maddison, historical statistics of the world economy, 1–2008 AD: GDP

	1	1000	1500	1600	1700	1820	1870	1900	1913	1950	1960	1970	1980	1990	2000	2006	2008
30 Western European countries	13.69	9.01	17.79	19.79	21.87	23.02	33.08	34.24	33.01	26.16	26.68	26.08	24.20	22.23	20.55	17.80	17.06
USA	0.26	0.43	0.32	0.18	0.14	1.81	8.85	15.83	18.93	27.28	24.27	22.38	21.11	21.39	21.89	19.61	18.61
Latin America	2.13	3.76	2.93	1.14	1.71	2.15	2.46	3.64	4.42	7.78	8.09	8.28	9.78	8.25	8.36	7.71	7.94
16 East Asian countries						55.66	35.09	25.37	22.39	15.88	17.55	19.66	21.77	27.79	33.01	38.17	39.19
China	25.45	22.68	24.88	28.96	22.30	32.92	17.08	11.05	8.83	4.59	5.24	4.63	5.20	7.83	11.77	16.78	17.48
India	32.02	27.84	24.36	22.40	24.44	16.04	12.14	8.64	7.47	4.16	3.88	3.41	3.18	4.05	5.18	6.11	6.70
Africa	7.62	11.32	7.76	7.04	6.92	4.49	4.07	3.35	2.91	3.80	3.57	3.55	3.61	3.33	3.20	3.28	3.40

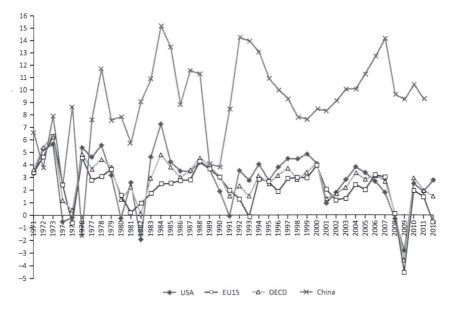

FIGURE 7.1 The development of GDP growth in China and other regions

number of transnational Chinese companies in lists of the largest companies in the world small (Nolan 2012, 66–67). Furthermore, two thirds of China's outward foreign direct investments (FDI) would go to Hong Kong, only very small shares to the West, and China would hardly participate in mergers and acquisitions of transnational companies (TNCs) (Nolan 2012, 97–98). Nolan argues that there are indications that China exports value created in the country to other countries more than benefitting internally.

> Despite widespread perceptions in the international media that China is buying the world, their presence in the high-income countries is negligible. [. . .] After three decades of capitalist globalization there is a tremendous disparity in business power between firms from high-income countries and those from developing countries. The companies that have established themselves at the core of the global business system almost all have their headquarters in the high-income countries.
>
> *Nolan 2012, 140*

Table 7.2 shows the growth of Mainland China's imports and exports. The data indicate how China has been transformed from a relatively self-sustaining economy into one that bases around one third of its economic activity on exports and imports and involvement in the capitalist world market. The start of the world economic crisis in 2008 meant that China faced difficulties to buy and sell on the

TABLE 7.2 Share of China's imports and exports in the GDP, data source: UNCTAD

	1970	1975	1980	1985	1990	1995	2000	2005	2008	2009	2011
Exports	2.6%	4.6%	10.5%	9.2%	15.5%	19.4%	23.4%	36.6%	34.9%	26.3%	30.6%
Imports	2.7%	4.6%	10.9%	13.2%	12.9%	17.0%	21.0%	31.2%	27.2%	22.0%	27.1%

world market so that its trade volume contracted. By 2011 it had, however, again relatively increased the share of imports and exports in the GDP.

In 2012, China exported agricultural and industrial products that had a total value of around US$2.0 trillion and services with a total value of around US$0.19 trillion (data source: Trade Map—International Trade Statistics). In the same years, it imported industrial and agricultural products with a total value of around US$1.9 trillion and services of around US$0.28 trillion (data source: Trade Map—International Trade Statistics). The statistics show that around 91 per cent of China's exports and 87 per cent of its imports are located in agriculture and the manufacturing industries.

Table 7.3 gives an overview of China's largest export and import sectors. China's exports are focused on electronic equipment and computing and other machinery as well as parts, circuits, and accessories for such technologies. Its imports are focused on machinery, energy, and raw materials. The export and import of services is relatively small in comparison to manufactured and agricultural products: The value of exported business services—the largest group of exported services—is smaller than the value of the third-largest sector in the export of manufactured and agricultural products (articles of apparel, accessories, knit or crochet). (data souce: Trade Map–International Trade Statistics).

Data shows that the most important products that China exports in the electronic equipment sector are appliances for line telephony and integrated circuits (data source: Trade Map—International Trade Statistics). In the realm of machinery, the most important Chinese exports are computers and computer parts. In the realm of apparel, the most important Chinese exports are suits, dresses, pullovers, jackets, and trousers. The largest importers of China's electronic products were in 2013 Hong Kong (33.1 per cent), the United States (14.8 per cent), Japan (6.2 per cent), and Korea (6.1 per cent). The largest importers of Chinese machinery were in 2013 the United States (22.6 per cent), Hong Kong (14.1 per cent), Japan (6.7 per cent), the Netherlands (5.5 per cent), and Germany (4.0 per cent). The United States (15.3 per cent), Japan (11.6 per cent), Hong Kong (7.4 per cent), Vietnam (4.9 per cent), and the United Kingdom (4.1 per cent) were in 2013 the largest importers of clothes manufactured in China (data source: Trade Map—International Trade Statistics).

TABLE 7.3 The five largest Chinese import and export sectors in manufacturing/agriculture and services (data source: Trade Map—International Trade Statistics)

Share of exported manufacturing and agricultural products, 2013		Share of exported services, 2012		Share of imported manufacturing and agricultural products, 2013		Share of imported services, 2012	
Electrical, electronic equipment	25.4%	Other business services	34.8%	Electrical, electronic equipment	22.5%	Travel	36.3%
Machinery, nuclear reactors, boilers, etc.	17.3%	Travel	26.1%	Mineral fuels, oils, distillation products, etc.	16.1%	Transportation	30.5%
Articles of apparel, accessories, knit or crochet	4.4%	Transportation	20.3%	Machinery, nuclear reactors, boilers, etc.	8.8%	Other business services	15.1%
Furniture, lighting, signs, prefabricated buildings	3.9%	Computer and information services	7.6%	Ores, slag, and ash	7.6%	Insurance services	7.3%
Optical, photo, technical, medical, etc. apparatus	3.4%	Construction services	6.4%	Optical, photo, technical, medical, etc. apparatus	5.5%	Royalties and license fees	6.3%

TABLE 7.4 China's exports in 2013, data source: National Bureau of Statistics of China 2014

Country	Exports in US$100 millions
EU	2,200
ASEAN	1,996
Republic of Korea	1,831
Japan	1,623
Taiwan	1,566
USA	1,525
Russia	396
India	170
Hong Kong	162

China's major export goods have in 2013 been data processing machines and accessories (value: US$1,822 million) and clothes and clothing accessories (value of US$1,770 million) (data source: National Bureau of Statistics of China 2014). Table 7.4 shows that the European Union has in 2013 been the major recipient of Chinese exports. In 2011, 52.4 per cent of all Chinese exports were foreign-funded (National Bureau of Statistics of China 2012).

Figure 7.2 shows the development of FDI flows into and out of China (Mainland China and Hong Kong combined). There has been a strong increase of FDI inflows and outflows since the end of the 1970s when Deng Xiaoping opened up the Chinese economy to the global capitalist system, which made it easier for foreign companies to invest in China. In 2012, China accounted for 14.5 per cent of the world's FDI inflows and 12.1 per cent of all FDI outflows (data source: UNCTAD).

Data from 2010 shows that 29.96 per cent of FDI inflows to China were located in an unspecified secondary sector, 28.82 per cent were business activities (6.2 per cent in real estate activities), 5.75 per cent were located in wholesale and retail trade, 3.6 per cent in chemicals and chemical products, 3.2 per cent in machinery and equipment, 2.9 per cent in electrical and electronic equipment, and 2.7 per cent in motor vehicles and other transport equipment (data source: Trade Map—International Trade Statistics). This statistical data is, however, incomplete and aggregated at a high level. It does not specify which industries are part of the "unspecified secondary sector" that makes up almost one third of all FDI inflows into China. We can therefore as an alternative indicator that provides some indication about the structure of FDI inflows to China have a look at data that specifies in which industries foreign companies that have affiliates in China are located. Table 7.5 shows the share of foreign transnational companies that have affiliates in specific Chinese industries. The data indicates that electronic equipment, trade computing and other machinery, clothing and metal production, and vehicle manufacturing are very important realms of foreign

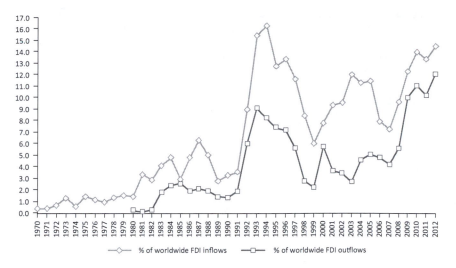

FIGURE 7.2 Development of China's foreign direct investment in- and outflows

direct investment in China and that manufacturing is much more important than services in FDI inflows to China. Chun Lin (2013, 58) cites data that shows that foreign capital controls large parts of the Chinese chemical, electronics, information and communications technology (ICT), machinery and motor industries. These data are an indication that foreign transnational corporations dominate China's export markets and use Chinese labour for the assemblage of electronic products and the finishing of clothes.

Table 7.6 shows that 9.1 per cent of all TNCs of the largest TNCs in the world were in 2013 located in China and that this is a relatively small share in comparison to the United States.

7.2.2. The Chinese Information Economy

A typical development of the productive forces in Western countries has in the past fifty years been the shrinking of the agricultural and manufacturing sectors and the increase of the share of the service, financial, and information industries in value added and employment (Fuchs 2011a, chapter 3.4; Fuchs 2014a, chapter 5). Tables 7.7 and 7.8 show that China's productive forces have since 1970 developed in such a way that agriculture has strongly declined its share in value added. At the same time, there was not, as in many parts of the West, a decrease of the manufacturing sector's value added share, but rather a simultaneous growth of the share of the manufacturing industries and the service sector in value added. China's urban metropolises are today industrial, financial, and informational centres, whereas poor rural parts are the primary locations of agriculture.

TABLE 7.5 Share of foreign transnational companies active in China in specific industries, year 2012; shown are industries with shares > 10%, total number of foreign parent companies (100%): 18,328, data source: Trade Map—International Trade Statistics

Industry	Share
Electrical and electronic equipment	29.3%
Wholesale and retail trade	21.9%
Machinery and equipment	19.4%
Textiles, clothes, leather	16.0%
Metal and metal products	15.9%
Motor vehicles and other transport equipment	14.3%
Business activities	11.5%

TABLE 7.6 Share of companies located in specific countries in the Forbes 2000 list of the world's largest transnational corporations (data source: Forbes 2000, 2013 list)

Country	Number of TNCs	Market Value	Sales	Profits	Assets
USA	542, 27.1%	37.9%	29.2%	35.9%	22.6%
Japan	251, 12.6%	6.7%	12.3%	4.5%	11.4%
China, Hong Kong	181, 9.1%	8.9%	9.1%	13.9%	11.7%
UK	95, 4.8%	5.9%	5.6%	4.7%	8.8%
Canada	65, 3.3%	3.1%	2.2%	3.0%	3.6%

TABLE 7.7 Development of the share of Mainland China's economic sectors in total value added, data source: UNCTAD, in %

	1970	1975	1980	1985	1990	1995	2000	2005	2011
Agriculture, hunting, forestry, fishing	35.3	32.5	30.2	28.0	26.8	20.0	15.1	12.1	10.1
Industry	40.2	45.5	48.2	42.5	41.1	47.3	45.9	47.4	46.8
Services	24.5	22.0	21.6	29.5	32.1	32.8	39.0	40.1	43.1

TABLE 7.8 Development of the share of Mainland China's and Hong Kong's economic sectors in total value added, data source: UNCTAD, in %

	1970	1975	1980	1985	1990	1995	2000	2005	2011
Agriculture, hunting, forestry, fishing	34.0	30.7	27.8	25.4	22.6	16.8	13.3	11.3	9.8
Industry	39.8	44.5	46.7	41.0	38.1	41.9	41.9	44.6	45.5
Services	26.2	24.7	25.6	33.5	39.2	41.3	44.8	44.2	44.7

One can measure the size of economic sectors either based on an industry approach that counts all employees independent of their occupation as working in an industry that produces a specific good, or an occupation approach that counts the number of people in the entire economy who have a certain occupation independent of the type of companies and branches they work in (Machlup 1962, 45). Tables 7.9 and 7.10 apply these two approaches for measuring the development of the size of the agricultural, industrial, and service sectors in China. The calculation was based on the following mapping of branches and occupations to economic sectors:

Agricultural sector:
Occupations: skilled agricultural, forestry, and fishery workers.
Branches: agriculture, forestry, fishing, and animal husbandry; mining and quarrying.

Industrial sector:
Occupations: craft and machine operation–related workers.
Branches: manufacturing; electricity and gas supply; water supply and remediation services; construction.

Service sector:
Occupations: legislators; senior officials and managers; professionals, technicians, and associate professionals; clerical support workers; service and sales workers.
Branches: wholesale and retail trade; transportation and storage; accommodation and food services; information and communication; finance and insurance; real estate; professional, scientific and technical services; support services; public administration and defense; compulsory social security; education, human health and social work services; arts, entertainment, and recreation; other services.

TABLE 7.9 Development of the Chinese economy's productive forces using the occupation approach for measuring employment shares in %, data source: Statistical Yearbook of the Republic of China 2011

	Agricultural occupations	*Industrial occupations*	*Service occupations*
2001	7.2	35.1	57.7
2002	7.2	33.7	59.1
2003	6.9	33.3	59.8
2004	6.2	33.3	60.5
2005	5.6	33.0	61.4
2006	5.2	32.4	62.4
2007	5.0	32.2	62.9
2008	4.8	31.8	63.4
2009	4.9	30.6	64.4
2010	4.9	30.5	64.6
2011	4.6	31.3	64.1

TABLE 7.10 Development of the Chinese economy's productive forces using the industrial approach for measuring employment shares in %, data source: Statistical Yearbook of the Republic of China 2011

	Agricultural sector	Industrial sector	Service sector
2001	7.6	36.5	55.9
2002	7.6	35.7	56.7
2003	7.4	35.4	57.2
2004	6.6	35.8	57.5
2005	6.0	36.3	57.7
2006	5.5	36.5	57.9
2007	5.3	36.7	57.9
2008	5.2	36.8	58.0
2009	5.3	35.8	58.9
2010	5.3	35.9	58.8
2011	5.1	36.3	58.6

Employment in agricultural and industrial occupations continuously decreased in relative terms in the years 2001 to 2011, whereas the share of service occupations increased from 57.7 per cent in 2001 to 64.1 per cent in 2011. Using the industry approach for measuring employment shows that employment in the industrial sector remained constant at around 35 per cent of total employment in the years 2001 to 2011, whereas the service sector's employment share increased from 56 per cent to 59 per cent and the agricultural sector's share decreased from 7.6 per cent to 5.1 per cent.

Table 7.11 outlines that in the information sector, China's TNCs accounted for 5.1 per cent of the world's largest TNCs in 2013.

TABLE 7.11 Financial shares of information companies that are located in specific countries, Forbes 2000 list of the world's largest transnational information corporations (data source: Forbes 2000, 2013 list). Sectors of the information industry: Communications equipment, computer hardware, computer services, computer storage devices, consumer electronics, electronics, Internet & catalogue retail, printing & publishing, semiconductors, software & programming, telecommunications services

Country	Number of TNCs	Market Value	Sales	Profits	Assets
USA	82, 32.4%	52.3%	36.1%	51.4%	38.9%
Japan	32, 12.6%	6.1%	18.4%	0.8%	15.5%
Taiwan	20, 7.9%	3.7%	7.7%	5.7%	3.8%
China, Hong Kong	13, 5.1%	6.2%	5.4%	8.0%	5.9%
France	11, 4.3%	2.0%	3.6%	0.9%	4.2%
UK	11, 4.3%	4.2%	3.3%	5.9%	4.9%
South Korea	10, 4.0%	3.8%	6.4%	7.1%	4.8%
Canada	7, 2.8%	2.0%	1.6%	2.2%	2.1%
Netherlands	6, 2.4%	1.2%	1.2%	1.5%	1.6%
India	5, 2.0%	2.0%	0.8%	1.6%	0.8%

Tables 7.12–7.17 show that in the information industry, China is the world's largest exporter of mobile phones and computers but plays a negligible role in the export of computer services, telecommunications services, printed media, and audio-visual media. This confirms the fact that China's economy, exports, and

TABLE 7.12 The largest exporters and importers of mobile phones in 2012 (data source: Trade Map—International Trade Statistics)

Country	Export share	Country	Import share
China	45.3%	USA	21.2%
Vietnam	8.0%	Hong Kong, China	10.5%
Republic of Korea	6.7%	Japan	6.7%
Hong Kong, China	6.1%	UK	4.8%
USA	4.1%	Germany	4.6%
Chinese Taipei	3.4%	United Arab Emirates	3.3%
Hungary	2.9%	France	3.1%
Germany	2.6%	Singapore	2.9%
Singapore	2.6%	Mexico	2.7%
Mexico	2.5%	India	2.2%

TABLE 7.13 The largest exporters and importers of computers in 2012 (data source: Trade Map—International Trade Statistics)

Country	Export share	Country	Import share
China	47.2%	USA	24.1%
USA	8.0%	China	9.8%
Hong Kong, China	5.4%	Hong Kong, China	6.3%
Mexico	5.3%	Germany	5.3%
Netherlands	4.5%	Netherlands	4.9%
Thailand	4.0%	Japan	4.8%
Germany	3.3%	UK	4.0%
Czech Republic	3.0%	France	2.8%
Malaysia	2.8%	Canada	2.6%
Singapore	2.7%	Mexico	2.3%

TABLE 7.14 The largest exporters and importers of computer services in 2011 (data source: Trade Map—International Trade Statistics)

Country	Export share	Country	Import share
Ireland	21.8%	USA	23.1%
India	21.5%	Germany	16.7%
Germany	9.2%	UK	5.7%
UK	5.7%	France	5.3%
USA	5.0%	Netherlands	4.4%
Israel	4.7%	Italy	4.4%
Sweden	4.1%	Brazil	4.0%
Finland	3.3%	Belgium	3.6%
Canada	3.0%	Sweden	3.1%
Belgium	2.1%	Spain	2.5%

TABLE 7.15 The largest exporters and importers of telecommunication services in 2011 (data source: Trade Map—International Trade Statistics)

Country	Export share	Country	Import share
USA	16.3%	USA	11.5%
UK	11.1%	UK	9.8%
Italy	8.2%	Italy	9.4%
France	8.1%	Germany	7.8%
Belgium	5.1%	France	6.6%
Kuwait	4.6%	Belgium	4.5%
Germany	4.2%	Saudi Arabia	3.9%
Luxembourg	3.3%	Spain	3.8%
Netherlands	3.0%	Russia	3.8%
Canada	2.5%	Sweden	3.0%

TABLE 7.16 The largest exporters and importers of newspapers, journals, and periodicals in 2012 (data source: Trade Map—International Trade Statistics)

Country	Export share	Country	Import share
USA	18.8%	Canada	15.7%
Germany	16.8%	Germany	8.0%
UK	10.0%	France	7.8%
France	9.2%	Switzerland	6.7%
Poland	5.8%	Belgium	5.2%
Netherlands	5.4%	China	4.0%
Belgium	5.3%	Russian Federation	3.8%
Italy	4.1%	Australia	3.7%
Spain	2.5%	Netherlands	3.6%
Czech Republic	1.8%	Austria	3.5%

TABLE 7.17 Top 10 exporters and importers of audio-visual and related services in 2010 (data source: WTO International Trade Statistics 2012, table III.40, the total volume refers to the combined import/export volume of the 10 analysed economies)

Country	Export share	Country	Import share
USA	48.1%	EU 27	60.5%
EU 27	39.8%	Canada	10.9%
Canada	6.9%	USA	7.5%
Russia	1.3%	Australia	4.7%
Argentina	1.2%	Brazil	4.3%
Norway	0.7%	Russian Federation	3.9%
Republic of Korea	0.7%	Japan	3.3%
Australia	0.5%	China	1.7%
China	0.4%	Korea, Republic of	1.6%
Hong Kong, China	0.4%	Argentina	1.6%

FDI inflows are more focused on manufacturing than services. The information industry consists of both hardware and content/software producers. China is strong in the manufacturing and export of hardware, but not so strong in the content and software industry.

Tables 7.18–7.20 analyse the economic structure of large TNCs headquartered in China (Mainland China and Hong Kong). Measured in terms of assets, profits, and market value, the majority of them are located in the finance industry. Energy and real estate are also relatively important sectors. The information industry is, besides several other industries such as construction, food, mobility, and metal, among those realms that have some importance, but are not major players (see Appendix 7.1 for a mapping of these industries to the categories used in the Forbes 2000 list). Within the 181 Chinese companies that are among the world's largest 2000 TNCs, the information sector companies accounted in 2013 for 1.4 per cent of the assets, 2.6 per cent of the profits, and 6.2 per cent of the combined market value.

TABLE 7.18 Share of specific industries in China's largest TNCs' total assets, data source: Forbes 2000, 2013 list, N = 181 Chinese TNCs

Industry	Assets share
Finance	81.1%
Energy	5.0%
Real estate	3.6%
Construction	2.6%
Metal	2.2%
Mobility	1.4%
Information	1.4%

TABLE 7.19 Share of specific industries in China's largest TNCs' total profits, data source: Forbes 2000, 2013 list, N = 181 Chinese TNCs

Industry	Profits share
Finance	52.0%
Energy	14.3%
Real estate	11.3%
Metal	5.1%
Mobility	3.1%
Construction	2.8%
Information	2.6%

TABLE 7.20 Share of specific industries in China's largest TNCs' total market value, data source: Forbes 2000, 2013 list, N = 181 Chinese TNCs

Industry	Market value share
Finance	40.9%
Energy	17.9%
Real estate	7.2%
Metal	6.7%
Information	6.2%
Mobility	4.4%
Food	3.6%
Construction	2.9%

Table 7.21 shows data for China's largest information TNCs. Search engine companies Baidu and Tencent, the operator of the instant messenger service QQ, and the mobile app WeChat are among these companies. They are two of the three social media companies analysed in section 3 of this chapter.

Understanding the Internet and social media in China requires us to understand China's relation to capitalism. The next section will give a theoretical introduction to this question.

7.2.3. China and Capitalism

China's strategy of urbanisation, privatisation, industrialisation, informatisation, the opening of the economy to foreign capital, and its export strategy came at a social price. China increased its GDP per capita from US$193 in 1980 to US$6,091 in 2012 (World Bank Statistics Online). On the one hand the GDP per capita increased and the share of the absolutely poor could be dramatically decreased. But on the other hand, as China became a richer country in absolute terms, the poorest 20 per cent's share of income halved and income inequality increased dramatically. The new rich and the new middle class benefited

TABLE 7.21 China's largest transnational information companies, data source: Forbes 2000, 2013 list, market values, profits, assets, and sales are in billion US$

Company	Industry	Country	Rank	Market Value	Profits	Assets	Sales
China Telecom	Telecommunications services	China	139	42	2.4	87.4	44.9
China Unicom	Telecommunications services	Hong Kong	217	32.4	1.1	82.8	39.5
Tencent Holdings	Computer Services	China	591	65	2	12.1	7
Lenovo Group	Computer Hardware	China	692	10.4	0.5	15.5	29.6
Baidu	Computer Services	China	960	29.7	1.7	7.3	3.5
ZTE	Communications Equipment	China	1165	6.5	-0.4	16.4	13.3
China Communications Services	Telecommunications services	China	1553	4.7	0.4	7.2	9.8
TCL Corp	Consumer Electronics	China	1613	3.4	0.1	12.8	11
Netease	Computer Services	China	1631	6.8	0.6	3.1	1.3
Great Wall Technology	Consumer Electronics	China	1745	0.2	0	8.5	15.2
Hikvision	Electronics	China	1948	12.3	0.2	1.3	0.8
TPV Technology	Computer Storage Devices	Hong Kong	1959	0.8	0.1	6.9	12

TABLE 7.22 China's social development, data sources: World Bank Statistics (1, 4), Millennium Indicators Database (2, 3), Qi (2014) (5)

		1980	1981	1985	1987	1990	1993	1995	1996	1999	2000	2005	2009	2010	2012
1	GDP per capita (US$)	193		292		314					949	1731		4433	6091
2	Population surviving on less than US$1 PPP/day					60.2%							11.8%		
3	Poorest quintile's share in national income					8.0%							4.7%		
4	Gini coefficient		29.1		29.9		35.5		35.7	39.2			42.1		
5	Labour share, %							51.4							45.6

much more and at the expense of the rural population and migrant workers. The Chinese labour share, the share of wages in the GDP, decreased from 51.4 per cent in 1995 to 45.6 per cent in 2012.

Most Marxist authors agree that China is today a country that is facing a clash between capitalism and socialism. They differ, however, in the overall assessment of the relationship between these two forces. There are two basic positions: a) that China is not a capitalist country, and b) that it is one.

7.2.3.1. Position 1: China Is Not a Capitalist Country, but a Socialist Market Economy

A first group of authors stresses the continuities of socialism in China and that overall it is not a capitalist country. Samir Amin argues that China-bashing is a contemporary bourgeois ideology and that China is not capitalist because "the capitalist road is based on the transformation of land into a commodity" (Amin 2013a, 16). Chinese peasants would not defend "the principle of private property" (Amin 2013a, 29). Petty production as well as small agricultural family production would have an important role in contemporary China. The cause of China's rise would not be foreign capital that has been invested in China since 1990 but the long-term build-up of a modern production system coupled with welfarist politics. This development would have been started under Mao. "I argue that if China is indeed an emerging power, this is precisely because it has not chosen the capitalist path of development pure and simple" (Amin 2013a, 25). Inequality would exist in China, but the country would also have managed to reduce poverty. Amin argues that China's rise is part of capitalism's "long period of decline" (Amin 2013b, 107), a "wave of independent initiatives of the countries of the South", in which "the 'emerging' countries and others, like their peoples, are fighting the ways in which the collective imperialism of the Triad [North America, Europe, Japan] tries to perpetuate its domination" (Amin 2013b, 117).

Giovanni Arrighi (2007, 4) argues that the rise of China may mean "an eventual equalization of power between the conquering West and the conquered non-West". Arrighi explains the crisis of the 1970s as a combination of inter-capitalist competition (Europe and Japan caught up economically with the United States) and a profit-squeeze stemming from successful working-class struggles. The United States would be militarily hegemonic, but China would have challenged its economic hegemony in terms of the worldwide economic value share and the United States' dependence on Chinese exports (the current-account deficit of the United States increased China's trade surplus) and credits. Arrighi (2007) shares Amin's assessment that "socialism in China has thus far neither won nor lost" (16), that "as long as the principle of equal access to land continues to be recognized and implemented, it is not too late for social action in contemporary China to steer evolution in a non-capitalist direction", and that "even if socialism has already lost out in China, capitalism, by this definition, has not yet won" (24).

Arrighi (2007) characterises contemporary China as a socialist market economy as imagined by Adam Smith. It would have advanced and maintained health care, education, and welfare (16).

> Contrary to widespread belief, the main attraction of the PRC for foreign capital has not been its huge and low-priced reserves of labor as such—there are plenty of such reserves around the world but nowhere have they attracted capital to the extent that they have in China. The main attraction, we shall argue, has been the high quality of those reserves—in terms of health, education, and capacity for self-management in combination with the rapid expansion of the supply and demand conditions for the productive mobilization of these reserves within China itself.
>
> *Arrighi 2007, 351*

Introducing competition would not have predominantly meant privatising state-owned enterprises (SOEs), but exposing them to competition with new private firms, community-owned enterprises, and international capital (356). Disagreeing with David Harvey's (2007) application of the notion of accumulation by dispossession to China, Arrighi (2007, 361–367) argues that China is facing accumulation without dispossession: the creation of communally owned township and village enterprises (TVEs) would have enabled a "relatively egalitarian distribution of land among households" (364), absorbed the rural surplus labour force, and advanced industrial production in rural areas. "China's economic success was built on the extraordinary social achievements of the Mao era" (370). This Maoist tradition that included the "economic and educational uplifting of peasantry" (374) would have also resulted in vast increases of per-capita income, life expectancy, and literacy. At the same time China would, however, face rising inequality between social groups and rural and urban areas (375), environmental degradation, and the diversion of rural land into industrial, real estate, or infrastructural zones, which would have advanced an "enormous upsurge of social unrest" (378).

Criticising Arrighi, Christopher Chase-Dunn (2010, 47–48) argues that even farmers not dispossessed of their land have become integrated into the capitalist world market and via outsourcing have become de-facto wageworkers for large companies. Leo Panitch (2010, 84) points out in this context that "unequal class-relations" have also developed within TVEs and that "TVEs have now been marginalised as the foundation of China's economic development". Richard Walker (2010) says that Arrighi does not take into account that many TVEs and SOEs have collapsed since the late 1990s, which would have increased the urban proletariat, and that he neglects the privatisation of land in Chinese cities and the growth of the speculative real estate market.

The discussion shows that it is a contested question within Marxist theory if China is a capitalist country or not. The question can only be answered by having a look at the distribution of value-added and employment between state-owned enterprises, worker-controlled enterprises, and privately controlled enterprises. Furthermore one cannot imply that the state or communities necessarily collectively control the first two types of firms. There can be mixed forms that involve shareholder ownership.

In 2013, state-owned companies made up 17.1 per cent of the profits in the Chinese manufacturing industry, collective enterprises 0.9 per cent, shareholding enterprises 42.0 per cent, enterprises controlled by foreign investors 16.4 per cent, and private Chinese enterprises 23.5 per cent (National Bureau of Statistics of China 2014). In contrast, there were no foreign investors and almost 100 per cent collective and state ownership in 1978 (Qiu 2009, 89: Table 4.2).

Huang (2008, 79) shows that the share of large privately owned TVEs in total TVE employment increased from 6.8 per cent in 1985 to 26.3 per cent in 2002, whereas the one of collectively owned TVEs decreased from 59.5 per cent in 1985 to 28.6 per cent in 2002. The number of TVEs run by small households increased from 33.7 per cent in 1985 to 45.0 per cent. A decreasing share of communist ownership and increasing shares of private-capitalist and petty bourgeois enterprises shape the structure of TVEs.

Huang (2008, 13–19) uses two different data sets (OECD, Guangdong Statistical Manual) and concludes that based on the first data set the share of capitalist value-added in China increased from 28.9 per cent in 1998 to 44.7 per cent in 2001 and 71.2 per cent in 2005, whereas in the second data set it increased from 31.8 per cent in 1998 to 38.8 per cent in 2001 and 50.8 per cent in 2005. In both cases indigenous and foreign-owned companies were included. Both analyses conclude that China's economy has an increasing share of capitalist ownership and is predominantly capitalist. SOEs and collective enterprises that have a mixed ownership status so that only a part of it is shareholder owned were in both analyses counted as being capitalist if the capitalist share in ownership was larger than 50 per cent. One can therefore say that the estimates are conservative and that actual capitalist ownership shares exceed the estimations. If a company is for example 49 per cent owned by capitalist shareholders and 51 per cent by workers, capitalist ownership shapes it to a significant degree.

If the data is correct, then both Arrighi and Amin overstate the socialist character of the Chinese economy. Capitalist, state, and communist (worker-controlled) forms of ownership and combinations thereof each control specific shares of the Chinese economy. There are indications that non-capitalist ownership is not dominant and has decreased. If this is the case, then China is at least predominantly a capitalist society.

7.2.3.2. Position 2: China Is a Capitalist Society with Specific Characteristics

A second group of authors stresses the rise of capitalism and neoliberal politics in China. In contrast to the first group of authors that point out continuities of socialism, these authors highlight discontinuities and how the logic of capitalism started penetrating China when Deng Xiaoping came to power in 1978. Chun Lin (2013, 47) pinpoints this position: "Abandoning socialism in the name of reform, however, is precisely what has been happening and is openly advocated by an intellectual elite speaking for the wealthy and powerful". At the same time these reforms would have been accompanied by the rise of new anti-capitalist struggles so that Chinese socialism "makes more sense as protest than as official language" (Lin 2013, 47). "The persistence of sweatshops, the collusion of money and power, the dictatorship of capital, and the reign of developmentalism all violate socialist promises" (Lin 2013, 87). Slavoj Žižek has made a similar assessment: "China as the emerging superpower of the twenty-first century thus seems to embody a new kind of capitalism: disregard for ecological consequences, disdain for workers' rights, everything subordinated to the ruthless drive to develop and become the new world force" (Žižek 2008, 191). Marxist literature sharing this assessment distinguishes three elements or explanations for characterising Chinese capitalism.

Market imbalances are the first such element. They result in the overproduction and underconsumption of commodities. Marx described an antagonism between single production and social need, i.e. an antagonism between the organisation of production in the individual factories or offices and the "anarchy" of production in society, i.e. the uncoordinated form of production:

> within capitalist production, the proportionality of the particular branches of production presents itself as a process of passing constantly of and into disproportionality, since the interconnection of production as a whole here forces itself on the agents of production as a blind law, and not as a law which, being grasped and therefore mastered by their combined reason, brings the productive process under their common control.
>
> *Marx 1894, 365*

This anarchy of production can result in overproduction or underconsumption of commodities:

> Since capital's purpose is not the satisfaction of needs but the production of profit, and since it attains this purpose only be methods that determine the mass of production by reference exclusively to the yardstick of production, and not the reverse, there must be a constant tension between the restricted dimensions of consumption on the capitalist basis, and a production that is constantly striving to overcome these immanent barriers.
>
> *Marx 1894, 365*

Hung Ho-fung says that the rise of China is due to "triple transformations of global capitalism in the late twentieth century" (Hung 2009, 13): "(1) the advent of a new international division of labor, (2) the twin decline of U.S. hegemony and the Cold War order, and (3) the general decline of antisystemic movements in the form of working-class-based, state-power-oriented mass politics" (Hung 2009, 2). A crisis of capitalism would have led corporations to look for global outsourcing possibilities in order to cut investment costs and increase profits.

Hung (2009, 2012) argues that since the 1990s there has been overproduction in the aluminium, car, cement, real estate, and steel industries in China. The Chinese economy is fairly localised and lacks coordination at the national level. "The buildup of excess capacity is exacerbated by the lack of geographical and intersectoral mobility of domestic enterprises, which increases their propensity to invest in already saturating localities and sectors" (Hung 2009, 192). Investments of state-owned enterprises would have typically been in single cities or provinces and state-owned banks would have supported this strategy with "lax lending practices" (Hung 2012, 219). Overproduction would have been combined with underconsumption caused by urban-rural inequality, unemployment in the manufacturing sector, rising income inequality from a Gini coefficient of 0.33 in 1980 to 0.45 in 2007, and a drop of the wage share from 53 per cent in 1998 to 41.1 per cent in 2005 (Hung 2012, 221). According to other calculations, the wage share dropped in China from a little less than 65 per cent in the early 1990s to around 45 per cent at the end of the first decade of the 2000s (ILO 2013, 45). China has only offset a crisis by basing its economy on cheap exports, predominantly to the United States (that absorbs around 30 per cent of all Chinese exports). Such exports are based on low wages. The start of the economic crisis in the United States resulted in a decrease of Chinese exports, to which the Chinese state answered with a stimulus package aimed at the urban economy. Hung doubts that "China's formidable export engine" that has thus far helped to offset a crisis "will last indefinitely" (Hung 2009, 196).

The second element that characterises Chinese capitalism is the overaccumulation of capital. Overaccumulation of capital means that capital has growth rates higher than investment possibilities in the key industries in which it operates. It is "a condition in which idle capital and idle labour supply [. . .] exist side by side with no idle way to bring these idle resources together to accomplish socially useful tasks" (Harvey 1990, 180). According to Harvey overaccumulation results from a combination of three factors:

a   The need to accumulate.
b   The exploitation of labour, the "class relation between capital and labour" (Harvey 1990, 180).
c   "Capitalism is necessarily technologically and organizationally dynamic" (Harvey 1990, 180); it requires rising productivity by technological innovations.

In situations of overaccumulation, high levels of productivity and exploitation allow to accumulate more capital than can be invested. Harvey explains overaccumulation as a combination of a) the class antagonism and b) the antagonisms between b1) necessary and surplus labour and b2) producers and means of production. Marx (1894, chapter 15) situates the overaccumulation of capital—"excess capital" that "coexists with a growing surplus population" (Marx 1894, 353)—in the context of the tendential fall in the rate of profit. "Simultaneously with the development of productivity, the composition of capital becomes higher, there is a relative decline in the variable portion as against the constant" (Marx 1894, 357).

> The rise in labour productivity consists precisely in the fact that the share of living labour is reduced and that of past labour increased, but in such a way that the total sum of labour contained in the commodity declines; in other words the living labour declines by more than the past labour increases. [. . .] The portion of value deriving from raw and ancillary materials must fall with the [rising] productivity of labour, since, as far as these materials go, this productivity is precisely expressed in the fact that their value has fallen. And yet it is precisely a characteristic of rising labour productivity that the fixed portion of the constant capital should experience a very sharp increase, and with this also the portion of value that it transfers to the commodities as wear and tear.
>
> *Marx 1894, 369–370*

Marx defines overaccumulation as "unoccupied capital on the one hand and an unemployed working population on the other" (Marx 1894, 359); "i.e. the expanded $C + \Delta C$ will not produce any more profit, or will even produce less profit, than the capital C did before its increase by ΔC" (Marx 1894, 360). At an aggregate level, the situation of increased capital without increased profits means, as Marx describes, that some capitalists continue to increase their profits, whereas others cannot compete and have stagnating profits.

> Overproduction of capital never means anything other than overproduction of means of production—means of labour and means of subsistence—that can function as capital, i.e. can be applied to exploiting labour at a given level of exploitation; a given level, because a fall in the level of exploitation below a certain point produces disruption and stagnation in the capitalist production process, crisis, and the destruction of capital. It is no contradiction that this overproduction of capital is accompanied by a greater or smaller relative surplus population. The same causes that have raised the productivity of labour, increased the mass of commodity products, extended markets, accelerated the accumulation of capital, in terms of both mass and value, and lowered the rate of profit, these same causes

have produced, and continue constantly to produce, a relative surplus population, a surplus population of workers who are not employed by this excess capital on account of the low level of exploitation of labour at which they would have to be employed, or at least on account of the low rate of profit they would yield at the given rate of exploitation.

Marx 1894, 364

Capital enjoying a higher level of productivity will be able to sell its commodities at a price higher than its individual value and will so achieve extra-profit. On the other hand, lower productivity would result in "swindling and general promotion of swindling, through desperate attempts in the way of new methods of production, new capital investments and new adventures, to secure some kind of extra profit, which will be independent of the general average and superior to it" (Marx 1894, 367).

David Harvey (2007) argues that the economic rise of China is based on a neoliberalism with Chinese characteristics that features heavy foreign direct investments combined with a low-wage economy and special economic zones focused on FDI; the fostering of urban and rural private companies as well as rural TVEs; state-owned corporation-managers' ownership of surplus products and extra-profits; the transformation of state enterprises into shareholding companies for fostering entrepreneurialism, competition, and free markets; and an export-oriented growth strategy focusing on the export of light industrial products (textiles, toys, plastics) and electronic consumer goods combined with low wages.

Hundreds of millions of rural migrants would flee from poverty and the dispossession of land that is turned into private property. As a result, they would become highly exploited workers in urban centres. Especially the rural land around larger cities would have been dispossessed for being turned into export-processing zones or urban modernisation projects (Harvey 2007, 146). Millions of workers in manufacturing and state-owned enterprises would have lost their jobs. "This labour force is vulnerable to super-exploitation and puts downward pressure on the wages of urban residents" (Harvey 2007, 127). China's urbanisation would have made the country dependent on the import of cement, coal, steel, oil and various metals. It would also have resulted in a growth of urban/rural income and wealth inequality. "Almost every city in the world has witnessed a building boom for the rich—often of a distressingly similar character—in the midst of a flood of impoverished migrants converging on cities as a rural peasantry is dispossessed through the industrialization and commercialization of agriculture" (Harvey 2012, 12).

The Chinese state and Chinese municipalities had to a large degree debt-financed the growth by making large investments into urbanisation projects involving a focus on real estate and construction, highways, subways, high-speed rail links, dams, shopping malls, airports, science parks, amusement parks, gated communities, golf courses, etc. These investments absorbed surplus-labour, but at the same time resulted in overbuilding, a speculative real estate market that drove up urban housing prices, and the creation of an asset bubble. "The danger lurks of a severe crisis of over-accumulation of fixed capital (particularly in the built environment)" (Harvey 2007, 141). The "overaccumulation of capital has been or is about to be transformed into an overaccumulation of investments in the built environment" (Harvey 2012, 58). Many assets in the built environment were overvalued (Harvey 2012, 65). So Harvey says that in China the composition of total capital changes in such a way that ever more fixed constant capital is created, especially buildings, infrastructure, and land. At the same time agricultural and manufacturing jobs tended to disappear via dispossessions and privatisations. The result in China has been "unoccupied capital on the one hand and an unemployed working population on the other" (Marx 1894, 359).

The new world economic crisis had an impact on China because its exports to a large degree go to the United States. As a result, Chinese exports declined in 2009 by 20 per cent (Harvey 2012, 61), to which the Chinese government reacted with further investments in urban and infrastructure projects in order to absorb the unemployed surplus-labour set free in the export industry (62). "Many investments, such as the huge shopping mall close to Dongguan, stand almost empty, as do quite a few of the high-rises that litter the urban landscape almost everywhere. And then there are the empty new cities waiting for populations and industries to arrive" (62). The expansion would have meant the rise of more and more irregular urban employment in China and the privatisation of Chinese state companies.

The third element that characterises Chinese capitalism is class antagonism. Marx and Engels see all history as a history of class struggles: "The history of all hitherto existing society is the history of class struggles" (Marx and Engels 1848, 35). Marx highlighted that under capitalism the distribution of wealth is unequal and the accumulation of capital is only possible at the cost of workers: "Political economy starts from labour as the real soul of production; yet to labour it gives nothing, and to private property everything" (Marx 1844, 81). He argued that as productivity increases the relative share of wages in the total value produced decreases:

> the increasing productivity of labour is accompanied by a cheapening of the worker, as we have seen, and it is therefore accompanied by a cheapening of the worker, even when the real wages are rising. The latter never rise in proportion to the productivity of labour.
>
> *Marx 1867, 753*

Marx's analysis has frequently been interpreted as a hypothesis of impoverishment of the dominated classes, i.e. that the development of the productive forces will result in impoverishment, which will cause social revolution. Marx, however, was speaking not about absolute, but about *relative* relationships. With the overall increase of wealth, the social situation of the dominated classes might improve although at the same time the relative share they receive tends to decrease. Class struggle can result in a relative lowering of wages so that ever more capital is present that cannot be invested (overaccumulation/overproduction of capital) or that commodities are available on the market that workers are not able to buy (overproduction and underconsumption of commodities). But class struggle can also increase the relative share of wages and decrease the relative share of profits. Marx writes therefore that

> crises are always prepared by a period in which wages generally rise, and the working class actually does receive a greater share in the part of the annual product destined for consumption. [. . .] It thus appears that capitalist production involves certain conditions independent of people's good or bad intentions, which permit the relative prosperity of the working class only temporarily, and moreover always as a harbinger of crisis.
>
> *Marx 1885, 486–487*

Crisis explanations that stress that rising wages result in falling relative profits have come to be known as profit-squeeze crisis theories.

A number of approaches describe China's economic growth as the consequence of the antagonism between capital and labour so that capital's power and exploitation of labour has been strengthened. Martin Hart-Landsberg (2010) argues for a class-based analysis of China. The post-1978 reforms would have turned China into a capitalism with Chinese characteristics that has an export-oriented economy and experiences the influx of transnational capital. Peter Nolan and Jin Zhang (2010) argue in this context that China's outward FDI is small. Also the operations of its banks would be comparatively small. The driving force would have been the "desire of transnational corporations to cheapen the production cost of goods classified as 'machinery and transportation equipment'" (Hart-Landsberg 2010, 18) in the areas of ICTs (computers; office machines; telecommunications, audio, and video equipment) and electrical equipment.

Minqi Li (2008a, 2008b) says in an analysis comparable to the one by Hart-Landsberg that the rising share of China in the world economy came along with the introduction of capitalism and privatisation. "A large, productive, and cheap labor force allows Chinese capitalists and foreign capitalists in China to profit from intense and massive exploitation" (Li 2008a, 27). The wage share would therefore have dropped from "51–52 percent in the 1980s to 38 percent in the early 2000s" (Li 2008a, 28). China's growth would in addition face ecological limits for the world's supply of fossil fuels (coal, natural gas, oil) that could become depleted.

John Bellamy Foster and Robert McChesney (2012) argue that China has reacted to the world economic crisis with massive state investments so that there was "an extraordinary increase in fixed investment" (Foster and McChesney 2012, 6). As a consequence, China would be a weak link in the world economy that "is rife with overinvestment in physical capital" (Foster and McChesney 2012, 7) and has created a Chinese financial bubble. This development would be combined with "the (super)exploitation of workers in the new export sectors" (Foster and McChesney 2012, 9) that has resulted in a falling wage share and rising inequality. "The core contradiction thus lies in the extreme form of exploitation that characterizes China's current model of class-based production" (Foster and McChesney 2012, 10). China would be "structured around the offshoring needs of multinational corporations geared to obtaining low unit labor costs by taking advantage of cheap, disciplined labor in the global South" (Foster and McChesney 2012, 14). Foster and McChesney stress that class antagonism is a major aspect of China's economy. They combine this element, however, with the focus on overaccumulation (a consequence of the antagonism between necessary and surplus labour and between producers and means of production).

7.2.4. Tendencies in the Development of China's Economy

We can summarise section 2's discussion in the form of some major tendencies that have shaped the Chinese economy:

- China has had continuously high GDP growth rates and a sharing rise in the global GDP since the 1980s.
- China has been transformed from a self-sustaining economy into an export-oriented economy. It predominantly exports telephone appliances, integrated circuits, computers, computer parts, and clothes.
- Since the opening of the Chinese economy to the capitalist world economy at the end of the 1970s, foreign direct investments into China have rapidly grown. The majority of China's foreign direct investments go to Hong Kong, whereas the shares of Western countries are rather small.
- Foreign transnational corporations dominate China's export markets and use Chinese labour for assemblage of electronic products and the finishing of clothes.
- In terms of value-added, China's productive forces have in the past forty years witnessed a decrease of agriculture and a dominance of manufacturing and services. The service sector is the dominant realm of employment.
- In 2013, China accounted for around 5 per cent of the largest information companies in the world and the United States for around 32 per cent. This is an indication that the US information economy plays a more important role in the world.
- China's information economy is strong in the manufacturing and export of hardware, but not so strong in the content and software industry.
- In 2013, the information sector accounted for 1.4 per cent of the largest Chinese TNCs. Finance's share was 81.0 per cent.
- China's strategy of urbanisation, privatisation, industrialisation, informatisation, the opening of the economy to foreign capital, and its export strategy came at the price of increasing inequality.

- Whereas some Marxist authors (e.g. Samir Amin, Giovanni Arrighi) hold that China is not a capitalist country but a socialist market economy, others (e.g. David Harvey, John Bellamy Foster, Martin Hart-Landsberg, Minqi Li, Chun Lin, Peter Nolan) argue that it is a capitalism with Chinese characteristics. Chinese capitalism would be characterised by neoliberalism, overaccumulation of capital, overproduction of commodities and infrastructure, a strong drop of the wage share accompanied by an increase of the capital share in the total economy, financialisation of the real estate market as a result of overaccumulation, social inequality coupled with an underconsumption tendency, and a new international division of labour that exploits Chinese workers—especially rural migrants—as cheap labour for increasing profits.
- One finds private capitalist companies, SOEs, TVEs, and family-run businesses. Collective ownership has decreased so that the Chinese economy is today predominantly controlled by private capitalist businesses.

Given this analysis of the Chinese economy, we can next analyse social media in China in the context of China's economy.

7.3. Capitalist Social Media in China: A Comparative Analysis

China has more than 600 million Internet users,[4] double the number of the United States. It is by far the country with the largest number of Internet users in the world. Table 7.23 gives an overview of the most used web platforms in China in 2014. It shows the 15 Chinese sites ranked among the 100 most accessed platforms in the world. For-profit companies run 12 of them. The Chinese state owns three of the dominant platforms. Two of them use advertising and therefore have commercial character. Commercial and profit logic dominate the Chinese Internet and Chinese social media just like it dominates the Internet in Western countries (Fuchs 2014b; Jin 2013).

Search engines, microblogs, and social networking sites are three important forms of contemporary social media (Fuchs 2014b). In this section, we will compare the political economy of the most important Chinese search engine (Baidu), microblog (Sina Weibo), and social networking site (Renren) to the political economy of Western equivalents (Google, Twitter, Facebook). Data show that in terms of global usage, these six platforms are the dominant Chinese and Western search engines, microblogs, and social networking sites in China and the West respectively.[5] I obtained financial data by collecting annual financial reports and proxy statements for various years for all six companies. The analysis focuses on profits, the role of advertising, the boards of directors, shareholders, and financial market values.

TABLE 7.23 Chinese web platforms that are among the 100 most accessed sites, data source: alexa.com, April 5, 2014

Platform	Rank	Character	Organisation	Type
baidu.com	5	For-profit	Baidu Inc.	Search engine
qq.com	7	For-profit	Tencent Holdings Ltd.	Instant messaging, online portal
taobao.com	11	For-profit	Alibaba Group	Online marketplace
sina.com.cn	14	For-profit	Sina Corp.	Online portal
hao123.com	16	For-profit	Baidu	Online portal
weibo.com	17	For-profit	Sina Corp.	Microblog
sohu.com	27	For-profit	Sohu.com Inc.	Online portal
360.cn	29	For-profit	Qihoo 360	Anti-virus tools
163.com	36	For-profit	NetEase Inc.	Online portal
soso.com	39	For-profit	Tencent Holdings Ltd.	Search engine
gmw.cn	60	Advertising	Guangming Newspaper, Chinese state	Online newspaper
xinhuanet.com	67	Non-commercial	Xinhua News Agency, Chinese state	News site
people.com.cn	79	Commercial (advertising)	People's Daily, Chinese state	Online newspaper
youku.com	85	Profit	Youku Inc.	Video hosting platform
china.com	92	Profit	China.com Inc.	Online news platform

7.3.1. Search Engines: Baidu and Google

Baidu is a Chinese search engine and web portal created in 2000 by Robin Li and Eric Xu. Baidu Inc. owns and operates it. Baidu became a public company listed on the NASDAQ, which focuses on tech companies, in 2005.[6] Its share-offering price was US$27.[7] Figure 7.3 shows that Baidu's profits have been rising steeply since 2004. There is a uniform income tax rate of 25 per cent for all Chinese enterprises, no matter if they are foreign-funded or not. There are, however, exceptions for specific companies in key industries. Some of Baidu's subsidiaries are considered to be high and new technology enterprises that have a preferential tax rate of 15 per cent (Baidu SEC Filings, Form-20F 2013, 78), and some of its subsidiaries are considered key software enterprises that pay a preferential tax rate of 10 per cent (79). In 2013, Baidu's combined tax rate was 15.01 per cent (79).

According to empirical data, Google in January 2014 accounted for 89.0 per cent of all Internet searches, Yahoo! for 2.7 per cent, Bing for 4.0 per cent, and Baidu for 0.9 per cent.[8] In China, Baidu accounted for 81.6 per cent of the search share in 2013 (Baidu SEC Filings, Form-20F 2013, 39). Not only was Google's share of searches larger than Baidu's, but also its 2013 profits were with US$12.9 billion (Google, SEC Filings, Form-10K 2013) more than seven times as large as the ones of Baidu (US$1.7 billion).

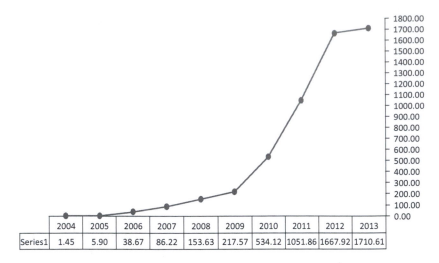

	2004	2005	2006	2007	2008	2009	2010	2011	2012	2013
Series1	1.45	5.90	38.67	86.22	153.63	217.57	534.12	1051.86	1667.92	1710.61

FIGURE 7.3 The development of Baidu's profits (data source: SEC filings, form 20-F), in million US$

Online advertising and marketing are the major sources of Baidu's revenues: 99.9 per cent in 2011, 99.7 per cent in 2012, and 99.6 per cent in 2013 (Baidu SEC Filings, Form-20F 2013, 74). In 2013, 91 per cent of Google's revenues came from advertising (Google SEC Filings, Form 10-K 2013, 9). Baidu uses pay for placement (P4P), which allows advertisers to place advertisements as popular search results that show up in association with specific keywords.

Table 7.24 shows that both Baidu and Google's board of directors interlock with other companies, especially venture capital and financial firms such as Dodge & Cox Funds, GSR Ventures, Kleiner Perkins Caufield & Byers, Madrone Capital Partners, Monex Group Inc., Sherpalo Ventures LLC, and technology and media companies such as Cisco, GluMobile, Intel, Lenovo, NetDragon, Netflix, NetQin Mobile Inc., and Zynga. This circumstance shows on the one hand that finance capital firms obtain decision power within companies. On the other hand it also illustrates that there is especially an interlocking with companies that do not compete with Baidu and Google, but that sell services or hardware that are complementary to search engines.

Table 7.25 shows Baidu and Google's main shareholders. The data indicate that CEOs and the main directors tend to hold relatively large amounts of shares and therefore also large shares of votes. Baidu's CEO Robin Yahong Li owns 31.6 per cent of all of Baidu's stock, whereas Google's CEO Larry Page controls 41.0 per cent of class B stock. Handsome Reward Limited (15.7 per cent of Baidu's stock) is a company owned by Robin Yahong Li that is based in the British Virgin Islands. Also financial investors such as Baillie Gifford & Co., BlackRock, and Fidelity own significant amounts of shares.

TABLE 7.24 Baidu and Google's board of directors and their interlocking positions, data sources: Baidu SEC Filings, Form 20-F 2013; Google, Proxy Statement 2014

Baidu's board of directors	Involvement in other companies	Google's board of directors	Involvement in other companies
Robin Yanhong Li, Chairman and CEO		Larry Page, CEO and Director	
Jennifer Xinzhe Li, Chief Financial Officer		Sergey Brin, Co-Founder and Director	
William Decker, Independent Director	PricewaterhouseCoopers, VisionChina Media Inc.	Eric E. Schmidt, Executive Chairman of the Board of Directors	
James Ding, Independent Director	GSR Ventures, NetQin Mobile Inc., Huayi Brothers Media Corporation	L. John Doerr, Director	Kleiner Perkins Caufield & Byers, Amyris Inc., Zynga Inc.
Nobuyuki Idei, Independent Director	Accenture, FreeBit Co Ltd., Lenovo Group, Monex Group Inc.	Diane B. Greene, Director	Intuit Inc., MIT Corporation
Greg Penner, Independent Director	Madrone Capital Partners, The Charter Growth Fund	John L. Hennessy, Lead Independent Director	Cisco Systems, Inc.
Dejian Liu, Director	NetDragon Websoft Inc., 91 Wireless Websoft Limited	Ann Mather, Director	Glu Mobile Inc., MoneyGram International Inc., Netflix Inc., Solazyme Inc., Dodge & Cox Funds
		Paul S. Otellini, Director	Intel Corporation
		K. Ram Shriram, Director	Sherpalo Ventures LLC
		Shirley M. Tilghman, Director	Princeton University

(continued)

TABLE 7.24 (continued)

Baidu's board of directors	Involvement in other companies	Google's board of directors	Involvement in other companies
		Nikesh Arora, Senior Vice President and Chief Business Officer	
		David C. Drummond, Senior Vice President, Corporate Development, Chief Legal Officer, and Secretary	
		Patrick Pichette, Senior Vice President and Chief Financial Officer	

TABLE 7.25 Baidu and Google's main shareholders, data sources: Baidu SEC filings, form 20-F 2013; Google, SEC filings, Proxy Statement 2014

Name	Baidu's stock (A and B)	Google's stock A	Google's stock B
Robin Yahong Li	15.9%		
All directors and executive officers	16.7%		
Handsome Reward Limited	15.7%		
Baillie Gifford & Co.	7.3%		
Larry Page			41.0%
Sergey Brin			40.1%
Eric E. Schmidt			10.9%
L. John Doerr			2.0%
All members of the board of directors			94.1%
BlackRock		5.4%	
Fidelity		6.7%	

Table 7.26 shows the development of Baidu and Google's share values on the NASDAQ stock exchange. There has been a long-term growth of both stock values. Both witnessed a large slump in 2008 after the start of the global financial and economic crisis. Google's stock value has been many times greater than that of Baidu, but the multiplication factor has become smaller over the years.

7.3.2. Microblogs: Sina Weibo and Twitter

Sina is a Chinese web portal founded in 1998. Sina Corp. owns and operates it. Sina became a public company listed on the NASDAQ in 2000[9] with

TABLE 7.26 Development of Baidu's and Google's NASDAQ stock value, data source: Yahoo! Finance

Date	Baidu's stock value (US$)	Google's stock value (US$)	Multiplication factor
August 8, 2005	$9.50	$145.01	15.3
August 7, 2006	$7.20	$184.43	25.6
December 10, 2007	$39.29	$345.33	8.8
December 1, 2008	$10.91	$142.14	13.0
January 18, 2010	$41.69	$275.28	6.6
January 31, 2011	$117.68	$305.80	2.6
January 9, 2012	$127.41	$312.81	2.5
March 18, 2013	$86.49	$405.56	4.7
April 4, 2014	$149.35	$545.25	3.7
June 15, 2014	$178.05	$551.76	3.1
October 24, 2014	$222.55	$548.90	2.5

a share-offering price of US$17.[10] It launched the microblog Weibo in 2009. Figure 7.4 shows that Sina struggled and made losses during the new economy crisis in 2000, then consolidated and increased its profits up to US$412 million in 2009, in the context of the global economic crisis again made losses in 2010 and 2011, and in 2012 and 2013 again achieved profits. Weibo can be seen as the Chinese microblogging equivalent of Twitter. Twitter has also been struggling financially: it became a stock-traded public company in November 2013, although its annual net losses were US$645.32 million in 2013 (Twitter SEC filings, form 10-K 2013). Weibo—a subsidiary of Sina—made losses of US$116.74 million in 2011, $102.47 million in 2012, and $38.12 million in 2013 (Weibo SEC filings, form F-1 registration statement). Sina in 2012 paid an effective tax rate of 18 per cent for its Chinese operations (Sina SEC filings, form 20-F for financial year 2012).

On December 31, 2013, Weibo had 129.1 million monthly active users (Weibo SEC filings, form F-1, registration statement) and Twitter 240.9 million (Twitter SEC filings, form 10-K: annual report for 2013). Advertising comprised 85 per cent of Twitter's revenues in 2012 and 89 per cent in 2013 (Twitter SEC filings, form 10-K: annual report for 2013). Advertising and marketing comprised 78.8 per cent of Weibo's revenues in 2013, 12.2 per cent from games, and 5.9 per cent from VIP membership services (Weibo SEC filings, form F-1, registration statement).

Table 7.27 shows that both Weibo and Twitter have directors who are either members of financial investment firms or other media companies in the sectors of mobile payments, entertainment, online shopping, or online storytelling.

Table 7.28 shows that both Sina and Twitter's stock values have been fluctuating. After reports that Weibo lost 28 million users in 2013, Sina's share lost value in February 2013.[11] Weibo argued that the rise of Tencent's mobile messaging application WeChat had to do with this loss.[12] In April 2014, Weibo—a subsidiary company of Sina—became a public company listed on the NASDAQ stock

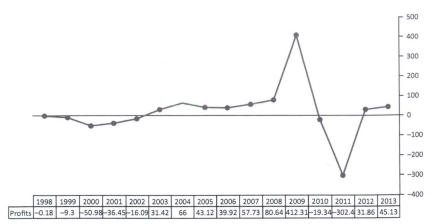

	1998	1999	2000	2001	2002	2003	2004	2005	2006	2007	2008	2009	2010	2011	2012	2013
Profits	-0.18	-9.3	-50.98	-36.45	-16.09	31.42	66	43.12	39.92	57.73	80.64	412.31	-19.34	-302.4	31.86	45.13

FIGURE 7.4   The development of Sina's profits (data source: SEC filings, forms 10–K, 20–F), in million US$

TABLE 7.27   Weibo and Twitter's boards of directors and their interlocking positions, data sources: Weibo SEC filings, amendment 2 to form F-1 registration statement, https://investor.twitterinc.com/directors.cfm (accessed on April 6, 2014)

Weibo's board of directors	Involvement in other companies	Twitter's board of directors	Involvement in other companies
Charles Chao, Chairman		Jack Dorsey, Chairman	Square Inc.
Hong Du, Director		Dick Costolo, CEO	
Yichen Zhang, Independent Director	CITIC Capital Holdings Limited	Peter Chernin	Chernin Entertainment LLC, Chernin Group LLC
Frank Kui Tang, Independent Director	FountainVest Partners	Peter Fenton	Benchmark Capital
Gaofei Wang, CEO		David Rosenblatt	1stdibs.com Inc.
Bonnie Yi Zhang, Chief Financial Officer		Evan Williams	Medium, Obvious Corp.
Jingdong Ge, Vice President of Marketing		Marjorie Scardino	
Yajuan Wang, Vice President of Business Operations			

exchange.[13] Twitter and Weibo have in common that they are both companies struggling to make wins with the help of targeted advertising. They both have become publicly traded companies although they made losses. There is a divergence between their positive stock values and their actual monetary losses. This divergence could be indicative of the existence of a social media financial bubble,

TABLE 7.28 Development of Sina (NASDAQ), Weibo (NASDAQ), and Twitter's (NYSE) stock values, data source: Yahoo! Finance

Date	Sina's stock value (US$)	Weibo's stock value (US$)	Twitter's stock value (US$)	Multiplication factor
April 17, 2000	$20.38			
April 16, 2001	$1.63			
April 15, 2002	$1.52			
April 14, 2003	$10.24			
April 12, 2004	$35.58			
April 11, 2005	$27.35			
April 17, 2006	$27.74			
April 16, 2007	$32.89			
April 14, 2008	$41.44			
April 13, 2009	$27.55			
April 12, 2010	$37.70			
April 11, 2011	$124.56			
April 16, 2012	$58.25			
April 15, 2013	$46.26			
Nov. 4/7, 2013	$76.04		$44.90	0.6
Dec. 2, 2013	$77.31		$40.78	0.5
Jan. 6, 2014	$85.72		$66.29	0.8
Feb. 3, 2014	$67.12		$65.25	1.0
March 3, 2014	$72.41		$53.71	0.7
April 4, 2014	$56.36		$43.14	0.8
April 17, 2014	$56.55	$20.24	$45.01	0.8 (Sina–Twitter), 2.2 (Weibo–Twitter)
June 15, 2014	$45.36	$19.21	$36.90	0.8 (Sina–Twitter), 1.9 (Weibo–Twitter)
October 24, 2014	$39.84	$18.27	$49.95	1.3 (Sina–Twitter) 2.7 (Weibo–Twitter)

in which financial values diverge from profits. If this bubble bursts, a financial crisis of the Internet economy could be the result.

7.3.3. Social Networking Sites: Renren and Facebook

Renren is a Chinese social networking site founded in 2005 by Joseph Chen. Renren Inc. owns and operates it. Renren became a public company listed on the New York Stock Exchange in 2011.[14] Its share-offering price was US$14.[15] Figure 7.5 shows that Renren's profits have been fluctuating between losses and wins.

In contrast to Renren, Facebook has had a steep growth of profits, culminating in a net income of US$1.5 billion in 2013 (Facebook SEC filings, form 10-K for financial year 2013). On December 31, 2013, Facebook had 1.23 billion monthly active users (Facebook SEC filings, form 10-K for financial year 2013). At the end of 2013, Renren had 206 million registered users (Renren SEC filings, form 20-F for financial year 2013). Renren is a very large platform, but has nonetheless less than a fifth of the number of Facebook users.

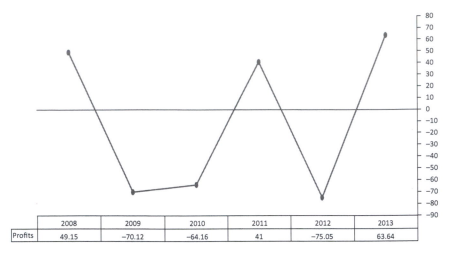

	2008	2009	2010	2011	2012	2013
Profits	49.15	−70.12	−64.16	41	−75.05	63.64

FIGURE 7.5 The development of Renren's profits (data source: SEC filings, form 20–F), in million US$

Software enterprises are in China exempt from paying income tax for two years if they have made losses in one specific year and a year later become profitable. Renren has been classified as a software company and therefore is due to previous losses exempt from income tax in 2013 and 2014 and enjoys a 50 per cent tax reduction from 2015 to 2017, which means an effective tax rate of 12.5 per cent because the enterprise income tax is 25 per cent in China (Renren SEC filings, form 20-F for financial year 2013).

Facebook generated 89 per cent of its 2013 revenues from advertising (Facebook SEC filings, form 10-K for financial year 2013). Renren has a business segment for social networking and one for online games. In 2013, the social networking segment accounted for 45.5 per cent of Renren's total net revenues (in comparison to 62.4 per cent in 2011). The online game segment made up 54.5 per cent of Renren's total net revenues in 2013 (37.6 per cent in 2011). Renren's social networking market derived 70.3 per cent of its total net revenues in 2013 from advertising (85.6 per cent in 2011) and 29.3 per cent from services such as virtual gifts on its video platform 56.com (acquired by Renren in 2011) as well as virtual gifts and VIP memberships on renren.com (all data: Renren SEC filings, form 20-F for financial year 2013). Whereas Facebook relies relatively purely on commodifying user data and is almost exclusively an advertising company, Renren has a mixed capital accumulation model that commodifies content, access, and users. Within its social networking business, it derived just like Facebook the vast majority of its revenues from targeted advertising.

Table 7.29 shows that some of directors of Renren and Facebook are also involved in financial investment firms such as Doll Capital Management, Business Growth Fund, General Atlantic, Andreessen Horowitz, BDT Capital

TABLE 7.29 Renren and Facebook's boards of directors and their interlocking positions, data sources: http://www.renren-inc.com/en/info/director.html (accessed on April 7, 2014), Renren SEC filings, form 20-F for financial year 2013; Facebook proxy statement 2014

Renren's board of directors	Involvement in other companies	Facebook's board of directors	Involvement in other companies
Joseph Chen, Chairman		Mark Zuckerberg, Chairman and CEO	
James Jian Liu, Executive Director		Sheryl K. Sandberg, Chief Operating Officer and Director	Walt Disney Company
David K. Chao	Doll Capital Management	David A. Ebersman, Chief Financial Officer	Ironwood Pharmaceuticals Inc., Castlight Health Inc.
Stephen Murphy	Jumeirah Group LLC, The Garden Centre Group, The Learning Clinic Ltd, The Business Growth Fund, Ashcombe Advisers LLP	David B. Fischer, Vice President, Business and Marketing Partnerships	
Katsumasa Niki	SoftBank Corp.	Marc L. Andreessen	Andreessen Horowitz, eBay Inc., Hewlett-Packard Company
Matthew Nimetz	General Atlantic LLC, Knight Capital Group Inc.	Erskine B. Bowles	BDT Capital Partners LLC, Carousel Capital LLC, Morgan Stanley, Belk Inc., Norfolk Southern Corporation
Chuanfu Wang	BYD Company Limited	Susan D. Desmond-Hellmann	The Gates Foundation, The Procter & Gamble Company
Hui Huang		Donald E. Graham	Graham Holdings Company
Jing Huang		Reed Hastings	Netflix Inc.
Lillian Liu		Peter A. Thiel	Thiel Capital, Founders Fund, Clarium Capital Management
Cao Miao			
Ripley Hu			
Juan Zhou			

Partners, Carousel Capital, Morgan Stanley, Thiel Capital, Founders Fund, Clarium Capital Management, and other companies. The latter comprise especially tech and media firms such as SoftBank, Walt Disney, eBay, HP, and Netflix. Table 7.30 shows that Renren and Facebook's CEO's Joseph Chen and Mark Zuckerberg own significant amounts of shares. Also financial firms such as Fidelity and Doll Capital Management control substantial quantities of shares. SB Pan Pacific Corporation, a subsidiary of SoftBank Corporation, is Renren's main shareholder. Joseph Chen holds the second largest amount of shares, followed by David Chao and Doll Capital Management. SoftBank is a Chinese Internet and telecommunications enterprise. Doll Capital Management is a Californian venture capital firm. Directors, finance capital enterprises, and tech firms are the most important owners of Renren. Especially directors and financial corporations control Facebook's shares.

Table 7.31 shows that Renren's stock has quickly lost value after the company's IPO on the NYSE in 2011, whereas Facebook's stock value has increased since its IPO in 2012. Since 2013 Renren's share value has remained relatively

TABLE 7.30 Renren and Facebook's main shareholders, data sources: Renren SEC filings, form 20-F for financial year 2013; Facebook Proxy statement 2014

Name	Renren's stock	Facebook's stock A	Facebook's stock B
Mark Zuckerberg			83.0%
All executive officers and directors as a group			83.3%
Dustin Moskovitz		2.3%	8.5%
Eduardo Saverin			9.3%
Fidelity		7.1%	
Joseph Chen	25.7%		
SB Pan Pacific Corporation [SoftBank Corporation]	37.6%		
Doll Capital Management	8.2%		
James Jian Liu	3.2%		
David K. Chao	8.4%		

TABLE 7.31 The development of Renren (NYSE) and Facebook's (NASDAQ) stock values, data source: Yahoo! Finance

Date	Renren's stock value (US$)	Facebook's stock value (US$)	Multiplication factor
May 4, 2011	$16.80		
May 18, 2012	$6.01	$38.23	6.4
May 17, 2013	$2.85	$26.25	9.2
Dec 24, 2013	$3.00	$57.96	19.3
March 10, 2014	$3.97	$72.03	18.1
April 4, 2014	$3.30	$56.75	17.2
June 13, 2014	$3.30	$64.50	19.5
October 24, 2014	$3.41	$80.67	23.7

constant, whereas that of Facebook has fluctuated. After there were fears that Facebook may lose users to mobile chat applications such as WhatsApp or WeChat, it bought WhatsApp for US$19 billion in February 2014.[16] This purchase may have been one of the factors resulting in Facebook's stock value climbing from US$53.53 on January 29, 2014, to US$72.03 on March 10. A month later, the share value was, however, down again to around US$55.

7.3.4. Corporate Social Media in China and the West

Combining the data presented in sections 7.3.1–7.3.3 allows us to conduct a comparative analysis of the political economy of corporate social media in China and the West.

Commercial and profit logic dominate the Chinese Internet and Chinese social media just like it dominates the Internet in Western countries. The major social media companies in China such as Baidu, Sina Weibo, and Renren are capitalist companies whose operations and economic structures are very similar to the ones of Google, Twitter, and Facebook. Both Weibo and Twitter have until 2014 not made any profits. Renren's profits and losses have been fluctuating, whereas Facebook's profits have been constantly growing. Baidu, Weibo, and Renren are just like Google, Twitter, and Facebook publicly traded companies. They reach out to international investors and are therefore like their US equivalents listed on US stock exchanges, which shows that they aim to attract Western finance capital. As discussed in section 7.2, Western capital is mainly interested in China as a cheap pool of labour for assembling phones, computers, computer equipment, and finishing clothes that are then exported to the West. China's information economy is therefore dominated by hardware-exporting companies, whereas software and Internet companies play a subordinated role. Given China's embedding into the capitalist world economy as an exporter of manufactured goods and a relatively cheap manufacturing labour pool, the interest of Western investors and finance capital to buy shares of Chinese companies and the interest of Western companies to advertise on Chinese social media may be limited. Baidu, Weibo, and Renren are platforms with a large Chinese user base, but given their relatively pure focus on China their profits and revenues can hardly compete with those of Western social media corporations that attract advertisers and investors in many countries.

Colin Sparks (2014) shows data that evidences that total advertising spending and ad spending per person in the BRICS (Brazil, Russia, India, China, South Africa) countries is only a small fraction of the ad volume in the United States. He argues that this circumstance has to do with the fact that the average consumer in the BRICS countries is rather poor. As an effect the ad revenues stay limited in these countries. One consequence is that indigenous social media platforms published in national languages have profits that are just a fraction of comparable US social media platforms.

Similar to Google, Twitter, and Facebook, large parts of Baidu, Sina, and Renren's revenues are generated by targeted online advertising. The basic capital accumulation model of social media companies both in China and the West is to turn user data (user-generated content, profile data, interest data, browsing data, social network data) into a commodity that is sold to advertisers (Fuchs 2014a, b). Baidu, Sina, and Renren are just like Google, Twitter, and Facebook primarily not communication platforms, but large advertising agencies. The logic of commerce, capitalism, and advertising dominates the Internet and social media both in China and the West. Free platform use makes it difficult for users to see the commodity logic underlying these platforms and the role their use has as unpaid digital labour that generates economic value. The basic exchange that social media corporations in China and the West organise is that they receive money in exchange for providing access to ad space that is targeted to users' interests.

Legally, targeted advertising is enabled by privacy policies and terms of use that are published on the websites of the platforms and to which users agree when registering their profiles. We can compare such policies and terms of Chinese and Western platforms:

- Baidu Privacy Notice: "Baidu will also provide you with a personalized service, such as to show you more relevant search results, or the more relevant marketing advertising of results."[17]
- Google Privacy Policy: "We use the information that we collect from all of our services to provide, maintain, protect and improve them, to develop new ones and to protect Google and our users. We also use this information to offer you tailored content—like giving you more relevant search results and ads."[18]
- Weibo Privacy Policy: "In addition, you acknowledge and agree that: within the scope permitted by existing laws and regulations, the microblog might use your personal non-privacy information for marketing and other use, including but not limited to: show or provide advertising and promotional materials on the microblogging platform; inform or recommend the microblogging service or product information to you; and other such information that we think you might be interested in depending on your usage of the micro-blogging service or products."[19]
- Twitter Terms of Service:[20] "The Services may include advertisements, which may be targeted to the Content or information on the Services, queries made through the Services, or other information."
- Renren Terms of Service: "Notices can be sent to users via e-mail or regular mail. The Thousand Oaks Company can send emails to users: information about changes of the Terms and Service, service changes or other important things. The Thousand Oaks Company reserves the right to present commercial advertising to all users of Renren.com."[21]
- Facebook Data Use Policy,[22] November 15, 2013, accessed on April 7, 2014:

We use the information we receive about you in connection with the services and features we provide to you and other users like your friends, our partners, the advertisers that purchase ads on the site, and the developers that build the games, applications, and websites you use. For example, in addition to helping people see and find things that you do and share, we may use the information we receive about you: [. . .] to measure or understand the effectiveness of ads you and others see, including to deliver relevant ads to you; [. . .]

We may also put together data about you to serve you ads or other content that might be more relevant to you. [. . .] So we can show you content that you may find interesting, we may use all of the information we receive about you to serve ads that are more relevant to you.

- WeChat[23] Terms of Service,[24] January 6, 2014, accessed on April 7, 2014:

You also agree that, as explained in more detail in our *WeChat Privacy Policy*, we use targeted advertising to try to make advertising more relevant and valuable to you. [. . .] We may use your information for the purpose of sending you advertising or direct marketing (whether by messaging within our services, by email or by other means) that offer or advertise products and services of ours and/or selected third parties." (http://www.wechat.com/en/service_terms.html).

The comparison shows that Chinese and Western social media companies use relatively similar terms of use and privacy policies that allow them to commodify a multitude of personal user data for commercial purposes. Commodification of user data is thereby a reality of social media usage in China and the West. Chinese and Western social media privacy policies and terms of use not only share similar economic goals, but also use a comparable ideological language that presents targeted advertising as advantageous for users by speaking of "relevant marketing advertising", "more relevant ads", "delivering relevant ads to you", "ads that might be more relevant to you", "targeted advertising make[s] advertising more relevant and valuable to you". Advertising and targeting are presented as desirable because they would allow users to get information about and to purchase relevant commodities. This ideology of "relevant ads" masks that advertising can have negative effects, such as the concealment of negative features and effects of products; the discrimination against competing products; the advancement of the concentration of the economy; the manipulation of human needs and desires; the statistical sorting of users into consumer groups so that the weak, the poor, people with low purchasing power, and people of colour are discriminated against; the enforcement of e.g. racist or sexist stereotypes; and the fostering of mass consumption of non-renewable resources that generates waste and aggravates the ecological crisis (for an overview see the contributions in Turow and McAllister 2009).

An interesting exception is the mobile chat application WhatsApp that says in its Terms of Service:[25] "We are not fans of advertising. WhatsApp is currently ad-free and we hope to keep it that way forever. We have no intention to introduce advertisement into the product, but if we ever do, will update this section." "These days companies know literally everything about you, your friends, your interests, and they use it all to sell ads. [. . .] Remember, when advertising is involved you the user are the product."[26] Given this criticism of advertising, it is interesting that WhatsApp was sold to Facebook for US$19 billion in February 2014.[27] Facebook derives 89 per cent of its revenues from advertising (Facebook SEC filings, form 10-K for financial year 2013). WhatsApp will be compelled to find a commodification strategy that allows making profits, and the future will tell whether this will mean the introduction of advertising and the change of WhatsApp's values towards advertising or not.

Both in China and the West, social media corporations' chairpeople and CEOs tend to be their largest shareholders, which gives them large financial and decision power. People such as Robin Li (Baidu), Larry Page (Google), Charles Chao (Weibo), Jack Dorsey (Twitter), Joseph Chen (Renren), or Mark Zuckerberg (Facebook) are not just managers working for a wage in order to grow the business, but are simultaneously capitalists who own parts of the company and are partly paid in the form of shares. Finance firms hold significant amount of shares and are via interlocking directorates represented in the board of directors of many Chinese and Western social media corporations. This circumstance is an indication that the capitalist information economy is both in China and the West not independent from the finance industry, but dependent on its investments, support, and loans, which results in an interconnection of informational capitalism and finance capitalism and a dependence of informational capital on finance capital. Also technology and media companies that do not directly compete but complement social media are connected to Chinese and Western social media corporations via interlocking directorates, which is an indication for the vertical integration of the capitalist media industry in China and the West.

Baidu, Sina/Weibo, and Renren are just like Google, Twitter, and Facebook listed on US stock markets and thereby connected to and dependent on finance capital that is invested in the form of share purchases into the social media corporations. So social media corporations have two economies: the advertising economy, in which they sell ads in order to accumulate capital; and the finance economy, in which they sell shares to investors and try to increase their stock market values. Baidu and Google have seen a long-term growth of their market value with a slump when the global capitalist crisis started in 2008. Renren's stock value has first dropped and then remained constantly low. Facebook's market value has since 2011 been rising, but is also fluctuating. Twitter and Weibo have in common that they are both companies struggling to make wins with the help of targeted advertising. They both have become publicly traded companies although they have until 2014 only made losses. There is a divergence between their positive stock values and their actual monetary losses.

Financial crises can start if finance bubbles burst. This can happen if there is a large divergence between actual profits and stock market valuation and investors lose confidence. The dot-com crisis in 2000 was an earlier expression of the high financialisation of the Internet economy, in which actual profits could not keep up with the promises of high stock market values. A new round of financialisation in the Internet industry has enabled the rise of social media while at the same time the new world economic crisis showed us how crisis-prone financial markets are. It is not easy to make profits with targeted advertising because the average click-through-rate is around 0.1 per cent (Comscore 2012): users only click on every one-thousandth online ad presented to them. And even then it is not clear if such clicks on targeted ads tend to result in purchases or not.

Targeted advertising is a high-risk business. Chinese social media corporations have also realised this circumstance and express warnings in their financial reports. Weibo writes:

> If we fail to retain existing customers or attract new advertisers and marketing customers to advertise and market on our platform or if we are unable to collect accounts receivable from advertisers or advertising agencies in a timely manner, our financial condition, results of operations and prospects may be materially and adversely affected. [. . .] Privacy concerns relating to our products and services and the use of user information could damage our reputation, deter current and potential users and customers from using Weibo and negatively impact our business. [. . .] The monetization of our services may require users to accept promoted advertising in their feeds or private messages, which may affect user experience and cause a decline in user traffic and a delay in our monetization. [. . .] New technologies could block our advertisements, desktop clients and mobile applications and may enable technical measures that could limit our traffic growth and new monetization opportunities.
>
> *Weibo SEC filings, form F-1, registration statement*

Baidu says:

> [T]hird parties may develop and use certain technologies to block the display of our customers' advertisements and other marketing products on our Baidu.com website, which may in turn cause us to lose customers and adversely affect our results of operations.
>
> *Baidu SEC Filings, Form-20F 2013, 5*

The future of the social media economy in China and the West is uncertain. It is clear that it is both in China and the West a highly financialised capitalist industry that depends on the influx of investments on finance markets and the confidence of advertisers that advertising works. There are many uncertainties associated with advertising capital accumulation models, especially concerning users' privacy concerns, the use of ad-block technologies and other limits to advertising, and the question if targeted ads are effective or not. The possibility of a dwindling investors' confidence after some trigger event and a resulting social media crisis cannot be ruled out because financialising and corporatising the Internet is accompanied by huge risks that both China and the West are facing.

7.4. China and Social Media Ideologies

There are different ways to define what an ideology is (Eagleton 1991). For the purpose of this work, ideology is understood as thoughts, practices, ideas, words, concepts, phrases, sentences, texts, belief systems, meanings, representations, artefacts, institutions, systems, or combinations thereof that represent and justify one group's or individual's domination and power by misrepresenting, one-dimensionally presenting, or distorting reality in symbolic representations (see Chapter 3 in this book for a discussion of foundations of ideology critique). One crucial dimension of the structure of ideologies has to do with norms and values. Ideologies present claims that have to do with the questions (Jupp 2006; van Dijk 1998, chapter 5; van Dijk 2011, 386, 395–396): What are our main values? How do we evaluate ourselves and others? What should (not) be done? This means that ideologies say something about what is considered to be good. At the same time they also say something about what is seen as bad or alternatively they leave out questions about negativity.

In order to assess which ideologies are associated with the commodity form of social media in China, I have conducted a discourse analysis of Baidu, Tencent (QQ, WeChat), Sina Weibo, and RenRen self-presentations as well as of interviews with these companies' CEOs Robin Li (Baidu), Ma Huateng (Tencent), Charles Chao (Sina, Weibo), and Joseph Chen (Renren). A search for suitable material resulted in a corpus of 13 texts. I reviewed these texts with the questions in mind: What does the company/CEO present as the main advantages of their platform? Are disadvantages presented? I identified passages that addressed these questions. I then compared the materials, identified how the statements relate to social media's power structures, and especially gave attention to the negative dimensions of social media that were not mentioned.

The main ideological claim of social media companies is that social media makes information and communication easier and allows everyone to participate.

- Robin Li (Baidu): "People can get information—on entertainment, politics, finance—much easier than before" (Watts 2005).
- Charles Chao (Sina Weibo):[28] "But with microblog, with Weibo, people start to not only create content themselves, but also to distribute content themselves. [...] In the future, you don't need a TV station to do the

live broadcasting. Everybody with a mobile phone can do live broadcasting. [. . .] We want to make it easy for people to access information, to share information."

- Joseph Chen (Renren): "people tend to communicate among their friends and sharing their instances in life";[29] "people tend to communicate among their friends and sharing their instances in life"; "The world is becoming more connected."[30]
- Ma Huateng (Tencent):[31] "All the popular commercialized products and services are the ones who can meet the ultimate needs of users."
- Baidu's self-description:[32] "the mission of providing the best way for people to find what they're looking for online", "We provide our users with many channels to find and share information."
- Sina Weibo's self-understanding:[33] Sina is designed to "allow users to connect and share information anywhere, anytime and with anyone on our platform" and provides "an array of online media and social networking services to our user to create a rich canvas for businesses and brand advertisers to connect and engage with their targeted audiences".
- Renren's self-understanding:[34] "Renren, which means 'Everyone' in Chinese, enables users to connect and communicate with each other, share information, create user generated content, play online games, watch videos and enjoy a wide range of other features and services. We believe real name relationships create a stronger and more enduring social graph that is essential in the mobile internet world and difficult to replicate. [. . .] Our vision is to re-define the social networking experience and revolutionize the way people in China connect, communicate, entertain and shop. To achieve this, we are focused on providing a highly engaging and interactive platform through technology that promotes connectivity, communication and sharing. The mobile internet is making the world more connected, and Renren stands at the forefront of this evolution."
- Tencent's (QQ, WeChat) self-understanding:[35] "It is Tencent's mission to enhance the quality of human life through Internet services." WeChat is a "value-added Internet, mobile and telecom services and online advertising under the strategic goal of providing users with 'one-stop online lifestyle services'" that provides users the possibility to "connect with friends across platforms".[36]

An associated claim is that social media make communication more open and transparent. Charles Chao (Sina Weibo) says Weibo is a space where users "talk, where they think, where they exchange intents of their ideas, their opinion", that it is "a very free platform for people to express themselves and exchange ideas" and that it helps China to "progress into a more open, more transparent society" (Talk Asia 2011). Chao argues Weibo enables transparency and enables a system of check and balance in society, which makes China's society much better. [. . .] Everybody will have the ability to report news and report what is happening. So it is made impossible almost to withhold information. [. . .] It makes information wider available. [. . .] This makes society much more open. [. . .] It makes everything much more transparent.[37]

Technological/instrumental rationality in capitalism has a double character. For Marx, the commodity and capital accumulation are based on the exploitation of labour power; it is the production and appropriation of surplus-value. Class society turns humans into instruments that in capital serve the dominant class's need of capital accumulation. At the same time, the commodity has a specific aesthetic and subjective appearance: the labour involved in its production disappears behind the commodity and money form; one can only see a thing devoid of social relations. The social is hidden behind the commodity form that appears natural and endless. Ideology operates the same way: It naturalises domination and exploitation by presenting them as best option, without alternative, essential, and natural.

Capitalist media are modes of reification and therefore expressions of instrumental/technological rationality in a manifold sense: First, they reduce humans to the status of consumers of advertisements and commodities. Second, culture is in capitalism to a large degree connected to the commodity form: there are cultural commodities produced by cultural wage-workers that are bought by consumers and audience commodities that the media consumers become themselves by being sold as an audience to the capitalist media's advertising clients. Third, in order to reproduce its existence, capitalism has to present itself as the best possible (or only possible) system and makes use of the media in order to try to keep this message (in all its differentiated forms) hegemonic. The first and the second dimension constitute the economic dimension of instrumental reason, the third dimension the ideological form of instrumental reason. Capitalist media are necessarily means of advertising and commodification and spaces of ideology. Advertisement and cultural commodification make humans an instrument for economic profit accumulation. Ideology aims at instilling the belief in the system of capital and commodities into human's subjectivity. The goal is that human thoughts and actions do not go beyond capitalism, do not question and revolt against this system, and thereby play the role of instruments for the perpetuation of capitalism. It is of course an important question to which extent ideology is successful and to which degree it is questioned and resisted, but the crucial aspect about ideology is that it encompasses strategies and attempts to make human subjects instrumental in the reproduction of domination and exploitation.

Social media ideology inverts commodity fetishism. In inverted commodity fetishism (Fuchs 2014a), the users do not immediately experience the commodity form because they do not pay money for accessing a commodity. Rather they get access without payment to social media platforms that are not commodities.

The commodity form takes place without an exchange that users are involved in: the platforms sell usage data to advertising clients who get targeted access to users' profiles that become ad spaces. It is rather difficult for users to think of corporate social media use as labour or exploitation because inverted commodity fetishism creates a social experience and social use-value for them and tries to ideologically hide the role of the commodity.

A common ideology that Chinese corporate platforms and their CEOs associate with social media is that it enables everyone to get and share information, to communicate, engage, produce and distribute content, and connect with others. A further claim is that producing, connecting, sharing, communicating, and engaging via social media enhances humans' quality of life and society's quality and transparency. In the analysed statements, there is an underlying assumption that social media makes society necessarily more open, transparent, and connected, whereas aspects of closure and power are not considered. If they are considered, they are only framed in such a way that social media empowers users. Chinese social media ideology reflects Henry Jenkins's concept of participatory culture that assumes that social media enables a culture "in which fans and other consumers are invited to actively participate in the creation and circulation of new content" (Jenkins 2008, 331) and there is "strong support for creating and sharing creations with others" (Jenkins et al. 2009, 5). The problem of this approach is the simplistic understanding of participation as content-creation and sharing that ignores the political connotation of participation as participatory democracy, a system in which all people own and control and together manage the systems that affect their lives (Fuchs 2014b, chapter 3). The engaging/connecting/sharing ideology is an ideology because it only views social media positively and is inherently technological-deterministic. It assumes that social media technologies as such have positive effects and disregards the power structures and asymmetries into which it is embedded.

This engaging/connecting/sharing ideology is, however, not just typical for Chinese corporate social media; it is a universal capitalist social media ideology that is used by social media companies, management gurus, and uncritical scholars and observers to justify the capitalist character of corporate social media as acceptable and good. The argument is that social media is fun for the users and allows them to do something with these platforms. It would be a form of cultural imperialism to describe this ideology as specific for China. It is in fact an ideology that comes along with the commodity form of social media. Western capitalist social media also advances it:

- Facebook says it provides "the power to share and to make the world more open and connected".[38]
- Google argues its goal is the organisation of "the world's information" in order to "make it universally accessible and useful" and "make money without doing evil".[39]

- YouTube conceives the essence of freedom as possibility "to connect, inform and inspire others across the globe and acts as a distribution platform for original content creators and advertisers large and small".[40]
- For Twitter, the freedom of social media is "to connect with people, express yourself and discover what's happening" and "give everyone the power to create and share ideas and information instantly".[41]
- Instagram says it is a "fast, beautiful and fun way to share your life with friends and family".[42]
- Pinterest describes itself as enabling "collecting and organising things you love".[43]
- LinkedIn claims it helps to "connect the world's professionals to make them more productive and successful".[44]
- tumblr says it enables you to "share the things you love".[45]
- VK sees itself as "a web resource that helps you stay in touch with your old and new friends".[46]

The language used by Western corporate social media platforms in order to describe their advantages resembles the one used by Chinese platforms and their CEOs. There is a focus on stressing how social media enables sharing, empowerment, connecting, opening, access, inspiring others, creating, informing, fun, collecting, and loving something. The engaging/connecting/sharing ideology is immanent to structures of representation of capitalist social media both in China and the West. It shows the similarities of ideological and corporate structures in these two parts of the world that are shaped by a universal capitalist ideology and universal capitalist interests.

The problem is, however, that capitalism is a class-divided society and that therefore inevitably not everyone benefits. Social media ideologies do not talk about outcasts, the poor, the unemployed, and the exploited. They ignores issues such as the exploitation of free labour; negative consequences of capitalism, advertising, and consumer culture; the fact that users create value on social media platforms but do not own these platforms; the asymmetrical power of visibility on social media that gives celebrities, companies, and governments much more visibility and attention than ordinary users (Fuchs 2014b).

B.J. Mendelson (2012) critically reflects in his book *Social Media Is Bullshit* on his 10-year experience as an Internet consultant: marketers want people to believe that social media can help organisations and individuals to increase their reputation. But in reality "almost nothing" works, "unless you have a multimillion-dollar budget and a healthy media presence" (Mendelson 2012, 11). Generating social media visibility requires "a big budget, lots of time, a team of people who know what they're doing, media exposure" (13) because the WWW "is essentially run by major corporations" (23). "The truth is that it's almost impossible for you to reach an audience of any significance [. . .] unless you have a strong network, millions to spend on advertising and publicity, or if the media likes you" (44). Mendelson argues that myths about the Internet that he based on what Harry G. Frankfurt (2005) calls "bullshit" spread through an "asshole-based economy" (Mendelson 2012, 54) that is furthered by cyber hipster, tech media and marketers, analysts, corporations, mainstream media, and users (74).

The engaging/connecting/sharing ideology is grounded in an individualistic and consumerist notion of freedom that sees freedom as social media's enablement of single users to communicate, create, consume, and share more. Corporate social media have hijacked the concept of free access and turned it into an ideology that tries to conceal the existence of a mode of capital accumulation that is based on the commodification of personal data and targeted advertising. Corporate social media present themselves as free, open, and social, but are in reality unfree, closed, and particularistic machines for the commodification of personal data that produce and sell targeted ads. The problem is that Internet companies, consultants, managers, and those who believe in their ideology do not see that freedom is, as Karl Marx stressed, a "realm of freedom" (Marx 1894, 958) that is not based on the logic of profitability and accumulation, but the principle "From each according to his ability, to each according to his needs!" (Marx 2000, 615), which implies that the "first freedom" of the media "consists in not being a trade" (Marx 1974, 41). The consequences of the reduction of the WWW's freedom to freedom of property, the market, and trade have been that the WWW is today first and foremost a shopping mall and a huge advertising space, in which the world's largest advertising agencies disguise themselves as "social media" and "mobile media" in order to garner and commodify personal data as "big data". The WWW is the world's biggest narcissistic self-presentation machine and individualising spectacle, in which users are not connected to WeTube, OurBook, OurSpace, but to YouTube, Facebook, MySpace, Weibo, and Renren in order to advertise their own selves to others. The task is to gain competitive advantages and accumulate reputation in order to be better "employable" and more successful. Individualism is designed into corporate "social" media platforms and has become a strategy of survival for many workers who tend to see themselves not as an exploited class, but reflect their existence as individual freelancers by conceiving themselves not as precarious workers, but as "knowledge professionals", "middle class", "makers", and "creatives".

If we go from the level of Internet companies' ideologies to the views of the users, there are indications that in China there are both a liberal middle-class practice and ideology of ICT, Internet, WWW, and social media usage as well as socialist working-class usage practices (Qiu 2009; Xing 2012; Wu 2012), including fake iPhones and bandit phones (*shanzhaiji*) (Qiu 2012).

An arbitrary grab for a bunch of books on one of my shelves dedicated to Internet research immediately results in a multitude of liberal Western authors decrying Internet surveillance and censorship in China: China is "operating extensive filtering practices" and "has one of the most sophisticated and pervasive filtering systems" (Nash 2013, 453). "Countries like China want as much control as they can get" in order to "create the first ICT-enhanced police state" (Sullins 2010, 125). China censors the Internet because it is "fearful of the effect of freely flowing information on their authoritarian control regime" (McNair 2009, 224). The Internet in China has "profound statist regulation and content surveillance" and is "monitored by the Propaganda Department, which bans all original content online" (Volkmer 2003, 321). "Iran, China and Malaysia [. . .] have instituted various kinds of restrictive internet policies" (Moore 1999, 41–42).

It does not much matter who these authors are as they were arbitrarily chosen and are just ideological sock puppets replaceable by thousands of others who make similar arguments in comparable publications. My criticism is also not that what they are saying is factually wrong. The point is rather that their arguments idealise the West in a highly ideological and cultural imperialist manner. Their arguments imply that the West is not operating Internet filtering, does not control the Internet, does not have ICT-enhanced police states, does not have authoritarian control regimes, and does not have restrictive Internet policies. Such arguments present the Chinese Internet as unfree and controlled and the Western Internet as free.

Such liberal authors do not want to see that there is not only state control of the Internet and free speech, but also a market control of the Internet and free speech that is instituted by capitalist companies that control power, visibility, attention, reputation, and capital in the context of the Internet and thereby deprive others of these resources. In addition, Edward Snowden's revelations have shown the existence of a surveillance-industrial complex in which Western state institutions such as the US National Security Agency (NSA) and the UK Government Communications Headquarters (GCHQ) collaborate with private security firms and Western communication companies, including AOL, Apple, Facebook, Microsoft, Paltalk, Skype, and Yahoo!, in order to collect user data "directly from the servers of these U.S. Service Providers".[47] Secret services have obtained detailed access to a multitude of citizens' activities in converging social roles conducted in converging social spaces. The US Prism programme is framed by the fact that since 9/11 there has been a massive intensification and extension of surveillance that is based on the naïve technological-deterministic surveillance ideology that monitoring technologies, big data analysis, and predictive algorithms can prevent terrorism. User data is in the surveillance-industrial complex first externalised and made public or semi-public on the Internet in order to enable users' communication processes, then privatised as private property by Internet platforms in order to accumulate capital, and finally particularised by secret services who bring massive amounts of data under their control that is made accessible and analysed worldwide with the help of profit-making security companies.

The social media surveillance-industrial complex shows that a negative dialectic of the Enlightenment is at play in contemporary society: the military-industrial complex constantly undermines the very liberal values of the Enlightenment, such as the freedoms of thought, speech, press, and assembly as well as the security of the people's persons, houses, papers, and effects. Prism shows how in supposedly liberal democracies dangerous forms of political-economic power negate Enlightenment values. Given these revelations, the argument that the Internet is politically free in the West and politically controlled in China has become ridiculous. Both in China and the West the Internet and social media are highly controlled by economic and political power.

It should also be noted that Internet control in China is taking place under a predominantly capitalist economic system, which shows that capitalism does not bring along democracy. In the West, neoliberal capitalism has also been accompanied by repressive state power that wages wars and has erected an extensive surveillance system based on the techno-deterministic ideology that surveillance can reduce crime and terrorism. Both in China and the West, "the market liberals depend on the repressive state" (Lin 2013, 93).

Chinese social media companies do not deny the existence of Internet control, censorship, and surveillance in China. They describe in their annual reports how these forms of control work. So for example Baidu says in its annual financial report (Baidu SEC Filings, Form-20F 2013):

> The Ministry of Public Security has the authority to order any local internet service provider to block any internet website at its sole discretion. From time to time, the Ministry of Public Security has stopped the dissemination over the internet of information which it believes to be socially destabilizing. The State Secrecy Bureau is also authorized to block any website it deems to be leaking state secrets or failing to meet the relevant regulations relating to the protection of state secrets in the dissemination of online information. Furthermore, we are required to report any suspicious content to relevant governmental authorities, and to undergo computer security inspections. If we fail to implement the relevant safeguards against security breaches, our websites may be shut down and our business and ICP licenses may be revoked.

Chinese Internet capitalists tend, as argued above, to argue that their platforms in the long term make China a freer, more transparent, and more open society. Besides this argument they think that the government's Internet control is needed and are therefore supportive of it. This political conviction may of course have economic motivations. But the decisive fact is that in Chinese Internet ideology, there is a fusion of neoliberal market ideology and state control just like in the ideology of Western conservatives who stress free markets and the technological fight against terrorism via an increase and extension of Internet surveillance. Being asked about censorship, Robin Li (Baidu) says: "As a locally operated company we need to obey the Chinese law. If the law determines that certain information is illegal, we need to remove it from our index" (Watts 2005).

Ma Huateng (Tencent) uses the euphemism of information security management for surveillance, control, and censorship:

> Question: How does Tencent approach the issue of freedom of speech and information online?
> Ma Huateng: In terms of information security management, online companies from any country must abide by a defined set of criteria, and act responsibly. Otherwise it might lead to hearsay, libel and argument among citizens—not to mention between countries. That's why the need for online management is increasingly urgent.[48]

Ma Huateng: "We are a great supporter of the government in terms of the information security. We try to have a better management and control of the Internet."[49] Being asked about censorship, Charles Chao (Sina Weibo) says that "we, as a company working in China—I think whatever we do, we follow the local law and the regulations" (Talk Asia 2011).

The reality of the Internet and social media both in the West and in China is that there are strong forms of economic and political control. The predominant ideology associated with these forms of control is that Chinese and Western social media corporations and uncritical observers present social media as a realm of individual freedom and participation. These terms are thereby deprived of their political meaning and reduced to the level of culture and individualism. Corporate social media's engaging, connecting, and sharing ideology deflects attention from social media and the Internet's power asymmetries and political-economic control structures that fuse authoritarian politics and neoliberal capitalism.

Given the capitalist and ideological control of the Internet and social media, the question is what can be done to save the Internet. To engage with this question, we have to think about China and social struggles today.

7.5. Towards an Alternative Internet and Truly Social Media in China and the World

China is in the West often viewed in a stereotypical manner as a monolithic regime that is centrally controlled by the state. This view neglects on the one hand commonalities between Western and Chinese capitalism; that in China, maybe more than in the West, community-controlled co-operatives that are characteristic for a decentralised democratic socialism have played a role (although their importance has due to Chinese capitalism been massively reduced); and that China is experiencing a large amount of social struggles that challenge the dominant order.

A better world can only be the result of social struggles. "The emancipation of the working class must be the work of the working class itself" (Marx and Engels 1879, 555). Given that capitalism is a global system, we have to look at contemporary working-class struggles for identifying seeds of a better society. For identifying Chinese working-class struggles in 2013 and the first quarter of 2014, I analysed the news and press releases published by China Labor Watch (https://www.chinalaborwatch.org/) and China Labour Bulletin (http://www.clb.org.hk/en/) during this period of time. The results are shown in Table 7.32.

TABLE 7.32 Reported strikes and worker protests in China in the period from January 2013 until March 2014, data sources: China Labour Bulletin: http://www.clb.org.hk/en/, China Labor Watch: https://www.chinalaborwatch.org/

Company	City	Date	Collective action
		January 2013	72 strikes and worker protests all over China
Yanchang Petroleum	Shaanxi	January 2013	600 auxiliary workers demand higher wages
High schools	Wuhan, Hubei, Guizhou, Zhejiang and Henan	January 2013	Strikes for pay increases
Foxconn, Xin Hai Yang Precision	Jiangxi	January 11, 2013	Strike for higher wages
Foxconn	Beijing	January 22, 2013	Strike for higher wages
		February 2013	32 strikes and worker protests all over China
	Guangzhou	February 2013	Street cleaners strike for higher wages
Ohms Electronics	Shenzen	February 27, 2013	Workers protest against fixed-term contracts
		March 2013	50 strikes and worker protests all over China
Honda	Nanhai	March 18, 2013	Workers strike for pay increases
		April 2013	65 strikes and worker protests all over China
	Guangdong, Henan	April 2013	Teacher strikes for wage increases
Motorola	Tianjin	April 2013	7,000 workers strike against low wages
Yamada	Jiangsu	April 27, 2013	Strike because of store closure
		May 2013	55 strikes and worker protests all over China
Samsung	Huizhou	May 2013	Protest in light of the suicide of a young female factory worker
Chinese Medicine University Hospital	Guangzhou	May-August 2013	Healthcare workers start a several-week-long protest against layoffs
		June 2013	38 strikes and worker protests all over China

(continued)

TABLE 7.32 (continued)

Company	City	Date	Collective action
Hop Lun	Dongguan	June 14, 2013	More than 1,000 women garment workers strike against pay cuts
		July 2013	78 strikes and worker protests all over China
Zhongji Pile Industry	Guangdong	July 2013	Workers detain five managers for five days in order to obtain full payment
		August 2013	67 strikes and worker protests all over China
		September 2013	40 strikes and worker protests all over China
Yantian and Shekou ports	Shenzen	September 2013	Dock workers strike for higher pay
Beigang Group	Jixi	September 16, 2013	Strike of more than 1,000 workers against wage arrears
Shili Electronics	Dongguan	September 17, 2013	Road blockage against unpaid social insurance contributions
		October 2013	53 strikes and worker protests all over China
CP Lotus stores	Beijing	October 2013	Work stoppage after takeover by Wumart
Industrial and Commercial Bank of China	Beijing	October 21, 2013	5,000 people protest against layoffs
		November 2013	42 strikes and worker protests all over China
Nokia	Dongguan	November 2013	3,000 workers strike and protest against layoffs
ASM	Shenzen	November 2013	5,000 semiconductor workers protest for wage increases
		December 2013	64 strikes and worker protests all over China
		January 2014	56 strikes and worker protests all over China
Doo Jung	Shenzen	January 11–14, 2014	Strike against labour violations
		February 2014	27 strikes and worker protests all over China
Weihai Sanjin	Weihai	February 2014	Ship workers strike and protest for the payment of pension and wage arrears
		March 2014	119 strikes and worker protests all over China

Ciyu Shoe Factory	Shenzen	March 10–19, 2014	6,000 workers strike against wage reductions
IBM Systems Technology Company	Shenzen	March 2014	1,000 workers strike against layoffs and wage cuts after the company was sold to Lenovo
Pepsi	Changchun, Chongqing, Xinjiang, Harbin, Xi'an, Lanzhou	March 2014	Pepsi workers strike against layoffs and cuts
Walmart	Changde	March 2014	Strike against shop closure
Samsung, Shanmukang Technology	Dongguan	March 2014	More than 1,000 workers strike for wage increases

The data indicate that from January 2013 until March 2014 at least 858 strikes and labour protests took place in China. In the years 2011–2013, 40 per cent of the strikes in China took place in the manufacturing sector (China Labour Bulletin 2014). A relatively large share (57 per cent) occurred in Guangdong that has seen a lot of closures and relocations of manufacturers (China Labour Bulletin 2014). Very active strike activity also occurred in transportation (26 per cent), construction (8 per cent), and education (6 per cent) (China Labour Bulletin 2014). China is not a monolithic society, but one with very active and vivid working-class struggles against exploitation.

Bo Xila was secretary of the Communist Party of China in Chongqing, a large southwestern city with almost 30 million inhabitants in its metropolitan area. He represents what some term the Chongqing model of Chinese development that is "looking to revitalize socialist ideas" and opposes the Guangdong Model that symbolises "a more free market approach, rising inequality, and an export orientation" (Zhao 2012b, 1). He became "the hero of many on the left in China" (Morley 2012). In September 2013, he was sentenced to life in prison because of corruption. Left-wing observers have considered his case "a political show trial" (Zhao 2012b, 2), whereas the People's Daily Online celebrated it as "China's determination to fight corruption in accordance with the law",[50] while even Western imperialist media concede that the trial was the Party's "chance to take him down" because "his admiration for Maoism, his ambition and his flamboyant, populist style had long been a worry for party leaders".[51] "Bo and his followers tried in particular to restore the spirit of a lost collectivism" (Lin 2013, 201). Under Bo Xila, Chongqing's satellite TV channel CQTV was decommercialised and abolished advertising in 2011 (Zhao 2012b, 10). It also introduced a weekly current affairs programme called "Public Forum on Common Prosperity" that was "the only large scale current affairs show dedicated to the theme of 'common prosperity'" (Zhao 2012a, 12).

In 2012, a grassroots "People's Proposal for China" circulated on the Chinese Internet and was supported by the left-wing Red China website. It demanded free education, fair payment for teachers, progressive real estate taxes, higher state expenditures for education, the establishment of a national anti-corruption online platform, the nationalisation of the coal industry, the closing down of highly exploitative enterprises, the enforcement of good working conditions, and a "self-reliant approach to economic development" that abolishes "any policy that serves foreign capitalists at the cost of the interest of Chinese working class" (Morley 2012).

The overview of social struggles, Bo Xila, and the People's Proposal shows how alive and vivid working-class struggles are in China. Zhao Yuezhi (2007) points out that neoliberalism with Chinese characteristics and Chinese digital neoliberalism do not signify a sealed fate, but are contested in the form of workers' and peasants' struggles that make use of ICTs as well as online publications and debates that support the emergence of a radical left. The struggles and riots at Foxconn are an expression that there are struggles that are "contesting the terms of China's digital revolution", they show "the unevenness and incommensurability of the digital age" in China and the world (Zhao 2007, 113).

Jack Qiu (2009, x) argues that China has "the largest exploited working class of the global information age". He therefore characterises China as undergoing a change that has resulted in the emergence of a working-class network society (Qiu 2009) that is especially characterised by what he terms the "information have-less: low-end ICT users, service providers, and laborers who are manufacturing these electronics" (Qiu 2009, 3–4). This class would consist of migrant workers (who have migrated from rural to urban areas), unemployed and underemployed workers, micro-entrepreneurs, youth, students, and retirees struggling to make a living. There are also "grey-collar" workers with highly repetitive jobs in industries such as software engineering, design, marketing, advertising, telecommunications, and customer services (Qiu 2009, 104–105, 93, 113).

Examples of websites related to the Chinese working class and its struggles are honghuacao (http://9hhc.com/), gongren menhu (http://chuizi.net, down since 2010 according to Wayback Machine—archive.org), gongren shige lianmeng (Workers' Poetry Alliance, http://www.laborpoetry.com), Red China (http://redchinacn.net), Utopia (http://zlk.wyzxsx.com/, http://www.wyzxwk.com/, http://www.wyzxsd.com/), or Mao Flag (http://maoflag.org).[52]

Jack Qiu says that the Chinese working class uses and adopts cheap ICTs that he calls "working class ICTs" (Qiu 2009): they include the sale of second-hand phones, refurbished computers, pirated DVDs, pirated software, and refilled printer cartridges, and the use of prepaid mobile phones, Internet cafés, Little Smart wireless phones, blogs, computer games, peer-to-peer networks, and QQ Internet messaging (one today can probably add the social networking site RenRen and the microblog Weibo). The purpose of the use of these ICTs would be networking for survival, entertainment, social relations, education, mutual support, and politics.

What characterises the working class is that it is not-capital: it does not own and control capital—it is therefore economically poor. Labour is "not-value", "not-capital", "not-raw-material", "not-instrument of labour", "not-raw-product" (Marx 1857/58, 295): it is "absolute poverty", which means an "exclusion from objective wealth" (Marx 1857/58, 296). At the same time labour is "the living source of value", the "general possibility" of wealth (Marx 1857/58, 296). Given that labour is not-capital and stands in a class antagonism with capital, working-class ICTs can be conceived as ICTs whose production and output is controlled and owned by workers, i.e. self-managed ICT companies. To the extent that Chinese workers create an informal economy in which they create ICTs (e.g. pirated DVDs), one can speak of the attempt of the information-have less to find ways to control ICT production. The category of working-class ICTs is theoretically interesting and can be quite fruitful. The question is if this notion should encompass the use of cheap ICTs that are sold by capitalist companies to workers. The basic logic for capital is that although these workers are poor, the fact that there are hundred millions of them creates a profitable market segment. These companies are, however, not worker-controlled and in fact exist by the exploitation of workers as well as the exploitation of users (the latter is the case if targeted or non-targeted advertising is used as capital accumulation model). The working class is universal in that its emancipation puts not only an end to capital, but to all classes. So working-class ICTs can conceptually be best defined as ICTs that try to explode the class character, i.e. ICTs that are collectively owned, controlled, operated, and used by the immediate producers and prosumers.

A concept of ICT use by the working class needs to reflect the difference between a class-in-itself and a class-for-itself, i.e. the difference between the working class in its position in the relations of production with any form of subjectivity and a politically conscious working class engaged in political struggles. One can use the two terms *proletariat* and *working class* to draw a distinction between the subjective and the objective class dimension, meaning that based on such a distinction, the working class is the politically conscious and politically (self-)organised struggling proletariat, the class-in-and-for-itself, a self-constituting collective political power. The becoming-working class of the proletariat is then a political process taking place in social struggles. The Communist Manifesto ends with the words "Proletarier aller Länder, vereinigt Euch!" (Proletarians of all countries, unite!) (Marx and Engels 1848, 493). This is an indication that Marx and Engels saw the working-class-in-itself as the proletariat. The proletariat is the not yet politically organised, not yet united, and a not yet conscious class. It has the potential to organise itself to become the working class that struggles for its own abolition and thereby the abolition of all classes and class society.

If one makes a theoretical distinction between the proletariat and the working class, then a differentiation between "proletarian ICTs" and "working class ICTs" can be made. For both, we find different aspects of a) production, b) distribution, and c) use of ICTs for economic, political, and cultural purposes. The proletariat uses ICTs for all sorts of purposes and in a context where the proletariat is large enough, this becomes a profitable industry, a kind of industry of selling cheap ICTs to proletarians. At the same time, if proletarian ICTs are organised by capital and in the form of commodities, exploitation and the deepening of class antagonism is a structural feature of proletarian ICTs. As the working class, proletarians have the interest not to be exploited because exploitation limits their opportunities and is the structural cause of inequality. So the becoming working-class of proletarians then entails specific features, namely that ICTs are used in working-class struggles. In addition, if the working class is the universal class that wants to overcome its exploitation and thereby all classes, then in the realm of ICTs it also stands for qualitatively different ownership and organisation structures of ICTs, namely ICTs that are no longer commodities but are worker controlled and owned, i.e. self-managed ICTs or commons-based ICTs. The notion of working-class ICTs then also entails the becoming-common (goods) of ICTs.

Commons are structures that all people control, produce, reproduce, and create. Therefore communication is also a commons. Communication is a social means of survival of humanity. Commodification therefore contradicts the essence of communication. Commodification stands in conflict with communicative work or the communications that we all produce in order to exist. A large part of the Internet is today based on commodity logic and capital accumulation. A political task today is to struggle for a commons-based Internet or working-class Internet.

There is a difference between proletarian digital media and working-class digital media. Proletarian digital media often feature capitalist ownership structures, although they can also be non-profit and non-commercial. Working-class digital media are media of struggle controlled by workers in processes of self-management. What a true working class struggles for is the abolishment of classes by the establishment of an economic democracy. Working-class media strive towards media of the commons just like working-class struggles strive towards a society of the commons.

Big-character posters were in twentieth-century China on the one hand working-class social media for public sphere communication, but were on the other hand politically contested. Mao (1957b, 467) wrote about big-character posters (大字报, dazibao, tatsepao): "We should put up big-character posters and hold forums." He characterised these posters the following way:

> The Tatsepao, or big-character poster, is [a] powerful new weapon, a means of criticism and self-criticism which was created by the masses during the rectification movement; at the same time it is used to expose and attack the enemy. It is also a powerful weapon for conducting debate and education in accordance with the broadest mass democracy. People write down their

views, suggestions or exposures and criticisms of others in big characters on large sheets of paper and put them up in conspicuous places for people to read.

Mao 1958

The big-character posters were a result of how "the masses have created a form of making revolution" (Mao 1957a, 484). "This year has seen a great development in our democratic tradition, and this form of speaking out freely, airing views fully, holding great debates and writing big-character posters should be handed down to future generations. It brings socialist democracy into full play. Democracy of this kind is possible only in socialist countries, not in capitalist countries" (Mao 1957a, 485). "Speaking out freely, airing views fully, holding great debates and writing big-character posters are the form best suited to arousing the initiative of the masses and enhancing their sense of responsibility" (Mao 1957a, 484).

The 1978/79 Beijing Spring movement made heavy use of big-character posters and other media (Xing 2012). The working class formed an important part of this movement (Xing 2012). The 1975 Chinese Constitution formulated under Mao the constitutional right to create big-character posters in public as part of the four big freedoms: "Speaking out freely, airing views fully, holding great debates and writing big-character posters are new forms of carrying on socialist revolution created by the masses of the people"[53] (article 13). This article was limited, however, by the formulation that these freedoms should "help consolidate the leadership of the Communist Party of China", which gave the CPC the power to censor *dazibao* (Sheng 1990, 242).

Big-character posters (*dazibao*) flourished during the 1957 Hundred Flowers Movement when Mao called for letting "a hundred flowers blossom" and "a hundred schools of thought contend" (Mao 1967, 134). *Dazibao* were often not accepted if they criticised Mao, and were part of the Mao personality cult in the 1960s when they became means for echoing Mao's voice across the country and a means of Mao for attacking his opponents such as Liu Shaoqi in the 1960s and Lin Biao—one of closest followers and designated successor of Mao in the 1960s—in the early 1970s (Sheng 1990; Li 2009; Churchill 2013). Mao thereby turned against his own idea that if one bans "the expression of wrong ideas, [. . .] the idea will still be there" and that one "should not use the method of suppression" to prevent "the bourgeoisie and petty bourgeoisie" from "expressing themselves" (Mao 1967, 138). Authors of some *dazibao*—such as the creators of the Li Yizhe *dazibao* that called for democracy, socialism, and human rights—were imprisoned (Sheng 1990). After Mao's death in 1976, *dazibao* were used in the Democracy Wall Movement and the protest movement in the late 1980s. Deng Xiaoping tolerated them as long as only the Cultural Revolution and Mao were criticised, but practically outlawed them in 1979 after the criticism had also turned against him (Sheng 1990; Li 2009; Churchill 2013). After the 1978/79 movement, Deng initiated the deletion of these freedoms in the reformulated 1980 Constitution (Xing 2012). The history of *dazibao* is a history of "effective vestiges of free speech" and the reality of "political dissent" (Sheng 1990, 234) as well as of political control.

Henry Siling Li (2009) argues that *dazibao* was a form of user-created content. He says that with the rise of the Internet and social media in China, popular expression "has migrated from brick walls to electronic walls" and that while user-created content "in the pre-internet stage tended to be politically oriented, in the internet age it is now more about fanfare and fun-making" (Li 2009, 57f).

Jürgen Habermas has argued that a public sphere turns into a "pseudo-public sphere" (Habermas 1989b, 162) or a "manufactured public sphere" (Habermas 1989b, 217) when it is controlled by political power, economic power, or commerce/advertising logic. *Dazibao* shows the reality of a contested public sphere in China that has involved public political expressions and struggles as well as political control of the *dazibao* under Mao and Deng. Social media have become a newly contested sphere that combines political control with forms of consumer and advertising culture that marginalise political speech and thereby constitute a form of economic control of the public sphere. *Dazibao* was contested, but in any case was a mass movement for political expression. Social media has the same potential, but commercial and state control limits and colonises its possible contributions to the establishment of a public sphere.

When Dallas Smythe wrote in the early 1970s about communication in China in his article "After Bicycles, What?" (Smythe 1994, 230–244), he took up Mao's idea of the big-character posters for thinking about how to democratically organise the broadcasting system. He spoke of a "two-way system in which each receiver would have the capability to provide either a voice or voice-and-picture response. [. . .] a two-way TV system would be like an electronic tatzupao system" (Smythe 1994, 231–232). These thoughts paralleled Hans Magnus Enzensberger's (1970) concept of emancipatory media use, Walter Benjamin's (1934, 1936/1939) idea of the reader/writer, and Bertolt Brecht's (1932) notion of an alternative radio formulated in his radio theory.

Brecht (1932) argued that the radio would advance public life if it were changed

> over from distribution to communication. The radio would be the finest possible communication apparatus in public life, a vast network of pipes. That is to say, it would be if it knew how to receive as well as to transmit, how to let the listener speak as well as hear, how to bring him into a relationship instead of isolating him. On this principle the radio should step out of the supply business and organize its listeners as suppliers.
>
> *Brecht 1932, 54*

Walter Benjamin (1936/1939, 28) said that printed letters to the editors would anticipate a situation in which literary license has become a common property.

"Thus, the distinction between author and public is about to lose its basic character. [. . .] At any moment the reader is ready to turn into a writer" (Benjamin 1936/1939, 28). This would be a socialisation of production because it would enable proletarians to speak and be an expression of proletarian expertise (Benjamin 1934). A media apparatus like the paper or the theatre would be the better, the more consumers become producers (Benjamin 1934, 243). Hans Magnus Enzensberger (1970) argued that an emancipatory use of media is characterised by a structure in which each receiver is a potential transmitter, programmes are produced collectively, the masses are mobilised, and there is feedback, political learning, decentralisation, and self-organisation. He said that the development of the media from distribution to communication and collective production systems would be "consciously prevented for understandable political reasons". For the mass of people becoming productive, "the elimination of capitalistic property relationships is a necessary, but by no means sufficient condition". In the capitalism of web 2.0, the mass has become productive, but the capitalistic property relations still exist.

It is interesting that Asian (Mao), European (Benjamin, Brecht, Enzensberger, Habermas), and North American (Smythe) critical thinkers came up with the same idea of how to organise a democratic communication system. They not only shared the insight that such a system must be non-capitalist and grassroots in character, but were also all socialist thinkers. These commonalities show that socialist democracy is a universalist idea opposed to capitalism and that a democratic media system is also a universal idea related to the struggle against capitalist and dominative media systems.

Mao had the idea of a media system that the people control in grassroots processes. Smythe applied this idea to electronic media for formulating a concept of alternative electronic media. Yuezhi Zhao (2011) points out the relevance of Smythe's article and his ideas of an alternative non-capitalist communication system for China. Given a world dominated by the logic of neoliberal capitalism (both in the West and China), she stresses inspired by Smythe the importance of establishing communications and societies that are based on non-capitalist logic. Zhao (2007, 92) argues that Smythe raised the question "After bicycles, what?" "in the context of China's search for a socialist alternative to capitalist modernity, with the hope that China would avoid the capitalist path of development". She says that although Smythe misjudged the political situation in China in the 1970s on a number of points, his intervention would continue to "offer a useful point of departure in analysing not only the deployment and development of ICTs in China during the reform era, but also the broad path of China's post-Mao development strategy and its sustainability" (Zhao 2007, 96). The question one would have today to ask in Dallas Smythe's manner about Chinese media would be: After mobile phones, what? (Zhao 2007). Whereas Smythe answered to the question "After bicycles, what?", that China should create a media structure that favours "public goods and services [. . .] against goods and services for individual, private use" (Smythe 1994, 243), ICTs would not only serve capitalist purposes, but would "by their very nature" be social and allow "alternative uses", including collective political action (Zhao 2007, 96). The reality of ICTs in China would show the antagonistic character of these technologies as both means of domination and protest.

The *dazibao*'s very idea that is related to Brecht, Benjamin, and Enzensberger's concepts of an alternative radio, the reader/writer, and emancipatory media use is a symbol for grassroots, participatory democratic media that the people control and that are embedded into a grassroots economy and grassroots politics, i.e. a participatory democracy. The reality of the *dazibao* was that as a medium it became embedded into asymmetric political and economic power structures and so its potentials were limited. If we, however, imagine social media to work like the ideal *dazibao*, then we can envision an Internet and social media that are controlled, owned, and operated by the users and not shaped by capitalist, commercial, advertising, or bureaucratic logic. Chinese working-class struggles and the history of communal economies in China show that there is active hope for life in participatory democracies beyond capitalism. A non-capitalist Internet and non-capitalist social media are not-yets, dreams that are not yet reality because of capitalist domination, but possibilities that can be turned into actualities by struggles for a participatory democratic Internet that supersedes the capitalist Internet.

7.6. Conclusion

Hu Zhengrong and Ji Deqiang (2014) argue that China's economic opening up was accompanied in media and journalism studies by the appropriation of Willbur Schramm-style administrative communication methods and theory that resulted in a "marginalisation of the critical school" (Hu and Ji 2014, 10). They call for a critical examination of this development and see the emergence of foundations of alternative paradigms. Daya Thussu (2014, 33) says that although there are counterflows from developing countries, the "US entertainment and information networks are the movers and shakers" of global media. The question that arises is therefore if with the increasing importance of China and India in the world, they can draw on their alternative traditions to strengthen critical media studies and a "development perspective less affected by the colonial mindset" (Thussu 2014, 40).

Critical media studies envision a media and Internet landscape that is not ruled by capitalist and state power. This chapter has tried to show that Western and the Chinese social media are not so different at all, but that rather both experience forms of capitalist and political control. A comparative political-economic analysis of the profits, the role of advertising, the boards of directors, shareholders, and financial market values of Baidu, Google, Sina Weibo, Twitter, Renren, and Facebook shows important commonalities of informational capitalism in China and the West. An analysis of Chinese and Western social media companies' discourses indicates the existence of an engaging, connecting, and sharing ideology that deflects attention from social media and the Internet's power asymmetries and political-economic control structures that fuse authoritarian politics and neoliberal capitalism both in China and the West.

Although often perceived as monolithic dictatorship in the West, there is a vivid reality of working-class struggles in China. These struggles and the concept of the big-character posters (*dazibao*) that resonates with visions of participatory media such as Brecht's notion of an alternative radio, Benjamin's idea of the reader/writer, Habermas's theory of the public sphere, and Enzenberger's concept of emancipatory media use allow us to envision an Internet and media that are truly and fully social, i.e. forms of participatory democracy that transcend capitalism.

For Mao, the dialectic is "the law of the unity of opposites" (Mao 1937, 311) and forms "the fundamental law of nature and of society and therefore also the fundamental law of thought" (Mao 1937, 345). Opposites would "on the one hand" be "opposed to each other, and on the other hand" be "interconnected, interpenetrating, interpermeating and interdependent" (Mao 1937, 338). "Without the bourgeoisie, there would be no proletariat; without the proletariat, there would be no bourgeoisie. Without imperialist oppression of nations, there would be no colonies or semi-colonies, without colonies or semi-colonies, there would be no imperialist oppression of nations" (Mao 1937, 338). From this understanding of dialectics, Mao derived his understanding of revolution as permanent revolution that is grounded in the concept that dialectical development means the endless destruction of the old that is eliminated and substituted by the new: "One thing destroys another, things emerge, develop, and are destroyed, everywhere is like this. If things are not destroyed by others, then they destroy themselves" (Mao 1964). "The life of dialectics is the continuous movement toward opposites" (Mao 1964). Therefore for Mao, the "struggle of mutually exclusive opposites is absolute" (Mao 1937, 342).

Although Mao argued that one-sidedness "is a violation of dialectics" (Mao 1967, 154), his own dialectic was one-sided in that he did not take into account Hegel's principles of negation of the negation and *Aufhebung* (sublation). Mao (1964) said:

> Engels talked about the three categories, but as for me I don't believe in two of those categories. (The unity of opposites is the most basic law, the transformation of quality and quantity into one another is the unity of the opposites quality and quantity, and the negation of the negation does not exist at all).

Sublation is at the same time uplifting, preservation, and elimination.

> At this point we should remember the double meaning of the German expression "*aufheben*". On the one hand, we understand it to mean "clear

away" or "cancel", and in that sense we say that a law or regulation is cancelled (*aufgehoben*). But the word also means 'to preserve', and we say in this sense that something is well taken care of (*wohl aufgehoben*).

Hegel 1830, §96)

The German "*aufheben*" ("to sublate" in English) has a twofold meaning in the language: it equally means "to keep", "to preserve" and "to cause to cease", "to put to an end". Even "to preserve" already includes a negative note, namely that something, in order to be retained, is removed from its immediacy and hence from an existence which is open to external influences. That which is sublated is thus something at the same time preserved, something that has lost its immediacy but has not come to nothing for that.

Hegel 1812, 82

Dialectical development is also a dialectic of preservation and elimination. The new cannot come out of nothing, but needs germ forms and elements in the old. The old does not fully vanish, but leaves its traces on the new. Mao's dialectic was one-sided because it only saw the role of elimination without its dialectical connection to preservation. A new society should not aim to fully eliminate the old one, but to preserve and transform its best elements. Society cannot go from something to absolutely nothing and then again to something. Sublation rather means that something new emerges so that nothing turns to something new, the old something is transformed, parts of it disappear, old parts and moments disappear, and a new something emerges. Mao read Lenin, but did not understand Hegel.

Slavoj Žižek (2008) argues that Mao's rejection of the dialectical notion of the negation of the negation resulted in a misunderstanding of revolution that insists "on the priority of struggle, of division, over every synthesis or unity" (185). The failure of the Cultural Revolution would therefore have been its destructiveness. Mao would have seen communist China as a restoration of the "old order" and would therefore have called for an "endlessly repeated negation" (194) so that "the final result of Mao's Cultural Revolution is today's unheard-of explosion of capitalist dynamics in China" (197).

For creating an alternative Internet not just in China, but the world, we need to rely on Hegel's concept of the dialectic. An Internet that is not controlled by companies, parties, or state institutions, but the users, cannot be fully transcendent but rather needs to start as part of social struggles in the here and now. It needs to be immanent-transcendent: non-commercial, non-profit online sites can be built now, but within capitalist societies they will always face limits set by corporate and state power. Therefore media charges need to support such alternative sites by struggling for progressive changes that help channel resources towards them so that they can ensure maintenance and visibility. The capitalist Internet is not social, but rather particularistically controlled by capitalist companies and political institutions whose power is interlinked. A particularly important role in this transnational cultural domination (Schiller 1991) of the Internet is played by large corporations such as Google, Baidu, Sina/Weibo, Twitter, Tencent, Facebook, and Renren.

"The idea of a participatory society and politics is indigenous to China, having been greatly fostered in the communist revolution" (Lin 2013, 105). Without

> any historically formed obsession with patents and copyrights, China can also be a relatively easy place to promote open source, open access, ad free information as a public good. The experimental project of Chinese socialism has the potential to encompass the intrinsically interconnected ideas of the commons, community, communism, communication and common culture.
>
> *Lin 2013, 166*

To make the Internet a truly and fully social medium, the world's workers as users and users as workers need to unite and struggle for an alternative global societal framework and working-class social media that upon their full realisation transcend the concept of class and enable a participatory grassroots Internet.

Part II of this book has looked at spatial aspects of social media's cultural political economy. An international division of digital labour (IDDL) organises the production of digital media technologies and content in global space in such a way that various forms of exploitation are interconnected (chapter 6). China plays a particularly important role in global capitalism (chapter 7). The way social media platforms are organised in China resembles the way they work in the West: economic and political power holders predominantly control these sites. China is contradictory and is also the site of large-scale labour struggles that question capitalist domination. It furthermore has a tradition of collective and communal ownership. Chinese working-class struggles can therefore inspire us to think about how to re-organise the economy and how an alternative Internet and alternative social media could look like. Part III of this book is devoted to thinking about alternatives and alternative social media through the lenses of the notions of the public sphere and public service media.

Appendix 7.1: Mapping of Forbes 2000's Industry Categories to Economic Sectors

Construction:
construction materials, construction services

Energy:
electrical equipment, diversified utilities, electric utilities, natural gas utilities, oil and gas operations, oil service and equipment

Finance sector:
diversified insurance, life and health insurance, major banks, property and casualty insurance, regional banks

Information sector:
communications equipment, computer hardware, computer services, computer storage devices, consumer electronics, electronics, Internet and catalogue retail, printing and publishing, semiconductors, software and programming, telecommunications services

Metal sector:
aluminium, diversified metals and mining, iron and steel

Mobility sector:
airline, auto and truck manufacturers, other transportation, railroad

Real estate:
real estate

Notes

Acknowledgement: I thank Na Yuqi for her assistance on this chapter. She made translations of excerpts from Chinese platforms' terms of use, helped me understand Chinese texts, and searched for specific information about the Internet in China.

1 Data source: http://www.alexa.com (accessed on April 8, 2014).
2 http://e-chaupak.net/database/chicon/1954/1954bilingual.htm (accessed on April 8, 2014).
3 http://english.people.com.cn/constitution/constitution.html (accessed on April 8, 2014).
4 http://www.zdnet.com/cn/china-has-618m-internet-users-80-percent-on-mobile-7000025291/ (accessed on April 5, 2014).
5 Data source: http://www.alexa.com, top 500 sites on the WWW (accessed on April 9, 2014).
6 http://ir.baidu.com/phoenix.zhtml?c=188488&p=irol-faq_pf#26140 (accessed on April 5, 2014).
7 http://ir.baidu.com/phoenix.zhtml?c=188488&p=irol-faq_pf#26140 (accessed on April 5, 2014).
8. http://www.statista.com/statistics/216573/worldwide-market-share-of-search-engines/ (accessed on April 5, 2014).
9 http://www.nasdaq.com/symbol/sina (accessed on April 6, 2014).
10 http://chinastockresearch.com/company-profiles/company-summaries/item/196-sina-corporation-sina/196-sina-corporation-sina.html (accessed on April 6, 2014).
11 http://www.bbc.co.uk/news/business-26588397.
12 http://thenextweb.com/asia/2013/02/20/sina-ceo-admits-fall-in-weibo-usage-due-to-wechat-competition-but-says-service-has-critical-mass/.
13 http://www.bbc.co.uk/news/business-26588397.
14 http://techcrunch.com/2011/05/04/chinese-social-network-renren-prices-743m-ipo-at-14-per-share-at-high-end-of-range/ (accessed on April 5, 2014).
15 http://techcrunch.com/2011/05/04/chinese-social-network-renren-prices-743m-ipo-at-14-per-share-at-high-end-of-range/(accessed on April 5, 2014).
16 http://www.theguardian.com/business/2014/feb/20/facebook-whatsapp-shares-stock-fall-acquisition-reaction (accessed on April 7, 2014).

17 http://www.baidu.com/duty/yinsiquan.html (accessed on April 7, 2014). Translation from Chinese: "百度还会向您提供个性化的服务，例如向您展现相关程度更高的搜索结果或者推广结果。"

18 https://www.google.co.uk/intl/en/policies/privacy/, version from March 31, 2014 (accessed on April 7, 2014).

19 http://www.weibo.com/signup/v5/privacy (accessed on April 7, 2014). Translation from Chinese: "此外，您已知悉并同意：在现行法律法规允许的范围内，微博可能会将您非隐私的个人信息用于市场营销，使用方式包括但不限于：在微博平台中向您展示或提供广告和促销资料，向您通告或推荐微博的服务或产品信息，以及其他此类根据您使用微博服务或产品的情况所认为您可能会感兴趣的信息。"

20 https://twitter.com/tos, version from June 25, 2012 (accessed on April 7, 2014).

21 http://renren.com/info/agreement.jsp, Renren Terms of Service (accessed on April 7, 2014). Translation from Chinese: "十四、通告所有发给用户的通告都可通过电子邮件或常规的信件传送。千橡公司会通过邮件服务发报消息给用户，告诉他们服务条款的修改、服务变更、或其它重要事情。同时， 千橡公司保留对人人网用户投放商业性广告的权利".

22 https://www.facebook.com/full_data_use_policy, version from November 15, 2013 (accessed on April 7, 2014).

23 Tencent Holdings Limited is a Chinese company operating online services such as the instant messenger QQ (launched in 1999) and the mobile phone-chat application WeChat (launched in 2011). WeChat is one of the first Chinese social and mobile media applications that is fully available in English and is therefore aimed at commodifying personal data on an international market of users.

24 http://www.wechat.com/en/service_terms.html, version from January 6, 2014 (accessed on April 7, 2014).

25 http://www.whatsapp.com/legal/, version from July 7, 2012 (accessed on April 7, 2014).

26 http://blog.whatsapp.com/index.php/2012/06/why-we-dont-sell-ads/ (accessed on April 9, 2014).

27 http://www.theguardian.com/technology/2014/feb/19/facebook-buys-whatsapp-16bn-deal (accessed on April 9, 2014).

28 http://www.youtube.com/watch?v=tlliivJKHk8 (accessed on April 9, 2014).

29 http://www.youtube.com/watch?v=yqnsYayo3fA (accessed on April 9, 2014).

30 http://www.bloomberg.com/video/86956830-renren-s-chen-on-growth-strategy-industry.html#ooid=Y1MG1rMzq3JTm2Bbe8-Vl88pjGfWPLbH (accessed on April 9, 2014).

31 http://videos.huffingtonpost.com/pony-ma-backstage-interview-at-disrupt-beijing-517389952 (accessed on April 9, 2014).

32 http://ir.baidu.com/phoenix.zhtml?c=188488&p=irol-homeprofile (accessed on April 9, 2014).

33 http://corp.sina.com.cn/eng/sina_intr_eng.htm (accessed on April 9, 2014).

34 http://ir.renren-inc.com/phoenix.zhtml?c=244796&p=irol-irhome (accessed on April 9, 2014).

35 http://www.tencent.com/en-us/at/abouttencent.shtml (accessed on April 9, 2014).

36 http://www.wechat.com/en/ (accessed on April 9, 2014).

37 http://www.youtube.com/watch?v=tlliivJKHk8 (accessed on April 9, 2014).

38 https://www.facebook.com/FacebookUK/info (accessed on April 10, 2014).

39 https://www.google.de/intl/en/about/company/philosophy/ (accessed on April 10, 2014).

40 http://www.youtube.com/yt/about/en-GB/ (accessed on April 10, 2014).

41 https://about.twitter.com/company (accessed on April 10, 2014).

42 http://instagram.com (accessed on April 10, 2014).

43 http://uk.about.pinterest.com/ (accessed on April 10, 2014).

44 http://www.linkedin.com/about-us (accessed on April 10, 2014).

45 https://www.tumblr.com/ (accessed on April 10, 2014).

46 http://vk.com/terms (accessed on April 10, 2014).

47 "NSA Prism Program Taps in to User Data of Apple, Google and Others". *The Guardian Online.* June 7, 2013. http://www.theguardian.com/world/2013/jun/06/us-tech-giants-nsa-data.

48 http://www.youtube.com/watch?v=pFV5-B65QJ8 (accessed on April 11, 2014).

49 http://videos.huffingtonpost.com/fireside-chat-with-pony-ma-with-sarah-lacy-517390007 (accessed on April 11, 2014).

50 "China's Commitment to Rule of Law". *People's Daily Online.* September 23, 2013. http://english.people.com.cn/90785/8407076.html (accessed on April 11, 2014).

51 "The Bo Xila Trial: End of the Road?" *The Economist.* September 28, 2013. http://www.economist.com/news/china/21586884-tough-sentence-popular-leader-end-road (accessed on April 11, 2014).

52 Some of these platforms have at times been censored: http://www.danwei.com/interview-before-a-gagging-order-fan-jinggang-of-utopia/ (accessed on April 10, 2014). "China Shuts Down Maoist Website Utopia". *The Guardian.* April 6, 2012. http://www.theguardian.com/world/2012/apr/06/china-maoist-website-utopia.

53 http://www.e-chaupak.net/database/chicon/1975/1975e.htm (accessed on April 11, 2014).

PART IV
Alternatives

8

SOCIAL MEDIA AND THE PUBLIC SPHERE

8.1. Introduction

Contributions to discussions of Internet, social media, and the public sphere often tend to stress new technologies' transformative power. Some examples:

- Yochai Benkler argues that there has been the emergence of a networked public sphere: "The easy possibility of communicating effectively into the public sphere allows individuals to reorient themselves from passive readers and listeners to potential speakers and participants in a conversation" (Benkler 2006, 213). "The network allows all citizens to change their relationship to the public sphere. They no longer need be consumers and passive spectators. They can become creators and primary subjects. It is in this sense that the Internet democratizes" (Benkler 2006, 272).
- Zizi Papacharissi describes the emergence of a "virtual sphere 2.0", in which citizen-consumers participate and express "dissent with a public agenda [. . .] by expressing political opinion on blogs, viewing or posting content on YouTube, or posting a comment in an online discussion group" (Papacharissi 2009, 244).
- Manuel Castells stresses the novelty of this sphere: "The construction of the new public sphere in the network society proceeds by building protocols of communication between different communication processes" (Castells 2009, 125).
- Jean Burgess and Joshua Green (2009, 77) argue that YouTube is a "cultural public sphere" because "it is an enabler of encounters with cultural differences and the development of political 'listening' across belief systems and identities".

Such contributions differ in how much they stress networking, dissent, novelty, and culture, but have in common that they are philosophically idealistic interpretations or revisions of Habermas's concept of the public sphere. They focus on political and cultural communication and ignore the public sphere's materiality and political economy that Habermas stressed. Consequently, they do not ask questions about ownership and do not see, as Nicholas Garnham stresses, that besides the focus on political communication a "virtue of Habermas's approach is to focus on the necessary material resource base for any public sphere" (Garnham 1992, 361). Habermas points out that the public sphere is a question of its members' command of resources (property, intellectual skills). "But even under ideally favorable conditions of communication, one could have expected from economically dependent masses a contribution to the spontaneous formation of opinion and will only to the extent to which they had attained the equivalent of the social independence of private property owners" (Habermas 1992, 434). The approaches discussed above do not ask the questions: Who owns Internet platforms? Who owns social media?

The contribution presented in this chapter challenges public sphere idealism. It argues for a materialist understanding and return to Habermas's original concept that encompasses the perspective of critical political economy as a foundation for the analysis of so-called "social media". Social media has since the mid-2000s become a buzzword and marketing ideology aimed at attracting users and investors to platforms such as Facebook, Twitter, YouTube, Wikipedia, LinkedIn, VKontakte, Blogspot, Weibo, Wordpress, Tumblr, Pinterest, or Instagram. Many people understand social networking sites, blogs, wikis, user-generated content sharing sites, and microblogs as social media. The term *social media*, however, brings up the question whether not all media are in one respect or another social. This depends on how one defines the social. As a consequence, one needs social theory in order to understand what is social about social media (Fuchs 2014b).

Sociality can mean that a) human thought is shaped by society, b) humans exchange symbols by communicating in social relations, c) humans work together and thereby create use-values, and d) humans form and maintain communities. These definitions of sociality correspond to the social theory concepts of social facts, social relations, co-operation, and community (Hofkirchner 2013; Fuchs 2014b, chapter 2). Described as information processes, sociality can be expressed as a threefold interconnected process of cognition (a), communication (b) and co-operation (c, d) (Fuchs 2014b, chapter 2). Media and online platforms reflect these forms of sociality to different degrees:

- Cognition: Reading books, watching the news or a film on TV, and listening to the radio involve just like Internet use the engagement with texts that reflect social contexts in society.
- Communication: Online communication is not new. Ray Tomlinson sent the first Internet email from one computer to the other in 1971.[1]

- Co-operation: Online communities are not new: already in the 1980s there were bulletin board systems such as the WELL. Computer-supported co-operative work (CSCW) became an academic field of studies in the 1980s, reflecting the role of the computer in collaborative work. The 1st ACM Conference on CSCW took place in December 1986 in Austin, Texas. The concept of the wiki is also not new: Ward Cunningham introduced the first wiki technology (the WikiWikiWeb) in 1995.

Online sociality is not new. A specific aspect of Facebook and related platforms is that they integrate tools that support various forms of sociality into one platform. They are tools of cognition, communication, and co-operation. How has the landscape of the World Wide Web (WWW) changed in the past 10 years? Table 8.1 presents an analysis of the most used websites in the world in 2002 and 2013.

In 2002, there were 20 information functions, 13 communication functions, and 1 cooperation function available on the top 20 websites. In 2013, there were 20 information functions, 15 communication functions, and 5 cooperation

TABLE 8.1 Information functions of the top 20 websites in the world, data source: alexa.com

December 9, 2002 (three-month page ranking based on page views and page reach)			December 11, 2013 (one-month page ranking based on average daily visitors and page views)		
Rank	Website	Primary information functions	Rank	Website	Primary information functions
1	yahoo.com	cogn, comm	1	google.com	cogn, comm, coop
2	msn.com	cogn, comm	2	facebook.com	cogn, comm, coop
3	daum.net	cogn, comm	3	youtube.com	cogn, comm
4	naver.com	cogn, comm	4	yahoo.com	cogn, comm
5	google.com[2]	cogn	5	baidu.com	cogn, comm
6	yahoo.co.jp	cogn, comm	6	wikipedia.org	cogn, comm, coop
7	passport.net	cogn	7	qq.com	cogn, comm
8	ebay.com	cogn	8	amazon.com	cogn
9	microsoft.com	cogn	9	live.com	cogn, comm
10	bugsmusic.co.kr	cogn	10	taobao.com	cogn
11	sayclub.com	cogn, comm	11	twitter.com	cogn, comm
12	sina.com.cn	cogn, comm	12	linkedin.com	cogn, comm, coop
13	netmarble.net	cogn, comm, coop	13	blogspot.com	cogn, comm
14	amazon.com	cogn	14	google.co.in	cogn, comm, coop
15	nate.com	cogn, comm	15	sina.com.cn	cogn, comm
16	go.com	cogn	16	hao123.com	cogn
17	sohu.com	cogn, comm	17	163.com	cogn, comm
18	163.com	cogn, comm	18	wordpress.com	cogn, comm
19	hotmail.com	cogn, comm	19	ebay.com	cogn
20	aol.com	cogn, comm	20	yahoo.co.jp	cogn, comm
		cogn: 20			cogn: 20
		comm: 13			comm: 15
		coop: 1			coop: 5

functions on the top 20 websites. The quantitative increase of collaborative features from 1 to 5 has to do with the rise of Facebook, Google+, Wikipedia, and LinkedIn: collaborative information production with the help of wikis and collaborative software (Wikipedia, Google Docs) and social networking sites oriented on community building (Facebook, Google+, LinkedIn). There are continuities and discontinuities in the development of the WWW in the period 2002–2013. The changes concern the rising importance of co-operative sociality. This transformation is significant, but not radical. One novelty is the rise of social networking sites (Facebook, LinkedIn, Google+, MySpace, etc.). Another change is the emergence of blogs (Wordpress, Blogger/Blogspot, Huffington Post), micro-blogs (Twitter), and file sharing and user-generated content web sites (YouTube), which have increased the possibilities of communication and information sharing in the top 20 US websites. Google has broadened its functions: It started as a pure search engine (in 1999), then introduced communication features in 2004 (Gmail) and its own social networking site platform (Google+) in June 2011.

This chapter contextualises social media in society with the help of the concept of the public sphere. The public sphere is just one way of achieving this aim; there are other social theory concepts (such as power, ideology, capitalism, democracy, participation, labour, control, surveillance) that need to be used together with the notion of the public sphere in a theory of the Internet and society (Fuchs 2008, 2014b). Section 2 discusses the concept of the public sphere, section 3 the role of the media in the public sphere, and section 4 social media and the public sphere. Section 5 draws some conclusions about how to advance from social media as a sphere colonised by capital and the state towards social media as public service, commons-based media, and a truly public sphere.

8.2. The Concept of the Public Sphere

Habermas (1989b, 1) stresses that if something is public it is "open to all". The task of a public sphere is that society can become engaged in "critical public debate" (Habermas 1989b, 52). The public sphere would therefore require media for information and communication and access by all citizens. The logic of the public sphere is independent of economic and political power (Habermas 1989b, 36): "Laws of the market [. . .] [are] suspended as were laws of the state." Habermas thereby stresses that the public sphere is not just a sphere of public political communication, but also a sphere free from state censorship and from private ownership. It is free from particularistic controls.

Both Jürgen Habermas (1989b) and Hannah Arendt (1958) stress that in pre-modern society the private realm was simultaneously the realm of the family and the economy. Modern society would have seen the rise of the capitalist economy and the modern state as relatively autonomous interconnected spheres. The economy became disembedded from the family and a separate sphere of modern society based on commodity production and wage labour emerged. The realm of the economy is mediated with the household as the realm of reproductive labour.

> The emergence of society—the rise of housekeeping, its activities, prob-
> lems, and organizational devices—from the shadowy interior of the house-
> hold into the light of the public sphere, has not only blurred the old
> borderline between private and political, it has also changed almost beyond
> recognition the meaning of the two terms and their significance for the life
> of the individual and the citizen.
>
> *Arendt 1958, 38*

The notion of the private became split into the sphere of private ownership in the economy and intimacy in the family. The economy started to no longer be part of private households, but became organised with the help of large commodity markets that go beyond single households. The modern economy became "a private sphere of society that [. . .] [is] publicly relevant" (Habermas 1989a, 19). It became a political economy. The British economist James Steuart formulated this change in 1767 in his book *An Inquiry into the Principles of Political Economy*— which was the first English book having the term "political economy" in its title—the following way: "What oeconomy is in a family, political oeconomy is in a state" (Steuart 1767). Political economy also became a field of study that analyses the production, distribution, and consumption of goods and considered the moral question of how the state and the economy shall best be related (Caporaso and Levine 1992).

The question that arises is how the public sphere that is sometimes also related to the concept of civil society is related to other realms of modern societies. Habermas (1987, 1989b, 2006) has stressed in many of his works that the public sphere is a kind of interface and intermediate sphere mediating between the economy, the state, and the realm of the family and intimacy. The "public sphere is a warning system with sensors that, though unspecialized, are sensitive throughout society" (Habermas 1996, 359). Modern society can be conceived as consisting of distinct and connected spheres: the economy is the sphere of the production of use-values, politics the sphere where collective decisions are taken, and culture the sphere where social meanings and moral values are created (Fuchs 2008). In modern society, these spheres are based on the accumulation of money, power and status (Fuchs 2008). In Habermas's (1984, 1987) theory, this distinction is reflected in his differentiation between the systems of the economy and politics and of the lifeworld. He assumes, however, that the cultural lifeworld is not shaped by power asymmetries, whereas in capitalist realities contemporary culture tends to be, as Pierre Bourdieu (1986a) stresses, a struggle over recognition and status. The public sphere/civil society connects culture, the economy, and politics and thereby creates sections of overlap between itself and these realms: the socio-political sphere, the socio-economic sphere, and the socio-cultural sphere.

Figure 8.1 visualises a model of modern society. The model is grounded in the social theory insight that the relationship between structures and actors is dialectical and that both levels continuously create each other (for dialectical solutions of the structure–agency problem in social theory, see: Archer 1995; Bhaskar 2008; Bourdieu 1986a; Fuchs 2003a, 2003b; Giddens 1984).

Habermas (1987, 320) mentions the following social roles that are constitutive for modern society: employee, consumer, client, citizen. Other roles, as e.g. wife, husband, houseworker, immigrant, convicts, etc. can certainly be added. So

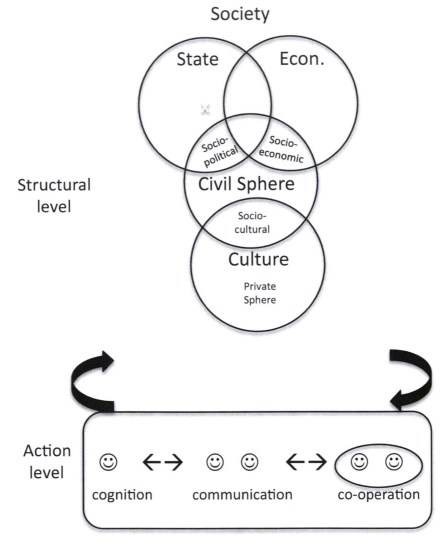

FIGURE 8.1 A model of modern society

what is constitutive for modern society is not just the separation of spheres and roles, but also the creation of power structures, in which roles are constituted by and connected to power relations (as e.g. employer-employee, state bureaucracy-citizen, citizen of a nation state-immigrant, manager-assistant, dominant gender roles, marginalised gender roles). Power means in this context the disposition of actors over means that allow them to control structures and influence processes and decisions in their own interest. In the modern economy, humans act as capital owners or workers. In the modern political system, they act as politicians or citizens. In the modern cultural system, they have the roles of friends, lovers, family members, and consumers. Modern society is not just based on a differentiation of social realms, but also a differentiation of social roles humans take on in these realms. In the public realm, humans do not act in isolation, but in common. For Hannah Arendt, the public sphere is therefore "the common world" that "gathers us together and yet prevents our falling over each other" (Arendt 1958, 52). In the public sphere, humans organise around specific interests as social groups. As groups they take on socio-economic, socio-political, and socio-cultural roles. Table 8.2 shows an overview of these roles in modern society. As modern society is based on structures of accumulation and a separation of roles within different realms, there are conflicts of interest over the control of property, collective decisions, and meanings that can result in social struggles. Economic, political, and cultural roles in modern society are organised in the form of classes, parties, and political groups, and communities of interest that compete over the control of property/surplus, collective decisions, and social meanings.

TABLE 8.2 Social roles in modern society

Political roles	Socio-political roles
citizen, politician, bureaucrat, political party member	privacy advocates, electoral reform advocate, feminist activist, gay-rights activists, anti-racist advocate, youth movement advocate, peace movement activist, anti-penitentiary advocate, anti-psychiatry activist, non-governmental organisation member/activist, non-parliamentary political activist (student groups, non-parliamentary fascist groups, non-parliamentary leftist groups, etc.)
Economic roles	**Socio-economic roles**
capital owner, entrepreneur, manager, employee, prosumer, self-employee	labour activist, union member, consumer protectionists, environmental activist
Private roles	**Socio-cultural roles**
lover, family member, friend, consumer, audience member, user	sports group member, fan community member, parishioner, member of a sect or cult, professional organisations and associations, self-help groups, neighbourhood association, etc.

Peter Lunt and Sonia Livingstone (2013) reflect on articles covering the topic of the public sphere that were published in the years 1979–2012 in the journal *Media, Culture & Society*. They say that Habermas faced many criticisms, including "his ideal of civic republicanism based on a form of direct democracy that could not accommodate the complexity and scale of modern society" and "his apparent blindness to the many varieties of exclusion (based on gender, class, ethnicity, etc.)" (Lunt and Livingstone 2013, 90). He would have revised his approach, recognising "a plurality of public spheres" and "the contested nature of public life" (Lunt and Livingstone 2013, 92) as well as the "importance of inclusivity, diversity, identity, the end of consensus government, distributed governance, and the complexity of social systems" (95).

Lunt and Livingstone point out doubts that can be summarised as three main criticisms of Habermas's notion of the public sphere:

- The working-class critique
- The postmodern critique
- The cultural imperialism critique

The *working class critique* stresses that Habermas focuses on the bourgeois movement and neglects popular movements that existed in the seventeenth, eighteenth, and nineteenth centuries, such as the working-class movement. Oskar Negt's and Alexander Kluge's (1993) notion of a proletarian (counter-) public sphere can be read as both a socialist critique and a radicalisation of Habermas's approach (see: Calhoun 1992, 5; Jameson 1988).

Such criticism should, however, see that Habermas acknowledged in the preface of *Structural Transformation* the existence of a "plebeian public sphere" like in the Chartist movement or the anarchist working class (Habermas 1989b, xviii) and that he pointed out that the "economically dependent masses" would only be able to contribute "to the spontaneous formation [. . .] of opinion [. . .] to the extent to which they had attained the equivalent of the social independence of private property owners" (Habermas 1992, 434).

Edward P. Thompson (1963) describes how Jacobin societies such as the London Corresponding Society fought for working-class representation in parliament, meeting in taverns such as the London Tavern, public houses, and public places. The London Corresponding Society (LCS) formed in 1792. Women were not allowed to attend the London debating societies in the first 30 years, which changed in the 1770s (Thale 1995). There was a 6 pence entry fee to the LCS meetings, so not everyone could attend. So it clearly was a public sphere with limits. There were around 650 participants at each weekly debate (Thale 1989). There were not just indoor, but also outdoor meetings. The LCS propagated Mary Wollstonecraft's feminist writings.

The working-class critique often also argues that Habermas idealises the bourgeois public sphere, which is, however, a misunderstanding. Habermas does not idealise the bourgeois public sphere, but rather applies an elegant dialectical logic to show that the bourgeois ideals and values find their own limits in the existence of stratified power relations and class. Habermas showed based on Marx (critique of the political economy: class character of the public sphere) and Horkheimer (ideology critique: manipulated public sphere) how the very concepts of the public sphere are stylised principles that in reality within capitalist society are not realised due to the exclusory character of the public sphere and the manipulation of the public sphere by particularistic class interests. Habermas's theory of the public sphere is an ideology-critical study in the tradition of Adorno's (2003) method of immanent critique that confronts the ideals of the public sphere with its capitalist reality and thereby uncovers its ideological character. The implication is that a true public sphere can only exist in a participatory society.

Liberal ideology postulates individual freedoms (of speech, opinion, association, assembly) as universal rights, but the particularistic and stratified character of unequal societies undermines these universal rights and creates inequality and therefore unequal access to the public sphere. There are specifically two immanent limits of the bourgeois public sphere that Habermas discusses:

- The limitation of freedom of speech and public opinion: if individuals do not have the same formal education and material resources available, then this can pose limits for participation in the public sphere (Habermas 1989b, 227).
- The limitation of freedom of association and assembly: big political and economic organisations "enjoy an oligopoly of the publicistically effective and politically relevant formation of assemblies and associations" (Habermas 1989b, 228).

Habermasian public sphere analysis with the help of the epistemological method of immanent critique compares an actual public sphere (its political economy and political communication) to the ideal and values of the public sphere that bourgeois society promises (freedom of speech, freedom of public opinion, freedom of association, freedom of assembly). The public sphere is a concept of immanent critique for criticising the shortcomings of societies. Habermas does not necessarily say that it exists everywhere, but that it should exist. Immanent critique compares proclaimed ideals to reality. If it finds out that reality permanently contradicts its own ideals, then it becomes clear that there is a fundamental mismatch and that reality needs to be changed in order to overcome this incongruity.

The bourgeois public sphere creates its own limits and thereby its own immanent critique. In capitalism,

> the social preconditions for the equality of opportunity were obviously lacking, namely: that any person with skill and "luck" could attain the status of property owner and thus the qualifications of a private person

granted access to the public sphere, property and education. The public
sphere [. . .] contradicted its own principle of universal accessibility.

Habermas 1989b, 124

Similarly, the equation of "property owners" with "human beings" was
untenable; for their interest in maintaining the sphere of commodity
exchange and of social labor as a private sphere was demoted by virtue
of being opposed to the class of wage earners, to the status of a particular
interest that could only prevail by the exercise of power over others.

Habermas 1989b, 124–125

"Under the conditions of a class society, bourgeois democracy thus from its very
inception contradicted essential premises of its self-understanding" (Habermas
1989b, 428). Thomas McCarthy interprets Habermas's approach as arguing that
the "Enlightenment's promise of a life informed by reason cannot be redeemed
so long as the rationality that finds expression in society is deformed by capitalist
modernization" (Habermas 1984, xxxvii).

That the public sphere is for Habermas (1989b) a critical concept is also
expressed by the related concept of the feudalisation of the public sphere. In
the *Theory of Communicative Action*, Habermas (1984, 1987) reformulated the
notion of the feudalisation of the public sphere as the colonisation of the lifeworld: "The thesis of internal colonization states that the subsystems of the
economy and state become more and more complex as a consequence of capitalist growth, and penetrate ever deeper into the symbolic reproduction of the
lifeworld" (Habermas 1987, 367). The "colonization of the lifeworld by system
imperatives [. . .] drive[s] moral-practical elements out of private and political
public spheres of life" (Habermas 1987, 325). The "imperatives of autonomous
subsystems make their way into the lifeworld from the outside—like colonial
masters coming into a tribal society—and force a process of assimilation upon
it" (Habermas 1987, 355).

The colonisation of the lifeworld (Habermas 1984, 1987) results in the centralisation of economic power (companies, market concentration, monopolies)
and political power (state, bureaucracy). *Bureaucratisation* is a transformation
through which "the state was infused into [civil] society (bureaucracy) and, in
the opposite direction, through which [civil] society was infused into the state
(special-interest associations and political parties)". *Monetarisation* and commodification transmogrify the public sphere into "a sphere of culture consumption" that
is only a "pseudo-public sphere" (Habermas 1989b, 162) and a "manufactured
public sphere" (Habermas 1989b, 217).

But the two concepts of feudalisation and colonisation are not just negative
forms of critique, but imply the possibility of a reversal—processes of decolonisation, lifeworldisation, commonification so that communicative action substitutes

the systemic logic of money and power and participatory democracy and spaces of co-operation emerge. Thomas McCarthy in the preface to the *Theory of Communicative Action* defines decolonisation as the "expansion of the areas in which action is coordinated by way of communicatively achieved agreement". It sets "limits to the inner dynamic of media-steered subsystems and to subordinate them to decisions arrived at in unconstrained communication" (Habermas 1984, xxxvii).

Are ideology or hegemony better and more critical terms than the public sphere? They are certainly both critical terms needed in a toolbox of a critical theory of society, but only focus on the manipulation of information and consensus to domination and tend to remain idealistic, whereas the public sphere is an economic and political concept that focuses on the inclusiveness of ownership and decision making. It allows stressing not only aspects of public discussion, but also the public or private ownership of crucial goods and services such as communications.

The postmodern critique points out that the public sphere has been a sphere of educated, rich men, juxtaposed to the private sphere that has been seen as the domain of women. Women, gays and lesbians, and ethnic minorities would have been excluded from the public sphere. It would therefore today be more promising that struggles against oppression take place in multiple subaltern counter-publics than in one unified sphere. The criticism also stresses that an egalitarian society should be based on a plurality of public arenas in order to be democratic and multicultural (Benhabib 1992; Fraser 1992; Eley 1992; Mouffe 1999; Roberts and Crossley 2004). Habermas agrees that his early account in *The Structural Transformation of the Public Sphere* (Habermas 1989b), originally published in German in 1962, has neglected proletarian, feminist, and other public spheres (Habermas 1992, 425–430).

The danger of the politics of pluralistic publics without unity is, however, that they tend to social struggle focus on mere reformist identity politics without challenging the whole that negatively affects the lives of all subordinated groups. They overlook that in an egalitarian society common communication media are needed for guaranteeing cohesion and solidarity and a strong democracy. Postmodernists and post-Marxists are so much occupied with stressing difference that they do not realise that difference can become repressive if it turns into a plurality without unity. One needs unity in diversity in order to struggle for participatory democracy and for maintaining this condition once it is reached. It is preferable and more effective to have a few widely accessible and widely consumed broad critical media than many small-scale special interest media that support the fragmentation of struggles. Nicholas Garnham argues in this context for the need of a single public sphere and says that the postmodernists risk "cultural relativism" if they do not see that democracy is in need of "some common normative dimensions" and "more generalized media" (Garnham 1992, 369).

The *cultural imperialism critique* stresses that the public sphere is a Western Enlightenment concept that Western societies use for trying to impose their political, economic, and social systems on other countries. Jim McGuigan formulates in this context a criticism of Nicholas Garnham's interpretation of Habermas: "We have to entertain the possibility that the global public sphere is a Western fantasy and perhaps a last gasp of its otherwise shaky bid for or to sustain global hegemony" (McGuigan 1998, 96).

Concerning the question if there is a global public sphere, Colin Sparks (1998) stresses that broadcasting is mainly national. "Global" stations such as CNN and BBC World reach limited audiences that are mainly located in the West. They also predominantly have Western-made and Western-focused contents. He therefore suggests to abandon the term "global public sphere" and to better use the term "imperialist, private sphere" (Sparks 1998, 122). The public sphere is not only about information and communication, but also about ownership. Therefore the existence of transnational forms of media and communication does not imply the existence of a global public sphere.

Public spaces and public spheres are not specific to the West. The public teahouse is an old cultural practice and space in many parts of the world, such as in China, Japan, Iran, Turkey, and the United Kingdom. Di Wang (2008) compares the early twentieth-century Chinese teahouse to the British public houses. It is a common space, where people from all walks of life go for different purposes. The Chinese word for teahouse is 茶倌 (cháguǎn). Chengdu (成都) is the capital of the southwestern Chinese province Sichuan (四川). It has about 7.7 million inhabitants in its urban core. "Teahouses in Chengdu, however, were renowned for their multiclass orientation. One of the 'virtues' of Chengdu teahouses was their relatively equality" (Wang 2008, 421). Women were first excluded, but by 1930 fully accepted. These teahouses were not just cultural spaces, but also political meeting points where political debates took place and political theatre pieces were performed, which attracted not only citizens, but also government spies. Wang (2008) discusses the role of the Chengdu teahouses during the 1911 Railroad Protection Movement. Public meeting places are spheres of civil engagement that can turn into political spaces of communication and protest.

The public sphere is both process and space: "In periods of mobilization, the structures that actually support the authority of a critically engaged public begin to vibrate. The balance of power between civil society and the political system then shifts" (Habermas 1996, 379). Juha Kovisto and Esa Valiverronen (1996) see the public sphere not as domain, but as process of counter-hegemonic struggles. A public sphere emerges where people struggle for a better society, and their struggle is a process of constituting the public that creates spatial domains of resistance in the public. The public sphere is simultaneously process and space. Social organisation turns into a public sphere when people act politically in common for a joint goal that fosters participatory democracy instead of economic and state power and when they use grassroots organisations and/or the occupation or creation of public space as political strategy. Neo-Nazis do not form a public sphere because their organisation structures and goals are authoritarian and opposed to participatory democracy.

The various Occupy movements are movements where protest and spaces of occupation converge. They created public spheres of political communication that they controlled in self-managed manner: Tahrir Square in Cairo, Egypt; Syntagma Square in Athens, Greece; Puerta del Sol in Madrid, Spain; Plaça Catalunya in Barcelona, Spain; Zuccotti Park in New York City; St. Paul's Cathedral's and Finsbury Square in London, etc. This creation of public spheres took place not just in the West, but in many parts of the world in times of global capitalist and societal crisis. In 2011, there were revolutions in Tunisia, Egypt, and Yemen as well as major protests in countries such as Albania, Algeria, Armenia, Australia, Azerbaijan, Bahrain, Belarus, Belgium, Bolivia, Burkina Faso, Canada, Chile, China, Colombia, Czech Republic, Cyprus, Denmark, Djibouti, Finland, France, Georgia, Germany, Greece, Hong Kong, Hungary, India, Iran, Iraq, Ireland, Israel, Italy, Jordan, Kuwait, Lebanon, Libya, Macedonia, Malawi, Malaysia, Maldives, Mauritania, Mexico, Mongolia, Morocco, Netherlands, New Zealand, Nigeria, Norway, Oman, Palestine, Portugal, Russia, Saudi Arabia, Slovenia, Somalia, South Africa, South Korea, Spain, Switzerland, Sri Lanka, Sudan, Syria, Turkey, the United Kingdom, the United States, Vietnam, and Western Sahara. Common aspects of these protests were that many of them used the tactic of making space public and political and that these protests took place in a common crisis of society. Resistance is as old as class societies, so public spheres have been formed as resisting publics throughout the history of class societies.

8.3. The Media and the Public Sphere

For Habermas (1984, 1987), a medium is an entity that enables social relations. He distinguishes between the steering media of money and power on the one hand and unmediated communicative action on the other hand. Niklas Luhmann (1995) in contrast to Habermas argues that all social systems are communication systems and organise their communication around specific media and binary codes such as money and the binary code paid/unpaid in the economy, or power and the binary code holding an office/not holding an office in politics. Communication is a social relation in which humans interact mutually with the help of symbols and thereby create meaning of each other and the world. It is a constitutive feature of society and all social systems. Communication requires and is not possible without media: storage media (information technologies) such as paper, tapes, film reels, computer hard disks, DVDs, web space; transport media (communication technologies) such as the telephone, television, radio, email; and collaborative media (technologies of co-operation) such as wikis and online communities.

Whereas property (such as money and other commodities) and power can certainly be seen as media of social relations, a specific feature of the media and communication system is that it communicates content created or co-created by human beings that is stored, interpreted, and re-interpreted in order to make meaning of the world. In modern society, the cultural system is not isolated, but culture is mediated by money in the culture industry and power in political communication. The cultural system has its own economy and politics.

Figure 8.1 points out that civil society and the public sphere are interfaces that connect culture, the economy, and politics through the socio-cultural, the socio-political, and the socio-economic sphere. All information media circulate ideas in public to a broad range of people. They are systems for publishing, i.e. the making public of information. Media address people with information as private individuals in their cultural role; as members of communities of interests in the socio-cultural sphere; as citizens or politicians in the political realm; as activists in the socio-political sphere; as owners, managers, or employees in the economic system; and as members of economic interest groups in the socio-economic realm. Confronted with content provided by the media, humans create, re-create, and differentiate meanings of the world in various social roles. Figure 8.2 shows the interactions of the media systems with other parts of modern society. Media create public information (news, entertainment, user-generated content, etc.) that confronts humans in various social roles, in which they make meaning of the world based on this information. In order to create cultural content, workers in the media system rely to a specific extent on humans in various social roles as information sources. These information sources tend to be asymmetrically distributed with politicians, governments, parties, celebrities, experts, companies, and managers playing a significantly more important role than everyday citizens. The media system also requires inputs from the economic system (financing in

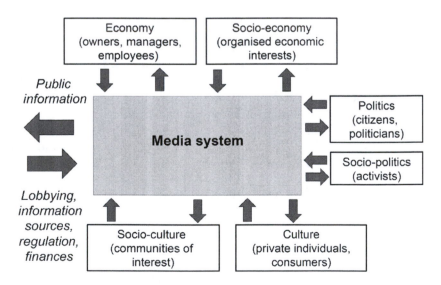

FIGURE 8.2 The media system in modern society

TABLE 8.3 Three political economies of the media (Murdock 2011, 18)

Organisation form	Capital	State	Civil Society
Structures	Commodities	Public Goods	Gifts
Structures	Prices	Taxes	Reciprocities
Agency	Personal Possession	Shared Use	Co-Creation
Agents	Consumers	Citizens	Communards
Moral values	Liberty	Equality	Mutuality

the form of loans, money paid for content or audiences, subsidies, donations) and the political system (laws, regulation).

Graham Murdock (2011) distinguishes between three political economies of the media in modern societies. Media can take on the form of commodities organised by capital, public goods organised by the state, and gifts organised by civil society (see Table 8.3).

Information media are specifically cultural in that they enable the creation, co-creation, diffusion, and interpretation of symbols, by which humans make meaning of the world. Raymond Williams has argued against cultural idealism and for cultural materialism: He opposes "the separation of 'culture' from material social life" (Williams 1977, 19). We "have to emphasise cultural practice as from the beginning social and material" (Williams 1989, 206). The production of culture is an economic activity of production that creates ideas and meanings as use-values. So culture is on the one hand always an economic process of production. On the other hand, culture is not the same as the economy. It is more than the sum of various acts of work; it has emergent qualities—it communicates meanings in society—that cannot be found in the economy alone. The economy is preserved in culture: culture is not independent from work, production, and physicality, but requires and incorporates all of them. Based on Williams we can therefore say that information media have a) their specific culture that stores and communicates information in public and helps produce meaning, and b) a specific mode of economic organisation of culture, a political economy of culture, that enables the ownership, control, production, diffusion, and consumption of information. The media have an economic and a cultural-political dimension; they are owned in specific ways and are channels for culture, political information, and debate: "A newspaper or a TV channel is at one and the same time a commercial operation and a political institution" (Garnham 1990, 110). Table 8.4 distinguishes two levels of the organisation of information media and introduces based on Graham Murdock's typology a distinction between capitalist media, public media, and civil society media.

The media system has a public role for making information public. Public culture is, however, mediated by political economy and ownership structures (see Table 8.4):

TABLE 8.4 Two levels of the three political economies of the media

	Capitalist media	Public service media	Civil society media
Economy (ownership)	Corporations	State institutions	Citizen control
Culture (public circulation of ideas)	Content that addresses humans in various social roles and results in meaning making	Content that addresses humans in various social roles and results in meaning making	Content that addresses humans in various social roles and results in meaning making

- *Capitalist media* are companies that single individuals, families, or shareholders own privately. They are culturally located in the public sphere, but at the same time they are part of the capitalist economy and therefore produce not only public information, but capital and monetary profit by selling audiences/users and/or content.
- *Public media* are funded by or with the help of the state and/or are created and maintained by a specific statute. They are seen as a public service that plays the role of providing political, educational, and entertainment information to citizens. They are as organisations located in or close to the state system.
- *Civil society media* are full parts of the public sphere. They are economically related to the state if they receive subsidies and often stand in an antagonistic relation to the capitalist economy and governments because as alternative media they tend to reject for-profit and commercial logic and to express alternative points of view that challenge governments and corporations. Citizens run, own, and control civil society media as common projects. They express alternative points of view on the level of culture and have alternative organisation models at the level of political economy (Sandoval and Fuchs 2010; Fuchs 2011a).

Media make information public on their cultural level, but only some of them are publicly controlled on the economic level by institutions that are funded with the help of the state or state legislation or civil society, whereas capitalist media are profit-making corporations based on private ownership.

Habermas (1989b) describes and criticises the commercialisation of the press since the middle of the nineteenth century, that the idea of profit generation was introduced to the media and advertising became common. The public sphere of the media would thereby have become undemocratic and a privatised realm controlled by powerful actors instead of citizens:

> The communicative network of a public made up of rationally debating private citizens has collapsed, the public opinion once emergent from

it has partly decomposed into the informal opinions of private citizens without a public and partly become concentrated into formal opinions of publicistically effective institutions. Caught in the vortex of *publicity that is staged for show or manipulation* the public of nonorganized private people is laid claim to not by public communication but by the communication of publicly manifested opinions.

Habermas 1989b, 248

In a media world dominated by capitalism, the "world fashioned by the mass media is a public sphere in appearance only" (Habermas 1989b, 171). Habermas critically observes that in capitalist media, publicity is not generated from below, but from above (Habermas 1989b, 177).

James Curran (1991) argues that before the 1850s there was a rich history of radical newspapers in the United Kingdom and that it was easy and cheap to create such media. Examples of the radical nineteenth-century UK press are: *Liberator, London Dispatch, Northern Star* (a Chartist newspaper that existed from 1837 until 1852 and had a circulation of around 50,000), *Political Register, Poor Man's Guardian, Reynolds News, Trades Newspaper, Twopenny Trash, Voice of the People, Voice of West Riding*, and *Weekly Police Gazette* (Curran and Seaton 2010, chapter 2). The radical press had an important role in radical politics and was associated with civil society groups such as the National Union of the Working Classes, the Chartist Movement, or the Society for Promoting the Employment of Women. Later advertising rose and it became ever more expensive to run a newspaper, so that the press shifted towards the right and the labour press came to an end in the twentieth century. Curran argues that the nineteenth-century press had "a radical and innovatory analysis of society" and "challenged the legitimacy of the capitalist order" (Curran 1991, 40). Habermas would dismiss the role of the radical press, whereas the nineteenth-century London press consisted of "conflicting public spheres" (Curran 1991, 42). Curran's position can be characterised as being close to Negt and Kluge's (1993) stress on a proletarian public sphere.

One should, however, see that Habermas's concerns about the economic colonisation of the life-world and the feudalisation of the media system show his worries about capitalist media and his preference for non-capitalist media. Habermas's notion of the feudalised public sphere reflects Marx's (1842, 175) criticism that the "primary freedom of the press lies in not being a trade". Slavko Splichal (2007) stresses in this context that Ferdinand Tönnies and Karl Bücher shared Marx's insight that media can only constitute a public sphere if they are non-commercial. The public sphere has never materialised "because of unequal access to communication channels, uneven distribution of communicative competence, and the reduction of public debates to a legitimisation of dominant opinions created by either the 'business type' or the 'government type' of power elites" (Splichal 2007, 242).

There are several problems with how capitalist media limit the public sphere:

- *Media concentration*: There is a tendency that market competition results in concentration. In the commercial media landscape, the mechanism of the advertising-circulation spiral enforces media concentration (Furhoff 1973).
- *Commercialised and tabloidised content*: Advertising-financed media tend to focus more on entertainment than news, documentaries, and educational programmes because this content is better suited for attracting advertisers (Jhally 1987; Smythe 1954; Williams 1990).
- *Power inequalities*: There are power differentials in commercial media that disadvantage individuals and groups that do not have significant shares of money, political influence, and reputation. These structures disempower citizens' voices and visibility:
  a   Private media ownership gives owners the possibility to influence media content.
  b   For-profit and advertising logic makes media organisations dependent on market and commodity logic and prone to exclude voices that question these logics.
  c   There is an educational and economic gap that can privilege educated and wealthy individuals in the consumption of demanding and costly culture.

There are general concerns about advertising culture (for an overview see the contributions in Turow and McAllister 2009):

- Advertising is product propaganda that conceals actual or possible negative features of products.
- Advertising only presents the products and ideologies of powerful companies and discriminates competing products and views and of less powerful actors, especially non-commercial and non-profit organisations.
- Advertising advances the concentration of the economy.
- Advertising advances media concentration (advertising-circulation spiral).
- Advertisers try to manipulate humans' needs, desires, tastes, purchasing, and consumption decisions.
- Advertising is mainly aimed at wealthy consumers.
- Advertising structures the corporate media as a filter in such a way that criticisms of corporate behaviour are avoided in order not to face loss of advertising clients.
- Advertisers try to calculate and make purely mathematical assumptions about human behaviour and interests (e.g. lives in a certain area, has a specific skin colour and age => has low income, no loan should be offered). They statistically sort consumers and users into groups and tend to discriminate especially

the weak, people with low purchasing power, and people of colour who as a consequence have disadvantages in society.

- Advertisements frequently contain and tend to enforce stereotypes, prejudices, and biases. Examples are classist, racist, and patriarchal stereotypes.
- Advertisements frequently present women in a sexist way.
- Advertising tends to violate consumer privacy and to use sensitive personal data for commercial purposes.
- Advertising fosters mass consumption of mostly non-renewable resources that end as waste in nature. Advertising aggravates the ecological crisis.
- Advertising fosters the programming of light entertainment and thereby advances the tabloidisation of the media as well as the undermining of public service media/content.

Habermas's (1991, 175–195) main concern about advertising is that it has the potential to de-politicise the public. This would on the one hand be due to particularistic interests: "The public sphere assumes advertising functions. The more it can be deployed as a vehicle for political and economic propaganda, the more it becomes unpolitical as a whole and pseudo-privatized" (Habermas 1991, 175). On the other hand the influence of economic logic on the media would result in tabloidisation: "Reporting facts as human-interest stories, mixing information with entertainment, arranging material episodically, and breaking down complex relationships into smaller fragments—all of this comes together to form a syndrome that works to depoliticize public communication" (Habermas 1996, 377). Private control of the media can easily result in an "uneven distribution of effective voice" (Couldry 2010, 145). The economic and political-cultural dimensions of the public sphere are in this respect connected: "Having a voice requires resources" (Couldry 2010, 7). Voice requires a material form (Couldry 2010, 9). In order to be heard and seen, one needs resources that enable media power. Media are the main mechanisms of creating voice and visibility in society. Private ownership of the media can harm the public visibility of and attention to citizens' voices.

There has been a tradition of public service broadcasting in Europe and other parts of the world that has been a crucial dimension of the modern media system in the twentieth and twenty-first centuries. Thinking of the BBC, most readers familiar with it will be able to come up with some points of criticism. It is remarkable, however, that since its inception in 1922 the BBC has by and large remained advertising-free in its United Kingdom–based core operations. Being advertising-free and funded either by a licence fee or taxes are features that the BBC shares with public broadcasting institutions in countries such as Finland, France, Spain, Sweden, and Norway. Mixed public broadcasting systems that combine state-organised funding with advertising exist in contrast in countries such as Austria, Denmark, Germany, Hungary, Italy, the Netherlands, Poland, and Portugal. France and Spain have in recent years phased out advertising-based funding on public broadcasting.

Public service media that are non-commercial and non-profit on the economic level embody values and relations "opposed to economic values and [. . .] essential to an operating democracy" (Garnham 1990, 111). Its cultural and political role is that it enables communication within the public sphere: "the collection and dissemination of *information* and the provision of a forum for *debate*" (Garnham 1990, 111). It has universal access obligations that enable "equal access to a wide range of high-quality entertainment, information and education" and ensure that "the aim of the programme producer is the satisfaction of a range of audience tastes rather than only those tastes that show the largest profit" (Garnham 1990, 120). Public service media's universal access principle means "the provision of a service of *mixed* programmes on *national* channels available to all" (Scannell 1989, 137).

By broadcasting and media in general, *public information comes into private households and private affairs become public*: "Broadcasting has created a public world of public persons who are routinely made available to whole populations. But at the same time it has brought private persons into the public domain" (Scannell 1989, 141). "Broadcasting, then, brings public life into private life, and private life into public life, for pleasure and enjoyment and enjoyment as much as for information and education" (Scannell 1989, 143). Besides these general characteristics, there are two important features of public media that distinguish them from privately controlled media:

- *Common culture*: They make culture commonly available to citizens. "European public service broadcasting has represented a real step forward in the attempt to create a common culture" (Garnham 1990, 126).
- *Public ownership*: Nicholas Garnham (1990, 132) stresses that public ownership and the non-profit and non-commercial status of the BBC is an important difference to the commercial media system that remains "the basis for its potential as a public service".

Habermas points out that the idea of the public sphere is connected to public services controlled and owned by the public: "In a democratic constitutional state, there are also public goods such as the undistorted political communication, that may not be tailored to the profit expectations of financial investors" (Habermas 2011, 101, translation from German[3]).

The BBC's structure reflects the commitment to the public sphere on a cultural and an economic level:

- *Common culture:*
- The BBC's Royal Charter[4] defines the BBC's public purposes: "The Public Purposes of the BBC are as follows—

    a   sustaining citizenship and civil society;
    b   promoting education and learning;

c   stimulating creativity and cultural excellence;

d   representing the United Kingdom, its nations, regions and communities;

e   bringing the United Kingdom to the world and the world to the United Kingdom;

f   in promoting its other purposes, helping to deliver to the public the benefit of emerging communications technologies and services and, in addition, taking a leading role in the switchover to digital television" (BBC Royal Charter, §3).

- The overall cultural task is "to inform, educate and entertain" (BBC Royal Charter, §5). The BBC Agreement[5] (§14, 1) further specifies that the "content of the UK Public Services taken as a whole must be high quality, challenging, original, innovative and engaging".

- *Public ownership:*
  The BBC's core activities are non-commercial: "The BBC as a corporation shall not directly provide any commercial services, but it may carry out other trading activities" (BBC Agreement §68, 1). The BBC is a public trust: "The Trust is the guardian of the licence fee revenue and the public interest in the BBC" (BBC Royal Charter, §22). Its core activities are advertising-free: "The BBC is not permitted to carry advertising or sponsorship on its public services. This keeps them independent of commercial interests and ensures they can be run purely to serve the general public interest. If the BBC sold airtime either wholly or partially, advertisers and other commercial pressures would dictate its programme and schedule priorities. There would also be far less revenue for other broadcasters. The BBC is financed instead by a TV licence fee paid by households. This guarantees that a wide range of high-quality programmes can be made available, unrestricted, to everyone" (BBC Advertising Policy[6]).

The Communications Act 2003 (§264, 6) defines public service in a rather idealist manner as providing information, entertainment, education, cultural diversity, fair and well-informed news reporting, sports and leisure interests, science, religion, beliefs, social issues, international affairs, specialist interests, programmes for children and young people, and regional diversity. It neglects aspects of a public economy and therefore opens a door to the commercialisation of the BBC. "This made the idea of funding public *content* rather than, or even instead of, public service *institutions* thinkable" (Lunt et al. 2012, 118).

In recent years, scholars committed to the concept of public service have responded to the challenge of digital media and the increasing commercialisation of the media by introducing the notion of public service media (PSM). These activities have especially been organised around the bi-annual RIPE Conference Series (Re-Visionary Interpretations of the Public Enterprise) that has been organised since 2002. The "PSB role as the central force preserving the cohesion of society clearly needs to be safeguarded and, crucially, *extended* to the online world" (Jakubowicz 2007, 35).

Bardoel and Lowe (2007) point out cornerstones of the concept of PSM:

- The extension of public service from broadcasting to the media in general.
- In the age of digital media, public service audiences should not be targets of transmitted information, but partners and participants.
- Neoliberalism has put public funding of public service under commercial and market pressures that question its legitimacy ("waste of public money", "lack of audience interest").

Slavko Splichal (2007) gives a concise definition of PSM:

> In normative terms, public service media must be a service *of* the public, *by* the public, and *for* the public. It is a service *of* the public because it is financed by it and should be owned by it. It ought to be a service *by* the public—not only financed and controlled, but also produced by it. It must be a service *for* the public—but also for the government and other powers acting in the public sphere. In sum, public service media ought to become "a cornerstone of democracy".
>
> *Splichal 2007, 255*

The European Commission (2009) uses the term *public service media* to stress that these media enrich "public debate and ultimately can ensure that all citizens participate to a fair degree in public life" (§10). "In this context, it must be recalled that the public service remit describes the services offered to the public in the general interest. The question of the definition of the public service remit must not be confused with the question of the financing mechanism chosen to provide these services" (§49).

The Committee of Ministers (2007) of the European Union defines public service media in the following way: "Public service media should offer news, information, educational, cultural, sports and entertainment programmes and content aimed at the various categories of the public and which, taken as a whole, constitute an added public value compared to those of other broadcasters and content providers."

Such policy definitions are, in contrast to the one provided by Splichal, idealist and culturalist. They ignore aspects of political economy that shape the way media are organised and can operate. They overlook the crucial implications of public ownership as well as of being non-profit and non-commercial. Idealist definitions of public service media advance the possibility to introduce the logic of commerce and commodification to public service and to ideologically and politically-economically mould them into the logic of capitalism. Cultural idealism is an ideology that harms a true understanding of public service media. Public service media require a cultural-materialist definition and understanding of the public in public service.

Table 8.5 introduces a model of public service media that operates on three dimensions. There are economic, political, and cultural dimensions of public service media: organisation, participation, and content. On each level, there is the production, circulation, and use of a specific good that is organised in line with the logic of public service. So for example public ownership of PSM is an economic aspect of the means of communicative production.

On the economic level, PSM are means of production, circulation, and consumption. PSM's means of production are publicly owned. The circulation of information is based on a not-for-profit logic. Consumption is made available in principle to everyone by giving citizens easy access to PSM's technology and information. On the political level, PSM make available inclusive and diverse political information that can support political debate and the achievement of political understanding. On the cultural level, PSM provide educational content that has the potential to support cultural debate and the achievement of understanding in society.

8.4. The Internet, Social Media, and the Public Sphere

The differentiation of modern society into various spheres, such as the capitalist economy, the state, civil society, and the sphere of the family and intimacy, has resulted in a division between what is considered the private sphere and the public sphere. The modern idea of privacy stands in the context of the division of spheres.

Historically, the division of labour has brought about separations of spheres such as work time/free time, work place/household, paid/unpaid, urban/rural, wage/reproductive labour, mental/physical labour, men/women, developed/developing world, and industry/agriculture. Such divisions of spheres are also

TABLE 8.5 A model of public service media

Sphere	Media	Production	Circulation	Use
Culture: social meaning	Content	Independence, unity in diversity, educational content	Cultural communication and debate	Cultural dialogue and understanding
Politics: collective decisions	Participation	Independence, unity in diversity (representation of minority interests and common affinity and reference points for society), political information	Political communication and debate	Political dialogue and understanding
Economy: property	Organisation and technology	Public ownership	Non-profit, non-market	Universal access, universal availability of technology

TABLE 8.6 Dualities associated with the private/public distinction (source: Garnham 2000, 174)

Private	Public
individual	social
family	society
economy	polity
civil society	state
lifeworld	systems world
agent/action	structure
everyday life	structure/system/power
nature	culture
feelings	reason
freedom	power
arts	sciences
personal	political
negative freedom	positive freedom

divisions of power. Nicholas Garnham (2000, 174) argues that the division between private/public is a typically "Western post-Enlightenment" thought and practice that is associated with a number of other divisions that are shown in Table 8.6.

In modern society, we associate the realms of intimacy/family and the economy as the realm of private ownership with the private realm, whereas we associate the state, civil society, and the media with the public realm. There are different definitions of privacy (Fuchs 2011b) that share as the least common denominator that they all have to do with the question if and which spaces, behaviours, communications, and data that concern individuals and groups should be available and accessible to others or not. According to Hannah Arendt, the distinction between the private and the public sphere is relevant for the privacy concept because it entails "the distinction between things that should be shown and things that should be hidden" (Arendt 1958, 72). Privacy has to do with the question of what dimensions of human life should be made visible to the public or should remain invisible. Many of us may feel uncomfortable about the idea that advertisers and employers get access to the health databases of our general practitioners and hospitals because we may fear that patients may get harmed. Figure 8.3 shows a research result that indicates that Internet users are sceptical about the sharing of health data.

We may not feel the same discomfort as in the case of health data sharing about the idea to abolish anonymous bank accounts in Switzerland that companies and wealthy people use for offshoring profits and income in order to evade paying taxes in their countries of residence. But both issues are discussed under the topic of privacy—health privacy and financial privacy.

The connection between privacy and private property becomes apparent in countries like Switzerland, Liechtenstein, Monaco, or Austria that have

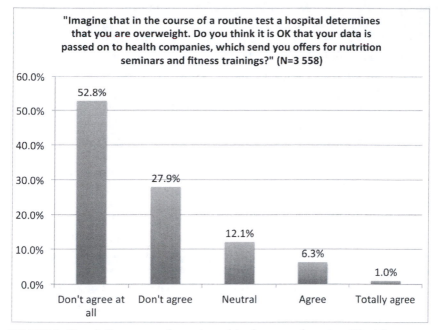

FIGURE 8.3 Result from research conducted in the research project "Social networking sites in the surveillance society" (see: http://www.sns3.uti. at, Kreilinger 2014)

a tradition of relative anonymity of bank accounts and transactions. Money as private property is seen as an aspect of privacy, about which the members of the public have no or only very restricted information. In Switzerland, bank secrecy is defined in the Federal Banking Act (§47). The Swiss Bankers Association sees bank anonymity as a form of "financial privacy"[7] that needs to be protected. It speaks of "privacy in relation to financial income and assets".[8] In most countries, information about income and the profits of companies (except for public companies) is treated as a secret, a form of financial privacy. The problem of secret bank accounts and transactions and the non-transparency of richness and financial flows is not only that secrecy can in the economy support tax evasion, black money, and money laundering but also that financial privacy masks wealth gaps. Financial privacy reflects the classical liberal account of privacy. So for example John Stuart Mill formulated a right of the propertied class to economic privacy as "the owner's privacy against invasion" (Mill 1848, 43).

A further criticism of the privacy concept has been that it helps to confine women to the household and shield domestic violence. Seyla Benhabib (1992, 89–90) says in this respect that the distinction between the private and public realm has "served to confine women and typically female spheres of activity like housework; reproduction; nurture and care for the young, the sick, and the elderly to the 'private' domain". Anita Allen summarises the feminist criticism of privacy in the following words: "Under fading regimes of patriarchy, privacy is the place where men lord over women and is the excuse that the state uses to justify letting them do it" (Allen 2003, 42). The right to bodily privacy can, however, also physically protect victims of violence from the offenders.

The brief discussion shows that discussing privacy requires us to ask: For whom shall privacy be guaranteed or limited, for which purpose, and in which context (Fuchs 2011b)? Privacy is a social, contextual, and relational moral value (Fuchs 2011b).

The emergence of "social media" is embedded into the trend that boundaries between the dualities of modernity have become somewhat liquid and blurred: we find situations where the distinctions between play and labour, leisure time and work time, consumption and production, private and public life, the home and the office have become more porous. Concepts such as digital labour, online prosumption, consumption work, produsage, crowdsourcing, freeconomy, or playbour (play labour) have been used to describe transformations in the media, culture, and society associated with social media. The liquefaction of boundaries is not, as Zygmunt Bauman (2005, 2000/2012) says in an overarching claim, the main feature of modernity today. It is more modest to assume that it is one of modernity's tendencies besides other features such as commodification, financialisation, informatisation, mediation, globalisation, or individualisation. I would therefore not speak of liquid life, liquid world, and liquid modernity, as Bauman (2005, 2000/2012) does.

Liquefaction may be the outcome of a number of developments in society:

- The globalisation of society, the economy, and culture.
- Increased mobility and the transnational flows of workers, people, capital, information, finance, goods, and services.
- Neoliberal policies that deregulate employment and relatively decrease wages, which makes people work longer hours.
- The rise of a flexible mode of production.
- The job crisis that makes people commute longer times and distances to and from their workplaces.
- The constant quest for reducing production and circulation costs in order to increase profits.

Two examples of liquefaction: Around 1 million people commute in and out of London every weekday by rail and bus.[9] Table 8.7 shows the results of a study that analysed how British rail passengers spend their time on the train and compared results for 2004 and 2010. This comparison is meaningful because the Amazon Kindle was introduced in the United Kingdom in 2009, Facebook in 2005, and the iPad in 2010.

TABLE 8.7 Activities that UK commuters spent some of the time doing while travelling by rail, 2004 and 2010, N = 26,221 (2004), 19,715 (2010), data source: Lyons et al. 2013

	Commuter activities 2004 (some of the time during journey)	Commuter activities 2010 (some of the time during journey)
Reading for leisure on outward journey	47%	46%
Window gazing, people watching on outward journey	50%	45%
Text messages and phone calls for personal reasons on outward journey	18%	32%
Working or studying on outward journey	27%	31%
Working or studying on return journey	29%	31%
Listening to music/radio/podcast on outward journey	12%	28%
Emails on outward journey		20%
Eating, drinking on outward journey	8%	12%
Non-personal text messages, phone calls on outward journey	7%	18%
Talking to other passengers on outward journey	11%	11%
Being bored on outward journey	13%	13%
Internet browsing on outward journey		13%
Sleeping on outward journey	16%	17%

The statistics show that commuters' most common activities have in 2010 been reading for leisure, gazing out of the window/watching people, working, using the phone for personal or non-personal reasons, listening to music or the radio, reading, and sending emails. These results indicate that the commuter train is simultaneously a public and a private space, where those on the way to their jobs engage in personal activities for leisure, work activities, and media use for both work and private activities. The commuter train is a liquid space, where work time and leisure time blur. For commuters the Internet and mobile phones play an important role as means of communication for both personal and work-related activities while on the move. Commuting is a mobile activity that brings people from their homes to their workplaces and back. Media are tools that allow commuters to use the daily commuting time for both work and leisure from mobile places, they are liquid technologies for the organisation of time and space.

According to statistics, there were 1.56 million freelancers in the United Kingdom in 2012, around 6 per cent of the total workforce (Kitching and Smallbone 2012). The largest group of freelancers—around 265,000 or 17 per cent—works in art, literature, and the media (Kitching and Smallbone 2012). It makes up 64.4 per cent of all people working in this sector in the United Kingdom. There were 93,300 (6 per cent) IT and telecommunications freelance professionals in 2011 (Kitching and Smallbone 2012). Freelancers generate around 8 per cent of the private sector's turnover (Kitching and Smallbone 2012).

Of UK freelancers 38 per cent work from home and other places, 26 per cent only at home, 33 per cent only outside of the home (Kitching and Smallbone 2012). For many freelancers, the home is at the same time the household for free time and the work place for leisure time. It is a liquid space. Broadcast Now conducted a UK Freelancer Survey in the media and cultural industries in 2012 (N = 656)[10] in which 21 per cent of the respondents worked more than 60 hours a week, nearly 50 per cent more than 50 hours, and 56 per cent 10 hours or more a day. 47 per cent earned less than £25,000. This shows that freelancers tend to work long hours. The liquefaction of the home and the work place and working time and leisure time they experience tends to be dominated by more time being occupied by labour. At the same time liquefaction does not mean a high income for most freelancers. Connected to the freelance economy is a crowdsourcing economy, in which companies try to find cheap or unpaid labour on the Internet with the help of platforms such as Amazon Mechanical Turk, eLance, oDesk, or PeoplePerHour.

The liquefaction of boundaries is not automatically good or bad, but under the current neoliberal framework the logic of private profit and state power colonises the blurring of boundaries so that the becoming-public of the private and the becoming-private of the public is colonised by the systems of the economy (commodification) and the state (bureaucratisation).

There are two constitutive features of how social media such as Facebook are connected to the liquefaction of boundaries (Fuchs and Trottier 2013).

Integrated sociality: Social media enable the convergence of the three modes of sociality (cognition, communication, cooperation) into an integrated form of sociality. This means for example on Facebook, an individual creates multi-media content like a video on the cognitive level, publishes it so that others can comment (the communicative level), and allows others to manipulate and remix the content, so that new co-operative content with multiple authorship can emerge. One step does not necessarily result in the next, but the technology has the potential to enable the combination of all three activities in one space. Facebook, by default, encourages the transition from one stage of sociality to the next, within the same social space.

Integrated social roles: Social media such as Facebook are based on the creation of personal profiles that describe the various roles of a human being's life. On social media like Facebook, we act in various roles (as friends, citizens, consumers, workers, colleagues, fans, etc.), but all of these roles become mapped onto single social media profiles that are observed by different people that are associated with our different social roles. This means that social media like Facebook are social spaces, in which social roles tend to converge and become integrated in single profiles.

A Facebook profile holds a1) personal data, a2) communicative data, a3) social network data/community data in relation to b1) private roles (friend, lover, relative, father, mother, child, etc.), b2) civic roles (socio-cultural roles as fan community members, neighbourhood association members, etc.), b3) public roles (socio-economic and socio-political roles as activists and advocates), and b4) sys-temic roles (in politics: voter, citizen, client, politician, bureaucrat, etc.; in the economy: worker, manager, owner, purchaser/consumer, etc.).

Figure 8.4 visualises social roles and information processes on social media.

Table 8.8 shows three basic antagonisms of contemporary social media. They are located in the realms of the economy, politics, and civil society. I will for each dimension discuss how it relates to the public and the private realms.

Social media's first contradiction concerns the economic level. Facebook's profits were US$1.5 billion in 2013 (SEC Filings, form 10-K, January 31, 2014). Google's profits were US$13.97 billion in the same time period (SEC Filings, form 10-K, annual report 2013). Twitter's net loss increased from US$79.4 mil-lion in 2012 to US$645.3 million in 2013 (SEC Filings, form EX-99.1, February 5, 2014). Given that Twitter is not making any profits, the question is if it was a wise decision to list the company on the New York Stock Exchange in autumn 2013. On the day that Twitter's annual losses were announced, its stock market value on the New York Stock Exchange dropped from US$65 on February 5, 2014, to US$50 on February 6 (data source: Yahoo! Finance). In contrast, Google's share price stood at the same time at almost US$1,200 and Facebook's share doubled its value from around US$30 in 2012 to above US$60 in February 2014 (data source: Yahoo! Finance). Where do corporate social media's profits come from?

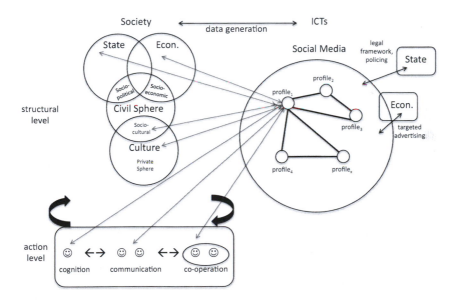

FIGURE 8.4 Social roles and information processes on social media (Fuchs and Trottier 2013)

TABLE 8.8 Three antagonisms of social media

Sphere	Antagonism between . . .	
Economy	users' interest in data protection and corporate tax accountability on the one side . . .	. . . and corporations' interest in user data's transparency/ commodification and corporate secrecy on the other side
Politics	citizens' interest to hold the powerful accountable and protect communications from powerful institutions' access on the one side . . .	. . . and on the other side power holders' interest to keep power structures secret and to criminalise the leaking and making public of any data about them.
Civil society	networked protest communication that creates political public spheres online and offline . . .	. . . and the particularistic corporate and state control of social media that limits, feudalises, and colonises these public spheres

On social media, users generate, upload, and update personal, communicative, and social network data stemming from their roles in the economy, politics, civil society, and culture. In addition, many social media platforms retrieve and store data about user behaviour on their sites and the Internet in general. The data is partly kept private (visible only to single users), semi-public (visible to a group), or public (visible to everyone). Most corporate social media's capital accumulation model is to turn private, semi-public, and public user data into a commodity that is sold to advertising clients that present targeted advertisements to users. Given that Facebook and Google's paid engineers alone only maintain platforms that without usage behaviour are devoid of sociality and economic value, it is reasonable to assume that corporate social media users are unpaid workers who generate economic value. In this context the notion of *digital labour* has been coined (see the contributions in Scholz 2013).

Dallas Smythe (1977) argued that in commercial broadcasting, audiences conduct labour that creates an audience commodity. On corporate social media, we can speak of an Internet prosumer data commodity generated by digital labour (Fuchs 2014a, chapters 4 and 11). It is qualitatively different from the audience commodity in a number of respects:

- Measuring audiences has in broadcasting and print traditionally been based on studies with small samples of audience members. Measuring user behaviour on corporate social media is constant, total, and algorithmic.
- Audience commodification on social media is based on the constant real-time surveillance of users.
- User measurement uses predictive algorithms (if you like A, you may also like B because 100,000 people who like A also like B).

- User prices are often set based on algorithmic auctions (pay per view, pay per click).

Turning user data into a private good controlled by social media companies is legitimated with the help of privacy policies. Some examples:

- *Google*: "We use the information that we collect from all of our services to provide, maintain, protect and improve them, to develop new ones and to protect Google and our users. We also use this information to offer you tailored content—such as giving you more relevant search results and ads" (Google Privacy Policy, version from June 24, 2013).
- *Facebook*: "We may use all of the information we receive about you to serve ads that are more relevant to you" (Facebook Data Use Policy, version from November 15, 2013).
- *Twitter*: "When you use Twitter to follow, tweet, search or interact with Tweets, we may use these actions to tailor Twitter Ads for you. For example, when you search for a specific term, we can show you promoted content related to that topic. We also might tailor ads using your profile information or location, which may be based on your mobile device location (if you've turned on location features) or your IP address. This helps us show you local ads and other ads that you might prefer. Twitter may also tailor ads based on information that our ad partners provide us, like browser-related information (a browser cookie ID) or a scrambled, unreadable email address (a hash)" (How Twitter Ads Work, version from December 12, 2013). "If you prefer, you can turn off tailored ads in your privacy settings so that your account is not matched to information shared by ad partners for tailoring ads" (Twitter Privacy Policy, version from October 21, 2013).
- *VKontakte*: "The Site Administration has the right to dispose of the statistical information relating to the Site operation as well as of the Users' information to ensure the targeted display of advertising information to different audiences of Site users" (VKontakte Terms of Service, version from December 12, 2013).
- *Weibo*: "Sina Weibo may use your non-private personal information for marketing purposes, including but not limited to present or provide you with the advertising and promotional materials on Sina Weibo platform, notify you of or recommend Sina Weibo service or product information, and/or any other information that might be of interest to you based on your use of Sina Weibo service or product" (Weibo Privacy Policy, version from December 12, 2013). "User agrees that Sina reserves the right to insert or add various kinds of commercial advertising or other types of commercial information (including but not limited to put advertisement on any web-page of Weimeng website), and, user agrees to accept product promotion or other relevant business information sent by Weimeng through email or

other measures" (Weibo Terms of Use, version from December 12, 2013).

- *Pinterest*: "We also use the information we collect to offer you customized content, including: [. . .] Showing you ads you might be interested in" (Pinterest Privacy Policy, version from December 12, 2013).
- *Instagram*: "We may use information that we receive to: [. . .] provide personalized content and information to you and others, which could include online ads or other forms of marketing" (Instagram Privacy Policy, version from January 19, 2013).

Google, Facebook, Twitter, VKontake, Weibo, Pinterest, and Instagram are some of the most used social media platforms in the world. They are all for-profit companies. One should not be mistaken by the fact that they offer communication services. They are not just communication companies, but also large advertising agencies. They sell targeted ads and guarantee themselves the right to commodify users' private, semi-public, and public data for this purpose in their privacy policies. Twitter limits this right somewhat by providing an opt-out option that allows users to have ads not "based on information shared by ad partners" (Twitter privacy settings, version from December 13, 2013). Targeted ads are, however, often based on data collected by the platform itself, not provided by ad partners, so that this constraint may only have limited effects.

Users, privacy advocates, and consumer protectionists tend to express concerns about corporate social media, especially about (see Fuchs 2014b):

- Very long or unlimited data storage;
- The lack of informed consent;
- Complex privacy policies and terms of use;
- Users' unpaid digital labour as business model;
- The privacy/free-access trade-off;
- The use of sensitive personal data for targeted advertising;
- The lack of consumer privacy in the light of personal data commodification;
- The lack of opt-in to and opt-out from targeted advertising;
- Liberal standard privacy settings;
- The difficulty of the full deletion of profiles;
- Networked data monitoring across platforms.

In a survey that was conducted as part of the research project "Social Networking Sites in the Surveillance Society" that I directed, around two thirds of the respondents felt that businesses handle personal data in inappropriate ways (Figure 8.5); 82.1 per cent said that web platforms should not use targeted advertising (Figure 8.6).

Such empirical data indicate that users feel that corporations in general violate consumer privacy and social media corporations in particular violate users' privacy by commodifying personal data. The economic value of the digital media

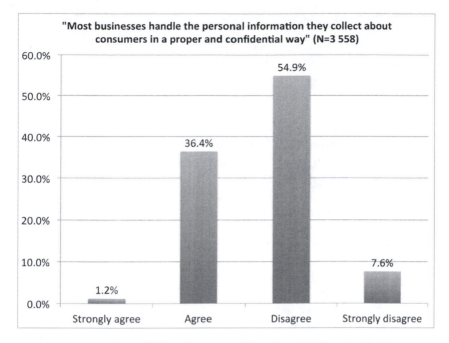

FIGURE 8.5 Research result from the project "Social networking sites in the surveillance society" (http://www.sns3.uti.at, Kreilinger 2014)

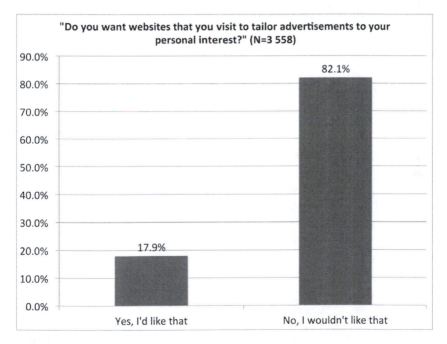

FIGURE 8.6 Research result from the project "Social networking sites in the surveillance society" (http://www.sns3.uti.at, Kreilinger 2014)

industry is generated by a complex global division of labour that includes not just users' unpaid digital labour, but also the digital labour of slaves extracting conflict minerals in Africa, hardware assemblers working often under toxic and extremely hard conditions, highly paid and highly stressed software engineers in the West, precarious call-centre workers, freelance digital media professionals, and e-waste workers facing dangerous conditions, etc. (Fuchs 2014a).

Social media corporations' managers often express the view that privacy is outdated. Google's executive chairman, Eric Schmidt said for example, "If you have something that you do not want anyone to know, maybe you should not be doing it in the first place"[11] (http://www.youtube.com/watch?v=A6e7wfDHzew, accessed on October 27, 2014). Facebook's co-founder and CEO, Mark Zuckerberg, said, "The goal of the company is to help people to share more in order to make the world more open and to help promote understanding between people."[12] Schmidt and Zuckerberg argue for massive data sharing on social media. They do not mention, however, that this sharing is not primarily a sharing of data with friends and the public, but a sharing with Google and Facebook that are the largest data processors and data commodifiers in the world, which explains not just the recent rise of the term "big data" but also social media companies' interest in hiding their commercial interests ideologically behind the ideas of sharing and openness. Their claims are double-edged if one considers for example that Mark Zuckerberg in 2013 bought four estates that surround his house in Palo Alto's Crescent Park neighbourhood for US$30 million. He is concerned about his privacy. Zuckerberg's logic is as simplistic as it is mistaken: "Privacy is good only if you can pay for it; it is not good if it makes Facebook or Google obtain less profits."

Social media corporations argue on the one hand against users' privacy, but on the other hand they are secretive about their own financial operations and by a complex global company structure try to establish financial privacy that makes their revenues and capital flows non-transparent. Google has its European headquarters in Ireland, from where it organises its European revenues. From Ireland profits are transferred to the Netherlands and from there to the Bermuda Islands, where Google does not need to pay any corporation tax.

Companies such as Google, Amazon, and Starbucks had to appear before the UK Public Accounts Committee in late 2012 to discuss the question if they avoided paying taxes in the United Kingdom.[13] Amazon has 15,000 employees in the United Kingdom, but its headquarters are in Luxembourg, where it has just 500 employees.[14] In 2011, it generated revenues of £3.3 billion in the United Kingdom, but only paid £1.8 million corporation tax (0.05 per cent).[15] Facebook paid £238,000 corporation tax on a UK revenue of £175 million (0.1 per cent) in 2011.[16]

Google has its headquarters in Dublin, but employs around 700 people in the United Kingdom.[17] Google's managing director for the United Kingdom and Ireland, Matt Brittin, admitted that this choice of location is due to the circumstance that the corporation tax is just 12.5 per cent in Ireland,[18] whereas in the United Kingdom it was 26 per cent in 2011.[19] Google had a UK turnover of

TABLE 8.9 Financial figures and estimates for Amazon, Facebook, and Google, data sources: UK revenues: *The Guardian Online, BBC Online*; worldwide: Amazon SEC Filings 2012, Form 10-K; Google SEC Filings 2012, Form 10-K; Facebook SEC Filings 2013, Form 10-K

Company	UK Revenue 2011 (£)	Worldwide Revenue 2011 (US$)	Worldwide Profit before Taxes 2011 (US$)	Gross Profit Rate 2011 (in % of revenue)	Estimated Gross UK Profit, 2011 (£)	UK Corporation Tax 2011 (£)	Estimated Tax Revenues at a Corporation Tax of 28%
Amazon	3.3 bn	48.077 bn	934 mn	1.9%	62.7 mn	1.8 mn	17.6 mn
Facebook	175 mn	3.711 bn	1.695 bn	45.7%	80.0 mn	238 000	22.4 mn
Google	395 mn	37.905 bn	12.326 bn	32.5%	128.4 mn	6 mn	36.0 mn

£395 million in 2011, but only paid taxes of £6 million (1.5 per cent).[20] While large media companies only pay a very low share of taxes, governments argue that state budgets are small, implement austerity measures, and as a result cut social and welfare benefits that hit the poorest in society.

In the House of Commons's Public Accounts Committee's inquiry on tax avoidance, Google's then UK managing director, Matt Brittin, admitted that this structure serves to pay low taxes. He said in the inquiry session conducted on May 16, 2013: "We talked about Bermuda in the last hearing, and I confirmed that we do use Bermuda. Obviously, Bermuda is a low-tax environment."[21] Confronted with Google's low level of corporation tax paid in the United Kingdom, its chairman, Eric Schmidt, said that "people we [Google] employ in Britain are certainly paying British taxes".[22] His logic here is that Google does not have to pay taxes because its employees do.

Whereas social media corporations advocate openness, sharing of user data, and an end of privacy in order to maximise profits, they claim closure, secrecy, and financial privacy when it comes to their own global finance, profit, and tax affairs.

Social media is facing an economic antagonism between users' interest in data protection and corporate tax accountability on the one side and corporations' interest in user data's transparency/commodification and corporate secrecy on the other side.

A comparable case from the world of the press that shows the contradictions of citizens and corporate interests is the UK phone hacking scandal, in which the *News of the World* newspaper monitored the communications of public figures and published the obtained data as parts of its stories in order to achieve monetary profits from increased sales, attention, and advertising revenues. The Leveson inquiry's report recommended a statutory regulation of the press that allows sanctions and fines in the case of privacy violations and libel. Stakeholders of the commercial press supported by the Tories opposed substantial legal measures with the argument that such laws would threaten the freedom of the press. The debate was shaped by an antagonism between the public's interest in protection from the media's invasion into citizens' lives and the press's interest in making monetary profits protected by wide-ranging freedoms that allow journalistic investigations that deeply penetrate into all aspects of the human world.

The second contradiction of social media is on the political level. Edward Snowden's revelations about the existence of global Internet surveillance systems such as Prism, XKey Score, or Tempora have shed new light on the extension and intensity of state institutions' Internet and social media surveillance. According to the leaked documents, the NSA in the Prism programme obtained direct access to user data from seven online/ICT companies: AOL, Apple, Facebook, Google, Microsoft, Paltalk, Skype, and Yahoo!.[23] The PowerPoint slides that Edward Snowden leaked talk about collection "directly from the servers of these U.S. Service Providers".[24]

Snowden also revealed the existence of a surveillance system called XKeyScore that the NSA can use for reading e-mails, tracking web browsing and users' browsing histories, monitoring social media activity, online searches, online chat, phone calls, and online contact networks, and follow the screens of individual computers. According to the leaked documents XKeyScore can search both meta-data and content data.[25] The documents that Snowden leaked also showed that the Government Communications Headquarter (GCHQ), a British intelligence agency, monitored and collected communication, phone and Internet data from fibre optic cables and shared such data with the NSA.[26] According to the leak, the GCHQ for example stores phone calls, e-mails, Facebook postings, and the history of users' website access for up to 30 days and analyses these data.[27] Further documents indicated that in co-ordination with the GCHQ also intelligence services in Germany (Bundesnachrichtendienst BND), France (Direction Générale de la Sécurité Extérieure DGSE), Spain (Centro Nacional de Inteligencia, CNI), and Sweden (Försvarets radioanstalt FRA) developed similar capacities.[28]

The concept of the military-industrial complex stresses the existence of collaborations between private corporations and the state's institutions of internal and external defence in the security realm. C. Wright Mills argued in 1956 that there is a power elite that connects economic, political, and military power:

> There is no longer, on the one hand, an economy, and, on the other hand, a political order containing a military establishment unimportant to politics and to money-making. There is a political economy linked, in a thousand ways, with military institutions and decisions. [. . .] there is an ever-increasing interlocking of economic, military, and political structures.
>
> *Mills 1956, 7–8*

Prism shows that the military-industrial complex contains a surveillance-industrial complex (Hayes 2012), into which social media are entangled: Facebook and Google both have more than 1 billion users and are probably the largest holders of personal data in the world. They and other private social media companies are first and foremost advertising companies that appropriate and commodify data on users' interests, communications, locations, online behaviour, and social networks. They make profit out of data that users' online activities generate.

They constantly monitor usage behaviour for this economic purpose. Since 9/11 there has been a massive intensification and extension of surveillance that is based on the naïve technological-deterministic surveillance ideology that monitoring technologies, big data analysis, and predictive algorithms can prevent terrorism. The reality of the murdering of a soldier that took place in the South-East London district of Woolwich in May 2013 shows that terrorists can use low-tech tools such as machetes for targeted killings. High-tech surveillance will never be able to stop terrorism because most terrorists are smart enough not to announce their intentions on the Internet. It is precisely this surveillance ideology that has created intelligence agencies' interest in the big data held by social media corporations. Evidence has shown that social media surveillance targets not just terrorists but has also been directed at protestors and civil society activists.[29] State institutions and private corporations have long collaborated in intelligence, but the access to social media has taken the surveillance-industrial complex to a new dimension: it is now possible to obtain detailed access to a multitude of citizens' activities in converging social roles conducted in converging social spaces.

Yet the profits made by social media corporations are not the only economic dimension of the contemporary surveillance-industrial complex: The NSA has subcontracted and outsourced surveillance tasks to around 2000 private security companies[30] that make profits by spying on citizens. Booz Allen Hamilton, the private security company that Edward Snowden worked for until recently, is just one of these firms that follow the strategy of accumulation-by-surveillance.

According to financial data (SEC Filings, http://investors.boozallen.com/sec.cfm), it had 24,500 employees in 2012 and its profits increased from US$25 million in 2010 to $84 million in 2011, $239 million in 2012, and $219 million in 2013, and $232 million in 2014. Surveillance is big business, both for online companies and those conducting the online spying for intelligence agencies.

Users create data on the Internet that is private, semi-public, and public. In the social media surveillance-industrial complex, companies commodify and privatise these user data as private property, and secret services such as the NSA driven by a techno-determinist ideology obtain access to the same data for trying to catch terrorists that may never use these technologies for planning attacks. For organising surveillance, the state makes use of private security companies that derive profits from organising the monitoring process. User data is in the surveillance-industrial complex first externalised and made public or semi-public on the Internet in order to enable users' communication processes, then privatised as private property by Internet platforms in order to accumulate capital, and finally particularised by secret services who bring massive amounts of data under their control that is made accessible and analysed worldwide with the help of profit-making security companies.

The social media surveillance-industrial complex shows that a negative dialectic of the enlightenment is at play in contemporary society: the military-industrial complex constantly undermines the very liberal values of the enlightenment, such as the freedoms of thought, speech, press, and assembly as well as the security of the people's persons, houses, papers, and effects. Prism and XKey Score show

how in supposedly liberal democracies dangerous forms of political-economic power negate enlightenment values.

Barack Obama commented on Prism that "you can't have a 100% security and also then have a 100% privacy and zero inconvenience".[31] He expressed the view that maximising state security requires minimising citizens' privacy and extending surveillance. The privacy-security-trade-off-model is flawed because it ignores that threats to state security tend to derive from power inequalities and social insecurities in the world. The solution is not to undermine civil liberties by implementing ever more surveillance technologies, but to foster equality and socio-economic security (human security) in the entire world.

The same institutions and politicians who want to minimise citizens' privacy and increase the state's access to personal data claim absolute secrecy for national security operations. Individuals and groups in civil society who oppose power asymmetries and inequalities in the world have made use of anonymous whistle-blowing on the Internet in order to make data about the operations of powerful institutions transparent to the public. The powerful try to keep their key operations secret in order to better be able to maintain and extend their power. Data about it is put under particularistic control, it is a kept secret. Whistle-blowers aim to make secret data about the powerful available to the public. WikiLeaks, Julian Assange, Bradley Manning, and Edward Snowden are the most important examples. WikiLeaks understands itself as a watchdog of the powerful that exposes their power by leaking information (see also Fuchs 2014b, chapter 9):

> WikiLeaks is a not-for-profit media organisation. Our goal is to bring important news and information to the public. [. . .] WikiLeaks interest is the revelation of the truth. Unlike the covert activities of state intelligence agencies, as a media publisher WikiLeaks relies upon the power of overt fact to enable and empower citizens to bring feared and corrupt governments and corporations to justice.[32]

Edward Snowden thinks that if the state threatens its citizens, the latter have to act and defend their rights:

> I grew up with the understanding that the world I lived in was one where people enjoyed a sort of freedom to communicate with each other in privacy without it being monitored, without it being measured or analyzed or sort of judged by these shadowy figures or systems anytime they mentioned anything that travels across public lines. [. . .] I don't want to live in a world where everything that I say, everything I do, everyone I talk to, every expression of creativity or love or friendship is recorded. [. . .] So I think anyone who opposes that sort of world has an obligation to act in the way they can.[33]

The US government and its allies oppose whistle-blowers in the name of national security and argue that military and secret service operations would have to remain secret. Barack Obama said about Snowden in this context that he is "putting at risk our national security and some very vital ways that we are able to get intelligence that we need to secure the country".[34] Military judge Denise Lind explained Bradley Manning's sentence of 35 years in prison in a special report by saying that Manning was "wrongfully and wantonly causing publication of intelligence belonging to the United States on the Internet knowing the intelligence is accessible to the enemy [. . .] The knowing conversions by PFC Manning deprived the United States government of the ability to protect its classified information".[35] After Wikileaks's 2010 disclosure of information about the US wars in Iraq and Afghanistan, Hillary Clinton commented:

> The United States strongly condemns the illegal disclosure of classified information. It puts people's lives in danger, threatens our national security, and undermines our efforts to work with other countries to solve shared problems. [. . .] want you to know that we are taking aggressive steps to hold responsible those who stole this information. [. . .] People of good faith understand the need for sensitive diplomatic communications, both to protect the national interest and the global common interest.[36]

The basic argument is that the US government has the right to keep data about its military and secret service operations, including the killing of civilians, secret. It argues that everyone making such secret information public threatens national security. The making public of secret state data would be a crime. Powerful actors have a schizophrenic attitude: They argue that they should have the power to monitor citizens' private, semi-public, and public data, but that citizens shall not have access to data about the state's internal and external defence activities and that their making public of such data is an offense that shall be penalised by several decades in prison.

On the political level of social media, there is an antagonism between civil society's interest to hold the powerful accountable and protect communications from powerful institutions' access on the one side and on the other side power holders' interest to keep power structures secret and to criminalise the leaking and making-public of any data about them.

The third antagonism of social media concerns the level of civil society. In 2011 revolutions and rebellions arose in many parts of the world. In political protests that aim to establish a better society, activists form political public spheres that give a voice to citizens' demands. So 2011 should have been called the year of public spheres. However, many called it the year of Twitter and Facebook revolutions, implying that it was social media that created the protest movements.

So for example *Foreign Policy Magazine* titled an article "The Revolution Will Be Tweeted"[37] and the *New York Times* wrote that the "Egyptian revolution began on Twitter".[38] There was talk about a "revolution 2.0" (Ghonim 2012) and in the scholarly world academics such as Manuel Castells (2012, 229) claimed that the "networked movements of our time are largely based on the Internet". I conducted an empirical study among activists who were involved in protests during 2011 in order to find out what role digital, social, mobile, and other media had. The online survey had 418 activist participants. The detailed results have been published in my book *OccupyMedia! The Occupy Movement and Social Media in Crisis Capitalism*. The survey contained one question that asked the respondents: "If you think back to a month in which you were involved in Occupy protests, then how often did you engage in certain media activities for trying to mobilise people for a protest event, discussion, demonstration or the occupation of a square, building, house or other space?" The results are shown in Table 8.10.

The data indicate that face-to-face communication, Facebook, email, phone, SMS, and Twitter are the most important media that Occupy activists employ for trying to mobilise others for protests. Activists use multiple media for mobilisation-oriented communication. These include classical interpersonal communication via phones, email, face-to-face, and private social media profiles as well as more public forms of communication such as Facebook groups, Twitter, and email lists. Posting announcements on alternative social media is much more uncommon than doing the same on Twitter and Facebook: Whereas 42 per cent of the respondents posted protest announcements frequently on their Facebook profiles, only 4.4 per cent did so on Occupii, 3.1 per cent on N-1, and 1.1 per cent on Diaspora*.

I also conducted a correlation analysis of the variables that cover protest mobilisation communication. Some of the correlation results are presented in Table 8.11.

Correlation analysis shows that a higher level of protest activity tends to result in a higher level of media use for protest mobilisation. Mobilisation in face-to-face communication tends to positively influence other forms of mobilisation communication such as social media use for spreading the word about protest events. The survey data is an empirical indication that contemporary protests are not social media rebellions and that at the same time digital and social media are also not irrelevant in these protests. Activists make use of multiple media, both offline and online, technologically mediated and unmediated, digital and non-digital. The 2011 protests were activities that created occupied squares as public spheres and that organised themselves and voiced political demands offline and online and as combination of both.

Of the survey respondents 69.5 per cent said that the big advantage of commercial social media such as Facebook, YouTube, and Twitter is that activists can reach out to the public and everyday people. Typically, respondents argued that "all the activists are already there [on social media], but so are regular people. I think it's one of the main goals of the Occupy movement to reach out to the rest of the 99%" (#63). At the same time 55.9 per cent of the respondents indicated that state and corporate surveillance of activist communication is a huge disadvantage and risk that commercial social media pose. Activists expressed this fear for example in the following ways: "My Twitter account was subpoena'd, for tweeting a hashtag. The subpoena was dropped in court" (#238). "Individuals I have supported have had Facebook accounts suspended, tweets catalogued as evidence against them, and this available information used for police to pre-emptively arrest them" (#270). "The other risk is that commercial sites might

TABLE 8.10 Frequency of usage per month of specific forms of communication in the mobilisation of protest

	Infrequently (0)	Medium (1-6)	Frequently (>6)
I had a personal face-to-face conversation in order to mobilise others.	15.0%	37.60%	47.40%
I sent an e-mail to personal contacts.	29.8%	40.40%	29.80%
I phoned people.	36.9%	39.50%	23.60%
I sent an SMS to my contacts.	49.7%	27.00%	23.30%
I posted an announcement on an email list.	46.2%	29.90%	23.90%
I posted an announcement on my Facebook profile.	25.2%	32.40%	42.00%
I posted an announcement on Facebook friends' profiles.	53.1%	21.10%	25.80%
I posted an announcement in an Occupy group on Facebook.	44.0%	20.50%	35.60%
I posted an announcement on Twitter.	52.0%	15.90%	32.10%
I created an announcement video on YouTube.	85.9%	11.10%	3.00%
I posted an announcement on my own profile on the social networking site Occupii.	86.1%	9.40%	4.40%
I posted an announcement on friends' profiles on the social networking site Occupii.	91.3%	7.40%	1.30%
I posted an announcement in an Occupy group on the social networking site Occupii.	85.3%	11.00%	3.70%
I posted an announcement on my own profile on the social networking site N-1.	90.9%	5.90%	3.10%
I posted an announcement on friends' profiles on the social networking site N-1.	93.3%	4.60%	2.20%
I posted an announcement in an Occupy group on the social networking site N-1.	93.9%	3.60%	2.50%
I posted an announcement on my own profile on the social networking site Diaspora★.	94.3%	4.70%	1.10%
I posted an announcement on friends' profiles on the social networking site Diaspora★.	95.7%	3.50%	0.80%
I posted an announcement in an Occupy group on the social networking site Diaspora★.	95.7%	3.20%	1.10%
I wrote an announcement on a blog.	69.0%	22.20%	8.80%
I informed people on meetup.com.	87.5%	10.70%	1.80%
I informed others by using one of the movement's chats.	73.8%	17.40%	8.90%
I posted an announcement on one of the movement's discussion forums.	67.6%	22.00%	10.30%
I made an announcement with the help of a Riseup tool (chat, email lists).	84.7%	11.00%	4.30%
I made an announcement on an InterOccupy teleconference.	86.1%	11.00%	2.80%
I made an announcement with the help of the OccupyTalk voice chat.	95.3%	2.90%	1.80%

TABLE 8.11 Correlations between the frequency of specific forms of protest mobilisation communication, activism intensity as well as political positioning (Spearman's rho)

	Intensity of activism, significance	Face-to-face conversations with friends	Announcement on my Facebook profile	Announcement video on YouTube
OccupyTalk	0.072, 0.232	-0.084, 0.161	0.098, 0.106	0.154*, 0.010
InterOccupy teleconference	0.283**, 0.000	0.111, 0.062	0.172**, 0.004	0.210**, 0.000
Riseup tool	0.290**, 0.000	0.189**, 0.002	0.104, 0.086	0.233**, 0.000
Movement discussion forum	0.335**, 0.000	0.206**, 0.001	0.319**, 0.000	0.293**, 0.000
Movement online chat	0.313**, 0.000	0.182**, 0.002	0.306**, 0.000	0.318**, 0.000
Meetup.com	0.066, 0.274	0.009, 0.876	0.193**, 0.001	0.130*, 0.031
Blog post	0.225**, 0.000	0.177**, 0.003	0.231**, 0.000	0.257**, 0.000
Occupy group on Diaspora*	0.059, 0.329	0.067, 0.265	0.093, 0.124	0.226**, 0.000
Friends' profiles on Diaspora*	-0.004, 0.941	0.015, 0.798	0.060, 0.322	0.263**, 0.000
Own profile on Diaspora*	0.020, 0.734	0.052, 0.387	0.072, 0.235	0.228**, 0.000
Occupy group on N-1	0.101, 0.092	0.033, 0.584	0.140*, 0.021	0.242**, 0.000
Friends' profiles on N-1	0.019, 0.748	0.029, 0.629	0.082, 0.175	0.240**, 0.000
Own profile on N-1	0.006, 0.926	0.051, 0.395	0.116, 0.052	0.204**, 0.000
Occupy group on Occupii	0.159**, 0.006	0.047, 0.424	0.231**, 0.000	0.325**, 0.000
Friends' profiles on Occupii	0.085, 0.143	0.020, 0.733	0.223**, 0.000	0.310**, 0.000
Own profile on Occupii	0.128*, 0.028	0.048, 0.410	0.278**, 0.000	0.346**, 0.000
Video on YouTube	0.294**, 0.000	0.167**, 0.004	0.305**, 0.000	–
Twitter	0.340**, 0.000	0.243**, 0.000	0.440**, 0.000	0.339**, 0.000
Occupy group on FB	0.481**, 0.000	0.304**, 0.000	0.697**, 0.000	0.349**, 0.000
Friends' FB profiles	0.307**, 0.000	0.371**, 0.000	0.708**, 0.000	0.354**, 0.000
My Facebook profile	0.337**, 0.000	0.318**, 0.000	–	0.305**, 0.000
eMail mailing lists	0.431**, 0.000	0.415**, 0.000	0.374**, 0.000	0.240**, 0.000
SMS	0.389**. 0.000	0.420**, 0.000	0.419**, 0.000	0.260**, 0.000
Phone calls	0.428**, 0.000	0.554**, 0.000	0.342**, 0.000	0.191**, 0.001
Personal e-mail	0.443**, 0.000	0.570**, 0.000	0.385**, 0.000	0.182**, 0.002
Personal conversation	0.497**, 0.000	–	0.318**, 0.000	0.167**, 0.004

collaborate with government or corporate interests to close down sites if a threat to their interests became apparent" (#11). "Facebook = Tracebook. [. . .] We're contributing to capitalism by putting our content for free [on these sites]" (#203).

Activists' use of corporate social media is facing a contradiction between possibilities for better communication and the risk of the corporate and state control of protest movements. Facebook, Google, and other corporate social media are making billions of dollars in advertising revenue every year. They are part of the 1 per cent. So why should the 99 per cent trust them and trust that these companies will deal with their data in a responsible manner? Edward Snowden's revelations about Internet surveillance show the dangers of the surveillance-industrial complex, in which Google, Facebook, and others collaborate with the National Security Agency (NSA).

Contemporary activists create public spaces of protest and make use of social media and face-to-face communication, online digital and offline non-digital media, in order to voice their political demands. At the same time they are confronted with the threat that both social media corporations and state institutions control corporate social media and thereby have the power to directly or algorithmically control political movements' internal and public communication capabilities.

Civil society is facing an antagonism between networked protest communication that creates political public spheres online and offline and the particularistic corporate and state control of social media that limits, feudalises, and colonises these public spheres.

8.5. Towards Alternative Social Media as a Public Sphere

The contemporary social media world is shaped by three antagonisms: a) the economic antagonism between users' data and social media corporations' profit interests, b) the political antagonism between users' privacy and the surveillance-industrial complex as well as citizens' desire for accountability of the powerful and the secrecy of power, and c) the civil society antagonism between the creation of public spheres and the corporate and state colonisation of these spheres.

In Habermas's terms, we can say that social media has a potential to be a public sphere and lifeworld of communicative action, but that this sphere is limited by the steering media of political power and money so that corporations own and control and the state monitors users' data on social media. Contemporary social media as a whole does not form a public sphere, but corporations and the state control and colonise it in a particularistic manner and thereby destroy the social media's public sphere potentials. The antagonistic reality of social media challenges classical liberalism's major assumptions.

John Locke (1690, 271), the founder of classical liberalism, argued that civil liberties and private property are natural laws and rights of human beings: "The *State of Nature* has a Law of Nature to govern it, which obliges every one: And

Reason, which is that Law, teaches all Mankind, who will but consult it, that being all equal and independent, no one ought to harm another in his Life, Health, Liberty, or Possessions". David Hume (1739) made private property a central element of liberal theory, arguing that justice and private property require each other mutually in any society.

The autonomy of the will is for Kant (1785, 109) "the supreme principle of morality". "The principle of autonomy is thus: not to choose in any other way than that the maxims of one's choice are also comprised as universal law in the same willing" (Kant 1785, 109). "Autonomy is thus the ground of the dignity of a human and of every rational nature" (Kant 1785, 101). Heteronomy would be the opposition of autonomy (Kant 1785, 95). Kantian autonomy means that people act freely if they accord to laws that they have given themselves (Habermas 2013, 70).

The consequence of Kant's principle of autonomy is the Golden Rule as categorical imperative:

> Act only according to that maxim by which you can at the same time will that it should become a universal law. [. . .] Act as though the maxim of your action were by your will to become a universal law of nature. [. . .] So act that you use humanity, in your own person as well as in the person of any other, always at the same time as an end, never merely as a means.
>
> *Kant 1785, 71, 87*

Habermas (2008, 140) argues that Kant's categorical imperative is reflected in the insight that freedoms are only limited by the freedom of others. Habermas (2011, 14) says that Kant's principle of autonomy and his categorical imperative are present in the *Universal Declaration of Human Rights*[39] §1: "All human beings are born free and equal in dignity and rights." As a further consequence of the principle of autonomy, Kant (1784, 4) saw the "public use of man's reason" for "addressing the entire reading public" as the main feature of the Enlightenment. It would enable "man's emergence from his self-incurred immaturity" (Kant 1784, 7). "The essence of such public reason is that it is always offered for possible critique by others" (Garnham 2000, 182).

John Stuart Mill (1859, 16) argued that there is a "portion of a person's life and conduct which affects only himself" and that this portion "is the appropriate region of human liberty". He derived from this assumption the liberties of conscience, thought, feeling, opinion, sentiment, expression, discussion, publication, tastes, pursuits, and association. He also propagated an individualism that gives humans the right to pursue their own good in their own way:

> No society in which these liberties are not, on the whole, respected, is free, whatever may be its form of government; and none is completely free in which they do not exist absolute and unqualified. The only freedom

which deserves the name, is that of pursuing our own good in our own way, so long as we do not attempt to deprive others of theirs, or impede their efforts to obtain it.

Mill 1859, 17

Mill (1848, 16–17) acknowledged that capitalism creates inequality and argued that freedom is preferable to equality:

> The perfection both of social arrangements and of practical morality would be, to secure to all persons complete independence and freedom of action, subject to no restriction but that of not doing injury to others: and the education which taught or the social institutions which required them to exchange the control of their own actions for any amount of comfort or affluence, or to renounce liberty for the sake of equality, would deprive them of one of the most elevated characteristics of human nature.

Based on the liberal principles of liberty, individualism, and private property, Adam Smith (1790) formulated the doctrine that the rich whom he considered to be naturally selfish "are led by an invisible hand to [. . .] advance the interest of the society" (215). He considered private property as fundamental human right and that one of the "most sacred laws of justice" (101) is to "guard his property and possessions" (102).

It becomes evident from this discussion that individual civil liberties are in liberal ideology connected to an individual right of private property that stands above considerations of socio-economic equality, which is not considered as a fundamental right. Marx formulated in this context the critique that the individualism advanced by classical liberalism results in egoism that harms the public good. The rights to private property of the means of production and to accumulate as much capital as one pleases would harm the community and the social welfare of others who are by this process deprived of wealth: "The right of property is thus the right to enjoy and dispose one's possessions as one wills, without regard for other men and independently of society. It is the right of self-interest" (Marx 1843a, 236). "Thus none of the so-called rights of men goes beyond the egoistic man, the man withdrawn into himself, his private interest and his private choice, and separated from the community as a member of civil society" (Marx 1843a, 236–237).

Crawford Macpherson (1962) has termed this critique of liberalism the critique of possessive individualism. Possessive individualism is the "conception of the individual as essentially the proprietor of his own person or capacities, owing nothing to society for them" (Macpherson 1962, 3). According to Macpherson, it is the underlying worldview of liberal theory since John Locke and John Stuart Mill. The problem of classical liberalism is that relatively unhindered private accumulation of wealth, as the neoliberal regime of accumulation has shown since the 1970s, comes into conflict with social justice and is likely to result in strong socio-economic inequality. The ultimate practical result of Mill's liberalism is an extreme unequal distribution of wealth.

Marx also criticised that liberalism is highly individualistic. He said in this context that Kant stresses autonomy and human will as individual principles and thereby sees individual reason and not social emancipation as the source of emanaipation from class:

> The key to the criticism of liberalism advanced by Saint Max and his predecessors is the history of the German bourgeoisie. [. . .] The state of affairs in Germany at the end of the last century is fully reflected in Kant's *Critik der practischen Vernunft*. While the French bourgeoisie, by means of the most colossal revolution that history has ever known, was achieving domination and conquering the Continent of Europe, while the already politically emancipated English bourgeoisie was revolutionizing industry and subjugating India politically, and all the rest of the world commercially, the impotent German burghers did not get any further than "good will". Kant was satisfied with "good Will" alone, even if it remained entirely without result, and he transferred the realisation of this good will, the harmony between it and the needs and impulses of individuals, to the world beyond. Kant's good will fully corresponds to the impotence, depression and wretchedness of the German burghers, whose petty interests were never capable of developing into the common, national interests of a class and who were, therefore, constantly exploited by the bourgeois of all other nations.
>
> *Marx and Engels 1845/46, 208*

The *Universal Declaration of Human Rights*[40] formulates the basic freedoms of thought (§18), opinion and expression (§19), and assembly and association (§20). It also defines the freedom of property: "(1) Everyone has the right to own property alone as well as in association with others. (2) No one shall be arbitrarily deprived of his property" (§17). Furthermore it defines social rights, such as that "Everyone, as a member of society, has the right to social security" (§22) and that "Everyone has the right to a standard of living adequate for the health and well-being of himself and of his family" (§25, 1).

The criticism of possessive individualism points out that the freedom of private property questions social rights and that therefore §17 stands in a fundamental antagonism to §§22 and 25. The *Charter of Fundamental Rights of the European Union* therefore limits the right to private property by the extension that "No one may be deprived of his or her possessions, except in the public interest and in the cases and under the conditions provided for by law, subject to fair compensation being paid in good time for their loss" (§17).[41] The *European Convention on Human Rights*[42] in a comparable way limits the freedom of private property by saying that a State may "enforce such laws as it deems necessary to control the use of property in accordance with the general interest or to secure the payment of taxes or other contributions or penalties" (article 1).

When Habermas argues that the stratification of ownership and education limits the freedom of speech and that the power of political and economic organisations limits the freedom of association and assembly (Habermas 1991, 227–228), he just like the criticism of possessive individualism points towards the liberal conception of the public sphere's specific limits.

Horkheimer and Adorno (1944/2002) argue that the liberal Enlightenment ideology turns into its own opposite that it initially questioned so that "irresistible progress is irresistible regression" (28). "Once harnessed to the dominant mode of production, enlightenment, which strives to undermine any order which has become repressive, nullifies itself" (Horkheimer and Adorno 2002, 73f). Although "freedom in society is inseparable from enlightenment thinking", the negative dialectic of freedom in capitalism is that the very concepts of enlightenment thinking, such as freedom, "no less than the concrete historical forms, the institutions of society with which it is intertwined, already contain[s] the germ of the regression which is taking place everywhere today" (Horkheimer and Adorno 2002, xvi). The freedoms proclaimed by liberal Enlightenment ideology find their actual violation in the practice of capitalism: the ideal of freedom turns into an opposite reality—unfreedom.

Alternative movements, groups, and individuals such as Anonymous (Fuchs 2013), WikiLeaks (Fuchs 2014b, chapter 9), Edward Snowden, Pirate parties, privacy advocates, media reform movements such as Free Press in the United States and the Media Reform Coalition in the United Kingdom, the free software and open access movement, the creative commons movement, hacker groups, data protection organisations, consumer protection organisations, state and corporate watchdog organisations, and human rights activists point out the limits of the classical liberal conception of the public sphere: the actual practices of data commodification, corporate media control, as well as corporate and state surveillance limit the liberal freedoms of thought, opinion, expression, assembly, and association. These movements and groups are twenty-first-century informational capitalism's negative dialectic of the Enlightenment. They show the difference of liberalism's proclaimed essence and its actual existence. If Anonymous, for example, argues in favour of the freedom of assembly and expression of the Occupy movement and criticises police violence against activists, then it, on the one hand, stays within the categories of liberal thought. At the same time it shows how within the United States, the country in the world that most stresses the liberal value of freedom, freedom is actually limited by state action, which drives liberal values ad absurdum and shows their actual contradictory existence. The aforementioned actors conduct a practical immanent political critique of liberalism. They, however, frequently miss taking this form of critique to the next step and advancing from immanent critique towards a transcendental critique that sees the limits of the realisation of liberal values and calls for the establishment of a participatory democracy. The freedoms that reality today negates can only be realised in a society of equals, a participatory democracy.

Social movements such as Occupy go one step further and do not simply demand privacy rights for citizens or freedom of speech, but rather also stress that socio-economic inequality, the contradiction between the 99 per cent and the 1 per cent, limits freedom. Occupy calls for the realisation of social rights together with individual rights in a realm of social and individual freedom that can best be described as participatory democracy.

But are there alternatives to the colonised Internet? Dal Yong Jin (2013) conducted an analysis of the most used Internet platforms and found that 98 per cent of them were run by for-profit organisations, 88 per cent used targeted advertising; 72 per cent had their home base in the United States, 17 per cent in China, 3 per cent in Japan, 4 per cent in Russia, 2 per cent in the United Kingdom, 1 per cent in Brazil, and 1 per cent in France. He concluded that there is a "platform imperialism", in which "the current state of platform development implies a technological domination of US-based companies that have greatly influenced the majority of people and countries" (Jin 2013, 154) and that "Chinese platforms [. . .] utilize the targeted advertising capital business model, which is not different from US Internet capitalism" (Jin 2013, 166). There were, however, two alternatives: BBC Online and Wikipedia. Reflecting Graham Murdock's (2011) distinction between three political economies, one can say that the Internet and social media are shaped by the logic of capitalism, public service, and civil society. The power of these models is, however, asymmetrical and heavily skewed in favour of a capitalist Internet and capitalist social media.

Wikipedia is "is a multilingual, web-based, free-content encyclopedia project supported by the Wikimedia Foundation and based on an openly editable model".[43] The Wikimedia Foundation is non-commercial and not-for-profit organisation. The BBC Agreement describes BBC Online as "a comprehensive online content service, with content serving the whole range of the BBC's Public Purposes".[44] On October 27, 2014, Wikipedia was the sixth most accessed website in the world and the ninth most visited in the UK.[45] BBC Online was the seventeenth most popular website in the world and the sixth most popular in the UK.[46] Wikipedia's civil society media model and BBC Online's public online service model differ from the for-profit models that have resulted in an Internet dominated by the logic of economic and political controls. They stand for the logic of a public service and commons-based Internet. What we need is not more market, advertising, and commerce on social media, but more platforms that are based on the logics of the commons and public service. We need more visibility for them. And we need more resources for them. We need the decolonisation of the world and the Internet so that they are less based on bureaucratic and economic power and more on communicative rationality and the logic of the public sphere. It is no problem if more private information becomes public for communicative purposes if companies, the state, and others do not have the power to misuse it and to harm citizens with it.

Graham Murdock (2014, 244) argues that resisting cultural commodification requires negatively "the resistance to commercial enclosure" and positively "a defence of commoning". The latter should take on the form of projects that establish digital commons—"a linked space defined by its shared refusal of commercial enclosure and its commitment to free and universal access, reciprocity and collaborative activity" (Murdock 2005, 227). Public service institutions, such as broadcasters, museums, libraries, and archives, are vast repositories of cultural commons. Making these commons available to the public in digital form and allowing the public to re-use and re-mix them for *non-commercial* purposes can advance both digital commons and participatory culture. It is essential that culture can only be participatory if it is non-commercial and non-profit, otherwise participation can turn easily over into crowdsourcing value-generation and therefore the economic exploitation of the public, which destroys all participation and creates merely pseudo-participation.

One argument against public service social media is that it could give the state more power to control user data and thereby further enhance state surveillance. Public service does not, however, automatically imply state control, but only state funding. Public service institutions are only truly public if they do not just have relative independence from the market, but also from government control of its contents. In order to minimise the state surveillance threat, user-generated content sites similar to YouTube that require large storage capacities, but do not contain lots of personal and communication data, could be increasingly organised by public service institutions such as the BBC and personal-data intensive social networking sites similar to Facebook by non-profit, non-commercial civil society organisations. We for example need a YouTube run by the BBC and a Facebook organised by Wikipedia or a global network of public universities.

There is no guarantee that civil society–run social media are less prone to collaboration with secret services than social media corporations such as Facebook and Google. They could by law be required to collaborate with secret services. Social media run by activists and civil society are, however, more likely to lobby against such requirements than companies because they share and directly support activists' interests.

Another concern about public service online media is how to sustain high-quality public service content online if there is user-generated content. On the one hand journalists providing high-quality news and reports can work for alternative online platforms if funding becomes available for their work. On the other hand it should increasingly be realised that citizens' participation in debate and cultural production is a crucial democratic quality in itself. A public service participatory media structure is a high quality feature of democracy.

Especially since the 2009 revision of the EU Broadcasting Communication (Brevini 2013, 112–118), there is a tendency in Europe to limit public service media organisations' capacity to offer online services. The basic thought is that the licence fee's economic power can harm capitalist media markets. This line of argument overlooks, however, that big monopoly corporations such as Facebook and Google largely control the Internet and that the actually existing power asymmetry on the Internet comes from the profit logic of the market that centralises and dominates the Internet.

In Austria, the country I originally come from, a new public service broadcasting law that regulates the ORF (Österreichischer Rundfunk, Austrian Broadcasting) came into effect in 2010. It was the outcome of the EU DG Competition's decision that Austria had to revise its online services in light of the 2009 EU Broadcasting Communication and after the Austrian Newspaper Association (Verband Österreichischer Zeitungen) filed a complaint to the EU that "ORF, using state funds, supplies online services such as games, dating services, computer and IT programs, GSM ring tones, sports platform and SMS services" and thereby causes a "pronounced distortion of competition to the detriment of newspaper publishers".[47]

The new ORF law regulates in §4e that the ORF is only allowed to provide an overview of daily news and content accompanying broadcasts (*sendungsbegleitende Inhalte*) online. §4f lists 28 online services that the ORF is not allowed to provide, including: forums, chats, user-generated content sites, social networks, or online services for specialist groups. The new law meant the end of several of the ORF's online services, such as the Futurezone (a news site for Internet politics) and the FM4 and Ö3 Chats (chat forums for users).

The BBC Charter and Agreement do not contain such direct regulations that limit the provision of social media and online services. But there is a public value test for the introduction of new services. The United Kingdom was the first European country to introduce an ex ante public value test that assesses with stakeholders if a new media service shall be introduced by a public service company or not in light of potential cultural and market impacts. The EU Commission obliged Germany, Denmark, the Netherlands, and Austria to introduce similar tests (Donders 2011).

The public value test consists of a public value assessment (PVA) that evaluates if a new service fulfils the BBC's public purposes and a market impact assessment (MIA): "Account will be taken of both 'negative' substitution effects and 'positive' market creation effects. The MIA considers the extent to which the BBC's proposals are likely to induce substitution away from competing services and the ways in which that substitution may reduce investment in new services, and potentially reduce choice for consumers and citizens" (Ofcom 2007, 2). "Were commercial providers to be deterred from seeking to offer competing services this would ultimately have the effect of reducing choice for listeners and viewers, to the detriment of the public interest as a whole" (Ofcom 2007, 3).

A crucial dimension is to assess if a potential BBC service limits the profitability of other media companies: "There is a very real concern that the BBC's services may distort competition" and because of the licence fee may make "commercial providers [. . .] unable to develop profitable offerings of their own" (Ofcom 2007, 11). "In the longer term, however, the negative impact on the revenues and profits of competing providers may lead to a reduction in investment and innovation. It could deter market entry by new providers or prompt existing suppliers to withdraw services. In other words, there may be longer term consequences which are detrimental to consumer interests" (Ofcom 2007, 13). Petros Iosifides (2010) shows that Ofcom's concern that public service media should be competitively provided is unique in Europe.

There are concerns that the BBC's licence fee can distort competition in the provision of online services. But the reality is that the logic of commerce distorts the capacity of the logic of public service and the commons to shape the Internet. Commerce has resulted in an antagonistic Internet dominated by targeted advertising and US communications companies that act as the world's largest advertising agencies, commodify data, and support state surveillance of citizens. The current system has resulted in Prism, XKey Score, and Tempora. Market impact assessments put limits on the possibility to create public service alternatives to the commercial Internet. As a result of the public value test, the BBC had to abolish online services, such as its online education service BBC Jam, because they were considered as competition for commercial providers. BBC's Video Nation, audience-generated videos that were shown on the BBC from 1993 to 2011 and web archived since 2011, had to close in 2011 because of cuts to the BBC Online's budget. The pilot of the BBC Creative Archive, the release of BBC archive material under a licence comparable to Creative Commons that enabled users to re-use it for non-commercial purposes, was discontinued in 2006, only a year after its introduction.

The United Kingdom and other European countries have a strong public service media tradition. Competing with Californian commercial social media companies is neither viable nor desirable. The best option is therefore that they focus on what they are good at, i.e. that they focus on creating public service and commons-based social media platforms. For this purpose existing laws would have to be adapted. Benedetta Brevini speaks in this context in her study of public service and the Internet in Europe of the need for Public Service Broadcasting 2.0—"a new policy framework and a new set for public service imperatives that can bring those ideals into the online world" (Brevini 2013, 156)—so that "the online world is to be infused with the same public service ethos characterized traditional broadcasting and served Europe well for over 50 years" (Brevini 2013, 157). The question is of course if one shall in this context speak of public service *broadcasting* online/2.0 because this may imply to define the Internet by not just normative, but also communicative features of broadcasting, or if it is not an advantage to speak of a public service Internet or public service social media.

Karen Donders sees the public value test as "an instrument that inherently curbs public broadcasters' independence to some extent and attaches a particular importance to the market aspect of public intervention" and "a panic reaction to deal with aggressive private sector lobbying against a new media remit of public broadcasters" (Donders 2011, 29–30). For Richard Collins, the United Kingdom's public value test is a Frankensteinian "regulatory tool designed to constrain and control public service broadcasters" (Collins 2011, 56; see also Barnett 2007). The call for public value tests is accompanied by the idea of top-slicing the licence fee so that parts of it are used for supporting public service content on commercial providers' media. "Top-slicing will not be the end of the BBC, but it may be the *beginning of the end*" (Iosifides 2010, 28).

Neoliberal austerity measures have been the mainstream political answer to the financial crisis that had resulted from the financialisation of the economy in combination with wage repression. First everyday people were deprived of wage increases and once the crisis hit the economy, their taxes were used to consolidate the banks and companies that are representatives of the system that deprived citizens in the first instance and then a second time.

These austerity measures in many countries mean cuts of public expenditure that hit the weakest and poorest. In Greece neoliberal responses to the capitalist crisis have resulted in the shutdown of the Hellenic Broadcasting Corporation and the layoff of its more than 2,500 employees. So neoliberalism deprives the people not just of material resources, but also of public communication resources.

Richard Collins (2010, 55–56) calls for "a radical shift in mentality—one that ceases to fetishise the traditional PSB and acknowledges the achievement and potential of the internet for delivery of public services and contents". Peter Goodwin argues that "for the BBC to survive in an increasingly web-based and digital world it needs to develop new web-based services" (Goodwin 2012, 70). A movement for public service media would need to be part of a larger project that challenges neoliberalism.

There are non-commercial and non-profit social media platforms such as Diaspora*, N-1, Occupii, InterOccupy, OccupyTalk, Occupy News Network, Occupy Streams, Riseup, Lorea, identi.ca, StatusNet, Quitter, Vinilox, Load Average, Thimbl, or Crabgrass that withdraw social media from corporate control and make state control of activist communication more difficult. My survey presented in the book *OccupyMedia! The Occupy Movement and Social Media in Crisis Capitalism* showed that activists tend to see such platforms as good alternatives to Facebook, Twitter, and YouTube because they do not profit from users' activities and have better privacy protection mechanisms. But at the same time they stress that the problem is that these platforms have a low reach, operating them is resource-intensive, and that there is the risk on these platforms to preach to the converted within an alternative ghetto that cannot reach a wider public. Activists said that such platforms are "owned and managed by us" and provide "more control of our content" (#413). They "are secure, they are not full of ads and they have clearer parameters and more sophisticated tools" (#113). "It is great to be focused and advertisement free. Also to have a network of like-minded individuals working together within a worldwide networked system. All great tools!" (#123).

But survey respondents also argued that operating, using, and maintaining alternative social media requires a large amount of different resources:

"The maintenance of such platforms might take lots of time from the people working with it" (#20). "Someone has to pay for them" (#41). "Well, hosting these can get expensive, and you are not guaranteed donations, which might pose a problem" (#329). "It requires time and man-power" (#364).

Alternative media, online and offline, are facing a political-economic dilemma: they are on the one hand self-managed and tend to be more independent from the interests of the power elite whose domination activists want to challenge, but at the same time they are facing the power of media monopolies and oligopolies as well as the problem of mobilising resources without state support and advertising. Alternative media are confronted with contradictions between critical voice and autonomy on the one side and resource precarity and lack of visibility on the other side (Sandoval and Fuchs 2010). As a consequence, the history of alternative media is also a history of voluntary self-exploitative labour. This circumstance is not activists' fault, but rather the consequence of the political economy of capitalism that limits the possibilities for civil society by making voice dependent on money and political resources. The oligopoly structure of social media has resulted in the circumstance that a few large transnational companies such as Facebook, Google, and Twitter control the vast majority of social media use. Given oligopoly control, it is very difficult to establish alternatives that question the very principles that capitalist media are built on. Capitalist media structures limit the liberal freedoms of speech, opinion, expression, association, and assembly. Liberalism is its own limit and immanent critique: liberal freedom of ownership limits citizens' liberal rights.

The survey respondents were very aware of the problems that alternative social media are facing. At the same time they saw the problems of how to organise alternative media in a capitalist world. The most popular suggestion is to collect voluntary donations. Voluntary donation models often face the problem of how to mobilise supporters and resources. There is the risk that only a small number of people donate continuously. Financial support can be highly uncertain and volatile, whereas organising a successful alternative project in and against the capitalist media world requires continuity and stability.

My view is that improving the resource reality of alternative media in general and alternative social media in particular is a crucial democratic question of our time. The key is to overcome privately controlled media oligopolies, which requires media reforms. Large multinational companies, including Google, Facebook, Amazon, and Apple, are avoiding paying taxes in a lot of the countries where they operate. This is not only unfair; it also increases the pressure for austerity measures in times of crisis.

One of the progressive media policy innovations that could help advancing media democracy is the *participatory media fee organised as a pubic sphere cheque*. If one takes the basic media reform funding idea of the UK Media Reform Coalition (http://www.mediareform.org.uk/), namely to tax large media corporations and to channel this income into non-commercial media, and combines it with elements of participatory budgeting, which allows every citizen to receive and donate a certain amount per year to a non-commercial media project, then elements of state action and civil society action could be combined: the power of the state would guarantee taxation of large companies, but the distribution of this income to media projects would be decentralised and put in the hands of citizens. Google, Facebook, and other large online media companies hardly pay taxes in many countries. The insight that users are digital workers and create economic value on corporate social media that are financed by advertising allows changing global tax regulations: Corporate social media platforms should have to pay tax in a specific country on that share of their revenues that corresponds to the share of users or ad-clicks/views in the country. Avoiding corporations' tax avoidance is a first step for strengthening the public sphere. The licence fee could be developed into a media fee paid by citizens and companies. It could be made more socially just than the licence fee by implementing it not as a flat but a progressive fee that varies based on salary and revenue levels. It is a matter of fairness that those who earn more contribute more to the organisation of the common interest and public good.

The media fee could partly be used for directly funding public service media's online presence and partly based on participatory budgeting for providing an annual voucher to every citizen that s/he must donate to a non-profit, non-commercial media organisation. So participatory budgeting should not be used for deciding if the BBC receives the full costs it needs for its operations. Additional income from the participatory media fee could, however, be distributed to alternative media projects with the help of participatory budgeting. Non-profit versions of Twitter, YouTube, and Facebook run either by institutions such as the BBC or by civil society could, based on such a model, serve the purpose of the public sphere and strengthen the democratic character of communications.

The Internet could become what Nancy Fraser terms a strong public sphere so that platforms are self-managed and "sites of direct or quasi-direct democracy, wherein all those engaged in a collective undertaking would participate in deliberations to determine its design and operation" (Fraser 1992, 135). Peter Dahlgren (1995) argues that a true public sphere requires a domain, in which "marginalized and oppressed groups would be assisted with financial and technical means to enable their participation on the advocacy domain" (Dahlgren 1995, 156). The system of a media fee combined with participatory budgeting could serve this purpose. It could enable alternative media to employ journalists, cultural workers, and technicians in order to operate a common media system in a viable manner.

Habermas (2008, 136–137) suggests to extend public service to the quality press and provide state subsidies to it:

> Concerning gas, electricity and water, the state is obliged to guarantee the population's supply with energy. Should it not also have such an obligation in the case of the type of "energy" without whose influx dysfunctions

emerge that damage the democratic state itself. It is not a "system error" when the state tries to protect the public good of the quality press in particular cases.[48]

Habermas 2008, 136–137, translation from German

The concept of the participatory budgeted media fee (the participatory media fee) extends Habermas's idea from the realm of the press to the realm of digital media and introduces an element of participatory democracy to parts of the allocation process.

Media reforms, participatory budgeting, and a reform of corporation tax could empower public service and alternative media's voice and visibility in the age of social media. It is time to occupy social media in order to withdraw them from corporate and state control and turn them into truly social media and a public sphere. Media reforms are needed for establishing a social media sphere that transcends particularistic control and represents the public interest so that the social potential of the media can be realised. Public service social media could overcome the Internet's antagonisms and serve the people.

Notes

Acknowledgement: This chapter is the extended printed version of Christian Fuchs's inaugural lecture for his professorship of social media at the University of Westminster that he took up on February 1, 2013. The event took place on February 19, 2014, at the University of Westminster.

1 See http://openmap.bbn.com/~tomlinso/ray/firstemailframe.html and http://openmap.bbn.com/~tomlinso/ray/ka10.html (accessed on December 12, 2013).

2 Google's main communicative feature, the email service Gmail, was launched in 2004.

3 „Im demokratischen Verfassungsstaat gibt es auch öffentliche Güter wie die unverzerrte politische Kommunikation, die nicht auf die Renditeerwartungen von Finanzinvestoren zugeschnitten werden dürfen" (Habermas 2011, 101).

4 http://downloads.bbc.co.uk/bbctrust/assets/files/pdf/about/how_we_govern/charter.pdf (accessed on December 11, 2013).

5 http://downloads.bbc.co.uk/bbctrust/assets/files/pdf/about/how_we_govern/agreement.pdf (accessed on December 11, 2013).

6 http://www.bbc.co.uk/aboutthebbc/insidethebbc/howwework/policiesandguidelines/advertising.html (accessed on December 12, 2013).

7 http://www.swissbanking.org/en/mobile/medienmitteilung-20130318 (accessed on December 12, 2013).

8 http://www.swissbanking.org/en/bankkundengeheimnis.htm (accessed on December 12, 2013).

9 http://londontransportdata.wordpress.com/2012/01/16/long-run-trend-in-commuting-into-central-london/ (accessed on December 12, 2013).

10 http://www.broadcastnow.co.uk/freelancer/freelancer-survey-2012-i-cant-do-this-much-longer/5043075.article (accessed on December 12, 2013).

11 http://www.youtube.com/watch?v=A6e7wfDHzew (accessed on December 13, 2013).

12 http://fuchs.uti.at/409/ (accessed on December 13, 2013).

13 "Starbucks, Google, and Amazon Grilled over Tax Avoidance". *BBC Online*. November 12, 2012. http://www.bbc.co.uk/news/business-20288077 (accessed on December 13, 2013).

14 Ibid.

15 "Amazon: £7bn Sales, No UK Corporation Tax". *The Guardian Online*. April 4, 2012. http://www.guardian.co.uk/technology/2012/apr/04/amazon-british-operation-corporation-tax. "Google, Amazon, Starbucks: The Rise of 'Tax Sharing'". *BBC Online*. December 4, 2012. http://www.bbc.co.uk/news/magazine-20560359 (accessed on December 13, 2013).

16 "Should We Boycott the Tax-Avoiding Companies?" *The Guardian Online*. Shortcuts Blog. October 17, 2012. http://www.guardian.co.uk/business/shortcuts/2012/oct/17/boycotting-tax-avoiding-companies (accessed on December 13, 2013).

17 "Google and Auditor Recalled by MPs to Answer Tax Questions". *The Guardian Online*. May 1, 2013. http://www.guardian.co.uk/technology/2013/may/01/google-parliament-tax-questions (accessed on December 13, 2013).

18 "Starbucks, Google and Amazon Grilled over Tax Avoidance". *BBC Online*. November 12, 2012. http://www.bbc.co.uk/news/business-20288077 (accessed on December 13, 2013).

19 In the UK, the main rate of corporation tax that applies for profits exceeding £1,500,000, was reduced from 28% in 2010 to 26% in 2011, 24% in 2012, 23% in 2013 and 21% in 2014.

20 http://www.bbc.co.uk/news/business-20288077 (accessed on December 13, 2013).

21 http://www.publications.parliament.uk/pa/cm201314/cmselect/cmpubacc/112/1305 16.htm (accessed on December 13, 2013).

22 http://www.bbc.co.uk/news/business-22245770 (accessed on December 13, 2013).

23 "NSA Prism Program Taps in to User Data of Apple, Google and Others". *The Guardian Online*. June 7, 2013. http://www.theguardian.com/world/2013/jun/06/us-tech-giants-nsa-data (accessed on December 13, 2013).

24 Ibid.

25 XKeyscore: NSA tool collects "nearly everything a user does on the internet'. *The Guardian Online*. July 31, 2013. http://www.theguardian.com/world/2013/jul/31/nsa-top-secret-program-online-data (accessed on December 13, 2013).

26 GCHQ taps fibre-optic cables for secret access to world's communications. *The Guardian Online*. June 21, 2013. http://www.theguardian.com/uk/2013/jun/21/gchq-cables-secret-world-communications-nsa?guni=Article:in%20body%20link (accessed on December 13, 2013).

27 Ibid.

28 GCHQ and European spy agencies worked together on mass surveillance. *The Guardian Online*. November 1, 2013. http://www.theguardian.com/uk-news/2013/nov/01/gchq-europe-spy-agencies-mass-surveillance-snowden (accessed on December 13, 2013).

29 "Spying on Occupy Activists". *The Progressive Online*. June 2013. http://progressive.org/spying-on-ccupy-activists (accessed on December 13, 2013).

30 "A Hidden World, Growing Beyond Control". *Washington Post Online*. http://projects.washingtonpost.com/top-secret-america/articles/a-hidden-world-growing-beyond-control/ (accessed on December 12, 2013)

31 "Barack Obama Defends US Surveillance Tactics". *BBC Online*. June 8, 2013. http://www.bbc.co.uk/news/world-us-canada-22820711 (accessed on December 13, 2013).

32 http://www.wikileaks.org/About.html (accessed on December 13, 2013).

33 http://mondoweiss.net/2013/07/i-dont-want-to-live-in-a-world-where-every-expression-of-creativity-or-love-or-friendship-is-recorded-full-transcript-of-snowdens-latest-interview.html (accessed on December 14, 2013).

34 http://stream.wsj.com/story/campaign-2012-continuous-coverage/SS-2-9156/SS-2-298484/ (accessed on December 14, 2013).

35 http://dissenter.firedoglake.com/2013/08/16/military-judge-announces-rationale-behind-verdict-in-bradley-mannings-trial/ (accessed on December 14, 2013).

36 http://www.state.gov/secretary/rm/2010/11/152078.htm (accessed on December 13, 2013).

37 "The Revolution Will Be Tweeted". *Foreign Policy Online.* June 20, 2011. http://www.foreignpolicy.com/articles/2011/06/20/the_revolution_will_be_tweeted#sthash.fzgJPMdN.dpbs (accessed on December 13, 2013).

38 "Spring Awakening. How an Egyptian Revolution Began on Facebook". *New York Times Online.* February 17, 2012. http://www.nytimes.com/2012/02/19/books/review/how-an-egyptian-revolution-began-on-facebook.html?pagewanted=all&_r=0 (accessed on December 13, 2013).

39 http://www.un.org/en/documents/udhr/ (accessed on December 13, 2013).

40 http://www.un.org/en/documents/udhr/ (accessed on December 14, 2013).

41 http://eur-lex.europa.eu/LexUriServ/LexUriServ.do?uri=OJ:C:2010:083:0389:0403:en:PDF (accessed on December 13, 2013).

42 http://www.echr.coe.int/Documents/Convention_ENG.pdf (accessed on December 13, 2013).

43 http://en.wikipedia.org/wiki/Wikipedia:About (accessed on December 13, 2013).

44 http://downloads.bbc.co.uk/bbctrust/assets/files/pdf/about/how_we_govern/agreement.pdf (accessed on December 11, 2013).

45 Data source: alexa.com (accessed on October 27, 2014).

46 Ibid.

47 European Commission: E/2 2008 (ex CP 163/2004 and CP 227/2005)—Financing of ORF. http://ec.europa.eu/competition/state_aid/cases/223847/223847_1014816_27_1.pdf (accessed on December 13, 2013).

48 „Wenn es um Gas, Elektrizität oder Wasser geht, ist der Staat verpflichtet, die Versorgung der Bevölkerung mit Energie sicherzustellen. Sollte er dazu nicht ebenso verpflichtet sein, wenn es um jene Art von 'Energie' geht, ohne deren Zufluss Störungen auftreten, die den demokratischen Staat selbst beschädigen? Es ist kein 'Systemfehler', wenn der Staat versucht, das öffentliche Gut der Qualitätspresse im Einzelfall zu schützen" (Habermas 2008, 136–137) (accessed on December 13, 2013).

9

CONCLUSION

How to think about the relationship of the economy and culture is an old problem of society, philosophy, and social theory. Already many ancient patriarchal societies were based on a separation of home and care work on the one side (culture) and hunting and gathering (economy) on the other side. This separation was not purely ideological, but came along with a gendered division of labour and gendered power structures that conceived women as emotional, caring, social, sensual, aesthetic, and weak, and men as the opposites. Although the economy has of course much changed, housework and low-paid service, social, and care work are strongly feminised employment sectors. The capitalist crisis increased the unemployment gender gap. In 2012, the worldwide female unemployment rate was 6.4 per cent and the male rate 5.8 per cent (ILO 2012). Especially the world's youth unemployment has been continuously high and at a rate above 11 per cent since 2012. In 2012, the world's youth female unemployment rate was 13.0 per cent and the male rate 12.4 per cent (ILO 2012). The ILO defines vulnerable employees as contributing family workers and own-account workers.[1] They are likely to have low incomes and face precarious labour conditions. They lack social security and trade union representation, and they experience discrimination. In 2012, 50.4 per cent of the world's female employment population and 48.1 per cent of the male employees were vulnerable workers (ILO 2012).

Comparing sectoral employment in the world, the female employment shares are especially high in education, health, and social work, whereas the male ones are high in manufacturing, construction, transport, storage, and communications (ILO 2012). In 1992, the relative majority of the world's female labour force worked in agriculture (48.8 per cent), whereas in 2012 the majority (47.4 per cent) is located in the service sector. Women are underrepresented in manufacturing (16.2 per cent of the female workforce, 25.9 per cent of the male workforce). Also the majority of male workers (41.3 per cent) conduct service jobs. The occupations in the service sector are heterogeneous in terms of skills, working conditions, wages, etc. Whereas men are in the service sector overrepresented in managerial and legislative occupations, women predominately work as clerks, shop and market sales assistants and in the health and education sectors (ILO 2012).

These data show that the patriarchal segregation of the economy has not ceased to exist and that this segregation operates along the dividing line of rationality and physical strength that are ideologically ascribed as male and emotionality and sociality that are ideologically ascribed as female. "Women dominate in 'care' occupations such as nursing, teaching, social care and especially child-care. Men tend to be concentrated in construction and management—areas associated with physical strength, risk-taking or decision-making" (ILO 2012, 27). The reality of the gender division of labour is by patriarchy ideologically legitimatised by a separation between what is conceived as male economic rationality and female cultural emotionality. Dualism is an ideology that is not just ideational, but has actual negative social effects.

Patriarchal discrimination of women in the economy and society is one of the effects of a dualistic conception of the relationship of culture and the economy. Classical idealism reduces the world to ideas. It sees spirit as the moving force of the universe and the human world. It reduces matter to mind. Mechanical materialism in contrast sees matter as determining the world, but as separate from consciousness. In contemporary social thought, this distinction between idealism and materialism is reproduced in culturalism that talks about culture without talking about the economy and a materialism that often focuses on the economy and sees the world of ideas as mere superstructure. The postmodern turn in the social sciences resulted in a neglect of connecting the study of identities to issues of class and capitalism. In contrast those who study the economy based on a materialist onto-epistemology frequently either give no or only minor attention to issues concerning culture, communication, the media, or the Internet. Raymond Williams describes a widely diffused way of thinking about the relationship of culture and the economy:

> instead of making cultural history material, [. . .] it was made dependent, secondary, "superstructural": a real of "mere" ideas, beliefs, arts, customs, determined by the basic material history. What matters here is not only the element of reduction; it is the reproduction, in an altered form, of the separation of "culture" from material social life.
>
> *Williams 1977, 19*

I remember countless mainstream social science conferences where Marx and any mentioning of capitalism and class were automatically derided as economistic, deterministic, and reductionist just like I remember countless Marxist and radical conferences, where culture, communication, and the media either played no role at all, played only a minor role, or were treated as a superstructural epiphenomenon that just distracts from "real things" such as discussing the capitalist crisis, the tendency of the profit rate to fall, the new imperialism, capitalism's global economic geography, neoliberalism, financial capital, urban crises and struggles, class theory, left strategies, world money, the state, etc. Almost 40 years after Dallas Smythe (1977) wrote his famous article "Communications: Blindspot of Western Marxism", communications is still a blind spot of Marxism just like Marxism is a blind spot of mainstream social sciences and humanities. I am not saying that the just-mentioned topics are unimportant and that communications is all that matters, but rather that communications stands in a dialectical relationship with all aspects of class, capitalism, space-time, domination, politics etc. and that those who are experts in studying communications therefore should take into account these broader contexts, whereas those who are experts on any other topic should among other dimensions also think about its communicative dimensions. The first happens naturally among critical communication scholars in the field of the political economy of communication, whereas the latter still needs more development and has a long way to go.

Raymond Williams challenged the separation of culture from the popular. He argued that bourgeois thinkers describe culture as the realm of cultivation, art, education, and the intellectuals and separate it off from working-class culture that is denounced as being ordinary, uncultivated, primitive, backward, and massified. "Yet, masses was a new word for mob, and the traditional characteristics of the mob were retained in its significance: gullibility, fickleness, herd-prejudice, lowness of taste and habit. The masses, on this evidence, formed the perpetual threat to culture" (Williams 1958, 298).

One point of this book has been that it has challenged dualistic thought in the contemporary study of culture and society. Such dualisms can be found when cultural and media theorists exclude digital media and software from the realms of the cultural and media industries/cultural labour (chapter 2), discourse analysts study ideology as independent from labour (chapter 3), social theorists separate life from work (chapter 2) or interaction and communication from work (chapter 3) or ideology from labour (chapter 3); when political economists analyse media capitalism's markets, class relations, and commodity structures independent from ideology (chapter 3), social theorists declare information labour, housework, circulation labour, corporate social media use, commercial media labour, service labour, sales labour, and prosumption labour as being unproductive, less productive than other labour, parasitic, value-consuming, or no labour at all (chapter 5), or when digital labour is confined to the realm of online content production and opposed to the physical labour required for producing digital media technologies (chapter 6).

The logical structure that such thought shares is that two categories are opposed and one is morally valued as being better or more important. Such dualisms are culture/technology, information labour/physical labour, digital labour/

industrial and agricultural labour, immaterial/material, circulation/production, consumption/production, superstructure/base, services/industry, communication/work, ideology/labour, unproductive/productive, reproductive/productive, immaterial/material, life/work. All of these dualities have to do with the relationship of culture and the economy. The approach taken in this book challenges dualism, culturalism, and economism by a dialectical cultural materialism that resists the logic of separation, but rather sees culture, ideas, information, knowledge, communication, ideology, circulation, consumption, and reproduction as inherently material, social, and economic. Matter is the totality of the development of systems in space-time. It is a causa sui that organises and produces itself on different organisational levels (Fuchs 2003c, 2008). Society is a specific organisational level of matter and within this level there are subsystems and sublevels that include culture, capitalism, informational capitalism, finance capitalism, etc. Matter is a process totality, its moments are not uniform but rather identical and at the same time different, i.e. they form dialectics, develop in a dialectical manner, and have emergent qualities. Raymond Williams argues in this context that a

> Marxist theory of culture will recognize diversity and complexity, will take account of continuity within change, will allow for chance and certain limited autonomies, but, with these reservations, will take the facts of the economic structure and the consequent social relations as the guiding string on which a culture is woven, and by following which a culture is to be understood.
>
> *Williams 1958, 269*

I have argued in part I of this book that culture is a realm of matter and is not immaterial. The brain is a physical organ inside the human body that produces emergent human ideas. Humans in communication and co-operation processes form culture as the body of emergent collective ideas, norms, values, and meanings that emerge from the synergies of human social relations, i.e. communication. Culture is not separate from the economy, not a superstructure, and not detached from physicality. It is part and parcel of the economy. Cultural goods are use-values that satisfy the human need to inform oneself, to make and create meaning of the world, to communicate, and to create something new. Culture is a specific form of work.

Culture is emergent in two specific ways:

1   Like all matter it develops dialectically and therefore there is the potential and actuality of the emergence of "new meanings and values, new practices, new relationships and kinds of relationships" (Williams 1977, 123).
2   Cultural production is a work process and in this respect identical to all work. It is, however, also specific, different, and emergent in relation to the economy because once produced, ideas, meanings, symbols, and communications take on roles inside and outside the economy and are embedded into social and power relations throughout society.

Information processes are material in that they develop as ideas, communications, and collaborations in space-time. Information is a semiosis of semioses and a dialectic of dialectics, in which individual, social, and societal dimensions develop and processes of cognition, communication, and co-operation interpenetrate, interconnect, interact, and interlock. Information is a cultural process and a cultural dialectic that does not take place outside of the economy. It is a work process that creates thoughts, meanings, and collective meanings and information products that take on relatively autonomous roles within society.

Ideology is a specific communication- and therefore also labour-process. A critical concept of ideology requires a normative distinction between true and false beliefs and practices. It understands ideology as thoughts, practices, ideas, words, concepts, phrases, sentences, texts, belief systems, meanings, representations, arte-facts, institutions, systems, or combinations thereof that represent and justify one group's or individual's power, domination, or exploitation of other groups or individuals by misrepresenting, ignoring, marginalising, excluding, rendering invisible, one-dimensionally presenting, or distorting reality in symbolic representations.

Ideology and labour do not have separate realms in the cultural and economic system, but rather form a dialectic:

1   Ideologies operate in and in relation to the economy in class societies: Wherever there is labour, there is class, and wherever there is class one finds a dominant class trying to defend its interests by making use of ideologies.

2   Ideology does not exist as an independent structure, but needs to be produced and reproduced by ideological workers such as consultants, managers, politicians, intellectuals, nationalists, racist, fascists, demagogues, conservatives, gurus, journalists, celebrities, etc. This does not mean, however, that all politicians, journalists, and intellectuals are ideologues, because ideology tends to be contested. There is the possibility and potential that critical workers produce critiques that challenge ideologies. Critical thought disseminated by critical media, progressive political groups and movements, critical intellectuals and teachers, critical associations, unions, and other institutions is in capitalism often confronted with an inherent resource inequality that poses disadvantages for critical thought production and dissemination in terms of personnel, money, attention, visibility, etc. Democracy and freedom of information are therefore in class societies always limited.

This book has focused on social media as a particular example case that can be studied with the help of cultural-materialist political economy. The concepts and reality of web 2.0 and social media emerged in the aftermath of the 2000 new economy crisis. This crisis was the result of the inherently antagonistic nature of the Internet's financialisation. Venture capital firms work in such a way that they invest large sums of money into start-up companies and thereby require specific roles, influences, and shares in these companies. As investors they compel firms to find commodification strategies in order to be profitable. Often an influx of venture capital results in companies becoming listed on the stock market because they have acquired the necessary capital for doing so. Financialisation can, however, drive up market values on stock markets without actual growth of monetary profits if the expectation is created that a company will become very profitable in the future. Divergences between share values and profits can create financial bubbles that burst when investors lose confidence, which occurs typically upon the failure of specific corporations so that massive doubts and uncertainties are triggered and spread in the financial economy.

eToys.com is an online toy retail website founded in 1997. Based on large venture capital injections by investors such as Highland Entrepreneurs' Fund III Limited Partnership, DynaFund L.P., idealab! Capital Partners, Bessemer Venture Partners, Sequoia Capital Moore Global Investments Ltd., Remington Investment Strategies L.P., and Multi-Strategies Fund, it made an initial public offering (IPO) on the stock market in 1999. It made huge losses of up to US$200 million and had to file for chapter 11 bankruptcy in 2001. It is just one of many Internet corporations that exploded during the 2000 dot.com crisis.

The new economy crisis made financial capitalists reluctant to invest into new Internet companies. Web 2.0 and later social media were ideological strategies to create the impression that the World Wide Web was re-invented and became entirely new so that new business opportunities had emerged. Social media was founded as an ideology aimed at convincing finance capitalists to invest in Internet companies and to attract advertising clients. Parts II and III of this book explored the organisation of social media labour and social media ideology in space-time. Corporate social media's political economy is an economy of time: it extends labour time into leisure time by turning user activity into value-generating labour, uses methods of absolute and relative surplus-value production, and creates the hope that targeted advertising will result in large profits in the future, which can create a distance between actual current profits and fictitious share values that are based on high expectations for future developments.

Despite having never made any profits, but just losses, microblog company Twitter became a publicly traded company in 2013. The Chinese microblog provider Weibo made an IPO in 2014 despite having just like Twitter never made any profits. Since the world economic crisis started in 2008, advertisers increasingly turned towards social media because targeting seems to be a more secure investment than investing in newspaper or broadcasting ads. Advertising-financed media involve many uncertainties, however. It is uncertain if users consider targeted ads as annoying or not, if they look at them at all, if they buy something after they have clicked on ads, if they tend to use ad block software, etc. A new round of financialisation of the Internet has come along with the rise of social media. If due to a trigger event investors lose the confidence that targeting advertising works and start pulling out their capital, the social media bubble could burst and an Internet economy crisis could be the outcome. The capitalist social media economy faces economic and political contradictions: there is an objective contradiction between fictitious share values and actual profits as well as a subjective contradiction between the users and the platforms. As long as the users trust the dominant corporate platforms and continue using them, their digital labour creates value that is potential monetary profit. But once they start turning against the dominant platforms, organise a mass exodus to non-commercial sites, or subvert commercialism by using ad block software, a crisis caused by users' class struggle could result.

Corporate digital and social media are embedded into an international division of digital labour, in which various forms of agricultural, industrial, and informational digital labour conducted in mines, sweatshops, factories, offices, on the move, at home etc. are anonymously networked and form necessary parts and conditions of digital, mobile, and social media's existence. Exploited labour is a core feature of the corporate Internet and social media economy. The political economy of China's social media such as Weibo, Renren, or Baidu is not so different from Western platforms such as Google, Twitter, and Facebook. They use comparable forms of user exploitation, targeted advertising, financialisation, and corporate interlocking with other companies, and they are participating in political control and surveillance. The exploitation of digital labour enables corporate social media in China, the West, and other countries. The Internet surveillance systems operated by the US National Security Agency, UK Government Communications Headquarters, and other secret services are the equivalents of the Chinese government's control of the Internet. Both the Chinese and the Western Internet are economically and politically highly controlled. They are not decentralised information systems, but information systems with highly centralised economic and political power structures.

A business model that uses unpaid digital labour does not simply work, but is rather prone to failures stemming from social media's objective and subjective antagonisms. It needs to be ideologically justified by ideological workers such as social media managers, consultants, the advertising industry, celebratory tech journalists, and intellectuals. Both in China and the West there is an engaging/connecting/sharing ideology that only stresses social media's informational, social, and communicative advantages in order to deflect attention from negative aspects such as user exploitation and surveillance. For the users, it is difficult to see that corporate social media use is a form of labour, value-generation, and exploitation because corporate social media's commodity form comes along with an inverse commodity fetishism that makes the commodity form invisible and hard to grasp and understand for users, and deflects attention from abstract user labour that creates value in class relations by focusing users' attention on the concrete activity of social networking. Also advertising itself contains ideologies that present commodities in a positive way and communicate feel-good meanings to consumers in order to try to make them buy and continuously consume these goods. For capital accumulation to work, these ideologies need to be produced by advertising departments or consultants and to be transported to potential consumers. On corporate social media, users are ideological transport workers who provide targeting data and online attention so that advertising ideologies can be transported to them. They are ideological transport workers.

On February 25, 2014, I attended the 2014 Technology for Marketing & Advertising fair in order to study social media ideologies and the work that produces and diffuses these ideologies. People working in companies' advertising, marketing, and public relations departments make up the main audience at such fairs. The keynote speakers and exhibiting companies therefore aim to create an atmosphere that makes the audience believe in how important it is to invest immediately into the newest advertising-marketing-land and public relations-innovations.

BBC's vice president of social media, Vincent Sider, spread the engaging/connecting/sharing ideology when he said that "fans want to get involved" and that "engagement will determine how much money we will make in the future". Incisive Media's managing director, John Barnes, argued that "data is the key driver" to "sustainable digital growth". He described user data commodification when he spoke of the need to "make the audience the purchase, not the platform". That data is the key driver to sustainable digital growth is marketing language for saying that capital accumulation on social media requires massive surveillance of users.

Facebook's global marketing manager, Catherine Flynn, argued that Facebook bought WhatsApp because it had for a long time not realised that "the world is mobile", whereas "it is never too late to be early". She admitted that Facebook is not really about communication, but is rather one of the world's largest advertising agents: "Facebook is one of the most effective marketing platforms on the planet." She presented large Facebook advertising campaigns by Pimm's, Cadbury Creme Egg, and Coca Cola in order to stress how innovative these campaign strategies were and to argue that other companies should imitate these strategies and therefore invest into ads and PR on Facebook. She withheld the information that getting likes and promoting specific pages is a matter of time, money, and special workforce that engages in a company's social media presence. Marketing idealogy aims to motivate investment into something whose economic benefits and efficiency are uncertain and highly contested.

Social media ideologues such as Sider, Barnes, and Flynn are workers employed by social media platforms, advertising agencies, or consultancies. Their job is to sell advertisements, advertising books, and strategies, and the ideologies that want to make companies, the public, and users believe that social media has advantages for everyone and no disadvantages at all. The most disturbing feature of all these talks on this day was that in over eight hours of ideological talk not a single time were concerns and possible disadvantages mentioned—neither by the ideologues nor by the audience. One key feature of social media ideologues is that they lack any degree of critical self-reflection.

Critical workers can challenge ideological work and the dominant class. Corporate social media are politically and economically highly controlled, which shows the need for alternatives. The struggle for alternatives needs to operate on economic, cultural, and political levels. Alternative, non-commercial, non-profit platforms need to be constructed as economic alternatives. Users need to be won and convinced on the cultural level to join and support alternative social media. Alternative platforms are, however, like all alternative media in capitalism structurally discriminated, which limits democracy, freedom of information and communication, which makes society unfree. Therefore political reforms such as a combination of a progressive media fee, capital taxation, a public sphere cheque, and participatory budgeting are needed in order to strengthen the resource base for alternative social media and other alternative media. Struggles for alternatives can draw inspiration from the class struggles fought by the Chinese working class against the capitalist class. Commons-based social media and public service social media are possible, needed, and necessary.

Let the work of social struggle begin and let's create one, two, many alternative social media projects and movements that struggle against the capitalist domination of communications and the world.

Notes

1 http://www.ilo.org/global/about-the-ilo/newsroom/features/WCMS_120470/lang--de/index.htm (accessed on April 21, 2014).

REFERENCES

Adorno, Theodor W. 2003 [1951]. Cultural criticism and society. In *Can one live after Auschwitz? A philosophical reader*, ed. Rolf Tiedemann, 146–162. Stanford, CA: Stanford University Press.

Adorno, Theodor W. 1988. *Ontologie und Dialektik*. Frankfurt am Main: Suhrkamp.

Adorno, Theodor W. 1968/2003. Late capitalism or industrial society? The fundamental question of the present structure of society. In *Can one live after Auschwitz?* ed. Rolf Tiedemann, 111–125. Stanford, CA: Stanford University Press.

Adorno, Theodor W. 1955. The sociology of knowledge and its consciousness. In *Prisms*, 37–49. Cambridge, MA: MIT Press.

Adorno, Theodor W. 1954. Ideology. In *Aspects of sociology,* ed. Frankfurt Institute for Social Research, 182–205. Boston: Beacon Press.

Agger, Ben. 2011. iTime: Labor and life in a smartphone era. *Time & Society* 20(1): 119–136.

Agger, Ben. 2004. *Speeding up fast capitalism. Cultures, jobs, families, schools, bodies*. Boulder, CO: Paradigm Publishers.

Allen, Anita. 2003. *Why privacy isn't everything: Feminist reflections on personal accountability*. Lanham, MD: Rowman & Littlefield. Althusser, Louis. 1970. Ideology and ideological state apparatuses (Notes towards an investigation). In *Lenin and philosophy and other essays*, 127–185. New York: Monthly Review Press.

Althusser, Louis. 1969. *For Marx*. London: Verso.

Althusser, Louis and Étienne Balibar. 1970. *Reading Capital*. London: NLB.

Amin, Samir. 2013a. China 2013. *Monthly Review* 64 (10): 14–33.

Amin, Samir. 2013b. *The implosion of contemporary capitalism*. New York: Monthly Review Press.

Andrejevic, Mark. 2013. Estranged free labor. In *Digital labor: The Internet as playground and factory*, ed. Trebor Scholz, 149–164. New York: Routledge.

Andrejevic, Mark. 2012. Exploitation in the data mine. In *Internet and surveillance. The challenges of web 2.0 and social media*, ed. Christian Fuchs, Kees Boersma, Anders Albrechtslund, and Marisol Sandoval, 71–88. New York: Routledge.

Andrejevic, Mark. 2007. *iSpy: Surveillance and power in the interactive era.* Lawrence: University Press of Kansas.

Aneesh, A. 2006. *Virtual migration: The programming of globalization.* Durham, NC: Duke University Press.

Anheier, Helmut K., et al., eds. 2010. *International encyclopedia of civil society.* Heidelberg: Springer.

Antunes, Ricardo. 2013. *The meanings of work: Essays on the affirmation and negation of work.* Chicago, IL: Haymarket.

Archer, Margaret S. 2002. Realism and the problem of agency. *Alethia* 5(1): 11–20.

Archer, Margaret S. 1995. *Realist social theory: The morphogenetic approach.* Cambridge: Cambridge University Press.

Arendt, Hannah. 1958. *The human condition.* Chicago, IL: University of Chicago Press. Second edition.

Arrighi, Giovanni. 2007. *Adam Smith in Beijing: Lineages of the twenty-first century.* London: Verso.

Árvay, János. 1994. *The Material Product System (MPS): A retrospective.* In *The accounts of nations*, ed. Z Kenessey, 218–236. Amsterdam: IOS Press.

Arvidsson, Adam. 2010. The ethical economy: New forms of value in the information society? *Organization* 17(5): 637–644.

Arvidsson, Adam. 2005. Brands: A critical perspective. *Journal of Consumer Culture* 5(2): 235–258.

Arvidsson, Adam and Eleanor Colleoni. 2012. Value in informational capitalism and on the Internet. *The Information Society* 28(3): 135–150.

Arvidsson, Adam and Nicolai Petersen. 2013. *The ethical economy. Rebuilding value after the crisis.* New York: Columbia University Press.

Banaji, Jairus. 2011. *Theory as history: Essays on modes of production and exploitation.* Chicago, IL: Haymarket Books.

Baran, Paul A. and Paul M. Sweezy. 1966. *Monopoly capital.* New York: Monthly Review Press.

Bardoel, Jo and Gregory Ferrell Lowe. From public service broadcasting to public service media. In *From public service broadcasting to public service media RIPE@2007*, ed. Gregory Ferrell Lowe and Jo Bardoel, 9–26. Gothenburg: Nordicom.

Barnett, Steven. 2007. Can the public service broadcaster survive? Renewal and compromise in the new BBC charter. In *From public service broadcasting to public service media. RIPE@2007*, ed. Gregory Ferrell Lowe and Jo Bardoel, 87–104. Gothenburg: Nordicom.

Bauman, Zygmunt. 2011. *Culture in a liquid modern world.* Cambridge: Polity Press.

Bauman, Zygmunt. 2005. *Liquid life.* Cambridge: Polity Press.

Bauman, Zygmunt. 2000/2012. *Liquid modernity.* Cambridge: Polity Press.

Bell, Daniel. 1974. *The coming of post-industrial society.* London: Heinemann.

Benhabib, Seyla. 1992. Models of public space: Hannah Arendt, the liberal tradition, and Jürgen Habermas. In *Habermas and the public sphere*, ed. Craig Calhoun, 73–98. Cambridge, MA: MIT Press.

Benjamin, Walter. 1936/1939. The work of art in the age of mechanical reproduction. In *Media and cultural studies: KeyWorks*, ed. Meenakshi Gigi Durham and Douglas M. Kellner, 18–40. Malden, MA: Blackwell.

Benjamin, Walter. 1934. Der Autor als Produzent. In *Medienästhetische Schriften*, 231–247. Frankfurt am Main: Suhrkamp.

Benkler, Yochai. 2006. *The wealth of networks.* New Haven, CT: Yale University Press.

Benner, Chris. 2002. *Work in the new economy: Flexible labor markets in Silicon Valley*. Malden, MA: Blackwell.

Beverungen, Armin, Steffen Böhm and Chris Land. 2015. Free labour, social media, management: Challenging Marxist organization studies. *Organization Studies* (forthcoming).

Bhaskar, Roy. 2008. *Dialectic: The pulse of freedom*. London: Routledge.

Biao, Xiang. 2007. *Global body shopping: An Indian labor system in the information technology industry*. Princeton, NJ: Princeton University Press.

Black, Bob. 1996. *The abolition of work* (1996 revised version). http://www.inspiracy.com/black/abolition/abolitionofwork.html (accessed October 27, 2014).

Bloch, Ernst. 1975. *Experimentum Mundi. Fragen, Kategorien des Herausbringens, Praxis*. Frankfurt am Main: Suhrkamp.

Bloch, Ernst. 1963. *Tübinger Einleitung in die Philosophie*. Frankfurt am Main: Suhrkamp.

Böhm, Steffen, Chris Land, and Armin Beverungen. 2012. The value of Marx: Free labour, rent and "primitive accumulation" in Facebook. Working paper: http://www.academia.edu/1571230/The_Value_of_Marx_Free_Labour_Rent_and_Primitive_Accumulation_in_Facebook (accessed October 27, 2014).

Bolaño, César and Eloy S. Vieira. 2014. The political economy of the Internet: Social networking sites and a reply to Fuchs. *Television and New Media*, first published on April 2, 2014 as doi:10.1177/1527476414527137.

Boltanski, Luc and Ève Chiapello. 2005. *The new spirit of capitalism*. London: Verso.

Boltanski, Luc and Axel Honneth. 2009. Soziologie der Kritik oder Kritische Theorie? In *Was ist Kritik?*, ed. Rahel Jaeggi and Tilo Wesche, 81–114. Frankfurt am Main: Suhrkamp.

Bourdieu, Pierre. 1986a. *Distinction: A social critique of the judgement of taste*. New York: Routledge.

Bourdieu, Pierre. 1986b. The (three) forms of capital. In *Handbook of Theory and Research in the Sociology of Education*, ed. John G. Richardson, 241–258. New York: Greenwood Press.

Bourdieu, Pierre. 1977. *Outline of a theory of practice*. Cambridge: Cambridge University Press.

Brecht, Bertolt. 1932. The radio as an apparatus of communications. In *Brecht on theatre*, ed. John Willett, 51–53. New York: Hill and Wang.

Brevini, Benedetta. 2013. *Public service broadcasting online: A comparative European policy study of PSB 2.0*. Basingstoke: Palgrave Macmillan.

Bruns, Axel. 2008. *Blogs, Wikipedia, Second Life and beyond: From production to produsage*. New York: Peter Lang.

Burgess, Jean and Joshua Green. 2009. *YouTube*. Cambridge: Polity Press.

Burston, Jonathan, Nick Dyer-Witheford and Alison Hearn, eds. 2010. Digital labour: Workers, authors, citizens. Special issue. *Ephemera* 10 (3/4): 214–539.

Caffentzis, George. 2013. *In letters of blood and fire*. Oakland, CA: PM Press.

Calhoun, Craig. 1992. Introduction: Habermas and the public sphere. In *Habermas and the public sphere*, ed. Craig Calhoun, 1–48. Cambridge, MA: MIT Press.

Caporaso, James A. and David P. Levine. 1992. *Theories of political economy*. Cambridge: Cambridge University Press.

Caraway, Brett. 2011. Audience labor in the new media environment: A Marxian revisiting of the audience commodity. *Media, Culture & Society* 33 (5): 693–708.

Carchedi, Guglielmo. 2014. Old wine, new bottles and the Internet. *Work Organisation, Labour & Globalisation* 8 (1): 69–87.

Carchedi, Guglielmo. 2012. *Behind the crisis: Marx's dialectics of value and knowledge*. Chicago, IL: Haymarket.

Carnoy, Martin, Manuel Castells, and Chris Benner. 1997. Labour markets and employment practices in the age of flexibility: A case study of Silicon Valley. *International Labour Review* 136(1): 27–48.

Castells, Manuel. 2012. *Networks of outrage and hope: Social movements in the Internet age.* Cambridge: Polity Press.

Castells, Manuel. 2009. *Communication power.* Oxford: Oxford University Press.

Castells, Manuel. 1996. *The rise of the network society.* Cambridge, MA: Blackwell.

Castree, Noel. 2009. The spatio-temporality of capitalism. *Time & Society* 18(1): 26–61.

Caves, Richard E. 2000. *Creative industries.* Cambridge, MA: Harvard University Press.

Chakravartty, Paula. 2004. Telecom, national development and the Indian state: A postcolonial critique. *Media, Culture & Society* 26(2): 227–249.

Chase-Dunn, Christopher. 2010. Adam Smith in Beijing: A world-systems perspective. *Historical Materialism* 18(1): 39–51.

China Labour Bulletin. 2014. Searching for the union. The workers' movement in China 2011–13. http://www.clb.org.hk/en/sites/default/files/File/research_reports/searching%20for%20the%20union%201.pdf.

Churchill, Pamela. 2013. Mao Zedong, the masses, and the art of calligraphy. Bug-character posters during the cultural revolution. *Cujah* 9(3). http://cujah.org/past-volumes/volume-ix/essay-3-volume-9/ (accessed October 27, 2014).

Cleaver, Harry. 2011. Work refusal and self-organisation. In *Life without money. Building fair and sustainable economies,* ed. Anitra Nelson and Frans Timmerman, 48–68. London: Pluto Press.

Cleaver, Harry. 2003. Marxian categories, the crisis of capital and the constitution of subjectivity today. In *Revolutionary writing. Common sense essays in post-political politics,* ed. Werner Bonefeld, 39–72. New York: Autonomedia.

Cleaver, Harry. 2002. Work is still the central issue! New words for new worlds. In *The labour debate. An investigation into the theory and reality of capitalist work,* ed. Ana Dienrstein and Michael Leary, 135–148. Hampshire: Ashgate.

Cleaver, Harry. 2000. *Reading Capital politically.* Edinburgh: AK Press.

Cleaver, Harry. 1992. The inversion of class perspective in Marxian theory: From valorisation to self-valorisation. In *Open Marxism. Volume II: Theory and practice,* ed. Werner Bonefeld, Richard Gunn and Kosmas Psychopedis, 106–144. London: Pluto Press.

CNN Global 500. 2012. Top companies. Biggest employers. http://money.cnn.com/magazines/fortune/global500/2012/performers/companies/biggest/ (accessed October 27, 2014).

Collins, Richard. 2011. Public value, the BBC and Humpty Dumpty words. In *Exporting the public value test. The regulation of public broadcasters' new media services across Europe,* ed. Karen Donders and Hallvard Moe, 29–37. Gothenburg: Nordicom.

Collins, Richard. 2010. From public service broadcasting to public service communication. In *RIPE@2009: The public in public service media,* ed. Gregory Ferrell Lowe, 53–69. Gothenburg: Nordicom.

Commander, Simon, Rupa Chanda, Mari Kangasniemi, and L. Alan Winters. 2008. The consequences of globalisation: India's software industry and cross-border labour mobility. *The World Economy* 31(2): 187–211.

Committee of Ministers. 2007. Recommendation CM/Rec(2007)3 of the Committee of Ministers to member states on the remit of public service media in the information society. https://wcd.coe.int/ViewDoc.jsp?id=1089759 (accessed October 27, 2014).

Comor, Edward. 2014. Value, the audience commodity, and digital prosumption: A plea for precision. In *The audience commodity in a digital age. Revisiting a critical theory of commercial media,* ed. Lee McGuigan and Vincent Manzerolle, 245–265. New York: Peter Lang.

Comor, Edward. 2011. Contextualizing and critiquing the fantastic prosumer: Power, alienation and hegemony. *Critical Sociology* 37(3): 309–327.

Comscore. 2012. *The power of Like2: How social marketing works*. White paper. http://www.comscore.com/ger/Insights/Presentations_and_Whitepapers/2012/The_Power_of_Like_2_How_Social_Marketing_Works (accessed on April 9, 2014).

Couldry, Nick. 2010. *Why voice matters: Culture and politics after neoliberalism*. London: Sage.

Cunningham, Stuart. 2005. Creative enterprises. In *Creative industries*, ed. John Hartley, 282–298. Malden: Blackwell.

Curran, James. 1991. Rethinking the media as a public sphere. In *Communication and citizenship: Journalism and the public sphere*, ed. Peter Dahlgren and Colin Sparks, 27–57. London: Routledge.

Curran, James and Jean Seaton. 2010. *Power without responsibility: Press, broadcasting and the Internet in Britain*. London: Routledge. Seventh edition.

D'Costa, Anthony. 2002. Uneven and combined development: Understanding India's software exports. *World Development* 31(1): 211–226.

D'Mello, Marisa and Sundeep Sahay. 2007. "I am a kind of nomad where I have to go places and places" . . . Understanding mobility, place and identity in global software work from India. *Information and Organization* 17(3): 162–192.

Dahlgren, Peter. 1995. *Television and the public sphere: Citizenship, democracy and the media*. London: Sage.

Dalla Costa, Mariarosa and Selma James. 1972. *The power of women and the subversion of community*. Bristol: Falling Wall Press.

Deuze, Mark. 2007. *Media work*. Cambridge: Polity.

Donders, Karen. 2011. The public value test: A reasoned response or panic reaction? In *Exporting the public value test. The regulation of public broadcasters' new media services across Europe*, ed. Karen Donders and Hallvard Moe, 29–37. Gothenburg: Nordicom.

Dossani, Rafiq and Martin Kenney. 2007. The next wave of globalization: Relocating service provision to India. *World Development* 35(5): 772–791.

Doyle, Gillian. 2013. *Understanding media economics*. London: Sage. Second edition.

du Gay, Paul, Stuart Hall, Linda Janes, Hugh Mackay and Keith Negus. 1997. *Doing cultural studies: The story of the Sony Walkman*. London: Sage.

Dyer-Witheford, Nick and Greig de Peuter. 2009. *Games of empire: Global capitalism and video games*. Minneapolis, MN: University of Minnesota Press.

Eagleton, Terry. 2000. *The idea of culture*. Oxford: Blackwell.

Eagleton, Terry. 1991. *Ideology: An introduction*. London: Verso.

Eagleton, Terry. 1989a. Introduction. In *Raymond Williams: Critical perspectives*, ed. Terry Eagleton, 1–11. Cambridge: Polity Press.

Eagleton, Terry. 1989b. Base and superstructure in Raymond Williams. In *Raymond Williams: Critical perspectives*, ed. Terry Eagleton, 165–175. Cambridge: Polity Press.

Ehrenberg, John. 1999. *Civil society. The critical history of an idea*. New York: New York University Press.

Eichstaedt, Peter. 2011. *Consuming the Congo: War and conflict minerals in the world's deadliest place*. Chicago, IL: Lawrence Hill Books.

Eisenstein, Zillah. 1979. Developing a theory of capitalist patriarchy and socialist feminism. In *Capitalist patriarchy and the case for socialist feminism*, ed. Zillah R. Eisenstein, 5–40. New York: Monthly Review Press.

Eley, Geoff. 1992. Nations, public and political cultures: Placing Habermas in the nineteenth century. In *Habermas and the public sphere*, ed. Craig Calhoun, 289–339. Cambridge, MA: MIT Press.

Endnotes Collective. 2013. The logic of gender: On the separation of spheres and the process of abjection. *Endnotes* 3: http://endnotes.org.uk/en/endnotes-the-logic-of-gender (accessed October 27, 2014).

Engels, Friedrich. 1892. Preface to the English edition of "The condition of the working class in England". In *Marx Engels Collected Works (MECW) Volume 27*, 257-269. London: Lawrence & Wishart.

Engels, Friedrich. 1886a. Engels to August Bebel in Plauen near Dresden. August 18, 1886. In *Marx Engels Collected Works (MECW) Volume 47*, 468-471. London: Lawrence & Wishart.

Engels, Friedrich. 1886b. Engels to Laura Lafargue in Paris. September 13, 1886. In *Marx Engels Collected Works (MECW) Volume 47*, 482-485. London: Lawrence & Wishart.

Engels, Friedrich. 1884. The origin of the family, private property and the state. In *Marx Engels Collected Works (MECW) Volume 26*, 129-276. London: Lawrence & Wishart.

Enzensberger, Hans Magnus. 1970 Baukasten zu einer Theorie der Medien. In *Baukasten zu einer Theorie der Medien. Kritische Diskurse zur Pressefreiheit*, 97–132. München: Fischer.

European Commission. 2009. Communication from the Commission on the application of state aid rules to public service broadcasting. http://eur-lex.europa.eu/LexUriServ/LexUriServ.do?uri=CELEX:52009XC1027%2801%29:EN:NOT (accessed October 27, 2014).

Fairclough, Norman. 2010. *Critical discourse analysis: The critical study of language.* Harlow: Pearson Education.

Fairclough, Norman. 1995. *Media discourse.* London: Hodder Education.

Fair Labour Association. 2012. *Independent investigation of Apple supplier, Foxconn.* http://www.fairlabor.org/sites/default/files/documents/reports/foxconn_investigation_report.pdf (accessed October 27, 2014).

Federici, Silvia. 2012. *Revolution at point zero: Housework, reproduction, and feminist struggle.* Oakland, CA: PM Press.

Fine, Ben, Heesang Jeon, and Gong H. Gimm. 2010. Value is as value does: Twixt knowledge and the world economy. *Capital & Class* 34(1): 69–83.

Fine, Ben and Alfredo Saad-Filho. 2010. *Marx's "Capital".* London: Pluto Press. Fifth edition.

Finnwatch. 2007. *Connecting components, dividing communities: The production of consumer electronics in the DR Congo and Indonesia.* makeITfair-Report: http://germanwatch.org/corp/it-tin.pdf (accessed October 27, 2014).

Finnwatch and Swedwatch. 2010. *Voices from the inside: Local views on mining reform in Eastern DRC.* makeITfair Report: http://somo.nl/publications-en/Publication_3586/at_download/fullfile (accessed October 27, 2014).

Foley, Duncan K. 2013. Rethinking financial capitalism and the "information" economy. *Review of Radical Political Economics* 45(3): 257–268.

Forbes 2000. 2014. *The world's biggest companies 2014.* http://www.forbes.com/global2000 (accessed October 27, 2014).

Fortunati, Leopoldina. 1995. *The arcane of reproduction: Housework, prostitution, labor and capital.* New York: Autonomedia.

Foster, John Bellamy and Robert W. McChesney. 2012. The global stagnation and China. *Monthly Review* 63 (9): 1–28.

Frankfurt, Harry G. 2005. *On bullshit.* Princeton, NJ: Princeton University Press.

Fraser, Nancy. 1992. Rethinking the Public Sphere. In *Habermas and the public sphere*, ed. Craig Calhoun, 109–142. Cambridge, MA: MIT Press.

Free the Slaves. 2011. *The Congo report. Slavery in conflict minerals.* http://www.freetheslaves.net/Document.Doc?id=243 (accessed October 27, 2014).

Freeman, Alan. 1998. Time, the value of money and the quantification of value. MPRA Paper No. 2217. http://mpra.ub.uni-muenchen.de/2217/ (accessed October 27, 2014).

Fröbel, Folker, Jürgen Heinrichs, and Otto Kreye. 1981. *The new international division of labour*. Cambridge: Cambridge University Press.

Fuchs, Christian. 2014a. *Digital labour and Karl Marx*. New York: Routledge.

Fuchs, Christian. 2014b. *Social media: A critical introduction*. London: Sage.

Fuchs, Christian. 2014c. Theorising and analysing digital labour: From global value chains to modes of production. *The Political Economy of Communication* 2(1): 3–27.

Fuchs, Christian. 2013. The Anonymous movement in the context of liberalism and socialism. *Interface: A Journal for and about Social Movements* 5(2): 345–376.

Fuchs, Christian. 2012a. Dallas Smythe today—the audience commodity, the digital labour debate, Marxist Political Economy and Critical Theory: Prolegomena to a digital labour theory of value. *tripleC: Communication, Capitalism & Critique* 10(2): 692–740.

Fuchs, Christian. 2012b. With or without Marx? With or without capitalism? A rejoinder to Adam Arvidsson and Eleanor Colleoni. *tripleC: Communication, Capitalism & Critique* 10(2): 633–645.

Fuchs, Christian. 2011a. *Foundations of critical media and information studies*. London: Routledge.

Fuchs, Christian. 2011b. Towards an alternative concept of privacy. *Journal of Information, Communication and Ethics in Society* 9(4): 220–237.

Fuchs, Christian. 2010. Labor in informational capitalism and on the Internet. *The Information Society* 26(3): 179–196.

Fuchs, Christian. 2009. A contribution to the critique of the political economy of transnational informational capitalism. *Rethinking Marxism* 21(3): 387–402.

Fuchs, Christian. 2008. *Internet and society: Social theory in the information age*. New York: Routledge.

Fuchs, Christian. 2003a. Some implications of Pierre Bourdieu's works for a theory of social self-organization. *European Journal of Social Theory* 6(4): 387–408.

Fuchs, Christian. 2003b. Structuration theory and self-organization. *Systemic Practice and Action Research* 16(2): 133–167.

Fuchs, Christian. 2003c. The self-organization of matter. *Nature, Society, and Thought* 16(3): 281–313.

Fuchs, Christian and Marisol Sandoval. 2014. Digital workers of the world unite! A framework for critically theorising and analysing digital labour. *tripleC: Communication, Capitalism & Critique* 12(2): 486-563.

Fuchs, Christian and Wolfgang Hofkirchner. 2009. Autopoiesis and critical social systems theory. In *Autopoiesis in organization theory and practice*, ed. Rodrigo Magalhaes and Ron Sanchez, 111–129. Bingley: Emerald.

Fuchs, Christian and Wolfgang Hofkirchner. 2005. Self-organization, knowledge, and responsibility. *Kybernetes* 34(1–2): 241–260.

Fuchs, Christian and Sebastian Sevignani. 2013. What is digital labour? What is digital work? What's their difference? And why do these questions matter for understanding social media? *tripleC: Communication, Capitalism & Critique* 11(2): 237–293.

Fuchs, Christian and Daniel Trottier. 2013. The Internet as surveilled workplayplace and factory. In *European data protection: Coming of age*, ed. Serge Gutwirth, Ronald Leenes, Paul De Hert, and Yves Poullet, 33–57. Dordrecht: Springer.

Furhoff, Lars. 1973. Some reflections on newspaper concentration. *Scandinavian Economic History Review* 21(1): 1–27.

Galtung, Johan. 1990. Cultural violence. *Journal of Peace Research* 27(3): 291–305.

Garnham, Nicholas. 2000. *Emancipation, the media, and modernity*. Oxford: Oxford University Press.

Garnham, Nicholas. 1992. The media and the public sphere. In *Habermas and the public sphere*, ed. Craig Calhoun, 359–376. Cambridge, MA: MIT Press.

Garnham, Nicholas. 1990. *Capitalism and communication: Global culture and the economics of information*. London: Sage.

Garnham, Nicholas. 1988. Raymond Williams, 1921–1988: A cultural analyst, a distinctive tradition. *Journal of Communication* 38(4): 123–131.

Garnham, Nicholas. 1979. Contribution to a political economy of mass communication. *Media, Culture & Society* 1(2): 123–146.

Ghonim, Wael. 2012. *Revolution 2.0. The power of the people is greater than the people in power*. New York: Houghton Mifflin Harcourt.

Giddens, Anthony. 1990. *The consequences of modernity*. Stanford, CA: Stanford University Press.

Giddens, Anthony. 1984. *The constitution of society: Outline of the theory of structuration*. Cambridge: Polity Press.

Gill, Rosalind. 2006. *Technobohemians or the new cybertariat?* Amsterdam: Institute of Network Cultures.

Gill, Rosalind. 2002. Cool, creative and egalitarian? Exploring gender in project-based new media work in Europe. *Information, Communication & Society* 5 (1): 70–89.

Glass, Robert L. 2006. *Software creativity 2.0*. Atlanta, GA: developer.* Books.

Global Slavery Index. 2013. *The global slavery index 2013*. Dalkeith (Western Australia): Walk Free Foundation.

Goodwin, Peter. 2012. High noon. The BBC meets "the West's most daring government". In *RIPE@2011: Regaining the initiative for public service media*, ed. Gregory Ferrell Lowe and Jeanette Steemers, 63–76. Gothenburg: Nordicom.

Gootnick, David. 2008. *Testimony before the Congressional Human Rights Caucus: The Democratic Republic of Congo*. March 6, 2008. Washington, DC: United States Government Accountability Office.

Gorz, André. 1982. *Farewell to the working class. An essay on post-industrial socialism*. London: Pluto Press.

Government of India, Ministry of Finance. 2011. *Economic survey 2009–2010*. http://indiabudget.nic.in/es2009–10/chapt2010/chapter.zip (accessed October 27, 2014).

Gramsci, Antonio. 1988. The Antonio Gramsci reader. In *Selected writings 1916–1935*, ed. David Forgacs. London: Lawrence and Wishart.

Gramsci, Antonio. 1971. *Selections from the prison notebooks*. New York: International Publishers.

Habermas, Jürgen. 2013. Demokratie oder Kapitalismus? Vom Elend der nationalstaatlichen Fragmentierung in einer kapitalistisch integrierten Weltgesellschaft. *Blätter für deutsche und internationale Politik* 5 (2013): 71–79. [English translation, online: http://www.resetdoc.org/story/00000022337 (accessed October 27, 2014)].

Habermas, Jürgen. 2011. *Zur Verfassung Europas. Ein Essay*. Frankfurt am Main: Suhrkamp.

Habermas, Jürgen. 2008. *Ach, Europa*. Frankfurt am Main: Suhrkamp.

Habermas, Jürgen. 2006. Political communication in media society. *Communication Theory* 16 (4): 411–426.

Habermas, Jürgen. 1996. *Between facts and norms. Contributions to a discourse theory of law and democracy*. Cambridge, MA: MIT Press.

Habermas, Jürgen. 1992. Further reflections on the public sphere and concluding remarks. In *Habermas and the Public Sphere*, ed. Craig Calhoun, 421–479. Cambridge, MA: MIT Press.

Habermas, Jürgen. 1989a. The public sphere: an encyclopedia article. In *Critical theory and society. A reader*, ed. Stephen E. Bronner and Douglas Kellner, 136–142. New York: Routledge.

Habermas, Jürgen. 1989b. *The structural transformation of the public sphere*. Cambridge, MA: MIT Press.

Habermas, Jürgen. 1987. *The theory of communicative action. Volume 2*. Boston, MA: Beacon Press.

Habermas, Jürgen. 1984. *The theory of communicative action. Volume 1*. Boston, MA: Beacon Press.

Habermas, Jürgen. 1976. *Zur Rekonstruktion des Historischen Materialismus*. Frankfurt am Main: Suhrkamp.

Habermas, Jürgen. 1969. *Technik und Wissenschaft als "Ideologie"*. Frankfurt am Main: Suhrkamp.

Habermas, Jürgen. 1968. Arbeit und Interaktion. Bemerkungen zu Hegels Jensener "Philosophie des Geisters". In *Technik und Wissenschaft als "Ideologie"*, 9–47. Frankfurt am Main: Suhrkamp.

Hall, Stuart, ed. 1997. *Representation: Cultural representations and signifying practices*. Los Angeles, CA: Sage.

Hall, Stuart. 1974/2003. Marx's notes on method: A "reading" of the "1857 introduction". *Cultural Studies* 17 (2): 113–149.

Hampton, Paul. 2008. *William Morris: Romantic or revolutionary?* http://www.workersliberty.org/story/2008/12/04/william-morris-romantic-or-revolutionary (accessed October 27, 2014).

Hardt, Michael and Antonio Negri. 2009. *Commonwealth*. Cambridge, MA: Belknap Press.

Hardy, Jonathan. 2014. *Critical political economy of the media: An introduction*. London: Routledge.

Hart-Landsberg, Martin. 2010. The U.S. economy and China: Capitalism, class, and crisis. *Monthly Review* 61 (9): 14–31.

Hartley, John. 2005. Creative industries. In *Creative industries*, 62–76, ed. John Hartley. Malden: Blackwell.

Harvey, David. 2014. *Seventeen contradictions and the end of capitalism*. London: Profile Books.

Harvey, David. 2012. *Rebel cities: From the right to the city to the urban revolution*. London:Verso.

Harvey, David. 2010. *The enigma of capital and the crises of capital*. London: Profile Books.

Harvey, David. 2007. *A brief history of neoliberalism*. Oxford: Oxford University Press.

Harvey, David. 2006. *Limits to capital*. London: Verso.

Harvey, David. 2005. *The new imperialism*. Oxford: Oxford University Press.

Harvey, David. 2001. *Spaces of capital: Towards a critical geography*. New York: Routledge.

Harvey, David. 1990. *The condition of postmodernity*. Cambridge, MA: Blackwell.

Harvie, David. 2005. All labour produces value for capital and we struggle against value. *The Commoner* 10: 132–171.

Hassan, Robert. 2012. *The age of distraction*. New Brunswick, NJ: Transaction Publishers.

Hassan, Robert. 2003. Network time and the new knowledge epoch. *Time & Society* 12 (2/3): 225–241.

Haug, Wolfgang Fritz. 1986. *Critique of commodity aesthetics*. Cambridge: Polity Press.

Hayes, Ben. 2012. The surveillance-industrial complex. In *Routledge handbook of surveillance studies*, ed. Kirstie Ball, Kevin D. Haggerty, and David Lyon, 167–175. Abingdon: Routledge.

Hegel, Georg Wilhelm Friedrich. 1830. *The encyclopaedia logic (with the Zusätze)*, trans. Theodore F. Geraets, Wallis A. Suchting, and Henry S. Harris. Indianapolis, IN: Hackett.

Hegel, Georg Wilhelm Friedrich. 1821. *Grundlinien der Philosophie des Rechts oder Naturrecht und Staatswissenschaft im Grundrisse*. Frankfurt am Main: Suhrkamp.

Hegel, Georg Wilhelm Friedrich. 1817. *Encyclopaedia of the philosophical sciences. Part 2: Philosophy of nature*. http://www.marxists.org/reference/archive/hegel/works/na/naconten.htm (accessed October 27, 2014).

Hegel, Georg Wilhelm Friedrich. 1812. *The science of logic,* trans. and ed. George Di Giovanni. Cambridge: Cambridge University Press.

Hegel, Georg Wilhelm Friedrich. 1805/1806. *Jenaer Systementwürfe III.* Hamburg: Felix Meiner Verlag.

Hegel, Georg Wilhelm Friedrich. 1803/1804. *Jenaer Systementwürfe I.* Hamburg: Felix Meiner Verlag.

Hesmondhalgh, David. 2013. *The cultural industries.* London: Sage. Third edition.

Hesmondhalgh, David and Sarah Baker. 2011. *Creative labour: Media work in three cultural industries.* London: Routledge.

Hofkirchner, Wolfgang. 2013. *Emergent information: A Unified Theory of Information framework.* Singapore: World Scientific.

Holloway, John. 1995. From scream of refusal to scream of power: The centrality of work. In *Open Marxism, Volume III: Emancipating Marx,* ed. Werner Bonefeld, Richard Gunn, John Holloway, and Kosmas Psychopedis, 155–181. London: Pluto Press.

Holman, David, Rosemary Batt, and Ursula Holtgrewe. 2007. *The global call centre report: International perspectives on management and employment.* http://www.ilr.cornell.edu/globalcallcenter/upload/GCC-Intl-Rept-UK-Version.pdf (accessed October 27, 2014).

Holz, Hans Heinz. 2005. *Weltentwurf und Reflexion: Versuch einer Grundlegung der Dialektik.* Stuttgart: J.B. Metzler.

Holzkamp, Klaus. 1985. *Grundlegung der Psychologie.* Frankfurt am Main: Campus.

Holzkamp-Osterkamp, Ute. 1983. Ideologismus als Konsequenz des Ökonomismus. Zur Kritik am Projekt Ideologietheorie (PIT). *Forum Kritische Psychologie* 11: 7–23.

Hong, Yu. 2011. *Labor, class formation, and China's informationized policy and economic development.* Lanham, MD: Rowman & Littlefield.

Hoofnagle, Chris Jay, Jennifer M. Urban, and Su Li. 2012. Privacy and modern advertising: Most US Internet users want 'Do Not Track' to stop collection of data about their online activities. http://papers.ssrn.com/sol3/papers.cfm?abstract_id=2152135 (accessed October 27, 2014).

Hope, Wayne. 2011. Crisis of temporalities: Global capitalism after the 2007–08 financial collapse. *Time & Society* 20 (1): 94–118.

Horkheimer, Max. 1930. A new concept of ideology? In *Between philosophy and social science,* 129–150. Cambridge, MA: MIT Press.

Horkheimer, Max and Theodor W. Adorno. 1944/2002. *Dialectic of enlightenment: Philosophical fragments.* Stanford, CA: Stanford University Press.

Howe, Jeff. 2008. *Crowdsourcing: Why the power of the crowd is driving the future of business.* New York: Three Rivers Press.

Hsiao, Hsin-Huang Michael and Cheng-yi Lin, eds. 2009. *Rise of China.* Abingdon: Routledge.

Hu, Zhengrong and Deqiang Ji. 2014. Retrospection, prospection and the pursuit of an integrated approach for China's communication and journalism studies. *Javnost – The Public* 20(4): 5–16.

Huang, Yasheng. 2008. *Capitalism with Chinese characteristics: Entrepreneurship and the state.* Cambridge: Cambridge University Press.

Hume, David. 1739. *A treatise of human nature.* Oxford: Oxford University Press.

Hülsmann, Michael and Nicole Pfeffermann, ed. 2011. *Strategies and communications for innovations: An integrative management view for companies and networks.* Heidelberg: Springer.

Hund, Wulf D. 1976. *Ware Nachricht und Informationsfetisch. Zur Theorie der gesellschaftlichen Kommunikation.* Darmstadt: Luchterhand.

Hund, Wulf D. and Bärbel Kirchhoff-Hund. 1980. *Soziologie der Kommunikation. Arbeitsbuch zu Struktur und Funktion der Medien. Grundbegriffe und exemplarische Analysen.* Hamburg: Rowohlt.

Hung, Ho-fung. 2012. Sixnomania: global crisis, China's crisis. *Socialist Register* 48: 217–234.

Hung, Ho-fung, ed. 2009. *China and the transformation of global capitalism*. Baltimore, MD: Johns Hopkins University Press.

Huws, Ursula. 2014. The underpinnings of class in the digital age: Living, labour and value. *Socialist Register* 50: 80–107.

Huws, Ursula. 2012. The reproduction of difference: Gender and the division of labour. *Work Organisation, Labour & Globalisation* 6 (1): 1–10.

Huws, Ursula. 2008. Break or weld? Trade union responses to global value chain restructuring. *Work Organisation, Labour and Globalisation* 2 (1): 1–10.

Huws, Ursula. 2003. *The making of a cybertariat: Virtual work in a real world*. New York: Monthly Review Press.

Huws, Ursula. 1999. Material world: The myth of the weightless economy. *Socialist Register* 35: 29–55.

Huws, Ursula and Simone Dahlmann. 2010. Global restructuring of value chains and class issues. In *Interrogating the new economy: Restructuring work in the 21st century*, ed. Norene J. Pupo and Mark P. Thomas, 65–91. Toronto: University of Toronto Press.

ICSSR (Indian Council of Social Science Research). 2012. *Structural changes and employment in the Indian economy*. http://isid.org.in/pdf/WP1202.pdf (accessed October 27, 2014).

Ilavarasan, Vigneswara. 2007. Is Indian software workforce a case of uneven and combined development? *Equal Opportunities International* 26 (8): 802–822.

ILO (International Labour Organization). 2013. *Global wage report 2012/13. Wages and equitable growth*. Geneva: International Labour Office.

ILO (International Labour Organization). 2012. *Global employment trends for women 2012*. Geneva: International Labour Organization.

Iosifides, Petros. 2010. Pluralism and funding of public service broadcasting in Europe. In *Reinventing public service communication. European broadcasters and beyond*, ed. Petros Iosifides, 9–22. Basingstoke: Palgrave Macmillan.

Jakubowicz, Karol. 2007. Public service broadcasting in the 21st century. In *From public service broadcasting to public service media. RIPE@2007*, ed. Gregory Ferrell Lowe and Jo Bardoel, 29–49. Gothenburg: Nordicom.

Jameson, Frederic. 1988. On Negt and Kluge. *October* 46: 151–177.

Jenkins, Henry. 2008. *Convergence culture*. New York: New York University Press.

Jenkins, Henry, Ravi Purushotma, Margaret Weigel, Katie Clinton, and Alice J. Robison. 2009. *Confronting the challenges of participatory culture*. Chicago, IL: MacArthur Foundation.

Jeon, Heesang. 2010. Cognitive capitalism or cognition in capitalism? A critique of cognitive capitalism theory. *Spectrum* 2 (3): 90–117.

Jessop, Bob and Stijn Oosterlynck. 2008. Cultural political economy: On making the cultural turn without falling into soft economic sociology. *Geoforum* 39(3): 1155–1169.

Jhally, Sut. 2006. *The spectacle of accumulation: Essays in culture, media, & politics*. New York: Peter Lang.

Jhally, Sut. 1987. *The codes of advertising*. New York: Routledge.

Jin, Dal Yong. 2013. The construction of platform imperialism in the globalization era. *tripleC: Communication, Capitalism & Critique* 11(1): 145–172.

Jobs, Steve. 2010. Interview at the 2010 D8 conference. http://www.youtube.com/watch?v=KEQEV6r2l2c (accessed October 27, 2014).

Jupp, Victor. 2006. Documents and critical research. In *Data collection and analysis*, ed. Roger Sapsford and Victor Jupp, 272–290. London: Sage.

Kant, Immanuel. 1785. *Groundworks of the metaphysics of morals: A German-English edition.* Cambridge: Cambridge University Press.

Kant, Immanuel. 1784. An answer to the question: What is Enlightenment? In *The idea of the public sphere. A reader,* ed. Jostein Gripsrud, Hallvard Moe, Anders Molander, and Graham Murdock, 3–8. Lanham, MD: Rowman & Littlefield.

Kant, Immanuel. 1781/1922. *Critique of pure reason.* New York: Macmillan. Revised second edition.

Katz, Katarina. 1997. Gender, wages and discrimination in the USSR: A study of a Russian industrial town. *Cambridge Journal of Economics* 21 (1): 431–452.

Keane, John. 2010. Civil society: Definitions and approaches. In *International encyclopedia of civil society,* ed. Helmut K. Anheier et al., 461–464. Heidelberg: Springer.

Kenny, Michael. 2007. Civil society. In *Encyclopaedia of governance,* ed. Mark Bevir, 91–95. London: Sage.

Kitching, John and David Smallbone. 2012. *UK freelance workforce, 2011.* Kingston upon Thames: Kingston University.

Kovisto, Juha and Esa Valiverronen. 1996. The resurgence of the critical theories of public sphere. *Journal of Communication Inquiry* 20 (2): 18–36.

Kreilinger, Verena. 2014. Research design & data analysis, presentation, and interpretation: Part two. *The Internet & Surveillance Research Paper Series #14.* Vienna: UTI Research Group.

Kücklich, Julian. 2005. Precarious playbour. *Fibreculture Journal* 5, http://five.fibreculture-journal.org/fcj-025-precarious-playbour-modders-and-the-digital-games-industry/ (accessed on February 13, 2013).

Land, Chris and Steffen Böhm. 2012. They are exploiting us! Why we all work for Facebook for free. http://snuproject.wordpress.com/2012/02/23/they-are-exploiting-us-why-we-all-work-for-facebook-for-free-via-p2p-foundation/ (accessed October 27, 2014).

Lash, Scott and John Urry. 1994. *Economies of signs & space.* London: Sage.

Lebowitz, Michael A. 1986. Too many blindspots on the media. *Studies in Political Economy* 21: 165–173.

Lefebvre, Henri. 2004. *Rhythmanalysis.* London: Continuum.

Lenin, Vladimir Ilyich. 1920. *Preface to the French and German editions of "Imperialism, the highest stage of capitalism".* http://www.marxists.org/archive/lenin/works/1916/imp-hsc/pref02.htm#fwV22E081 (accessed October 27, 2014).

Lenin, Vladimir Ilyich. 1917a. Imperialism, the highest stage of capitalism. In *Essential works of Lenin,* ed. Henry M. Christman, 177–270. New York: Dover.

Lenin, Vladimir I. 1917b. State and revolution. In *Essential Works of Lenin,* ed. Henry M. Christman, 271–364. New York: Dover.

Li, Henry Siling. 2009. The turn to the self: From "big character posters" to YouTube videos. *Chinese Journal of Communication* 2 (1): 50–60.

Li, Minqi. 2008a. An age of transition: The United States, China, peak oil, and the demise of neoliberalism. *Monthly Review* 59 (11): 20–34.

Li, Minqi. 2008b. *The rise of China and the demise of the capitalist world-economy.* London: Pluto Press.

Lin, Chun. 2013. *China and global capitalism: Reflections on Marxism, history, and contemporary politics.* Basingstoke: Palgrave Macmillan.

Linebaugh, Peter. 2011. Foreword to the 2011 edition. In *William Morris: Romantic to revolutionary, Edward P. Thompson,* vii–xliii. Pontypool: The Merlin Press. Reprinted with a New Foreword.

Locke, John. 1690. *Two treatise of government*. Cambridge: Cambridge University Press.

Luhmann, Niklas. 1995. *Social systems*. Stanford: Stanford University Press.

Lukács, Georg. 1986. *Werke. Band 14: Zur Ontologie des gesellschaftlichen Seins. 2. Halbband*. Darmstadt: Luchterhand.

Lukács, Georg. 1971. *History and class consciousness: Studies in Marxist dialectics*. Cambridge, MA: MIT Press.

Lunt, Peter and Sonia Livingstone. 2013. Media studies' fascination with the concept of the public sphere: Critical reflections and emerging debates. *Media, Culture & Society* 35 (1): 87–96.

Lunt, Peter, Sonia Livingstone, and Benedetta Brevini. 2012. Changing regimes of regulation. Implications for public service broadcasting. In *RIPE@2011: Regaining the initiative for public service media*, ed. Gregory Ferrell Lowe and Jeanette Steemers, 113–128. Gothenburg: Nordicom.

Lyons, Glenn, Juliet Jain, Yusak Susilo, and Stephen Atkins. 2013. Comparing rail passengers' travel time use in Great Britain between 2004 and 2010. *Mobilities* 8 (4): 560–579.

Machlup, Fritz. 1962. *The production and distribution of knowledge in the United States*. Princeton, NJ: Princeton University Press.

Macpherson, Crawford B. 1962. *The political theory of possessive individualism*. Oxford: Oxford University Press.

Mandel, Ernest. 1990. Karl Marx. In *Marxian economics*, ed. John Eatwell, Murray Milgate, and Peter Newman, 1–38. London: Palgrave Macmillan.

Manzerolle, Vince and Lee McGuigan, ed. 2014. *The audience commodity in a digital age: Revisiting a critical theory of commercial media*. New York: Peter Lang.

Mao, Tse-tung. 1967. *On literature and art*. Peking: Foreign Languages Press.

Mao, Tse-tung. 1964. Talk on questions of philosophy. http://www.marxists.org/reference/archive/mao/selected-works/volume-9/mswv9_27.htm (accessed October 27, 2014).

Mao, Tse-tung. 1958. Introducing a co-operative. http://www.marxists.org/reference/archive/mao/selected-works/volume-8/mswv8_09.htm (accessed October 27, 2014).

Mao, Tse-tung. 1957a. Be activists in promoting the revolution. In *Selected works of Mao Tsetung, Volume V*, 483–497. Peking: Foreign Language Press.

Mao, Tse-tung. 1957b. Beat back the attacks of the bourgeois rightists. In *Selected works of Mao Tsetung, Volume V*, 457–472. Peking: Foreign Language Press.

Mao, Tse-tung. 1937. On contradiction. In *Selected works of Mao Tse-Tung, Volume 1*, 311–347. Peking: Foreign Language Press.

Marcuse, Herbert. 1979. Children of Prometheus: 25 theses on technology and society. In *Philosophy, psychoanalysis and emancipation. Collected papers of Herbert Marcuse, Volume 5*, ed. Douglas Kellner and Clayton Pierce, 222–225. London: Routledge.

Marcuse, Herbert. 1967a. Art in the one-dimensional society. In *Art and liberation: Collected papers of Herbert Marcuse, Volume 4*, ed. Douglas Kellner, 113–122. London: Routledge.

Marcuse Herbert. 1967b. Society as a work of art. In *Art and liberation: Collected papers of Herbert Marcuse, Volume 4*, ed. Douglas Kellner, 123–129. London: Routledge.

Marcuse, Herbert. 1965. Remarks on a redefinition of culture. In *The essential Marcuse. Selected writings of philosopher and social critic Herbert Marcuse*, ed. Andrew Feenberg and William Leiss, 13–31. Boston, MA: Beacon Press.

Marcuse, Herbert. 1964. *One-dimensional man: Studies in the ideology of advanced industrial society*. London: Routledge.

Marcuse, Herbert. 1958. *Soviet Marxism: A critical analysis*. New York: Columbia University Press.

Marcuse, Herbert. 1941a. *Reason and revolution: Hegel and the rise of social theory*. Amherst, NY: Humanity Books.

Marcuse, Herbert. 1941b. Some social implications of modern technology. In *Technology, war and fascism: Collected papers of Herbert Marcuse, Volume 1*, ed. Douglas Kellner, 41–65. London: Routledge.

Marx, Karl. 2000. *Selected writings*, ed. David McLellan. Second edition. Oxford: Oxford University Press.

Marx, Karl. 1980. *Das Kapital. Kritik der politischen Oekonomie. Urfassung von 1867*. Hildesheim: Gerstenberg Verlag.

Marx, Karl. 1974. *On freedom of the press & censorship*, ed. Saul K. Padover. New York: McGraw-Hill.

Marx, Karl. 1894. *Capital Vol. III*. London: Penguin.

Marx Karl 1885. *Capital Vol. II*. London: Penguin.

Marx, Karl. 1867. *Capital Vol. I*. London: Penguin.

Marx, Karl. 1865. *Value, price, and profit*. http://www.marxists.org/archive/marx/works/1865/value-price-profit/index.htm (accessed October 27, 2014).

Marx, Karl. 1862/63. *Theories of surplus value. Part 1*. London: Lawrence & Wishart.

Marx, Karl. 1861–63. Economic manuscripts of 1861–1863. In *Marx Engels Collected Works (MECW) Volume 30*. London: Lawrence Wishart.

Marx, Karl. 1859. Contribution to critique of political economy. In *Marx Engels Collected Works, Volume 29*, 257–417. New York: International Publishers.

Marx, Karl. 1857/58. *Grundrisse*. London: Penguin.

Marx, Karl. 1853. The future results of British rule in India. In *Marx Engels Collected Works (MECW) Volume 12*, 217–222. London: Lawrence Wishart.

Marx, Karl. 1851/52. The eighteenth Brumaire of Louis Bonaparte. In *Karl Marx and Friedrich Engels, Selected works in one volume*, 93–171. London: Lawrence & Wishart.

Marx, Karl. 1847. *The poverty of philosophy*. London: Lawrence.

Marx, Karl. 1844 [English]. *Economic and philosophic manuscripts of 1844*. Mineola, NY: Dover.

Marx, Karl. 1844 [German]. Ökonomisch-philosophische Manuskripte. In *MEW, Band 40*, 465–588. Berlin: Dietz.

Marx, Karl. 1843a. On the Jewish question. In *Writings of the young Marx on philosophy and society*, 216–248. Indianapolis, IN: Hackett.

Marx, Karl. 1843b. Toward the critique of Hegel's philosophy of law: Introduction. In *Writings of the young Marx on philosophy and society*, 249–264. Indianapolis, IN: Hackett.

Marx, Karl. 1842. On freedom of the press. In *Marx Engels Collected Works (MECW) Volume 1*, 132–181. London: Lawrence Wishart.

Marx, Karl and Friedrich Engels. 1879. The manifesto of the three Zurichers. In *The Marx-Engels Reader*, ed. Robert C. Tucker, 549–555. Second edition. New York: W. W. Norton & Company.

Marx, Karl and Friedrich Engels.1848 [English]. Manifesto of the Communist Party. In *Selected works in one volume*, Karl Marx and Friedrich Engels, 35–62. London: Lawrence & Wishart.

Marx, Karl and Friedrich Engels. 1848 [German]. Manifest der kommunistischen Partei. In *MEW, Band 3*, 459–493. Berlin: Dietz.

Marx, Karl and Friedrich Engels. 1845/46. *The German ideology*. Amherst, NY: Prometheus Books.

Maxwell, Richard. 1991. The image is gold: Value, the audience commodity, and fetishism. *Journal of Film and Video* 43 (1–2): 29–45.

Maxwell, Richard and Toby Miller. 2012. *Greening the media*. Oxford: Oxford University Press.

McGuigan, Jim, ed. 2014. *Raymond Williams on culture & society: Essential writings*. London: Sage.

McGuigan, Jim. 1998. What price the public sphere? In *Electronic empires. Global media and local resistances*, ed. Daya Kishan Thussu, 108–124. London: Hodder Arnold.

McGuigan, Jim and Marie Moran. 2014. Raymond Williams and sociology. *The Sociological Review* 62(1): 167-188.

McNair, Brian. 2009. The internet and the changing global media environment. In *The Routledge handbook of Internet politics*, ed. Andrew Chadwick and Philip N. Howard, 217–299. New York: Routledge.

Mendelson, B. J. 2012. *Social media is bullshit*. New York: St. Martin's Press.

Mies, Maria. 1986. *Patriarchy & accumulation on a world scale: Women in the international division of labour*. London: Zed Books.

Mill, John Stuart. 1859. On liberty. In *On liberty and other essays*, 5–128. Oxford: Oxford University Press.

Mill, John Stuart. 1848. *Principles of political economy. And: Chapters on socialism*. Oxford: Oxford University Press.

Miller, Toby, Nitin Govil, John McMurria, Richard Maxwell, and Ting Wang. 2004. *Global Hollywood 2*. London: British Film Institute.

Mills, C. Wright. 1956. *The power elite*. Oxford: Oxford University Press.

Moore, Richard K. 1999. Democracy and cyberspace. In *Digital Democracy: Discourse and decision making in the information age*, ed. Barry N. Hague and Brian D. Loader, 39–58. London: Routledge.

Morley, Daniel. 2012. Splits in the Chinese ruling class. http://www.marxist.com/splits-in-the-chinese-ruling-class.htm (accessed October 27, 2014).

Morris, William. 1894. How I became a socialist. In *The collected works of William Morris. Volume 23: Signs of changes: Lectures on socialism*, 277–281. Cambridge: Cambridge University Press.

Morris, William. 1893. Communism. In *The collected works of William Morris. Volume 23: Signs of changes: Lectures on socialism*, 264–276. Cambridge: Cambridge University Press.

Morris, William. 1885. How we live and how we might live. In *The collected works of William Morris. Volume 23: Signs of changes: Lectures on socialism*, 3–26. Cambridge: Cambridge University Press.

Morris, William. 1884a. A factory as it might be I. *Justice*, May 17. http://www.marxists.org/archive/morris/works/1884/justice/10fact1.htm (accessed October 27, 2014).

Morris, William. 1884b. Useful work versus useless toil. In *The collected works of William Morris. Volume 23: Signs of changes: Lectures on socialism*, 98–120. Cambridge: Cambridge University Press.

Morris, William. 1884c. Work in a factory as it might be III. *Justice*, June 28: 2. http://www.marxists.org/archive/morris/works/1884/justice/13fact3.htm (accessed October 27, 2014).

Mosco, Vincent. 2009. *The political economy of communication*. Second edition. London: Sage.

Mosco, Vincent and Catherine McKercher. 2009. *The laboring of communication: Will knowledge workers of the world unite?* Lanham, MD: Lexington Books.

Mouffe, Chantal. 1999. Deliberative democracy or agonistic pluralism? *Social Research* 66 (3): 745–758.

Moulier-Boutang, Yann. 2012. *Cognitive capitalism*. Cambridge: Polity Press.

Murdock, Graham. 2014. Commodities and commons. In *The audience commodity in a digital age*, ed. Lee McGuigan and Vincent Manzerolle, 229–244. New York: Peter Lang.

Murdock, Graham. 2011. Political economies as moral economies: Commodities, gifts, and public goods. In *The handbook of the political economy of communications*, ed. Janet Wasko, Graham Murdock, and Helena Sousa, 13–40. Chichester: Wiley-Blackwell.

Murdock, Graham. 2005. Building the digital commons: Public broadcasting in the age of the Internet. In *Cultural dilemmas of public service broadcasting*, ed. Per Jauert and Gregory F. Lowe, 213–230. Gothenburg: Nordicom.

Murdock, Graham. 1978. Blindspots about Western Marxism. A reply to Dallas Smythe. *Canadian Journal of Political and Social Theory* 2 (2): 120–129.

Murdock, Graham and Peter Golding. 2005. Culture, communications and political economy. In *Mass media and society*, ed. James Curran and Michael Gurevitch, 60-83. London: Hodder Arnold.

Napoli, Philip M. 2009. Media economics and the study of media industries. In *Media industries: History, theory, and method*, ed. Jennifer Holt and Alisa Perren, 161–170. Chichester: Wiley-Blackwell.

Nash, Victoria. 2013. Analyzing freedom of expression online: Theoretical, empirical, and normative contributions. In *The Oxford handbook of Internet studies*, ed. William H. Dutton, 441–463. Oxford: Oxford University Press.

NASSCOM (National Association of Software and Services Companies. 2012. *The IT-BPO sector in India. Strategic review 2012. Executive summary.* http://www.nasscom. in/sites/default/files/researchreports/SR_2012_Executive_Summary.pdf (accessed October 27, 2014).

National Bureau of Statistics of China. 2014. *Statistical communiqué of the People's Republic of China on the 2013 national economic and social development.* http://www.stats.gov.cn/ english/PressRelease/201402/t20140224_515103.html (accessed March 29, 2014).

National Bureau of Statistics of China. 2012. *Statistical communiqué of the People's Republic of China on the 2011 national economic and social development.* http://www.stats.gov.cn/ english/NewsEvents/201202/t20120222_26575.html (accessed March 29, 2014).

Negri, Antonio. 2008. *Reflections on empire*: Cambridge: Polity Press.

Negri, Antonio. 1991. *Marx beyond Marx: Lessons on the Grundrisse.* New York: Autonomedia.

Negri, Antonio. 1982. Archaeology and project: The mass worker and the social worker. In *Revolution retrieved: Selected writings on Marx, Keynes, capitalist crisis & new social subjects 1967–83*, 199–228. London: Red Notes.

Negri, Antonio. 1971. Crisis of the planner-state: Communism and revolutionary organisation. In *Revolution retrieved: Selected writings on Marx, Keynes, capitalist crisis & new social subjects 1967–83*, 91–148. London: Red Notes.

Negt, Oskar and Alexander Kluge. 1993. *Public sphere and experience: Toward an analysis of the bourgeois and proletarian public sphere.* Minneapolis: University of Minnesota Press.

Negt, Oskar and Alexander Kluge. 1972. *Öffentlichkeit und Erfahrung. Zur Organisationsanalyse von bürgerlicher und proletarischer Öffentlichkeit.* Frankfurt am Main: Suhrkamp.

Nest, Michael. 2011. *Coltan.* Cambridge: Polity Press.

Nielsen. 2013. *Paid social media advertising: Industry update and best practices 2013.* New York: Nielsen.

Noah, Harold J. 1965. The 'unproductive' labour of Soviet teachers. *Soviet Studies* 17 (2): 238–244.

Noam, Eli. 2009. *Media ownership and concentration in America.* Oxford: Oxford University Press.

Nolan, Peter. 2012. *Is China buying the world?* Cambridge: Polity Press.

Nolan, Peter and Jin Zhang. 2010. Global competition after the financial crisis. *New Left Review* 64: 97–108.

Ofcom. 2012. *International communications market report 2012.* http://stakeholders.ofcom. org.uk/binaries/research/cmr/cmr12/icmr/ICMR-2012.pdf (accessed April 5, 2013).

Ofcom. 2007. Methodology for market impact assessments of BBC services. http://stakeholders.ofcom.org.uk/binaries/research/tv-research/bbc-mias/bbc-mia-meth.pdf (accessed December 8, 2013).

Offe, Claus. 1985. New social movements. Challenging the boundaries of institutional politics. *Social Research* 52 (4): 817–867.

Panitch, Leo. 2010. Giovanni Arrighi in Beijing: An alternative to capitalism? *Historical Materialism* 18 (1): 74–87.

Papacharissi, Zizi. 2009. The virtual sphere 2.0: The internet, the public sphere, and beyond. In *Routledge handbook of Internet politics,* ed. Andrew Chadwick and Philip N. Howard, 230–245. New York: Routledge.

Pasquinelli, Matteo. 2010. The ideology of free culture and the grammar of sabotage. In *Education in the creative economy: Knowledge and learning in the age of innovation,* ed. Daniel Araya and Michael Peters, 285–304. New York: Peter Lang.

Paul, Christopher. 2011. *Strategic communication: Origins, concepts, and current debates.* Santa Barbara, CA: Praeger.

Peirce, Charles Sanders. 1958. *Collected papers: Volume 2.* Cambridge, MA: Harvard University Press.

Peirce, Charles Sanders. 1955. *Philosophical writings of Peirce,* ed. Justus Buchler. New York: Dover.

Pellow, David N. and Lisa Sun-Hee Park. 2002. *The Silicon Valley of dreams: Environmental injustice, immigrant workers, and the high-tech global economy.* New York: New York University Press.

Pfeiffer, Sabine. 2013. Web, value and labour. *Work Organisation, Labour & Globalisation* 7 (1): 12–30.

Picard, Robert G. 2009. A note on the relations between circulation size and newspaper advertising rates. *Journal of Media Economics* 11 (2): 47–55.

Porter, Michael. 1985. *Competitive advantage: Creating and sustaining superior performance.* New York: Free Press.

Postone, Moishe. 2003. The Holocaust and the trajectory of the twentieth century. In *Catastrophe and meaning. The Holocaust and the twentieth century,* ed. Moishe Postone and Eric Santner, 81–114. Chicago, IL: University of Chicago Press.

Postone, Moishe. 1993. *Time, labor, and social domination: A reinterpretation of Marx's critical theory.* Cambridge: Cambridge University Press.

Postone, Moishe. 1980. Anti-Semitism and National Socialism: Notes on the German reaction to "Holocaust". *New German Critique* 19 (1): 97–115.

Poulsen, Frank. 2011. *Blood in the mobile.* DVD documentary. Berlin: good!movies.

Qi, Hao. 2014. The labor share question in China. *Monthly Review* 65 (8): 23–35.

Qiu, Jack L. 2012. Network labor: Beyond the shadow of Foxconn. In *Studying mobile media. Cultural technologies, mobile communication, and the iPhone,* ed. Larissa Hjorth, Jean Burgess, and Ingrid Richardson, 173–189. New York: Routledge.

Qiu, Jack L. 2010. Deconstructing Foxconn. Documentary film. http://vimeo.com/ 17558439.

Qiu, Jack L. 2009. *Working-class network society: Communication technology and the information have-less in urban China.* Cambridge, MA: MIT Press.

Reveley, James. 2013. The exploitative web: Misuses of Marx in critical social media studies. *Science & Society* 77(4): 512–535.

Rigi, Jakob and Robert Prey. 2015: Value, rent, and the political economy of social media. *The Information Society* 31. Forthcoming.

Ritzer, George and Nathan Jurgenson. 2010. Production, consumption, presumption: The nature of capitalism in the age of the digital "prosumer". *Journal of Consumer Culture* 10 (1): 13–36.

Roberts, John Michael and Nick Crossley. 2004. Introduction. In *After Habermas: New perspectives on the public sphere*, ed. Nick Crossley and John Michael Roberts, 1–27. Malden, MA: Blackwell.

Robinson, Bruce. 2015. With a different Marx: Value and the contradictions of web 2.0 capitalism. *The Information Society* 30. Fothcoming.

Rosa, Hartmut. 2012. *Weltbeziehungen im Zeitalter der Beschleunigung. Umrisse einer neuen Gesellschaftskritik*. Frankfurt am Main: Suhrkamp.

Rosa, Hartmut. 2005. *Beschleunigung. Die Veränderung der Zeitstrukturen in der Moderne.* Frankfurt am Main: Suhrkamp.

Rossi-Landi, Ferruccio. 1983. *Language as work and trade. A semiotic homology for linguistics & economics*. South Hadley, MA: Bergin & Garvey.

Rossi-Landi, Ferruccio. 1977. *Linguistics and economics*. The Hague: Mouton.

Roy, Arundhati. 2003. *Confronting empire*. World Social Forum, Porto Alegre, Brazil, on January, 27, 2003. http://www.sustecweb.co.uk/past/sustec11–4/following_speech_by_arundhati_ro.htm (accessed October 27, 2014).

Saad-Filho, Alfredo. 2002. *The value of Marx: Political economy for contemporary capitalism.* London: Routledge.

SACOM (Students & Scholars against Corporate Misbehaviour). 2012. *New iPhone, old abuses. Have working conditions at Foxconn in China improved?* http://www.scribd.com/doc/106445655 (accessed October 25, 2013).

SACOM (Students & Scholars against Corporate Misbehaviour). 2011a. *Foxconn and Apple fail to fulfill promises. Predicaments of workers after suicides.* http://sacom.hk/wp-content/uploads/2011/05/2011–05–06_foxconn-and-apple-fail-to-fulfill-promises1.pdf (accessed October 25, 2013).

SACOM (Students & Scholars against Corporate Misbehaviour). 2011b. *iSlave behind the iPhone. Foxconn workers in Central China.* http://sacom.hk/wp-content/uploads/2011/09/20110924-islave-behind-the-iphone.pdf (accessed October 25, 2013).

SACOM (Students & Scholars against Corporate Misbehaviour). 2010. *Workers as machines. Military management in Foxconn.* http://sacom.hk/wp-content/uploads/2010/11/report-on-foxconn-workers-as-machines_sacom.pdf (accessed October 25, 2013).

Salzman, Ryan. 2011. Civil society. In *21ˢᵗ century political science: A reference handbook*, ed. John T. Ishiyama and Marijke Breuning, 193–200. London: Sage.

Sandoval, Marisol. 2014. *From corporate to social media: Critical perspectives on corporate social responsibility in media and communication industries.* New York: Routledge.

Sandoval, Marisol. 2013. Foxconned labour as the dark side of the information age: Working conditions at Apple's contract manufacturers in China. *tripleC: Communication, Capitalism & Critique* 11 (2): 318–347.

Sandoval, Marisol and Christian Fuchs. 2010. Towards a critical theory of alternative media. *Telematics and Informatics* 27 (2): 141–150.

Scannell, Paddy. 2007. *Media and communication*. London: Sage.

Scannell, Paddy. 1989. Public service and modern public life. *Media, Culture and Society* 11 (2): 135–166.

Schiller, Dan. 1996. *Theorizing communication: A history*. New York: Oxford University Press.

Schiller, Herbert I. 1991. Not-yet the post-imperialist era. In *International communication. A reader*, ed. Daya Kishan Thussu. Oxon: Routledge.

Schmiede, Rudi. 1996. Informatisierung und gesellschaftliche Arbeit – Strukturveränderungen von Arbeit und Gesellschaft. In *Virtuelle Arbeitswelten. Arbeit, Produktion und Subjekt in der „Informationsgesellschaft"*, 107–128. Berlin: edition sigma.

Schmitt, Gary J., ed. 2009. *Rise of China*. New York: Encounter Books.

Scholz, Roswitha. 2000. *Das Geschlecht des Kapitalismus. Feministische Theorien und die postmoderne Metamorphose des Patriarchats*. Bad Honnef: Horlemann.

Scholz, Trebor, ed. 2013. *Digital labor: The Internet as playground and factory*. New York: Routledge.

Sennett, Richard. 1998. *The corrosion of character: The personal character of work in the new capitalism*. New York: W.W. Norton & Company.

Sheldon, Garrett Ward. 2001. *Encyclopedia of political thought*. New York: Facts on File.

Sheng, Hua. 1990. Big character posters in China: A historical survey. *Journal of Chinese Law* 4 (2): 234–256.

Smith, Adam. 1790. *The theory of moral sentiments*. London: Penguin.

Smythe, Dallas W. 1994. *Counterclockwise*. Boulder, CO: Westview Press.

Smythe, Dallas W. 1977. Communications: Blindspot of Western Marxism. *Canadian Journal of Political and Social Theory* 1 (3): 1–27.

Smythe, Dallas W. 1954. Reality as presented by television. In *Counterclockwise. Perspectives on communication*, 61–74. Boulder, CO: Westview Press.

SOMO (Centre for Research on Multinational Corporations). 2007. *Capacitating electronics: The corrosive effects of platinum and palladium mining on labour rights and communities*. makeITfair Report. http://somo.nl/publications-nl/Publication_2545-nl/at_download/fullfile (accessed October 27, 2014).

Sparks, Colin. 2014. Deconstructing the BRICS. *International Journal of Communication* 8: 392–418.

Sparks, Colin. 1998. Is there a global public sphere? In *Electronic empires: Global media and local resistances*, ed. Daya Kishan Thussu, 91–107. London: Hodder Arnold.

Sparks, Colin. 1996. Stuart Hall, cultural studies and Marxism. In *Stuart Hall. Critical dialogues in cultural studies*, ed. David Morely and Kuan-Hsing Chen, 71–101. London: Routledge.

Splichal, Slavko. 2007. Does history matter? Grasping the idea of public service at its roots. In *From public service broadcasting to public service media. RIPE@2007*, ed. Gregory Ferrell Lowe and Jo Bardoel, 237–256. Gothenburg: Nordicom.

Stalin, Josef V. 1938. Dialectical and historical materialism. http://www.marx2mao.com/Stalin/DHM38.html (accessed October 27, 2014).

Statistical Yearbook of the Republic of China. 2011. Nantou City: Directorate-General of Budget, Accounting and Statistics.

Steuart, James. 1767. *An inquiry into the principles of political economy*. http://www.marxists.org/reference/subject/economics/steuart/index.htm (accessed October 27, 2014).

Sullins, John. 2010. Rights and computer ethics. In *The Cambridge handbook of information and computer ethics*, ed. Luciano Floridi, 116–132. Cambridge: Cambridge University Press.

Sum, Ngai-Ling and Bob Jessop. 2013. *Towards a cultural political economy: Putting culture in its place in political economy*. Cheltenham: Edward Elgar.

Talk Asia. 2011. Interview with Charles Chao. *CNN Online* transcript, *CNN Talk Asia*, August 3, 2011, http://transcripts.cnn.com/TRANSCRIPTS/1108/03/ta.01.html (accessed October 27, 2014).

Teixeira, Rodrigo Alves and Tomas Nielsen Rotta. 2012. Valueless knowledge-commodities and financialization: Productive and financial dimensions of capital autonomization. *Review of Radical Political Economics* 44 (4): 448–467.

Thale, Mary. 1995. Women in London debating societies in 1780. *Gender & History* 7 (1): 5–24.

Thale, Mary. 1989. London debating societies in the 1790s. *The Historical Journal* 32 (1): 58–86.

Thompson, Edward P. 2011. *William Morris: Romantic to revolutionary*. Pontypool: Merlin Press. Reprinted with a New Foreword.

Thompson, Edward P. 1994. *Persons & polemics: Historical essays*. London: Merlin Press.

Thompson, Edward P. 1991. *Customs in common*. Pontypool: Merlin Press.

Thompson, Edward P. 1978. *The poverty of theory and other essays*. New York: Monthly Review Press.

Thompson, Edward P. 1967. Time, work discipline, and industrial capitalism. *Past and Present* 38: 56–97.

Thompson, Edward B. 1963. *The making of the English working class*. New York: Vintage Books.

Thompson, John B. 1995. *The media and modernity: A social theory of the media*. Cambridge: Polity Press.

Thussu, Daya Kishan. 2014. De-americanising media studies and the rise of "Chindia". *Javnost – The Public* 20 (4): 31–44.

Toffler, Alvin. 1980. *The third wave*. New York: Bantam.

Touraine, Alain. 1985. An introduction to the study of social movements. *Social Research* 52 (4): 749–787.

Tronti, Mario. 1962. *Arbeiter und Kapital*. Frankfurt am Main: Verlag Neue Kritik.

Turow, Joseph and Matthew McAllister, eds. 2009. *The advertising and consumer culture Reader*. New York: Routledge.

UNHDR. 2011. *United Nations Human Development Report 2011*. New York: Palgrave Macmillan.

Upadhya, Carol and A.R. Vasavi. 2008. Outposts of the global information economy: Work and workers in India's outsourcing industry. In *In an outpost of the global economy: Work and workers in India's information technology industry*, ed. Carol Upadhya and A.R. Vasavi, 9–49. New Dehli: Routledge.

Urry, John. 1994. Time, leisure and social identity. *Time & Society* 3 (2): 131–149.

U.S. Geological Survey Statistics. 2012. http://minerals.usgs.gov/minerals/pubs/commodity *(accessed October 25, 2013)*.

van Dijk, Teun, ed. 2011. *Discourse studies: A multidisciplinary introduction*. London: Sage. Second edition.

van Dijk, Teun. 2009. *Society and discourse: How social contexts influence text and talk*. Cambridge: Cambridge University Press.

van Dijk, Teun. 2008. *Discourse & power*. Basingstoke: Palgrave Macmillan.

van Dijk, Teun. 1998. *Ideology. A multidisciplinary approach*. London: Sage.

Vercellone, Carlo. 2010. The crisis of the law of value and the becoming-rent of profit. In *Crisis in the global economy*, ed. Andrea Fumagalli and Sandro Mezzadra, 85–118. Los Angeles, CA: Semiotext(e).

Vercellone, Carlo. 2007. From formal subsumption to general intellect: Elements for a Marxist reading of the thesis of cognitive capitalism. *Historical Materialism* 15 (1): 13–36.

Virilio, Paul. 1999. *Polar inertia*. London: Sage.

Volkmer, Ingrid. 2003. Media systems and journalism in the global network paradigm. In *Democracy and new media*, ed. Henry Jenkins and David Thorburn, 309–330. Cambridge, MA: MIT Press.

Walker, Richard. 2010. Karl Marx between two worlds: The antinomies of Giovanni Arrighi's Adam Smith in Beijing. *Historical Materialism* 18 (1): 52–73.

Wang, Di. 2008. The idle and the busy: Teahouses and public life in early twentieth-century Chengdu. *Journal of Urban History* 26 (4): 411–437.

Watts, Jonathan. 2005. The man behind China's answer to Google: Accused by critics of piracy and censorship. *The Guardian Online*, December 8, 2005. http://www.theguardian.com/technology/2005/dec/08/piracy.news (accessed October 27, 2014).

Weeks, Kathi. 2011. *The problem with work: Feminism, Marxism, antiwork politics and postwork imaginaries*. Durham, NC: Duke University Press.

Weingart, Brigitte. 1997. *Arbeit – ein Wort mit langer Geschichte*. http://www.ethikprojekte.ch/texte/arbeit.htm (accessed November 10, 2013).

Werlhof, Claudia von. 1991. *Was haben die Hühner mit dem Dollar zu tun? Frauen und Ökonomie*. München: Frauenoffensive.

Williams, Raymond. 1990. *Television*. London: Routledge. Second edition.

Williams, Raymond. 1989. *What I came to say*. London: Hutchinson Radius.

Williams, Raymond. 1983. *Keywords*. New York: Oxford University Press.

Williams, Raymond. 1981. *The sociology of culture*. Chicago, IL: University of Chicago Press.

Williams, Raymond. 1980/2005. Advertising: The magic system. In *Culture and materialism*, 170–194. London: Verso.

Williams, Raymond. 1979. *Politics and letters: Interviews with* New Left Review. London: Verso.

Williams, Raymond. 1977. *Marxism and literature*. Oxford: Oxford University Press.

Williams, Raymond. 1975. "You're a Marxist, aren't you?" In *Resources of hope*, 65–76. London: Verso.

Williams, Raymond. 1973. Base and superstructure in Marxist cultural theory. In *Culture and materialism*, 31–49. London: Verso.

Williams, Raymond. 1961. *The long revolution*. Cardigan: Parthian.

Williams, Raymond. 1958. *Culture & society, 1780–1950*. New York: Columbia University Press.

Withalm, Gloria. 2006. Ferruccio Rossi-Landi. An overview on his ideas on social reproduction and innovation. *Trans* 16, http://www.inst.at/trans/16Nr/01_2/withalm16.htm (accessed October 27, 2014).

Wodak, Ruth and Michael Meyer, ed. 2009. *Methods of critical discourse analysis*. London: Sage. Second edition.

Wu, Changchang. 2012. Micro-blog and the speech act of China's middle class: The 7.23 train accident case. *Javnost – The Public* 19 (2): 43–62.

Xing, Guoxin. 2012. Online activism and counter-public spheres: A case study of migrant labour resistance. *Javnost – The Public* 19 (2): 63–82.

Zerdick, Axel et al. 2000. *E-conomics: Strategies for the digital marketplace*. Berlin: Springer.

Zhao, Yuezhi. 2012a. Introduction to "Communication and class divide in China". *Javnost – The Public* 19 (2): 5–22.

Zhao, Yuezhi. 2012b. The struggle for socialism in China: The Bo Xila Saga and beyond. *Monthly Review* 64 (5): 1–17.

Zhao, Yuezhi. 2011. The challenge of China: Contribution to a transcultural political economy of communication for the twenty-first century. In *The handbook of political economy of communications*, ed. Janet Wasko, Graham Murdock, and Helena Sousa, 558–582. Malden, MA: Wiley-Blackwell.

Zhao, Yuezhi. 2007. After mobile phone, what? Re-embedding the social in China's "digital revolution". *International Journal of Communication* 1: 92–120.

Žižek, Slavoj. 2012. *The year of dreaming dangerously*. London: Verso.

Žižek, Slavoj. 2010. *Living in the end times*. London: Verso.

Žižek, Slavoj. 2009. *First as tragedy then as farce*. London: Verso.

Žižek, Slavoj. 2008. *In defense of lost causes*. London: Verso.

Žižek, Slavoj. 1989. *The sublime object of ideology*. London: Verso. Second edition.

INDEX